S0-BAH-641

THE UNITED NATIONS SERIES

ROBERT J. KERNER, GENERAL EDITOR

SATHER PROFESSOR OF HISTORY IN THE
UNIVERSITY OF CALIFORNIA

◇

CZECHOSLOVAKIA
EDITED BY ROBERT J. KERNER

THE NETHERLANDS
EDITED BY BARTHOLOMEW LANDHEER

POLAND
EDITED BY BERNADOTTE E. SCHMITT

BELGIUM
EDITED BY JAN-ALBERT GORIS

CHINA
EDITED BY HARLEY FARNSWORTH MAC NAIR

NEW ZEALAND
EDITED BY HORACE BELSHAW

BRAZIL
EDITED BY LAWRENCE F. HILL

AUSTRALIA
EDITED BY C. HARTLEY GRATTAN

◇

Other volumes in preparation

AUSTRALIA

AUSTRALIA

Chapters by K. H. Bailey, F. A. Bland, E. H. Burgmann, Herbert
Burton, S. J. Butlin, Colin Clark, H. C. Coombs, John G. Craw-
ford, R. M. Crawford and G. F. James, K. S. Cunningham, Sir
Frederick Eggleston, A. P. Elkin, L. F. Fitzharding, Brian Fitz-
patrick, Ross Gollan, C. Hartley Grattan, H. M. Green, Gordon
Greenwood, J. Macdonald Holmes, T. H. Kewley, Gavin Long,
Eris O'Brien, Vance and Nettie Palmer, Lloyd Ross, Bernard
Smith, Clive Turnbull, E. Ronald Walker, John M. Ward

EDITED BY C. HARTLEY GRATTAN

UNIVERSITY OF CALIFORNIA PRESS
BERKELEY AND LOS ANGELES · 1947

THE LIBRARY
COLBY JUNIOR COLLEGE
NEW LONDON, N. H.

DU
110
G8

UNIVERSITY OF CALIFORNIA PRESS
BERKELEY AND LOS ANGELES
CALIFORNIA

◇

CAMBRIDGE UNIVERSITY PRESS
LONDON, ENGLAND

COPYRIGHT, 1947, BY
THE REGENTS OF THE UNIVERSITY OF CALIFORNIA

28419

PRINTED IN THE UNITED STATES OF AMERICA
BY THE UNIVERSITY OF CALIFORNIA PRESS

TO THE MEMORY OF
ARTHUR PHILLIP, ESQUIRE
1738–1814
CAPTAIN-GENERAL IN AND OVER
HIS MAJESTY'S TERRITORY OF NEW SOUTH WALES
FROM 1788 TO 1792
WHO AS FOUNDING GOVERNOR
BESET BY DIFFICULTIES OF ALL KINDS
NEVERTHELESS HAD A VISION OF
THE LAND'S BRILLIANT FUTURE
A GREAT AND GOOD MAN
FULLY EQUAL TO THE BURDEN OF BEING
THE FATHER OF A COUNTRY

The United Nations Series

THE UNITED NATIONS SERIES *is dedicated to the task of mutual understanding among the Allies of the Second World War and to the achievement of successful coöperation in the peace. The University of California offered the first volumes of this series as a part of its contribution to the war effort of this state and nation and of the nations united in the greatest conflict known to history; it offers the later volumes, of which this is one, to the peace effort; and it heartily thanks the editors of the respective volumes and their collaborators for their devoted service and for their efforts to present an honest, sincere, and objective appraisal of the United Nations.*

ROBERT J. KERNER
General Editor

Editor's Preface

ANY BOOK *which is the product of many hands always exhibits merits and faults peculiar to its kind. It is the editor's hope that in this particular example the meritorious features completely overshadow the possible inadequacies. The essays included are products of varying temperaments, reflect various styles of writing, and are based on differing systems of interpretation (from purely subjective to semi-Marxist), and therefore give differing assessments of men and events. Each contributor is responsible for his own opinions. In no instance should they be assumed to be those of other contributors, or of the editor. The book is what the contributors have made it. The editor has merely acted as an "honest broker," aiming at offering to the public a fairly comprehensive account of a country with which, for many years, he has been intimately associated.*

In this connection it should perhaps be noted here that all the contributors to this volume, save one, are Australians actively engaged in professional work in or for their native or adopted land. The single exception is the editor, an American who has been interested in the study of Australian affairs since 1927, always as a journalist to whom the Australian has been but one of several fields he has cultivated, though the one which has never in two decades suffered from fluctuations of enthusiasm. The editor certainly has no objection to being thought an Australian, but he is nevertheless rather concerned that the Australians not have to take responsibility for him through the inadvertence of ignorance on the part of others. The prospective inclusion of his name in the Australian Who's Who *is perhaps an earnest of the fact that to the Australians he is the good friend he certainly intends being.*

[ix]

The theme of this book is the evolution of Australia from colonial dependence to ever-increasing national self-reliance. This theme was not imposed upon the contributors by the editor, or any other outsider, but was selected by the writers quite independently of one another, a circumstance which strongly supports its validity. Two decades ago, when the editor first visited Australia, it is doubtful if it would have received such general, unsolicited support from so various a company; five decades ago, in the 1890's when, as this record reports, Australian nationalism first found strong expression, it would have received support in certain quarters only, not universally; but today there are few dissenters indeed and their influence is steadily declining. It is to be hoped that readers will closely observe how this underlying theme is worked out in the various essays, dealing as they do with several specialized fields.

It is important, at this time, to realize why the Australians think of themselves as a distinctive people. The country cannot be fully understood unless it is clearly realized that it is a separate nation as well as an associate of the British Commonwealth. Its character is increasingly that of a small, strong, self-conscious, self-reliant autonomous nation in a world dominated by great powers, but in which nevertheless the small powers have a place and a voice if they have the fortitude, to make that place and use their voice.

The editor has not felt it necessary to worry too much about the repetition of certain facts in successive essays. As a rule the facts are presented in differing contexts and thus have a special meaning each time. Moreover, there is always the possibility that the essays may be read in isolation from one another, and the absence of vital information from one, though it is available in another, might cause readers to entertain misconceptions. There is, too, a certain pedagogical value in reiteration. However, an effort has been made to confine the full development of particular data to a single essay, reducing subsequent references to as brief a compass as possible.

It may be respectfully suggested that a useful approach to this book would be first to read the general historical essays, contained in Part Two, and then to proceed to the specialized essays as professional interest or personal whim suggest.

The gathering of the essays for the volume was begun in wartime and continued after the war ended. Delays, inseparable from books of this kind, were multiplied by the fact that the editor worked 10,000 miles removed from his collaborators. It is doubtful if the job would ever have been brought to a successful end had not David Bailey, of the staff of the Sydney Morning Herald, acted on the editor's behalf in Australia in stirring contributors to action. Even when confined to the hospital, as he was for a period, to the intense concern of his numerous friends, Mr. Bailey kept conscientiously to his task, voluntarily assumed. Words of tribute are a shockingly inadequate return for so signal a service. The editor also wishes to thank the general editor, Professor Robert J. Kerner, for his patience, tolerance, and good sportsmanship in all his relations with the editor over the long months after the book was scheduled for the United Nations Series and it unluckily moved forward at a snail's pace. And, finally, the editor wishes to thank most heartily all those Australians who as contributors, expediters, or sympathetic by-standers helped make this book, at last, a reality.

C. HARTLEY GRATTAN

Katonah, New York
August 5, 1947

Contents

[xiii]

Contents

Public Law, University of Melbourne, 1931–1947, and Dean, Faculty of Law, 1938–1942; Adviser, Australian Delegation at the Imperial Conference, 1937; member, Australian Delegation to the League of Nations Assembly, 1937; member, Aliens Tribunal, 1941; Adviser, Australian Delegation to the United Nations Conference, San Francisco, 1945; Rapporteur, Sixth Committee (Legal), General Assembly, United Nations, 1946.

By Ross Gollan, M.A.

On the staff of the Sydney *Morning Herald* since 1923; political correspondent at Canberra, 1940–1946; M.A. (Sydney).

CHAPTER VIII

By F. A. Bland, M.A., LL.B.

Professor of Public Administration, University of Sydney, since 1935; B.A., LL.B., M.A. (Sydney); attended London School of Economics; Chairman of the Local Government Examining Committee, New South Wales; Chairman of the Public Service Examinations Committee, New South Wales; Visiting Professor of Government, New York University, 1929–1930; editor, *Public Administration*, Journal of the Australian Regional Groups, Institute of Public Administration; editor, *Government in Australia*, a collection of documents (2d ed., Sydney, 1944); author of *Shadows and Realities of Government* (1923), *Planning the Modern State* (2d ed., 1945), *Budget Control* (3d ed., 1938); contributor to learned journals.

CHAPTER IX

By Sir Frederick Eggleston

Kt. cr., 1941; retired public servant; Envoy Extraordinary and Minister Plenipotentiary from Australia to China, 1941–1944; Envoy Extraordinary and Minister Plenipotentiary from Australia to the United States, 1944–1946; educated at Wesley College, Melbourne, and Leys School, Cambridge, England; admitted as barrister and solicitor to bar of Victoria, 1897; served in A.I.F., 1916–1919; on staff of Australian Delegation to the Peace Conference, Paris, 1919; Member of Legislative Assembly, Victoria, 1920–1927; Minister for Water Supply and Minister for Railways, 1924–1926; Attorney-General and Solicitor-General, 1924–1927, in Victorian State Governments; Chairman of the Commonwealth Grants Commission, 1933–1941; Chairman of the Committee to consider the amalgamation of Papua and New Guinea, 1939; member of the Commonwealth Advisory Board on Investments, 1939; Chairman, Australian delegations to I.P.R. conferences, 1927, 1929, 1936; editor, *The Australian Mandate for New Guinea* (Melbourne, 1928); author (with E. H. Sugden), *Life of George Swinburne* (Sydney, 1931), *State Socialism in Victoria* (London, 1932); contributor to many journals.

PART FOUR: ECONOMIC AND SOCIAL
DEVELOPMENT

Senior Lecturer in Economic History, University of Melbourne,
since 1930; Sub-Dean of Faculty of Economics and Commerce and
Head of Department of Economic History, University of Melbourne,
since 1944; B.A. (University of Queensland); Queensland Rhodes
Scholar, 1922; B.A., M.A. (Oxford); M.A. (hon. c.) (Melbourne);
contributed to *The Peopling of Australia: Further Studies* (Melbourne, 1933), *The Future of Immigration into Australia and New
Zealand* (Sydney, 1937); contributor to learned journals.

Counsellor at the Australian Legation, Paris; member of the Australian Delegation to the Peace Conference, Paris, 1946; B.A., M.A.,
(Sydney); Ph.D. (Cambridge); Fellow of the Rockefeller Foundation,
1931–1933; Lecturer in Economics, University of Sydney, 1927–1938;
Economic Adviser to the New South Wales Treasury, 1938–1939;
Professor of Economics and Economic Adviser to the state govern-
ment, Tasmania, 1939–1942; Chief Economic Adviser and Deputy
Director-General, Commonwealth Department of War Organiza-
tion of Industry, 1942–1945; Chief of Country Programs Branch,
U.N.R.R.A., Washington, D.C., 1945; author of *Australia in the
World Depression* (London, 1933), *Unemployment Policy, with
Special Reference to Australia* (Sydney, 1936), *War-time Econom-
ics, with Special Reference to Australia* (Melbourne, 1939), *From
Economic Theory to Policy* (Chicago, 1943), etc.; contributor to
learned journals.

Director, Commonwealth Bureau of Agricultural Economics, Canberra; M.Ec. (Sydney); Lecturer in Agricultural Economics, University of Sydney, 1934–1941; Economic Adviser, Rural Bank of New
South Wales, 1935–1943; Commonwealth Fund Service Fellow in
the United States, 1938–1940; Honorary Economic Adviser, New
South Wales Department of Agriculture, 1941–1942; Honorary Adviser, Commonwealth Department of War Organization of Industry, 1942–1943; Director of Research, Commonwealth Department
of Post-War Reconstruction, 1943–1946; co-author (with Colin
Clark), *The National Income of Australia* (Sydney, 1938); contributor to learned journals.

Contents

List of Illustrations

MAPS

[xxiii]

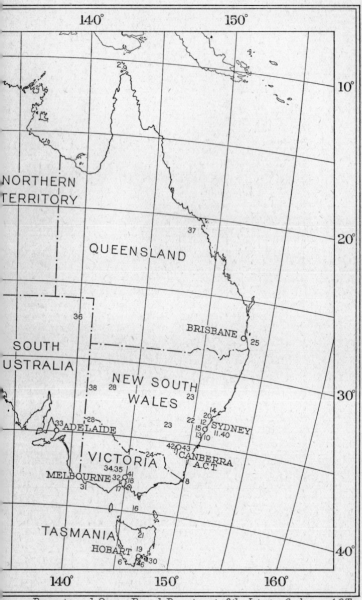

Property and Survey Branch, Department of the Interior, Canberra. A.C.T.

KEY TO NUMBERED MAP ON PRECEDING PAGES

1. 1606   The "Duyfken" in the Gulf of Carpentaria.
2. 1606   Torres sailed through Torres Strait.
3. 1616   Hartog at Shark Bay.
4. 1622   The "Leeuwin" at Cape Leeuwin.
5. 1627   The "Gulden Zeepaert" at Streaky Bay.
6. 1642   Tasman discovered Tasmania.
7. 1688   Dampier at Buccaneer Archipelago.
8. 1770   Cook sighted eastern coast.
9. 1770   Cook took possession of all the eastern coast at Possession Island.
10. 1788   First settlement at Botany Bay.
11. 1788   Settlement moved to Sydney.
12. 1789   First agricultural work on the Hawkesbury River.
13. 1790   First land grant at Parramatta.
14. 1796   Coal discovered at Port Stephens.
15. 1797   Macarthur's first experiments with sheep breeding near Parramatta.
16. 1798   Bass Strait discovered.
17. 1802   Port Phillip discovered.
18. 1803   First attempt to settle on shores of Port Phillip.
19. 1803   Settlement at Risdon, Tasmania (Hobart).
20. 1804   Founding of Newcastle.
21. 1806   Founding of Launceston.
22. 1813   Crossing of the Blue Mountains.
23. 1817–1823   Land beyond the Blue Mountains opened up by Oxley's exploration.
24. 1824   Hume and Hovell go overland toward Port Phillip.
25. 1825   Settlement at Moreton Bay (Brisbane).
26. 1826   Settlement at Albany.
27. 1827   Stirling at the Swan River.
28. 1829–1830   Sturt discovered the Darling and Murray rivers.
29. 1830   Founding of Perth.
30. 1832   Founding of Port Arthur, convict settlement.
31. 1834   The Hentys at Portland.
32. 1835   Batman and Fawkner at Port Phillip and the founding of Melbourne.
33. 1837   Founding of Adelaide.
34. 1851   Gold discovered at Ballarat.
35. 1854   Eureka Stockade.
36. 1861   Burk and Wills die at Cooper's Creek.
37. 1864   First sugar crops in Queensland.
38. 1883   Silver discovered at Broken Hill.
39. 1892–1893   Gold discovered at Coolgardie and Kalgoorlie.
40. 1901   Federation proclaimed at Sydney.
41. 1901   First Federal Parliament met in Melbourne.
42. 1908   Site of Canberra, the Federal Capital, selected.
43. 1927   Opening of Federal Parliament at Canberra.

AUSTRALIAN NATIONAL ANTHEM

THE COMMONWEALTH has never formally and officially adopted a national anthem. The song most commonly used on occasions when a national anthem may appropriately be played or sung is "Advance Australia Fair," both the words and the music of which were composed about 1878 by P. D. McCormick. The words are given below. This anthem enjoys considerable popularity with the people. Second in popular regard is "Australia," words by Mrs. C. J. Carleton, music by C. Linger, which dates from 1887. A third contender, "My Country," by Dorothy Mackellar, is superior to both as a piece of verse, but it has yet to be set to music of equal quality. The words of the latter two are printed immediately preceding the Bibliography of this book.

ADVANCE AUSTRALIA FAIR

By P. D. McCORMICK

Australia's sons, let us rejoice,
For we are young and free,
We've golden soil and wealth for toil,
Our home is girt by sea,
Our land abounds in nature's gifts,
Of beauty rich and rare.
In history's page let every stage
Advance Australia fair.

  Chorus:

In joyful strains then let us sing,
Advance Australia Fair.

When gallant Cook from Albion sail'd
To trace wide oceans o'er,
True British courage bore him on
Till he landed on our shore.
Then here he raised Old England's flag,
The standard of the brave;
With all her faults, we love her still,
Britannia rules the wave.

While other nations of the globe
Behold us from afar,
We'll rise to high renown and shine
Like our glorious southern star.
From England, Scotland, Erin's Isle,
Who come our lot to share,
Let all combine with heart and hand
To advance Australia fair.

Should foreign foe e'er sight our coast,
Or dare a foot to land,
We'll rouse to arms like sires of yore
To guard our native strand.
Britannia then shall surely know,
Beyond wide ocean's roll,
Her sons in fair Australia's land
Still keep a British soul.

Part One:

THE SCENE

CHAPTER I

Land and People

BY J. MACDONALD HOLMES

A USTRALIA is an island continent, long remote from the densely populated centres of the Old and the New World, but today at a crossroads south of the equator of both world air and world sea routes. It lies between East Longitude 113° 9′ and 153° 39′ (or between seven and one-half and ten hours' time difference from London) and between South Latitude 10° 41′ and 43° 39′, but, being surrounded by great oceans, has a more temperate climate than the latitudinal position would suggest when compared with corresponding positions in the Northern Hemisphere. Australia has a total area of 2,974,581 square miles, measures approximately 2,400 miles from east to west and 2,000 miles from north to south, and has about 10,000 miles of coast line. Its western gateway, Fremantle, is approximately 5,000 miles from Cape Town on the west. Its northern port, Darwin, is 1,900 miles from Singapore, and is approximately 5,000 miles from Japan, by way of Hong Kong.

Ships from London, via Suez, traverse 10,000 miles to Fremantle and some 12,500 miles to Sydney; via the Cape, the distances are 10,850 and 13,400 miles, respectively. The sea route from Sydney to the United States of America (Los Angeles) via New Zealand, Fiji, and the Samoan and Hawaiian Islands covers 7,500 miles. The distance from Sydney to New Zealand (Auckland) is 1,274 miles across the Tasman Sea, and to Panama the distance is 6,512 miles; through to London by that route is 12,500 miles.

Despite this marked isolation from the large land masses, Australia is, by virtue of air services, only a few days by flying boat from London via India, or from the California coast.

[3]

In area, Australia is more or less equivalent in size and in compact shape to the United States of America, and about twenty-five times the size of Great Britain. The mainland and the island of Tasmania comprise the Commonwealth of Australia, but in addition Australia controls Papua (90,540 square miles), the Mandated Territory of New Guinea (100,000 square miles), and several neighbouring islands in the Pacific Ocean, as well as the Australian Antarctic Dependency covering an area of something like 2,500,000 square miles.

Australia is a most compact continent, and although it "broke away" from Africa and Asia in the early history of the configuration of the land masses, it shows in its rock structures and topographic surface evidences of the main mountain-building movements and varieties of denudation forces pertaining to the world as a whole. A synoptic picture of the history of Australia in this regard would epitomise the geological history of the world. Some areas show excellent mountain forms, others great deserts. There are some ancient rock types with abundant mineral wealth and also enormous areas of rich alluvial plains. While in some respects the mountains are not comparable to the Alps, the Rockies, or the Andes, there are snow landscapes of great beauty, as at Mount Kosciusko and Mount Buffalo, with rugged slopes and peaks eminently satisfactory to the artist and climber. There is the infinite variety and charm of the desert, and the luxuriant growth and exotic abundance of the Tropics.

Structurally, Australia consists, first, of a central core of high mountain ranges composed of ancient metamorphic quartzites and granite domes. This is surrounded by very extensive plains of horizontal rocks consisting of Tertiary quartzites and sandstones with intervening areas of parallel sand ridges, as in the Simpson Desert. Outwards beyond the core, especially to the east and south, there are extensive plains of recent alluvium underlain by Tertiary limestones. Thus around the margins of the centre there are many areas whose surface consists of stony ("gibber") plains of quartzite or of limestone, soilless and almost devoid of vegetation.

Outwards again and nearing the coast are an infinite variety of granitic, metamorphic (slates and schists), and sedimentary zones such as the Grampians, the Australian Alps, and Carpentaria. Many of these zones are the chief mineral-bearing areas of Australia.

Interspersed with and overlying these basal rocks are more recently formed volcanic rocks such as basalts, denuded to such an extent that they now form isolated mountains and have weathered to form many of the richest soil belts. Elsewhere there are isolated areas, sometimes of considerable extent, consisting of coal-bearing rocks, especially in coastal Queensland and on the central coast of New South Wales. These give rise to the commercial coal fields (listed from north to south) of Bowen, Ipswich near Brisbane, the Hunter Valley, Lithgow and Bulli coal fields near Sydney, and Collie in Western Australia. The brown-coal area of Yallourn, which gives most of Victoria its electricity, is of comparatively recent geological formation, and there are several similar areas in Australia yet to be developed.

Eastern Australia consists of deep valleys carved out of once high plateaux. The remnants of these plateaux appear as continuous sculptured ranges. Between the ranges are wide valleys now undulating slopes out of which have been carved other valleys, and these contain the present-day rivers. So characteristic is this of eastern Australia that the statistical divisions for administrative purposes bear the prefixes coast, plateau, western slopes, and central plains. Furthermore, the eastern plateaux are so close to the coast that their spurs form cliffed headlands and their valleys riverine plains flanked by sandy beaches, while torrential rivers leave little opportunity for estuarine ports, excluding one or two exceptional cases. Nevertheless the scale of affairs is large, so that much of the dairying, timber, sugar, and tropical fruit industries are to be found on the eastern coast.

On the other hand, the western slopes of the plateaux are smooth, yet often too steep for the plough, but when cleared of their natural forest and woodland they have become the world's chief merino wool-growing region.

In contrast with the south, the northern coasts of Australia frequently have low mud-and-sand plains and gently undulating country. For topographic reasons many of the coast roads pass over high headlands almost along the water's edge, giving remarkable vistas; others are ten or more miles inland, seeking easy ways across wide and deep rivers or avoiding dry sandy stretches. Many towns said to be on the coast are, strictly speaking, many miles inland at a suitable

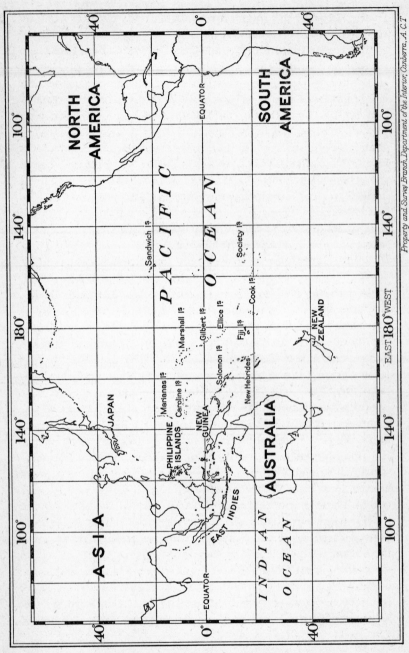

"AUSTRALIA AND THE SOUTHWEST PACIFIC"

Property and Survey Branch, Department of the Interior, Canberra, A.C.T

river crossing. So too, inland roads seek the open plains rather than the tortuous river bank.

The coastal plateau-ranges have been called the Great Divide to signify the parting of the western-flowing rivers from those of the east. There is considerable variation in the height of the Divide; for example, Mount Bartle Frere on the Atherton Tableland in Queensland is 5,438 feet in altitude, and Mount Roberts and Wilson's Peak, in the Macpherson Ranges near the northern border of New South Wales, are about 4,000 feet. The highest peak, Mount Kosciusko in southern New South Wales, is 7,328 feet. The New England Plateau in northern New South Wales is about 9,000 square miles in extent and has an elevation which varies between 2,000 and 5,000 feet. The Blue Mountains country in central New South Wales lying to the west of Sydney varies between 4,460 and 3,000 feet. In Victoria, Mount Bogong is 6,509 feet, and Feathertop, Hotham, Buffalo, and Buller are elevated areas and important tourist and sporting centres. Near Melbourne are the Dandenong Ranges of just over 2,000 feet, with charming fern gullies and native bushland, Mount Donna Buang (4,080 ft.) at Warburton, and Mount Macedon (3,325 ft.) at Macedon, both of which are within fifty miles of Melbourne. In the west of the State, the Grampians are a sandstone range with peaks rising to 3,029 feet. Elsewhere in Victoria there are isolated highlands rising to a little more than 2,000 feet. These highlands contain tourist resorts for fishing, shooting, and winter sports.

South Australia and the Northern Territory may be considered together so far as their topography is concerned. Of the combined areas, the principal highlands are the Mount Lofty Ranges (2,334 ft.), alongside Adelaide, and the Flinders Range, north of Adelaide, which runs roughly north and south for about 200 miles and then rises to 4,000 feet in St. Mary's Peak; and the Macdonnell Ranges and Musgrave Ranges near Alice Springs, with an altitude of about 5,000 feet at Mount Woodroffe. The well-grassed Barkly Tableland, part of which lies in the Northern Territory and part in Queensland, is an area more than 1,000 feet above sea level.

Western Australia lies almost entirely between 1,000 and 2,000 feet above sea level, with its greatest altitude at Mount Bruce (4,000 ft.), near the coast just north of the Tropic of Capricorn. In the Kimberley district in the north of the State are other mountains

ranging to 2,800 feet at Mount Hann. In the extreme south, the
Stirling Ranges rise to 3,640 feet, while the Darling Ranges near
Perth, which are a tourist attraction, rise little more than 1,000 feet
above sea level.

The land-surface pattern of Australia has been a major factor in
the pattern of her farming industries, especially in placing surplus
farming production for export in areas far removed from the coastal
ports. (Fig. 1)

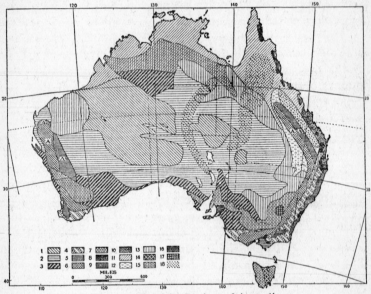

Fig. 1. Productivity Regions of Australia.

1, desert; 2, desert fringe, scrublands; 3, sparse woodland, mallee; 4, plateau
woodland and valley forest; 5, dairy- and beef-cattle regions; 6, sheep and wheat
belt (regions marked A are sparser occupations); 7, wheat and sheep belt; 8, rain-
forest; 9, sugar-plantation belt; 10, dairying, tropical fruits—bananas, pine-
apples, and sugar cane; 11, savannah woodland; 12, brigalow scrub and woodlands;
13, savannah, sparse sheep and cattle in New South Wales; 14, sheep, sparse agriculture and fruit-growing; 15, rain-forest, sclerophyllous forest, and moorland;
16, mountain forest, grassland, and pasture; 17, wheat almost solely; 18, stock-
cattle assembling regions and direction of southward movement.

This map is based on many statistically plotted distribution maps, the
vegetation maps, and numerous traverses in eastern Australia. Regions marked
A are of lesser importance.

Since Australia lies across the South Tropic, its climate partakes of both equatorial and temperate characteristics. In winter the cold influences from the south can be felt in Queensland and even in Darwin, and in summer the north monsoonal influences can give even Victoria a hot spell, temperatures soaring in summer to above 105° F. But for most of the year, throughout Australia, ordinary English clothing is required, and fires in the evenings. Rainfall is

TABLE 1
SEASONAL INCIDENCE OF RAINFALL
(Altitudes in feet, rainfall in inches)

Station	Alt.	Jan.	Feb.	Mar.	Apr.	May	June	July	Aug.	Sep.	Oct.	Nov.	Dec.	Year
Queensland														
Harvey Creek........	Coast	30.9	22.2	32.2	22.2	13.2	8.0	4.2	5.4	3.7	3.8	8.1	11.7	165.6
Brisbane...........	137	6.3	6.2	5.6	3.6	2.8	2.6	2.3	2.1	2.1	2.6	3.7	4.8	44.7
Charleville..........	975	2.6	3.3	3.3	1.5	1.5	1.2	0.8	0.6	0.8	1.3	1.4	2.3	20.6
New South Wales														
Sydney...........	146	3.7	4.2	4.8	5.6	5.1	4.8	4.8	3.0	2.9	3.2	2.8	2.9	47.9
Broken Hill.........	1,000	0.7	0.7	0.7	0.8	0.9	1.2	0.6	1.0	0.7	0.8	0.6	0.6	9.3
Melbourne..........	115	1.9	1.8	2.2	2.3	2.2	2.1	1.9	1.8	2.4	2.7	2.2	2.3	25.6
Western Australia														
Broome...........	63	5.0	6.4	3.8	1.4	0.4	1.2	0.3	0.0	0.1	0.0	0.9	3.5	23.0
Perth..............	197	0.3	0.3	0.7	1.7	4.9	6.6	6.4	5.6	3.3	2.1	0.8	0.6	33.3
Northern Territory														
Darwin............	97	15.9	13.0	10.1	4.1	0.7	0.1	0.1	0.1	0.5	2.2	4.8	10.3	61.8
Alice Springs........	2,000	1.8	1.7	1.2	0.7	0.7	0.6	0.4	0.4	0.4	0.7	1.0	1.6	11.1
Coolgardie..........	1,389	0.4	0.7	0.6	0.6	1.3	1.2	0.9	0.9	0.6	0.7	0.5	0.6	9.2
Tasmania														
Hobart.............	160	1.8	1.5	1.6	1.8	1.9	2.2	2.1	1.8	2.1	2.2	2.5	1.9	23.6
South Australia														
Adelaide...........	140	0.7	0.7	1.0	1.8	2.8	3.1	2.7	2.5	2.0	1.7	1.2	1.0	21.2

frequent and abundant, but a high evaporation rate reduces its economic significance. Days are mild and sunny in winter, cold in the south and not too warm in the north. In the Centre, dry days are in endless succession, and even elsewhere drought may become extensive in area and in duration. Contrasts are greatest in the Centre, where extensive deserts occur, but even here conditions often result in a rich type of cattle country, as in the Macdonnell Ranges and the Kimberleys. The Southeast Trade winds, so-called, scarcely make their presence felt in Australia, but the westerlies and the Northwest and Northeast monsoons influence the south and north respectively. When these north and south influences combine, rains fall throughout Australia and even the desert may have ten inches in a week.

The influence of altitude on rainfall is generally negligible, but there is considerable change in temperature with height, especially between day and night temperatures. Thus the highland ranges and plateaux offer to the dwellers on the coast an easily accessible respite from too great summer heat and humidity. Holiday resorts, schools, and colleges make use of this factor in the environment.

The seasons in Australia are in general the reverse of those of the Northern Hemisphere: summer, December, January, February; autumn, March, April, May; winter, June, July, August; spring, September, October, November. Seasonal incidence of rainfall can best be shown by the figures for a selection of Australian towns (see table 1).

The rainfall pattern of the continent as a whole is as shown in table 2. (It should be noted that over an area of 2,777 square miles no records are kept.)

TABLE 2
Average Annual Rainfall Distribution

Average annual rainfall (inches)	New South Wales (sq. mi.)	Victoria (sq. mi.)	Queensland (sq. mi.)	South Australia (sq. mi.)	Northern Territory (sq. mi.)	Western Australia (sq. mi.)	Tasmania (sq. mi.)	Total (sq. mi.)
Less than 10	48,749	nil	80,496	310,660	140,500	486,952	nil	1,067,357
10 to 15....	78,454	19,270	81,549	36,460	132,780	255,092	nil	603,605
15 to 20....	55,762	13,492	111,833	19,940	63,026	94,101	304	358,458
20 to 25....	45,140	14,170	143,610	8,620	49,157	44,340	3,844	308,881
25 to 30....	30,539	15,579	99,895	3,258	41,608	31,990	3,016	225,885
30 to 40....	33,557	14,450	61,963	1,036	37,642	59,520	5,027	213,195
More than 40	18,171	10,923	91,154	96	58,907	3,925	11,247	194,423
Total area	310,372	87,884	670,500	380,070	523,620	975,920	23,438	2,971,804

In central Australia there may be many consecutive days with the temperature near 100° F., and in the wintertime bright sunny days with frost during the night. Similarly, the difference between day and night temperatures may be as great as the difference on the average between summer and winter on the coast. In any season of the year, even in summer, it is possible to get cold spells when an overcoat is welcome, and in places like Sydney a hot summer day is frequently followed by a drop in temperature which gives vitality to the Australian climate.

Only in the cooler, temperate regions of the southeast and south-west and in Tasmania is the cold season well marked. More than one-third of Australia—1,149,320 square miles—is within the Tropics, the remaining 1,825,261 square miles being in the Temperate Zone. The extreme range of shade temperature in summer and winter over a large inland area is only 81°, as compared with 153° in North America and 171° in Siberia. Over the greater part of the continent, within the Temperate Zone, the climate resembles that of California, Southern France, or Italy. Cattle graze in the open all the year round, and it is only in the winter months in the mountain country of the southeastern corner of the continent and in Tasmania that snow falls. A difference between Australia and countries in the Northern Hemisphere is the absence of severe winters.

It is of interest to compare climatic statistics for various cities in Australia and in other countries. Tables 3 and 4 will bear examination in this connection. Actually some temperature at a moment of

TABLE 3

AVERAGE TEMPERATURES FOR A REPRESENTATIVE SET OF AUSTRALIAN TOWNS
(Altitudes in feet, temperatures in degrees Fahr.)

Station	Alt.	Jan.	Feb.	Mar.	Apr.	May	June	July	Aug.	Sep.	Oct.	Nov.	Dec.	Year	Range
Cape York	69	80.4	80.6	80.2	80.1	80.1	77.5	76.6	76.1	77.0	79.7	81.1	81.7	79.3	5.6
Charleville	975	82.8	80.2	75.8	68.8	60.2	53.5	51.0	56.5	62.8	71.6	77.4	80.2	68.4	31.8
Brisbane	137	77.2	76.5	74.3	70.3	64.5	60.2	58.5	60.4	65.3	69.8	73.6	76.4	68.9	18.7
Sydney	146	71.6	71.0	69.2	64.5	58.6	54.3	52.3	54.8	58.8	63.4	67.0	70.0	63.0	19.3
Broken Hill	1,000	78.6	78.2	72.0	64.0	56.6	51.1	49.2	52.6	58.4	65.9	72.9	76.6	64.7	29.4
Alice Springs	2,000	83.3	82.0	76.6	68.1	59.7	54.4	52.6	58.2	65.5	73.3	79.0	82.3	69.6	30.7
Perth	197	73.5	74.1	71.1	66.4	60.4	56.2	55.0	55.9	58.0	60.9	65.4	70.6	64.0	19.1
Melbourne	115	67.5	67.2	64.7	59.6	54.1	50.3	48.5	51.0	53.9	57.5	61.3	64.5	58.3	19.0
Adelaide	140	74.2	74.0	69.9	64.0	57.7	53.4	51.5	53.8	57.0	61.9	67.0	71.1	62.9	22.7
Darwin	97	83.8	83.4	84.0	84.1	81.8	78.9	77.4	79.4	82.6	85.3	85.8	85.1	82.6	8.4
Broome	63	85.9	85.4	85.4	83.1	76.4	71.2	70.3	72.4	77.0	81.0	84.6	85.9	79.8	15.6
Hobart	160	62.0	62.2	59.4	55.4	50.6	47.1	45.7	48.1	50.8	54.0	57.3	59.8	54.3	16.5

time may be lower than stated, but not the daily average at the point of observation at the usual time of reading the instruments. For example, although the lowest temperature on record for Sydney is 35.7°, temperatures lower than 32° have occurred.

The most urgent necessity in Australia is to obtain a good water supply. In coastal regions, rivers are usually torrential and only beginning to be brought under control; there is an abundance of rainfall to fill earth dams and household tanks from roof water.

The area of Australia that may be classed as arid, viz., with an annual rainfall of five to ten inches, is about a third of its total area. About another third surrounding it has up to fifteen inches of rainfall. Large-scale public works have therefore had to be constructed

TABLE 4

CLIMATIC STATISTICS FOR CITIES IN AUSTRALIA AND ELSEWHERE COMPARED

City	Average annual rainfall (inches)	Temperature (degrees Fahr.)			
		Mean summer	Mean winter	Highest on record	Lowest on record
Australia					
Canberra.................	23.15	67.8	43.9	104.2	14.0
Perth....................	34.73	73.2	56.1	112.2	34.2
Adelaide................	21.15	72.9	53.1	116.3	32.0
Melbourne...............	25.55	66.6	50.0	114.1	27.0
Sydney..................	47.06	71.0	54.3	108.5	35.7
Brisbane.................	44.90	76.7	59.8	108.9	36.1
Hobart..................	24.05	61.4	47.0	105.2	27.0
Other countries					
London..................	23.80	60.8	39.9	94.0	9.0
Edinburgh...............	25.21	55.9	39.0	90.0	6.0
Dublin..................	27.66	39.1	42.8	87.0	13.0
Paris....................	22.68	63.5	37.9	101.1	19.5
Berlin...................	22.72	64.8	33.0	98.6	13.4
New York...............	44.63	71.4	31.8	102.0	13.0
Bombay..................	70.54	82.7	74.7	100.2	53.2
Singapore................	91.99	81.2	78.6	94.2	63.4
Shanghai................	45.00	78.0	41.1	102.9	10.2
Tokio...................	61.45	74.8	39.2	91.0	29.7
Capetown................	25.50	68.1	54.7	102.0	34.0
Wellington...............	39.86	61.9	48.7	88.0	28.6
Ottawa..................	33.51	66.6	14.0	98.0	33.0
Buenos Aires............	38.78	72.7	50.9	104.0	25.3

to control the headwaters of inward-flowing streams, and there are such dams as the Eilden, the Hume (1,250,000 acre ft.), the Wyangala (304,000 acre ft.), and the Burrinjuck (770,000 acre ft.).

The headwaters and catchment areas of most of the inland rivers are found in the eastern highlands. They usually have an abundance of water most seasons of the year and offer facilities for trout fishing. Later on, the rivers have to find their way across extensive semiarid areas where tributaries are few. There may be eleven feet of water when the water is low, and rising from the water level are steep banks, tree-covered, for another twenty feet, so that the river appears to be travelling in a great ditch. When the river is in flood it may rise over the bank and spread far and wide over the surrounding country. The fascinating things about the river bridges of Australia are the long approaches and the height they appear to stand above the river level.

Along the banks of the rivers and for a zone on either side are remarkable belts of *Eucalyptus rostrata* or river gum. Elsewhere the vegetation may be low and sparse, and so there is an enlivening contrast for the traveller. Many of the smaller rivers are dry for months on end, and their clean sand beds, with the occurrence of deep waterholes, sheltered by the tall gums, are fascinating places for picnics, which are a characteristic feature of rural life. The banks close to the water level are often higher than the surrounding country, and the rivers, when ponded back, offer themselves for extensive irrigation schemes. On the Darling, the Murrumbidgee, and the Murray and its Victorian tributaries, and in South Australia, there are often very large irrigation settlements.

In South Australia and Western Australia there are extensive lakes, but only after very wet seasons do they contain water. Usually, they are simply extensive salt pans. Some are used for commercial salt and gypsum production.

The most remarkable water phenomena in the Commonwealth are the inland artesian water areas, the greatest separate unit being 570,000 square miles. These great geological basins have recently been proved to have a slightly greater extent than formerly realised, and to have on their margins a number of important high-level basins. It should be noted that the land surface where the largest of these geological basins occurs is an inland elevated region of 700 feet altitude and is generally a series of plains and hills covered with Mitchell grass or savannah woodland. Agricultural development from artesian water has not taken place, because artesian water is not a sufficient substitute for rainfall and it often contains much mineral matter.

The essential function of artesian water is the augmentation of pluvial water supplies for grazing and pastoral purposes. Occasionally, individuals may grow fruit or vegetables with artesian water, and on rare occasions small towns (e.g., Broome in Western Australia) may use artesian water for domestic supply. The region developed by artesian bores is much less than the geological water-bearing area. In Queensland the chief district is near Hughenden and Winton; in New South Wales, between Coonamble and the Queensland border; and in the mallee region of Victoria.

The costs of development are indicated by the depth to which artesian bores are put down. The maximum depth at which water has been found is 6,000 feet and the minimum 10 feet, with a frequency of 1,000 to 2,000 feet.

The flow of water has declined in virtually all the bores since they were first put down, owing to an increase in the number of bores and a diminution in the reserve of water. This decrease is usually stated to be 3 per cent per annum. The water is definitely known to be derived from the rainfall in eastern Queensland. Its continuation is therefore assured, and reliable conservation schemes ensure the maintenance of a permanent resource.

To the early pioneers in Australia the landscape was heavily forested. Around the coast in certain localities there are areas of dense evergreen forest of tall cedar trees and creeping vines. Elsewhere there is the characteristic evergreen eucalypt with its hundreds of species. Beyond the mountains extend wide belts of pine woodland and red, yellow, and grey box trees. Extensive grass plains are not characteristic and there is nothing comparable to the wide prairies of Canada and the United States. Instead, there are large areas of scrub vegetation consisting of belts of acacias called mallee or mulga and wide plains of low bushes called saltbush and bluebush. The Australian trees, even the scrub trees, offer a considerable variety in commercial timbers, especially for veneers for furniture. Almost every plant and tree in Australia is edible to sheep and cattle, and the great wool and cattle industries of Australia are in large part built up on a herbage and scrub pasturage rather than on improved grassland. The original Australia, therefore, was a woodland-and-forest environment.

The total effect of one hundred and sixty years of development has been that 47 per cent of the population is in metropolitan cities, about 17 per cent in provincial cities and towns, and 36 per cent is classified as rural. Whereas the percentage increase in rural population between 1921 and 1933 was 17 per cent, that for the metropolitan growth was 33 per cent. This is a measure of the increase in urbanisation taking place in Australia. The figures for New South

Wales are typical of the change in emphasis from rural to metropolitan dominance. In 1861 the metropolis had 27 per cent of the total population, while 13 per cent was in country towns and 59 per cent in rural areas. By 1891 the percentages were, respectively: metropolis, 34 per cent; towns, 32 per cent; rural, 34 per cent. In 1921 the rural population had dropped to one-fifth of the total.

Australia was peopled principally from Europe, and the main influx of population took place after 1850. Between that time and

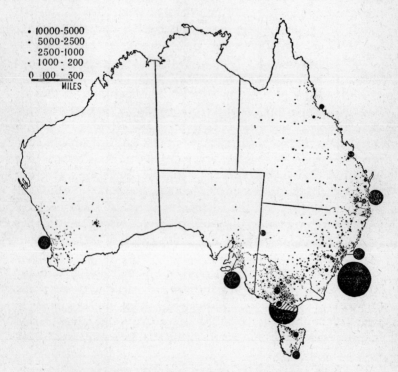

Fig. 2. Population Distribution Pattern of Australia in 1921.

Although this map was constructed from the figures for the 1921 census, the pattern for 1946 would not be appreciably different. The larger circles would be slightly increased in area. This is a proportional dot map in which the area of each circle represents the number of people in the locality as shown. Note the large number in each capital city; also, the widespread distribution inland of towns of a population of 5,000 to 10,000 or more. There is an additional wider distribution of the smaller population units than this map is able to show.

1911, when the first Commonwealth-wide census was taken, there was a change in the constitution of the population. In the earlier period the majority were immigrants, principally from Europe, and the native-born were in the minority. It was not until about 1871 that the Australasian-born exceeded those of British and foreign birth together. In 1891 the local-born were 69 per cent of the population, and the immigrants, 31 per cent. In 1921, 49 per cent of the immigrant population had resided in Australia for less than twenty years. By 1933 the figure had dropped to 45 per cent. At the 1911 census, of the total population of the Commonwealth, 81 per cent were born in Australia. At the 1933 census the figure had risen to 87 per cent.

The distribution of the population at the 1921 census is shown in figure 2 (p. 15). A map of the 1933 census would not be appreciably different.

Of all the states and territories the Northern Territory has the greatest percentage of rural population, namely, 66 per cent, and this figure would be higher were full-blooded aboriginals included.

The original native population has disappeared from the more settled areas and the present aborigine population is mainly dispersed as follows: northwestern Western Australia, 35 per cent; Northern Territory, 20 per cent; Queensland, 20 per cent. The remainder of the aborigines are in small groups in the remote rural areas of New South Wales and South Australia.

An effort has been made to relate population to resources, especially on a regional pattern over Australia. For example, governmental regional committees divided Queensland into about twenty regions, New South Wales into eighteen, Victoria into fifteen. These regions are designed so that each would have a community of interest and a balance of resources and activities. The regions are of different sizes and the populations they support vary between 50,000 and 100,000, though sometimes less. None of the regions is self-sufficient, though many of them could balance their budgets on two or three dominant industries.

Australia is a country in a transitional stage from primary production for export as one of the world's chief granaries to a continent in which industrialisation bids fair to outmode the earlier economic pattern.

Part Two:

HISTORICAL BACKGROUND

CHAPTER II

The Coming of the British to Australia, 1770-1821

BY ERIS O'BRIEN

FROM THE ages of antiquity geographers had suggested the existence of a great continent in the Southern Hemisphere, and on medieval maps "Terra Australis" was a familiar marking. The first practical approach to a solution of the problem occurred in the sixteenth century when Portuguese explorations extended eastward, north of Australia, toward the Pacific, and in 1520 when Ferdinand Magellan's Spanish expedition rounded South America and crossed the Pacific westward. Subsequent expeditions in the Pacific tended in a northeasterly direction and missed the Australian continent lying in the southeast. Among these a Spanish expedition led by Pedro Fernandez de Quiros in 1606 mistook an island in the New Hebrides group for the continent, calling it "Austrialia del Espiritu Santo," but an officer of that expedition, Luis Vaez de Torres, continued this voyage further westward and, without discovering the continent, sailed through the narrow strait that bears his name and separates Australia from New Guinea. This discovery remained unexploited until 1770.

Contemporary Dutch explorations were more successful. William Janszoon in 1606 discovered a section of the north coast of Australia, and between 1616 and 1627 Dutch industry practically determined the west coast and the south coast as far as 133° E. The final important Dutch contribution was made in 1642 by Abel Tasman, who, in an endeavour to find a southern sea route to America, touched upon the south coast of the island which was named for him, Tasmania, and then discovered New Zealand.

Although the positions of the north, west, and south coasts of the continent had thus been determined with reasonable accuracy, the eastern boundary remained unknown until a British scientific expedition, with James Cook (1728–1779) as commander and Joseph Banks (1743–1820) as scientist, was commissioned to explore the South Pacific area and locate the Southern Continent. Sailing by way of Cape Horn, Cook demonstrated the insularity of New Zealand, and then, proceeding westward, discovered the east coast of Australia on April 20, 1770, at a point 37° S. In a remarkable journey Cook accurately charted this eastern coast to its extreme northern tip and sailed into the strait discovered by Torres in 1606. On two subsequent expeditions he proved that no continent other than Australia existed in the South Pacific. In 1779 he was murdered by natives in the Sandwich (Hawaiian) Islands.

The new British possession, described as New South Wales or New Holland, aroused little interest in England until its convenience as a penal settlement became apparent. Transportation had been adopted in England as a statutory punishment in the sixteenth century, and for a century and a half large numbers of prisoners were sent regularly to the American Colonies; but when these colonies revolted in 1775 the convenient American outlet was closed. Proposals to reform the criminal law, to impose sentences of hard labour instead of transportation, or to modernise and extend gaol accommodation failed to impress Parliament, which, however, in 1784 authorised the Government to determine by an Order in Council whatever place it might fix upon for the establishment of a new penal settlement. Meanwhile, an expedient had to be adopted: the prisoners sentenced to transportation were confined on hulks moored in the Thames.

As early as 1779, Joseph Banks had suggested Botany Bay in New South Wales as a suitable place for a penal settlement at which prisoners could become self-supporting. In 1783 and 1785 similar proposals were made, suggesting also that "American Loyalists" should be allowed to settle there. But it was only after an abortive attempt to found a penal settlement in southern Africa that William Pitt's Government on December 6, 1786, issued an Order in Council authorising the establishment of a penal settlement on "the eastern coast of New South Wales." The decision was not a grand gesture of colonisation, but an avowed attempt to "remove the inconvenience" of overcrowded gaols. Captain Arthur Phillip, R.N. (1738–1814), a man long experienced in naval service, humane, with broad vision and the capacity to act on his own initiative, was fortunately selected to act as governor and planner of the new settlement.

Unlike the previous conception of transportation, under which a property interest in the services of sentenced prisoners was vested in transporting contractors who sold these interests to private employers, such property interests were now vested solely in the governor after the arrival of the convicts at their destination, and the governor was empowered to use these services in public works or to assign them to settlers for the duration of the sentences.

The majority of those transported were the inevitable products of the agricultural and industrial changes that had recently occurred in England, precipitating unemployment and creating social conditions that contributed to an increase in crime. No attempt was made to rehabilitate petty offenders. Under the drastic penal code the punishment of transportation, imposed for periods of life or fourteen or seven years, could be inflicted for trifling offences, such as stealing property valued above one shilling. The fact that about eighty per cent of those first sent to Australia belonged to the seven-years category indicates, not unreasonably, a minor degree of guilt; but because it was customary to commute sentences from execution to life transportation and from fourteen years to the minimum level of seven, it may be necessary to modify this conclusion somewhat. Nevertheless, throughout the history of transportation to Australia, which ended on the eastern coast in 1838, the disproportionate severity of the transportation penalty can be assumed generally, and particularly as applied to men transported for political disturbances.

On May 13, 1787, Phillip's expedition, known as "the First Fleet," which comprised eleven small ships totalling less than 4,000 tons, sailed from England. The prisoners on board numbered approximately 586 men, 192 women, and 13 children of convicts, and the free (officials, marines, and crews) were 695. January 18–20, 1788, after a voyage of eight months, during which only 32 had died, the Fleet entered Botany Bay, a week before the arrival of a French exploring expedition under the Comte de La Pérouse. Meanwhile, Phillip, dissatisfied with the barrenness of Botany Bay, had discovered at Port Jackson "the finest harbour in the world, in which a thousand sail of the line may ride in perfect security," and there on January 26 he unfurled the British flag and founded the settlement of Sydney.

The formative period of Australian history to 1821 divides into three sections, each of which marks a stage in determining whether the new settlement would be predominantly penal or free. The first section (1788–1792), as briefly sketched below, deals with the foundation of the penal settlement, in which the servitude and the rehabilitation of prisoners by land settlement were the main concerns. The second (1793–1809) notes the rise of private enterprise and the breaking of the penal system. The third (1810–1821) describes the attempt made to restore the authoritative rule of a penal settlement and the subsequent compromise effected between the then numerous body of free and freed settlers, who wanted constitutional concessions, and the Government, which wanted to continue transportation indefinitely.

The official task assigned to Arthur Phillip was to establish a penal settlement with the aid of prison labour and the enterprise of freed convicts, and to make it self-supporting as soon as possible and capable of receiving unpredictable numbers of transported prisoners in future. Phillip's ambition, however, was to lay the foundations of an outpost of empire.

The difficulties confronting him in this vast, unexplored country were enormous. With totally inadequate supplies of food, stock, seed, and farming utensils, he had to provide for, and regulate, a community of 1,030 persons comprising officials and marines and 548 male and 188 female convicts. Despite severe rationing and the transfer of convicts to Norfolk Island, which he immediately occupied, starvation threatened the settlement until the arrival of the first store-ship in 1790.

From 1778 to 1823 Australia was a Crown Colony of the extreme type in which governors ruled absolutely, their proclamations having temporarily the force of law but requiring endorsement by the contracting British ministerial department for their permanent validity. The settlement was conducted on military lines. The governor was assisted in administration by a few officials, such as a lieutenant-governor and a judge-advocate. The court of criminal jurisdiction consisted of the judge-advocate and six naval or military officers, and the civil jurisdiction was conducted by a judge-advocate together with two magistrates appointed by the governor. This type of judicial procedure remained in force until 1814.

The immediate problems arising out of the penal nature of the settlement were the control and employment of convicts and the rehabilitation of them when freed. The controls broke down immediately when the officers and marines refused to supervise the convicts, necessitating the appointment of supervisors from the convict ranks. Although a move was made in 1790 to solve this disciplinary lack by the creation of a special body of troops, known as the New South Wales Corps, a conflict between the officials and the governing authority continued until the removal of this specially dedicated military body twenty years later.

Generally speaking, the convicts, 4,312 of whom arrived during Phillip's administration, were undesirable types for colonisation. Large numbers were medically unfit and scarcely any were experienced in agriculture or trades. Realising the dead weight of them, Phillip complained: ". . . sending out the disordered and helpless clears the gaols, but it is obvious that this settlement, instead of being a colony which is to support itself, will, if the practice is continued, remain for years a burthen to the Mother Country." Such expressions as this are significant of Phillip's policy. In the original British plan, free settlement had been vaguely envisaged, but by his constant and emphatic advocacy of it as an immediate necessity to supplement the deficient system of land settlement by former prisoners Phillip challenged the predominantly penal purpose of the settlement at the outset and shaped the course of its development.

Convicts in servitude were maintained by the public stores and employed chiefly in forming the township at Sydney or in public farming at the Parramatta settlement about fifteen miles from Sydney. In the earliest period the conditions of their employment were not unreasonable, though punishments for misconduct were summary and severe. The brutalities and excesses commonly associated with the Australian penal system were generally limited to convicts who had committed breaches of the law after transportation, in respect of which severe exemplary sentences were imposed, as in the case of the Irish political prisoners who threatened a minor rebellion in 1804, or were inflicted under the summary jurisdiction of prejudiced and unqualified magistrates. Systematic adoption of severity occurred particularly in the penal stations specially set up to receive recidivists and incorrigibles, such as the Hunter River coal mines, Norfolk Island (particularly after 1821), and Tasmania (particularly after 1825). The excesses of the penal system and its failure to reform a majority of the convicts can be attributed mainly to the recurring element of incorrigibles among those transported, and weakened control after Governor Phillip's administration.

Important concessions originated by Phillip to encourage industry and reformation were the assignment and the emancipation of prisoners. Under the assignment system, which continued with modifications until 1841, convict labour was made available to settlers; but the system later deteriorated into a loosely controlled practice under which convicts were often assigned to masters who profited by the cheap labour and contributed little in return. Apart from the large number of convicts who became free by the expiry of their sentences, others, known as "emancipists,"[1] were granted remissions conditionally on their remaining in the colony for the duration of the sentence. This concession also was abused later when emancipations were made readily in consideration of a convict's education and former social standing or as a solace to those who believed their sentences had expired. Incidentally, it should be observed that the lack of precise information relative to the sentences of many transported prisoners caused embarrassment to prisoners and governors up to 1834.

To those who were freed by servitude or emancipation, land grants of thirty acres—more if they were married or had children—could be made, and assistance in labour and equipment was provided. As part of the plan of settlement, land grants of sixty acres were made also to minor ratings of the official establishment who desired to become settlers. Conditions of residence and cultivation were imposed on all settlers. Convinced that the expansion of the colony depended on a more competent class of settlers, Phillip strongly urged Great Britain to adopt a policy of free immigration and supported the request of the officers of the settlement that they be authorised to receive grants of land.

---

[1] This term was later used to denote anyone who had been in servitude.

Phillip's policy of colonisation, based on the principle of a peasant proprietorship of the land, might have proved an interesting
experiment had it not been completely overturned immediately
after his resignation. He granted 8,000 acres to 172 settlers, and at
his departure 1,800 acres were under cultivation. Only 102 of these
settlers were former convicts. One of them, James Ruse, after his
emancipation in 1789, became the first Australian settler and contrived to support a family on a small area of land without public
assistance. The rare repetition of his example, however, indicated
the general unsuitability of the convicts for the purposes of colonisation.

When Phillip resigned in 1792, settlements had been made at
Norfolk Island, Sydney, and Parramatta. The population was 4,322,
which included 255 children and 2,377 males and 684 females who
had been transported.

After Phillip's departure in 1792, the appointment of a successor
was delayed for three years and the administration unfortunately
devolved on Lieutenant-Governors Francis Grose (1792–1794) and
William Paterson (1794–1795), who were successively in command
of the New South Wales Corps. Moreover, Phillip's petition that
officers should be authorised to receive grants of land had just been
granted. Hence, power and opportunity were presented to these
men.

Grave social and political disorders ensued, not because the
officers elected to engage in agricultural and commercial pursuits,
but because they unscrupulously exploited their opportunities to
the disadvantage of the struggling populace. They took complete
control of trade; commandeering the cargoes of ships, they entered
into a combine to retail the implements of labour and the necessities of life to the populace at fantastic profits. Under such circumstances, settlers were compelled to sell their grain to the traders in
discharge of debts. Also, because the importation and distillation
of spirits had come under the control of the military, all classes of
the population were encouraged to barter their possessions in exchange for spirits, on which the percentages of profit could be com-
puted in thousands. Besides consolidating their position as traders,
the official class made grants of land to themselves, and considerably
extended some of them by appropriations of land belonging to

their debtors. Moreover, having power over the distribution of convict labour, they so greatly exploited the labour market that when
Governor John Hunter arrived in 1795 he found scarcely any convict labour available for public works.

During this short interregnum, fundamental social, economic,
and political changes were made, and it soon became evident that
development would not follow indefinitely on the lines of Phillip's
plan of a controlled peasant proprietorship. This fact demonstrated
that the predominantly penal purpose of the settlement, so far as
this had been envisaged in Great Britain, must be modified so that
free enterprise could be recognised alongside transportation. The
most serious challenge of all, however, was directed against the
absolute control of the Crown, and around this aspect of the situation a bitter conflict ensued until 1810.

During that period unsuccessful attempts to restore control to
the Crown were made by three governors, John Hunter (1795–1800),
Philip Gidley King (1800–1806), and William Bligh (1806–1808).
But before we consider this conflict, the growth of the settlement in
territory and population should be noted.

The coast of Tasmania had been explored in 1798, and between
1801 and 1803 the Australian continent was circumnavigated by
Matthew Flinders. The Sydney settlement was confined to the coast,
but after settlement had been attempted at Port Phillip in 1802, the
colonisation of Tasmania was begun in 1803, and at Newcastle in
1804 the coal industry was permanently begun by the labour of
convicts. Between 1792 and 1810 only about 7,000 convicts were
transported, but among them was a new element of political offenders, most of whom were Irish. The presence of these gave a degree
of respectability to the penal population, justifying concessions
such as early emancipation; nevertheless, resenting their penal condition, some of the convicts became malcontents and were subjected
to rigorous punishment.

In order to cope with the expanded settlement and to provide
opportunities for the rapidly increasing number of expirees, the
three governors determined to break the monopolistic power of the
official section. Governor Hunter accomplished little more than the
restoration of the civil court. It was obvious that reforms were impossible in circumstances where the policing and administration

of trade and labour restrictions were the responsibility of officers whose personal interests were opposed to such reforms. Governor King, however, achieved a measure of reform by imposing severe penalties on the traffickers in spirits, by restricting the assignment of convicts, and by setting up government and new private stores to compete with the traders. By 1806 social and economic conditions had improved; settlers then numbered 646, occupying 83,000 acres of land, on some of which—this is important—more than 20,000 sheep were grazing.

Of the 646 settlers, however, fewer than 100 belonged to the free class; and 36,000 of the 83,000 acres of granted land were held by twenty-nine officers of the civil and military services. Nevertheless, social and economic conditions were on the verge of change. Emancipists had already invaded the trading sphere. The members of the "exclusive" section, however, now including civil as well as military officers and a few progressive immigrant settlers of importance, were astutely visioning the overwhelming advantages of the pastoral industry. Their leader was John Macarthur (1767–1834), who as an officer of the New South Wales Corps had received his first land grant in 1794 and had begun importing sheep as early as 1796. His prestige had long been established, not only as the instigator and shrewd director of the opposition to governors, but also as the wealthiest trader, the greatest of the landholders, and the expert pioneer of the wool industry. At this stage he forecast that twenty years hence the sheep flocks of Australia would number five millions. Although the prediction was far from accurate, he would be able fifteen years hence to export to England 150,000 pounds of the finest merino wool from his own sheep.

So determined a man rode roughshod over colonial governors and carried his party with him. Governor King contrived to send him to England for court martial, but he convinced British opinion so effectively about the prospects of the wool industry that he returned with breeding rams from the King's own flocks and a permit to choose 5,000 acres of land anywhere in the settlement. Here was evidence of a new conflict in influential British opinion, which, while realising the necessity for restoring the prestige of the Crown in the colony and stabilising the penal purpose of the colony, had also become interested in the commercial prospects it evidenced.

Shortly after his return, having resigned his commission and further antagonised local authority by selecting his land grant from a valuable government reserve, Macarthur was confronted with the newly arrived Governor, William Bligh (1754–1817), who had previously attained celebrity as a man of determination in the incident of the "Mutiny of the Bounty" (1789).

Bligh's stern and restrictive policy, appreciated with much justice by the smaller settlers, made inevitable a test of strength between him and the anti-Government group. The opportunity came for both parties when the Governor arrested Macarthur for trading irregularities. Macarthur refused to be tried by a judge-advocate who was in his debt, and the objection was upheld by the six officers who, with the judge-advocate, constituted the court. When the Governor rearrested Macarthur and threatened to arrest the six officers, the Commandant of the New South Wales Corps, Lieutenant-Colonel Johnston, released Macarthur, and at his suggestion arrested the Governor on January 26, 1808. Bligh was kept a prisoner until the end of 1809, when he was released on condition that he would proceed to England.

Meanwhile, the settlement was administered by officers of the New South Wales Corps, who lavishly granted 194 absolute and 164 conditional emancipations, together with 75,000 acres of land. The irregular land grants were surrendered to the succeeding governor, but practically all were ratified immediately.

In the next twelve years, under the benevolent autocracy of Governor Lachlan Macquarie (1761–1824), the settlement made remarkable economic and social progress. But although much of this progress must be attributed to the initiative and rare capacity of the Governor, due regard must be had for the facts that the settlement had in 1810 a population of about 12,000, including more than 700 settlers, and great economic and agricultural progress had already been achieved through the efforts of the free and the freed. Macquarie began his career wisely by disbanding the troublesome New South Wales Corps, setting in its place a regiment under his own command. Protest against the principle of autocratic rule continued, but a degree of unity was always evident in the identical ambitions of the Governor, the "exclusives," and the "emancipists" to convert the settlement into a colony of economic importance.

Hitherto, the settlement had been confined to the seacoast by a low but impenetrable range of mountains thirty miles from Sydney. The condition was admirable for a vast gaol. In 1813 this barrier was crossed, revealing the existence of great fertile plains beyond, "changing the aspect of the colony from a confined, insulated tract of land to a rich and extensive continent" and opening the way for extensive pastoral settlement. The prospect was pleasing to the ambitious Governor as well as to enterprising settlers. Under his energetic direction, 276 miles of roads were made; scores of new townships were begun in New South Wales and Tasmania; the future city of Sydney was planned; the Bank of New South Wales was established; convict barracks, public buildings, schools, hospitals, and churches, some of them imposing and beautiful in design, were built. Legal procedure was reformed by the establishment of a civil court, and both the civil and criminal jurisdictions were placed under the control of legally qualified judges. Population increased threefold and the economic life of the settlement advanced.[2]

Despite such evidences of progress a serious cleavage in policy existed between the Governor and the free settlers. Macquarie believed that the colony should be developed chiefly by convict and emancipist enterprise, thereby ensuring its original purpose as a reformatory for prisoners. The free settlers, however, emphasised the importance of free settlement and looked to immigration to rid the colony of its penal characteristics and the associated autocratic rule of governors. Both parties refused to make the inevitable compromise.

In fairness to the Governor, the nature and extent of the penal problems which he had to solve for the public benefit should be appreciated, and this can be done by analysing the vital statistics of the colony at the end of 1821. Excluding officials, the total population of New South Wales and Tasmania was 36,968. The total of adults who had come free or had been born free in the settlement

---

[2] At the end of his career Macquarie made the following comparisons between the conditions existing in 1810 and those at the end of 1821: population increased from 11,590 to 38,778; cattle, from 12,442 to 102,939; sheep, from 25,888 to 290,158; acreage tilled, from 7,615 to 32,267; customs duties levied, from £8,000 to £38,000. The total land held by the free and the freed was stated to be 654,000 acres, of which Macquarie had granted 240,000 acres. In 1821, wool was exported for the first time, to an amount estimated at 200,000 lbs.

was only 4,492. There were also 8,416 children, of whom 5,859 were
the offspring of the transported. During his term of office transported
prisoners were nearly twice as numerous as those who had come to
the country between 1788 and 1810. In 1821 there still remained
16,062 convicts in servitude. He had not only to absorb these through
a big programme of public works, but also to provide opportunities
for their future in freedom. Moreover, apart from the prisoners,
there were 7,938 former convicts, free by expiry of sentence or by the
various forms of remission, who were exercising the rights of free
citizens in the settlement. Obviously, the rehabilitation of this preponderant penal section of the community demanded particular
attention from the Governor.

Two distinct free classes existed, however, and the "exclusives"
ostracised the "emancipists" effectively from social relations. Consequently, the Governor established the principle that "once a convict
had become a free man he should in all respects be considered on a
footing with every other man in the country, according to his rank
in life and character." Some of these emancipists had been merely
political prisoners. Among all classes of them could be found professional men, trained for the church, the law, and medicine. Several
had become wealthy through farming and trade, and a few were
reputed to have incomes of £3,000.[3]

Macquarie's prejudice in favour of the emancipists led him into
several excesses. He not only refused to recognise the contribution
which the free settlers had made, but also discouraged free immigration. Pursuing a stubborn policy, he left himself open to criticism in
the colony and in England by improvidently granting remissions to
prisoners and authorising the employment of emancipists in the
magistracy and the legal profession. Consequently, in 1819 John
Thomas Bigge (1780–1843) was appointed by the House of Com-
mons to make in Australia a thorough investigation into the affairs
of the colony.

Before Bigge presented his *Reports*, Macquarie resigned. The
three *Reports* (1822, 1823) were an exhaustive survey of Australian

---

[3] Statistics supplied by them in 1821 to support their claim for social recognition stated that they had 29,000 acres in cultivation and 212,335 acres in pasture;
sheep, 174,179; estimated capital, £150,000; estimated total of all their property,
£1,123,600. (Cf. *Historical Records of Australia*, Series 1, Vol. X, p. 549.)

history and progress since 1788, but they failed to recognise that the comparatively advanced economic condition of the colony warranted a readjustment of policy to enable free enterprise to develop normally alongside a more restricted British scheme of penal settlement. The statistics published in his *Reports,* however, made the conclusion obvious, even if unstated, and quite unused by Bigge in formulating his recommendations.

CHAPTER III

The Triumph of the Pastoral Economy, 1821-1851

BY JOHN M. WARD

NEW SOUTH WALES in 1821 was still a penal colony. Her prison-farm economy was varied by the trade and industry of only a small number of free settlers and emancipists. Observation of these facts prompted John Thomas Bigge, who had been sent out by the British Government two years earlier to report on the state of the colony, to assume that New South Wales would remain a mere "receptacle for convicts." His instructions had made this assumption, and only in the infant wool industry could Bigge find any suggestion that it might need amendment. His conclusions were based on misinterpretation of the facts. He did not appreciate the significance of the increase in the free population. He did not even remark the degree to which a free economy was already functioning.

In 1820 only half the adults in New South Wales were convicts. A further third were emancipists and convicts conditionally at liberty on tickets of leave. A sixth of the population had come into the colony as free settlers, or had been born there. The increase in the free population had produced a vast potential of change even before Bigge came to New South Wales in 1819. Petitions asking for trial by jury and economic concessions had been sent to London in 1819 and 1821, as a result of which the colonists had been granted extended trading rights. Grants of land had been made to the emancipists right from the first and not a few of them had been able to develop their interests far beyond the stage of peasant proprietorship originally envisaged by the Government. By 1821 the emancipists had secured a large share of the wealth of the country. Their growing investments in trade, agriculture, and the pastoral industry strikingly demonstrated the degree to which a private-enterprise economy was growing up inside the walls of the prison farm. In 1821 emancipists were cultivating nearly three times as much land as were the free settlers.

In economic matters there was a marked identity in the interests of the free settlers (the exclusives) and the wealthy emancipists—an identity which their strained social relations generally obscured. What both groups sought was to develop the colony with men of capital as the proprietors and with convicts as their servants. Despite the operation of the assignment system under which convicts were set to work for free men, the ambitions of both the exclusives and the wealthy emancipists conflicted fundamentally with the penal-colony policy, which had been strongly reaffirmed during the governorship of Macquarie.

This conflict and the rift between the exclusives and the emancipists were the main problems confronting Governor Macquarie's successor, Sir Thomas Brisbane (1773–1860), who was appointed in 1821. Brisbane was intended to introduce reforms arising out of Bigge's recommendations, but, as Bigge's *Reports* were not available when his instructions were drafted, no changes in policy were introduced until he had been in the colony more than a year.

The first instalment of reform was the New South Wales Judicature Act, 1823 (4 Geo. IV, cap. 93). Partly based on Bigge's *Reports*, the Act was also influenced by the emancipist petition of 1821. It redressed several of the emancipists' complaints concerning their legal status and provided for some regulation of the assignment of convicts to private employers. But the main provisions were those intended to restrict the powers of the Governors. The Act established a small Legislative Council to advise the Governor, and also set up a Supreme Court. Civil juries were introduced for civil cases, but, because of the predominantly convict character of the population, the so-called "military juries" were preserved for criminal cases. The Act also separated the administrations of New South Wales and Van Diemen's Land (Tasmania).

These changes accomplished little in relation to fundamental social and economic problems. They merely made administrative

THE LIBRARY
COLBY JUNIOR COLLEGE
NEW LONDON, N. H.

28419

adjustments and small concessions to the increasing proportion of free men in the colony. Some of the exclusives saw in the Council a potential check on the emancipist leanings of the Governors. The emancipists themselves benefited directly. But the Act did not touch the conflict of private enterprise with the Government's penal-colony policy, or the social gulf between the wealthy free settlers on the one hand and the emancipists and poor settlers on the other.

Official policy could not long remain silent on matters of such importance. In 1824 Governor Brisbane was ordered to make land grants of as much as four square miles to free settlers, each granted area being proportioned either to the amount of money the immigrant was prepared to spend on his estate or to the number of labourers he was prepared to employ. This instruction represented a sharp break with the earlier policy of making large grants only in exceptional cases. Partly in order to finance more extensive transportation, Brisbane was also empowered to sell Crown lands under a tender system. The full swing of the pendulum away from the small-estates policy came in 1825 with the instructions to the new Governor, Lieutenant-General (Sir) Ralph Darling (1775–1858), which permitted grants of between 320 and 2,560 acres to private persons and expressly permitted the sale of Crown land in lots up to 4,000 acres at not less than five shillings an acre.

The new policy comprised in these instructions plainly favoured large-scale development by private interests. Its adoption is to be attributed to changing conditions in both New South Wales and Great Britain. In New South Wales the way to a change of land policy had been opened by pastoral development, especially wool-growing, which necessitated extensive sheep runs. In Great Britain the change in land policy flowed from the increase of English imports of Australian wool, coinciding with which came a revival in English emigration and overseas investment. British capital, having emerged from the depression at the end of the Napoleonic Wars, was in an expansive mood. Australia seemed to offer a good field for investment. In 1824 the Australian Agricultural Company received its charter. The Company was to be granted extensive areas of land at a nominal quit rent and a monopoly of coal-mining in New South Wales in return for an investment of £1,000,000 in the colony and for employing convicts. The Van Diemen's Land Company, estab-

WILLIAM CHARLES WENTWORTH
1792–1872

SIR HENRY PARKES
1815–1896

lished by Royal Charter in 1825, received more than 400,000 acres
for a quit rent of £468. Individual settlers of substance were encouraged to go out to the colony by a system of Colonial Office orders on
the Governors for land grants.

A period of rapid expansion followed the change in economic
policy. Wool exports in 1831 were fifteen times as great as they had
been in 1821, the first year in which wool was exported in commercial quantities. The increase in the number and quality of sheep led
to a rapid opening of new territories for grazing.

Exploration proceeded apace. Three main problems were pressing to be solved. The most important was to find an easy road northward to the rich Liverpool Plains which John Oxley (1781–1828)
had crossed in 1818. The second problem was to push exploration
southward beyond the River Lachlan and westward beyond the
Monaro Plain. The third problem, the problem of the rivers, arose
out of the second. Where did the big inland rivers of New South
Wales end? Was there an inland sea? Was the heart of Australia
desert or fertile? Allan Cunningham (1791–1839), the botanist,
solved the first problem in 1823 and went on to explore the rich
tableland of the Darling Downs in 1827–1828. The task of pushing
exploration southward was begun by the sheepmen, looking, it has
been said, "not for glory but for grass." Formal exploration to the
south was undertaken by Alexander Hamilton Hume (1797–1873)
and William Hilton Hovell (1786–1875) in their journeys on the
Murrumbidgee, the Murray, and to Port Phillip. South of the Murray, exploration was continued by Angus McMillan (1810–1865) in
1839 and by the Pole, Count Paul Edmund de Strzelecki (1796–1873)
in 1840. The problem of the rivers was virtually solved by the explorations of Captain Charles Sturt (1795–1869) on the Murrumbidgee, the Murray, and the Darling, and by the work of Sir Thomas
Livingstone Mitchell (1792–1855) on the Darling. The inland areas
of the centre of Australia were probed by Edward John Eyre (1815–
1901) and by Sturt. In northeastern Australia a great series of explorations was carried out in the 1840's by Mitchell, Dr. Ludwig
Leichhardt (1813–1848), and Edmund B. Kennedy (1817–1848).

It was the search for new land of economic worth which underlay
most of the explorations. In New South Wales especially, settlers
and sheepmen quickly followed exploration in every direction,

their flocks and herds spreading out fanwise from Sydney over the interior. But the search for new land did not of itself account for the entire expansion of settlement in the 1820's. The growing determination to exclude other powers from the continent stimulated official interest in long-distance exploration by land and by sea and in the planting of new settlements. Bathurst and Melville Islands (off the northwest coast) were annexed and outposts were established between 1824 and 1827 at Westernport in the southeast and Albany in the far southwest, in order to clinch British claims to the whole of Australia. Elsewhere, official policy reflected a blend of expanding pastoral economics and of the old penal-colony system. When Governor Brisbane planted a settlement at Moreton Bay (Queensland) in 1824, he intended it partly as a place of punishment for recalcitrant convicts, partly as the nucleus of further economic development. A combination of the policies of laying claim to the whole continent and of extending settlement for the sake of investment led to the annexation of the Swan River Territory in 1829, together with a formal declaration that the whole of Australia was British territory.

The leaders and principal beneficiaries of the great pastoral expansion of the 1820's were men possessing substantial capital, whose emigration from Great Britain had been much encouraged by the Home and Colonial governments. The avowed policy was to develop the country through the opening up of large estates, preferably in the hands of free settlers. Special assistance was given to well-established investors with capital. In 1829 it was reported that any intending settler who had satisfied the Colonial Office of his financial standing could receive "the usual grant of 2,560 acres of land at his option." Land was available also by sale. More than six times as much land was alienated from the Crown in the 1820's as had been disposed of during the first thirty-two years of the colony's existence.

That the colony developed rapidly under the new policy cannot be gainsaid. But there were some disturbing social and political implications, which had become apparent by the end of the decade. Government policy was obviously strengthening the hands of the wealthy capitalists. Those of the emancipists who belonged to this group sought social recognition through political change. Less wealthy emancipists sought reform for the sake of economic opportunity. Throughout Darling's term of office (1825–1831) the emancipist movement gained strength under the vigorous leadership of William Charles Wentworth (1793–1872), the young explorer, barrister, and writer, the first Australian-born leader of major stature. So strongly was the administration attacked by the *Australian* and the *Monitor* newspapers that in 1827 Darling began a series of attempts to restrict the liberty of the press. In the same year the emancipist party prepared petitions to the King and Parliament asking for a representative legislature and trial by jury and protesting against the privileged position of the exclusives. Useful support was received from the efforts of Sir Francis Forbes (1784–1841), the first Chief Justice of the colony, to bring about the establishment of constitutional government. Forbes brought to the colony liberal theories of representative government.

The Colonial Office was convinced that reform was necessary, but was not prepared to change fundamental policy in spite of the fact that free economies were by that time firmly established in the Australian colonies. The new Act, 9 Geo. IV, cap. 83, which applied to both New South Wales and Van Diemen's Land, introduced reforms without effecting fundamental change. Further restrictions were imposed on the powers of the Governors by an increase in the size of the Legislative Council (to permit the addition of more non-official members) and by the abolition of certain special powers of legislation reserved by the Act of 1823. Taken in conjunction with the establishment of an Executive Council in 1825, these reforms provided in some degree a potential check on the Governors' powers, although in practice the Legislative Council represented only the exclusives for many years. Judicial changes made in the Act of 1828 foreshadowed the institution two years later of an alternative method of trial by civil jury in criminal cases. Military juries were not finally abolished until 1839.

The changing nature of the colony during the 1820's made a deep impression on British policy. New South Wales was so obviously prosperous in comparison with the depressed state of England that there was a growing tendency to regard it not merely as a receptacle for convicts but as a valuable source of aid for the harassed Mother Country. The root of the distress in England was then generally thought to be superabundant population. Why, it was asked, should not prosperous New South Wales, with its increasing opportunities for free immigrants and its shortage of labour, relieve Great Britain of her surplus workers? Labourers and mechanics should be encouraged to emigrate, rather than men of capital such as those who had gone to Australia in the 1820's.

One solution of the problem of finding labour for the colonies was that of Edward Gibbon Wakefield (1796–1862). In his *Letter from Sydney* (1829) and succeeding works Wakefield developed a theory of colonisation which greatly influenced the development of the British Empire. The three leading principles of his scheme were the sale of colonial lands instead of land grants, the application of the proceeds of sale to emigration from the Mother Country, and the granting of some form of self-government to British possessions overseas. Wakefield held that the colonies possessed an insufficient labour supply because even the working classes were able to acquire land freely and set up on their own account. If land were sold at a sufficient price, he contended, the number of proprietors would be smaller, development would be better coördinated, and the labour problem would be solved.

Wakefield's theories soon obtained some measure of support at the Colonial Office. The dismal failure of the 1828 attempt to settle Western Australia on the basis of generous land grants lent further force to his arguments in their application to Australia. It became generally accepted in British official circles that the existing land-grant system in Australia was bad, that greater emigration was necessary for the sake of England itself, and that the growing economic strength of the colony should be used to relieve the distress of the Mother Country.

These three conclusions were merged in a single policy by the new Colonial Secretary, Viscount Goderich (later the Earl of Ripon). Goderich proposed that land grants be abolished for the future and that the proceeds of land sales (beyond what was needed for the administration of the colony) be used to finance emigration from Great Britain. Under the Ripon Regulations of February, 1831, sale by auction at a minimum price of five shillings per acre replaced the old land-grant system. An Emigration Commission established in June was sending out emigrants within four months. For the first time a consistent effort was being made to encourage large-scale free emigration to Australia.

Emigration proceeded at a high rate for the next ten years. Between 1832 and 1842 about 70,000 immigrants, of whom nearly four-fifths were assisted by the Government, arrived in Eastern Australia. The quality of the immigrants, however, was often less satisfactory than their quantity. "A good deal of disappointment," wrote the Governor in 1835, "has arisen . . . from the want of a correct understanding in England as to the persons in request here."

Dissatisfaction with the loose supervision of the London Emigration Committee (a voluntary body) led to a demand for colonial control of emigration. As a result a new bounty system was introduced in 1835. Settlers in Australia would be paid a bounty for bringing out suitable migrants. No bounty would be paid unless the migrants were certified as suitable on their arrival in Sydney. Some improvement in the quality of immigrants resulted from the appointment of an Official Agent for Emigration to replace the unofficial London Emigration Committee.

The surprising feature is that the migrants were as well absorbed in the colony as they were. The people whom the British Government wished to send out were not generally the type needed in Australia. Only the high level of demand for both rural and urban labour, which resulted from the rapid expansion of settlement, made immigration a working success.

In actual fact the amount of new country being opened up was greater than even the expansion of the pastoral industry necessitated. The Ripon Regulations themselves were partly responsible for the avidity with which land was taken up. The policy of the Regulations being to get in as much revenue as possible, no limits were placed on any settler's purchases of land. As a result wealthy farmers and graziers bought up the Crown lands which they had been holding since Darling's time under a licencing system. So common was this procedure that before long hardly any pasture land remained for newcomers inside the so-called Nineteen Counties within which Darling and his successors had attempted to confine settlement. (The Nineteen Counties comprised the area along the Pacific coastline from Moruya to the Manning and later to Port Macquarie, spreading inland to the Wellington Valley and Yass.)

Under the double stress of a high price for land and the absorption of the best grazing land in the Nineteen Counties, newcomers and those of the old settlers who did not buy up big pastoral estates within the prescribed area simply moved outside the Nineteen Counties and ran their sheep without permission on the unlimited areas which lay beyond. No Government could stop them. A man with sheep or cattle went where he pleased and obtained land for nothing. The opening up of land beyond the Nineteen Counties began the much-discussed "squatting" of 1835–1850.

Originally a "squatter" was simply a person who illegally occupied Crown land near alienated estates and plundered the stock of legitimate settlers. There had been squatters even in the Nineteen Counties. When the big landholders moved into the prohibited zone, poorer men followed them and squatted on the fringes of big holdings, there to earn a living by dubious methods.

After 1835 the outflow of the flocks and herds over the boundaries of the Nineteen Counties became so great that in the process men of all ranks pushed off into the interior with sheep. At first the respectable pastoralists who crossed the borders of the Nineteen Counties in search of grass were designated "settlers" and the undesirables who accompanied them were stigmatised as "squatters." But eventually the term "squatter" was applied to any person of means who depastured his flocks and herds on the Crown lands beyond the Nineteen Counties. The term ceased to be invidious and became honorific.

Governor Richard Bourke (1777–1855) understood that it was impossible to prevent this form of squatting, and Acts of Council in 1832 and 1833 afforded it a limited recognition. But the Colonial Office was less sagacious. The Ripon Regulations had been partly based on a "concentration theory" of settlement. According to the prevailing Wakefield doctrine, squatting represented a wanton dissipation of resources. Bourke, however, persisted in his attitude, and in 1836 the Legislative Council of New South Wales passed the Squatting Act (7 William IV, No. 41), which enabled any respectable man to occupy Crown lands without breaking the law. For a licence fee of £10 a year a squatter could stock as many acres of Crown land as he pleased. Boundary disputes were to be settled by officials known as Commissioners of Crown Lands. In 1839 the ad-

ministration was tightened up by the establishment of a Border
Police, to be paid from the proceeds of a poll tax on stock.

In bursting the bounds of the old concentration policy Bourke
threw the Colonial Office into confusion. Only two years before,
Parliament had passed the South Australia Act, embodying some
elements of the Wakefield scheme. Land was to be sold in the new
colony of South Australia at not less than twelve shillings per acre,
although the current price in New South Wales was only five shillings. The concentration policy was to be rigidly applied. In the
same month that Bourke introduced his Squatting Act, the first
settlers were arriving in South Australia.

The wrath of the Wakefield group at Bourke's disregard of their
principles was extreme. But neither the cherished theories of the
Wakefield group nor the interests of the new colonial experiment in
South Australia could be permitted to outweigh the claims of the
pastoral industry, on which England relied to keep New South
Wales prosperous.

Similar conflicts of English policy and Australian development
were raised by the early settlements in Victoria. In the name of the
concentration policy, Thomas Henty had been refused leave to purchase land at Portland Bay in 1834. But settlers from Van Diemen's
Land nevertheless crossed Bass Strait in search of new land, and in
1835 John Batman (1800–1839) and John Pascoe Fawkner (1792–
1869) established themselves at Port Phillip. Recognising that occupation was inevitable, the Government eventually abandoned the
concentration policy there and decided to throw open the whole
district to settlement.

The changes in land policy clearly demonstrated the rapidity
with which free enterprise had developed in Eastern Australia
beyond the realisation of the Colonial Office. Actually, land was
only one of the many subjects in respect of which the emergence of
the pastoral economy in Australia and changing conditions in
England were constantly raising new problems for British policy.
In 1838, when Sir George Gipps (1791–1847) became Governor of
New South Wales, the main problems were land control, "transportation" (deportation), immigration, and the control of colonial
revenue. Local interests, with varying degrees of unanimity, asserted
that all these problems should be solved by a local Parliament.

The fundamental problem was that of transportation. The pastoral economy had reached the stage in 1838 at which it was not merely in conflict with the penal purposes of the colony, but was inconsistent with them. This fact was recognised by at least a few of the shrewder employers in New South Wales, who perceived that convict labour was not always cheap and that transportation was a hindrance to the emigration on which they would have to depend for adequate labour of the right kind. In Whitehall also the economic aspects of transportation were well understood. Now that the pastoral industry had made New South Wales and Van Diemen's Land prosperous, British policy was to build up emigration and it was generally recognised that transportation and large-scale emigration were incompatible.

This conclusion was reinforced by the rapid growth in the free population. Assisted migration had produced a new social class in Australia, the emergence of which later obliterated many of the legacies of convictism, including the emancipist problem. The 75,000 settlers who reached New South Wales between 1836 and 1850 provided not only free workingmen, but also the nucleus of a middle class. It was the middle class, whose cause was so vigorously expounded by Dr. John Dunmore Lang (1799–1878), the forceful Presbyterian divine, which provided one of the strongest political forces opposed to transportation.

Knowing that transportation was coming to an end, the British Government readily acquiesced in the appointment of a Select Committee on Transportation in April, 1837. The Committee did not report until 1838, when it strongly condemned the barbarities of the assignment system and, doubting the deterrent effects of transportation, recommended its abolition. Actually, the Government had already decided to abolish transportation, the decision being taken just eight days after the Committee was appointed. Formal abolition of transportation to the mainland was made by an Order in Council of May, 1840. Transportation to Van Diemen's Land did not cease until 1853.

In the colonies themselves opinion was sharply divided on the transportation question. The whole issue was complicated by the emancipist problem and by the certainty that there would be no further progress toward self-government while transportation continued. (Thus Van Diemen's Land was excluded from the constitutional reforms of 1842 on the ground that a penal colony could not be self-governing.)

Australian opinion seems to have carried little weight in the making of the final decision. It is clear that the British Government had determined in April, 1837, to abandon transportation. Yet the issue was still being hotly debated in the colony in 1840. Even after 1840 some of the wealthy landowners, taking advantage of interruptions to immigration, agitated for the resumption of transportation. Though the British authorities were willing, public opinion in Australia demonstrated in 1844 and 1849 that no further transportation to New South Wales would be practicable.

Deprived of further convict labour, colonial employers relied increasingly on the bounty system of immigration introduced by Governor Bourke in 1835. Bounty immigrants were preferred to assisted immigrants, not only because they were cheaper to bring out, but because they were content with lower wages.

Heavy calls on the land and emigration fund in 1839–1840 combined with the onset of the financial crisis of 1841–1843 to bring to a head the fiscal problems of the colony. The immediate trouble concerned the expenditure of land-sales revenue, which was controlled by the Colonial Office alone. Protest after protest had been made in New South Wales against the use of such revenue for any purposes other than the immigration needed to sustain the labour supply. Opposition was particularly directed against the use of land revenue for police and gaol expenditure. The exclusives and the emancipists combined in their demand for local control of the revenue from land.

Constitutional adjustment was obviously overdue in New South Wales. Transportation had ceased. All classes were demanding representative institutions and greater local self-government. The only important division of opinion in the colony on this issue was whether the representative institutions should be those sought by the wealthy exclusives and emancipists or those sought by the great mass of public opinion, then dominated by the free settlers who had come out as assisted immigrants and sought a free Australia.

In 1842 there were British attempts to solve the land problem, the constitutional problem, and the problem of land revenue. By the Land Sales Act free grants were abolished throughout Australia and provision was made for sale by auction at increased minimum prices and for private sale of large areas. Land revenue was to be at the disposal of the Crown, subject to the expenditure of at least half of it on emigration. The Constitution Act (5 and 6 Vic., cap. 76) broadened the basis of nonofficial representation in the Legislative Council, but laid down that elected members were to be chosen by voters having freehold property worth £200 or equivalent qualifications. The elected members themselves had to possess freehold estate in New South Wales to the value of £2,000, or £100 a year. The Governor and Legislative Council were expressly excluded from legislating for the control of Crown lands or of revenue derived from them.

These changes brought little satisfaction. The burning questions of the day regarding land had been decided against the wishes of the most influential colonists. The majority were almost equally dissatisfied with the property qualifications which confined the Legislative Council to the wealthy. But the principal objection was to the increase of the upset price of Crown land and the failure to grant the squatters' demand for preëmptive rights.

For several years powerful squatting interests had insisted that the British Government should either surrender all control over Crown lands or else reverse its policy. By 1840 the squatters were making common cause with the wealthiest and most conservative groups, legally entrenched in the Nineteen Counties, in order to secure proper recognition in Great Britain of the needs of Australian capital. The spokesman of the squatters was Wentworth, who had led the emancipist agitation for the Act of 1828. Wentworth, a squatter himself, pointed out that under the existing land law squatters had no security of tenure and no inducement to stabilise the staple industry of the country. The squatters demanded compensation for improvements, security of tenure, and the right to buy portions of their runs. Governor Gipps, who took a more balanced view of the land question than either his superiors in London or the squatters in New South Wales, sympathised with the demand for security of tenure. But he also recognised that the squatters were using large areas of land at nominal charges and were making high profits.

It seemed to Gipps that the most reasonable tenure would be leasehold. He wished to maintain the existing rights of the squatters while removing such abuses as the grouping of several runs under a single licence fee. On April 2, 1844, Gipps promulgated a simple code allowing the squatters to remain beyond the Nineteen Counties as before but requiring a separate licence fee for each run. No run would exceed 20 square miles or carry more than 4,000 sheep. A day after these regulations were announced, the details of Gipps's policy of land purchase were made public. This policy was designed to meet the squatters' demand for preëmptive rights over portions of their runs. It was provided that after five years' occupation a squatter could buy 320 acres of his run. The purchase would preserve his rights to the rest of the run for eight years, when a further 320 acres would have to be purchased. On failure to complete a purchase, the run would become vacant. Any person could claim the unpurchased balance, the previous occupant receiving merely compensation for improvements.

The proposals were reasonable, but the time was inopportune. Smarting under their losses in the depression of 1841–1843 and continued bad seasons, the squatters resented all efforts at control. A militant Pastoral Association was formed and petitions were sent to England, where the increasing importance of Australian wool won much support for the squatters' case. In Australia it was the obligatory character of the purchase system which was specially attacked. When the whole issue of land control became confused with the claim for responsible government, there was even talk of rebellion.

With the return of better seasons and more prosperous conditions, calm judgment again prevailed and the firmness of Gipps was rewarded. It was recognised that the land-purchase proposals really amounted to a leasehold tenure coupled with a right of purchase. By 1847 it was possible for the British Government to solve the major land problems by an Order in Council, issued under the Waste Lands Occupation Act of 1846. The old system of restricting sales to the Nineteen Counties was abandoned. Different leasehold tenures with varying rights of purchase were granted in the "settled" districts near the towns, the "intermediate" lands next to them, and the "unsettled" lands of the far interior. Substantially, the squatters received the leases and preëmptive rights for which they had fought. The Order in Council was extended with only slight variations to South Australia and Western Australia. The squatters' battle for recognition was over.

In fact, the zenith of the pastoral domination of Australia was also passing. By 1850 there were complaints that agriculture was being obstructed by the pastoralists' occupation of the best land. Van Diemen's Land and South Australia, in which farming had always predominated, were supplying New South Wales and Victoria with part of their breadstuffs. A further attack on pastoral supremacy was developing in the coal of New South Wales and the copper of South Australia.

The general prosperity of the colonies, the ending of transportation, and the rapid increase of their populations were overt facts reinforcing the claims being made for constitutional change. Van Diemen's Land and South Australia, still governed by nominee councils, were persistently demanding self-government. Victoria was still part of New South Wales and was fighting hard for complete separation, a measure of which had already been won. Even in New South Wales the Legislative Council had not played the active rôle expected of it in 1842.

In 1850 the British Government attempted to remedy all these constitutional grievances. Under the Australian Colonies Government Act, 1850, Victoria was separated from New South Wales and the separation of Queensland from New South Wales was foreshadowed. The most important change was that which conferred on all the Australian colonies the right of preparing constitutions of their own. Having established their economic position, the colonies were thus put in a position to work out their own political destinies.

CHAPTER IV

The Gold Rushes and the Aftermath, 1851-1901

BY R. M. CRAWFORD AND G. F. JAMES

B Y THE MIDDLE of the century, the pastoralists or "squatters" dominated the economic life and government of the Australian colonies. At its end, the Australian economy still rode mainly "on the sheep's back," and the power of the squatters was still great in government. Yet in those fifty years there had come to be very widely accepted in Australia a set of democratic assumptions that were not theirs.

By 1851 the squatters' flocks supplied more than half of Britain's imported wool and gave a livelihood to nearly half a million Australians. In a country where scarcity and uncertainty of the water supply made the significant ratio that of acres per sheep and not sheep per acre, the grazing lands were inevitably the "big man's frontier." Theirs was the dominant wealth of the colonies, and theirs, too, the dominant voice in government.

The Australian Colonies Government Act of August, 1850, recognised these facts. It empowered the various colonies to formulate plans for their own future constitutions, to decide their own franchise, and even to control their own tariffs. But neither Whitehall nor the squatters had the slightest desire to "sow the seeds of a future democracy," and, had this act been delayed a year, it might have aroused anxious misgivings both among those who had demanded it and those who drafted it as a natural step in colonial evolution. It was intended for comparatively simple pastoral communities; but almost immediately it became evident that its consequences would have to be worked out in completely unforeseen conditions. For in

1851 the discovery of rich gold fields in New South Wales and Victoria brought to Eastern Australia what were for those small communities vast numbers of people and whirled Australia into social and economic revolution.

For fifteen years, from 1851 to 1865, an average of two and a half million ounces of gold was exported from New South Wales and Victoria alone, at an average price of £4 per ounce. The industry and commerce of the Northern Hemisphere were demanding every assistance that financial institutions could provide, and banks purchased eagerly every ounce of gold available. Bank rates fell, capital became abundant, and migration to the Australian colonies made no insignificant contribution to the new markets that completed the cycle of economic stimulus.

Victoria, containing the most prolific fields, was most fully transformed by the gold rushes; but no adjacent colony escaped their influence. Ships left Adelaide and Launceston crowded with hopeful diggers flocking from the colonies of South Australia and Van Diemen's Land to the fields of Ballarat and Bendigo; and raced back in ballast to overload again. Economically, both South Australia and southern New South Wales were annexed to the Victorian diggings, and flocks were again "overlanded" across the Murray. But they were no longer flocks in search of pasture; they were flocks which would not be shorn, destined for the crude slaughter-houses amid the canvas townships of the gullies.

An older colony might have been better able to meet the strain of the overwhelming rushes than the newly established colony of Victoria with its inexperienced legislature and its undeveloped administration. In the decade from 1851 to 1861, Victoria's population jumped from 77,000 to 540,000, outstripping that of New South Wales, which in the same period rose to 350,000. Melbourne quickly became the most populous city in Australia. The pressing immediate problem was the accommodation, feeding, and policing of the incoming crowds; the more permanent was their employment when the surface alluvial gold petered out.

The problem of housing the new numbers was frantically and imperfectly solved with canvas and corrugated iron. Their feeding was an opportunity for those who saw more profit in supplying the diggers than in digging. The proceeds from cartage to the diggings at

£80 per ton from Melbourne lifted more than a few former diggers
and immigrants into the ranks of small landowners, small manufacturers, or subcontractors on the public works that Victoria's sudden
urbanisation demanded. The administration and policing of this
swollen community was a more stubborn problem. Lieutenant-
Governor C. J. Latrobe (1801–1875) might well fear that the colony
might "parallel California in crime and disorder." In fact, surprise
at the good order of the diggings was to be a recurrent motif of the
Governor's despatches until grievances goaded the diggers into
revolt; but Latrobe was meagrely enough equipped with police and
officials to administer a quiet pastoral colony, and his police and
officials, as much infected by gold fever as anyone else, deserted
readily. But from one source or another Latrobe managed in time
to replace them and add to them. Unfortunately, his new police
covered their inexperience with a provocative arrogance which
went ill with the self-reliant character of many of the diggers.

For on the diggings men of all classes and all occupations rubbed
shoulders. Here was the most varied frontier phase of Australian
history. Intelligence, adaptability, determination, and personality
quickly brought men to leadership in those fluid communities The
diggers included many of informed and vigorous political views
who had refused to be docile whether as English Chartists, Irish
home rulers, or Continental rebels of '48. Quiet acceptance of a
government which did not represent them could not be expected of
such men, particularly if they became aware of government only
through irritation and injustice.

Their immediate grievance was the collection of the miner's
licence fee. The levy in Victoria and New South Wales of 30 shillings per month took too little from the successful and bore heavily
on the unsuccessful, while it failed to meet the cost of administering
the fields. The sense of unfairness was raised to seething indignation
by the arrogance and brutality of the licence hunts carried out by
the police. By 1854 the yield per digger was declining sharply from
the first days of hope, and in the frustration of their hopes the tem-
per of the diggers rose to the danger point. They formed a Ballarat
Reform League, which linked familiar Chartist demands for political democracy with the demand to end licence fees. An intensified
hunt for unlicenced diggers at this juncture was merely provocative;

the diggers burned their licences and threw up an armed stockade flying the blue flag spangled with the stars of the Southern Cross, the flag of the "Republic of Victoria." On Sunday morning, December 3, 1854, troops stormed the Eureka Stockade, and, with the loss of some thirty lives, the "rebellion" was over. This quickly brought Council and Executive to realism. An enquiry had already been planned. Within four days it was commissioned; and its report is one of the most valuable surveys of this phase of Australian history. Within six months a miner's "right" costing £1 a year together with an export duty had replaced the monthly licence fee in Victoria; and the miner's right carried with it the right to vote.

In Australian labour history, the Eureka Stockade has been built into a legend. Although the "rebellion" was a blow struck by small independent capitalists against official policy, rather than by wage-earners against organised capital, the legend is not wholly wrong, for the Eureka Stockade did bring to a head the inevitable conflict between traditional monopoly and democracy.

This was the period, between 1850 and 1856, when, in accordance with the Act of 1850, new constitutions were drafted by the Legislative Councils of New South Wales, Victoria, South Australia, and Tasmania. The majorities in the Councils were mainly concerned with gaining complete control over purely colonial matters, while retaining the protection that a property qualification might give to those with a stake in the country. But the times were against them. Even the drafts for the new constitution conceded a wide franchise for elections to the lower house, and by 1858 the ballot and manhood suffrage for the lower house had been accepted in all four southeastern colonies. Here was the measure of the change wrought by the radical immigration of the gold decade.[1]

But these concessions to democracy were incomplete. In each instance a fairly democratic lower house was checked by an upper house strongly representative of property. William Charles Wentworth had even suggested a hereditary colonial peerage; but it was

---

[1] Western Australia was to receive a similar stimulus from gold discoveries in the 1880's, culminating in the granting of responsible government in 1890. In its earlier years it had failed to attract immigrants and had welcomed convicts from 1850 to 1868 as a solution of its labour shortage. As a receptacle of convicts it had been condemned to remain a Crown Colony for an unusually long period.

laughed out of court as "a bunyip aristocracy," though his purpose was to keep control in the hands of those men of wealth whom he regarded as the country's backbone and its only true leaders. Indeed, every attempt to use the power of the state to solve the economic problems of the new population was carried through against the obstruction of propertied upper-house majorities appealing to laissez-faire against what seemed to them dangerous steps toward state socialism. It would be surprising if the situation had been otherwise; but it is this conflict which makes clear the relation of the economic and social development of the period with its politics.

The dominant problem was the permanent employment of a greatly enlarged population. Many persons were quick to realise either that they were unsuited to the rough, uncertain life of the diggings, or that gambling for gold could not be a lifetime employment. Some could be taken up immediately to replace those who had fled from employment to seek gold. But contemporaries noticed the sturdy independence that marked many of them, and their resistance to becoming dependent wage-earners. The immediate cry was for land, so that as farmers they might combine security with independence. But the first land act intended to unlock the land was not passed until 1861.

What happened to the diggers, meanwhile? Only the most general answer can as yet be given. Many left the declining fields to try their luck elsewhere, a proportion of them slipping imperceptibly into the rôle of transitory diggers, moving on, with intervals of casual work, to New Zealand, to Queensland, even as old men to the thirsty diggings of Kalgoorlie and Coolgardie in Western Australia, and to Alaska and the Yukon. In 1859, 45,000 people left Victoria, some returning to their earlier homes, others moving on still further. Many who remained found work equipping the newly swollen community with hotels, schools, roads and bridges, railways, fencing for sheep runs, houses, shops, and the building materials required for all these purposes. Some were absorbed as schoolteachers, doctors, and so on. Many moved about the country, following the rotation of casual employment in shearing and harvesting. It is to this time that we can look as the main source if not the beginning of the tradition, prominent in Australian literature, of the itinerant worker, be he swaggy or bagman, shearer or fruit-picker.

But none of these palliatives could satisfy the demand for a secure livelihood, and throughout the 'sixties and 'seventies one can trace the swelling cry for land and industrial employment. Indeed, that demand was never fully satisfied, and the disillusionment that came on top of high hopes of this new land explains much of the utopian fervour of later Australian shearers, miners, and industrial workers.

It was exasperating to diggers in New South Wales and Victoria to see, hard by their diggings, unused land and to know that these colonies were importing their food not only from neighbouring South Australia but from distant California. If diggers turned farmers could transform Californian valleys into smiling farms, why should they not do the same in Victorian gullies? But there was a difference. The Australian lands were not simply the property of aborigines whose claims could be waved aside; they were in large part in the hands of squatters whose claims were harder to overcome. It is true that in general the squatters were not the owners of their runs, but lessees of Crown lands. But they or their fathers were pioneers who had "mixed their hard labour" with these lands, which were theirs by right, they thought, whatever the technicalities. Many of them were little able to imagine the diggers' point of view. Although, after initial difficulties, they had gained from the gold rushes a handy market for mutton and could ease their labour shortage in time by fencing their runs, the new population of radical diggers was a noisy intrusion on their quiet and security.

The public-spirited imagination of men like John Robertson (1816–1891), the New South Wales squatter, author of the land acts of 1861, bore fruit after almost a decade of struggle in bills intended to make land available for farming at easy rates. In New South Wales the upper house had to be swamped with Government nominees before its opposition could be overcome. Between 1861 and 1865 there were passed in New South Wales and Victoria various land acts having aims similar to those of the American Homestead Act of 1860. They enabled intending farmers to select from 40 to 640 acres of land at £1 an acre on easy terms and on condition of occupancy. In general the New South Wales acts were tenderer on the squatters' interests than those of Victoria, where a greater proportion of arable land was in the hands of the squatters and the problem of accommodating new numbers was more pressing.

The intended results were not achieved. The increase in the area of cultivated land was tiny as compared with the area of land sold under these acts. Fifteen and a half million acres were sold in New South Wales between 1862 and 1883; the area cultivated increased only by a little more than three hundred thousand acres. In Victoria, better results were achieved after a revised act of 1865, but not before the earlier acts had given the squatters large parts of the rich Western District in fee simple.

For the squatter was not ready to stand by while selectors divided up his run. The squatter could himself turn selector, using hired "dummies" as well as members of his own family, for the New South Wales acts enabled anyone over two years of age to select. In the dry interior, the squatter who could in this way select land by river, creek, billabong, or water hole, was safe from intruders. It proved, in fact, difficult to enforce provisions meant to ensure occupation by farmer selectors. So the squatters gained ownership of vast areas on the easy terms intended for diggers with little or no capital.

The squatter, however, did not have it all his own way. If he could "pick the eyes" of his run, so could others. Even his own "dummy" might turn blackmailer, and the acts enabled other people who had no intention of farming to indulge in "peacocking" with no other aim than to be bought off by the squatter at a good profit. In the bitter war that took place during the twenty years of free selection the squatter had the advantage of being able to call more readily on cash, since to the banks he was the safer investment; but he won his battle with the selector at the cost of a debt which has burdened the Australian pastoral industry.[2]

---

[2] The land-selection laws of the southern states contributed indirectly to the pastoral occupation of Queensland. Moreton Bay was, by the late 'fifties, the centre of a pastoral population of about 30,000, whose agitation for independence from the control of the government at Sydney ended in the proclamation of a separate colony of Queensland in 1859. In the 'sixties, this colony was invaded by squatters from the southern colonies, where all available runs were occupied and where the efforts to subdivide holdings in the interests of land-hungry diggers made the squatters' security seem precarious. By the 'seventies, occupation had followed explorers into areas where drought was a constant menace, and where the pastures were more suited to cattle than to sheep. Queensland became and remained the chief cattle area of the continent, and when the tapping of artesian water vastly increased the sheep-carrying area, the rapid growth of population during the 'eighties, from 211,000 to 392,000, carried this young community into third place among the Australian colonies.

Of course there was more genuine selection than the meagre figures of increased cultivation reveal; for in fact a great deal of selection came to be for running sheep on a small scale as well as for agriculture, and a great number of the selections recorded in the land offices conceal a story of years of high hopes waning into surrender as would-be selectors realised that the squatters were not their only enemies in this arid land. For, so far as the free-selection acts were intended to build up a self-sufficient peasantry, they did not allow for the impossibility of that imperfect ideal in a country of long, dry summers. If the intention was commercial farming, the selector was handicapped, except in favoured districts, by high costs and an intractable land. The age of railway building was only just beginning and transport by bullock dray was costly and slow. Seasons were unpredictable and drought common. The deficiencies of Australian soils were not yet understood. Indeed, the selectors were commonly to find, as others have, from Phillip's starvation days to this latter day of soil erosion, that Australian land is to be conquered only with knowledge gained by toil, bitter experience, and patient study.

Science and invention were to give Australian agriculture new hope, but they followed the development of commercial farming and did not create it. Commercial farming developed rapidly in South Australia without the warmhearted, blundering attempts at legislative nurturing which marked the eastern states, for the fertile lands of that colony were close to the port of Adelaide and their dry summers proved more suitable for ripening wheat than did the wet coastal lands at first favoured in the eastern states. High costs of labour were reduced by labour-saving devices such as Ridley and Bull's stripper, which cut down the cost of harvesting perhaps to one-tenth and was the forerunner of the harvesters of later years. The Victorian market stimulated a rapid increase in South Australian farming, which produced Australia's third export of significance to Britain—wheat. By 1870 South Australian wheat had displaced American wheat in the Australian market, and by 1880 it had surpassed the share of Canadian wheat in the British market—only after the practical farmers, however, had been forced by an alarming fall in the yield per acre to listen to the scientists and to dress their land with superphosphate. The end of the century saw the Cambridge-trained mathematician, William J. Farrer (1845–1906), breeding rust- and drought-resisting wheats suitable to Australian conditions. The development of the present-day wheat belt of eastern, southern, and western Australia has rested on railway-building and agricultural research, both of which were actively pursued during the last thirty years of the century.

These things came too late to help the selector. The selection laws did settle a number of farmers on the land, but the number was much smaller than the legislators had hoped, and many were forced to quit or to drag out their days in the miserable slow defeat described in fiction by Henry Lawson (1867–1922). Land and climate, high costs, and the entrenched interest of the squatters were more effective factors than well-intentioned laws.

But the cost of defeat was serious for these Australian communities. It need not cause surprise that squatters fearing the loss of what they regarded as their own should have resorted to perjury as a matter of course in their war with the selectors, but the result was a lowering of standards of conduct and of respect for law, and a deepening of social hostility between the squatters as a class and the selectors, together with the shearers and labourers who were socially akin to them. "Class has been pitted against class," reported the Sydney *Bulletin* of January 29, 1881, "each trying to remedy its wrongs by committing greater wrongs. . . . The universal principle of 'grab all' now prevails." Apart from South Australia with its even balance of farming, mining, and pastoral communities, the Australian colonies had from their foundation been deeply riven societies. The gulf between convicts and free settlers had been obliterated in the fluid gold-fields society, but it was succeeded by that between working-class immigrants and the upper classes of squatters, merchants, and a few professional or official families. As a result of the late settlement of the Australian colonies, the working and lower middle-class immigrants came from societies already growing familiar with the world movement of self-assertion on the part of these classes. Local traditions of forced labour and local conflicts over squatter attempts to bring in cheap labour or to retain outworn Masters' and Servants' Acts kept this assertion alive. The gold rushes reënforced it with the frontier type of experience, and always there was the mere fact of transplantation to shake old acquiescence, if it had not been already weakened. So, although the squatter might exercise absolute rule over his own station, and although he might enjoy a short-lived supremacy in legislative assemblies and a longer one in the upper houses, he did not enjoy a superiority accepted as axiomatic or of right. Still less did he do so after a generation of class war over the land acts. The spectacle of wholesale dummying destroyed respect for the landed proprietor among those defeated in the struggle. "Between the self-valuation of the latter-day squatter," wrote Tom Collins (Joseph Furphy, 1843–1912) in *Such Is Life,* "and that of his contemporary wage-slave, there is very little to choose. Hence the toe of the blucher treads on the heel of the tan boot, and galls its stitches." The feeling which was to mark the shearers' strikes of the early 1890's owed something to this background.

The possible dangers of this broad gulf had not gone unrecognised. Men like the Rev. John Dunmore Lang (1799–1878) had hoped to bridge it by bringing out small settlers and "decent mechanics" who would form a sturdy and independent lower middle class. A similar aim marked the proposals of a Scotch ex-digger, David Syme (1827–1908), who as proprietor of the Melbourne newspaper, the *Age,* proposed in the 1860's to solve the digger problem by building up Victorian industry behind a tariff wall. It was at the heart of Syme's plan that the tariff should protect not only Australian industry but the Australian industrial worker. He expounded with unwearied repetition that idea of a "fair and reasonable" standard of living, which came to be the axiom to which at least lip service must be paid in all Australian political controversy and social legislation.

From 1860, with the dour determination that enabled him in time to make and unmake governments, Syme preached his ideas in the *Age* newspaper without cease or concession. His views gained supporters in Melbourne, Geelong, and the mining towns; indeed, many of the diggers hailing from the United States and Europe were already accustomed to the idea of protection. At length, in 1865, the Victorian Premier, James McCulloch (1819–1893), decided to take the plunge.

His halting protective tariff became law in 1866 only after a prolonged and bitter struggle between the lower and upper houses.

From the outset it was evident that the conflict was less concerned with the virtues or vices of protection than with the rival claims of wealth and democracy to rule. Diggers and immigrants wanting jobs supported protection and carried the day by weight of numbers. Merchants and, on the whole, the squatters supported free trade. From the beginning, the tariff proposals appeared as part of an attack on the power of the wealthier classes to block popular reforms through their control of the upper house. McCulloch was already at loggerheads with the upper house over his proposal to reform it by reducing the property qualification and by shortening the period of office from ten to five years. Knowing that his tariff bill would be amended out of existence, he tacked it to an appropriation bill which the Legislative Council could not amend and which it could reject only at the cost of taking responsibility for leaving the government without supply for essential services. The Council accepted the challenge and laid the bill aside. The fight was on. The government resorted to means of doubtful legality to pay for government services, thereby enabling the upper house and its supporters to raise the cry of demagogic tyranny. "Arbitrary power," declared one of them,[3] "had been placed in the hands of the Executive."

The free-trade Melbourne newspaper, the *Argus,* appealed in leader after leader to "the aristocracy of labour" against "its democracy." But it was disappointed in its preëlection hope that the intelligent operatives would "resent any unnecessary interference on the part of the state, with their unquestionable right to dispose of the produce of their labour, when, where, and how they themselves may think fit, without let or hindrance";[4] by an overwhelming vote in support of McCulloch's Ministry they demanded just that interference. The appeal of a laissez-faire notion of liberty weighed less with the majority of voters than the demand for security. McCulloch's tariff was only a cautious beginning, but by 1877 Victoria was an out-and-out protectionist colony.

This was the cause of much intercolonial friction and hostility. The tariffs of the other colonies were primarily designed for raising revenue, and New South Wales in particular remained a free-trade

---

[3] Quoted, Melbourne *Argus,* November 29, 1865.
[4] *Argus,* December 1, 1865.

colony; unlike Victoria, she had a vast hinterland awaiting development, her flocks increased steadily, railways and new breeds of wheat opened up the western plains, and her coal fields supplied a sound basis for local industries. Although Victoria's tariff fostered a greater variety of industries, New South Wales from 1870 onward, with its more extensive resources, drew steadily nearer to Victoria's population figure. Victoria reached the million mark first, but by 1892 both New South Wales and its capital, Sydney, had regained their lead in population. Their tariff differences accentuated their rivalry and, particularly in the Murray basin, caused much irritation which contributed to the rather negative movement toward federation, regarded by many of its supporters as a way out of difficulties rather than as a great national ideal.

The spreading assumption that Australia must be a country providing its inhabitants with a fair and reasonable standard of living is evident also in another question which occupied the colonists throughout this period. That was the question of non-European immigration and, in particular, of Chinese immigration. Prejudice, born of ignorance, grew into active hostility. The Chinese had been imported as coolies in the 1840's, but they first came in large numbers during later years of the gold decade when the yield from alluvial washing was already beginning to decline. Disappointed diggers vented their discontent on the most obviously different people on the fields, the Chinese, of whom there were 42,000 in Victoria in 1859. The Chinese offended the more because they were expert "tailers," industriously working over claims abandoned by European diggers. Anti-Chinese demonstrations, beginning in 1854, flared up into serious riots at Lambing Flat in New South Wales in 1861 and on Queensland fields during the Queensland gold rushes of the 'seventies.

Until the 'seventies, opposition to Chinese immigration drew its impetus mainly from the miners, and thereafter from urban and maritime workers who felt the security and standards of their employment threatened. This fear was given point when mine owners used Chinese to break a strike at Clunes in 1873, an action which was the occasion of the federation of the Victorian miners' unions in the Amalgamated Miners' Association of Victoria in 1874. The fear of the Chinese as a menace to employment and wage standards was evident, also, in the strike of the New South Wales Seamen's Union in 1878 against the employment of Chinese on ships of the Australian Steam Navigation Company. In this stand the seamen were supported by the Queensland Government, which, alarmed by the rush of Chinese to the new Queensland gold fields, threatened to withdraw its mail subsidy from the Australian Steam Navigation Company.

Chinese immigration was opposed not only by workers, but by other sections of Australian society. The opposition was compounded of rational alarm and muddled prejudice. Chinese poverty and frugal standards of living might threaten Australian living standards. Their immigration was largely male, and much of the heated discussion which flared up in the 'seventies and 'eighties expressed fears of their sexual behaviour, their opium-smoking, and their gambling. Again, could people of alien manners and values, people of what one politician described as "a servile race," be assimilated without grave damage to Australian British civilisation? Beyond these more particular fears was a vague sense of vast numbers just to the north of Australia, which gave rise to talk of a "yellow flood." And through all the heated discussion ran a good deal of pseudo-biological nonsense.

Such fears were given effect in laws intended to limit or prevent Chinese immigration. Victoria led the way in 1854, and by 1886 every colony had passed laws discriminating against the Chinese. It is true that there was vacillation on the part of Queensland, South Australia, and Western Australia, which had large tropical areas which some of their governments hoped to develop with Oriental labour. As the century neared its end, the Chinese question was merged in the wider question of "White Australia," concerning the restriction of Indian, Pacific, and Japanese immigration as well. By that time the only question accepted in the colonies as open to debate was the method of exclusion.

Colonial governments unskilled in the niceties of international intercourse had acted with brutal directness rather than with diplomacy, on many occasions acutely embarrassing the British Government in its relations with the Government of China. The Australian reply to British expostulations was expressed by Sir Henry Parkes (1815–1896), Premier of New South Wales and prominent

in the anti-Chinese campaign: ". . . we have an indisputable right
to expect the Imperial Government to consult and protect our
separate and peculiar interests . . . by the exercise of the powers
of treaty on our behalf . . . if protection cannot be afforded, the
Australian Parliaments must act from force of public opinion in
devising measures to defend the colonies."[5] The colonial stand was
accepted implicitly in the Anglo-Japanese commercial treaty of
1894, which contained a clause allowing the colonies to dissent
from it. In this fashion, the "White Australia" question marked a
further advance of the colonies toward complete self-government.

It also marked their progress toward federation, for it was the
occasion of several intercolonial conferences both of governments
and of trade-union organisations, and it brought home to the colonists their common character and their common danger.

The Natal Dictation Test had been adopted by New South
Wales, Tasmania, and Western Australia in 1897 as less open to
objection, and Joseph Chamberlain had urged it on all the colonial
premiers in London for Queen Victoria's Jubilee in 1897. A modified form of this test was adopted by the first Parliament of the
Commonwealth. By this means, no particular nationality was excluded, but immigrants of any nationality might be required to
pass a dictation test in a European language.

While Chinese who wanted to come to Australia were being
kept out, Pacific Islanders who did not want to come were being
brought in against their will. It was after their successful use in
1864 on a sugar plantation in Queensland that the Kanaka traffic
became regular, and by 1900 about 47,000 Kanakas had been
brought in. This traffic in what the Chinese called "buying men"
was subject to the gravest abuses. Queensland and Imperial laws
were passed to control the recruiting of the employment and the
return of the Kanakas to their homes. So far as their treatment in
Queensland was concerned, these laws met with varying success,
but they could not touch the root problem, the crimes accompanying the recruitment of the natives.

The British Admiralty reported to the Colonial Office its belief
that no proper control could ever be exercised over the recruiting

---

[5] Quoted in T. A. Coghlan, *Labour and Industry in Australia* (Oxford University Press, 1915), Vol. III, p. 1341.

of islanders and that their "collection and shipment" were "likely, from the nature of the work, to fall into the hands of an unscrupulous and mercenary set who . . . would not hesitate to commit acts of piracy, kidnapping and murder."[6] The event proved the correctness of this forecast, and attempts at inspection and supervision were futile. Ships of many nations took part, and the jurisdiction of the British High Commissioner of the Pacific, ineffective over his own nationals in remote islands, did not run to foreigners outside British territory.

The growth of this trade in men was paralleled by a growing outcry against it, drawing its strength from outraged humanity, alarm at the stigma on colonial honour, and, particularly on the part of the workers, a fear of a lowering of wage and living standards.

The North Queensland planters met attempts to control or end the Kanaka traffic with a demand for the separation of North Queensland and later of Central Queensland as autonomous colonies. There were many good arguments in favour of this, but it arose directly from a desire to escape the cramping control of Brisbane governments. It was, in fact, a demand that the North Queensland planters should be allowed to establish a plantation society based on semislave labour free from the control of governments which were subject to the prevailing Australian notions of a fair and reasonable standard of living, of equality of opportunity and political democracy; and as such it was attacked. Its end, already planned, was hurried on by federation and the Commonwealth Parliament's adoption of the policy of "White Australia."

The sharpening of radical ideas and demands among immigrants was a familiar story in the lands receiving immigrants during the nineteenth century. But whereas in America the expanding frontier bred individualism, the peculiar difficulties of the Australian continent encouraged the belief that it was the government's duty to bring about the desired conditions. This was inevitable, as even some believers in laissez-faire recognised. The system of assisted immigration implied a promise on the part of the state to provide employment. The sudden access of numbers in the gold decade

---

[6] Quoted in Myra Willard, *History of the White Australia Policy* (Melbourne University Press, 1923), pp. 143–144.

created problems which demanded legislation to provide land
and work. And small men could cultivate this dry country successfully only with the provision of railways and irrigation, prereq-
uisites which are found in practice to depend on government
action. It was only their experience that private enterprise could
not finance and build railways in this dry continent that drove very
reluctant governments into the railway business.

But particular governments were from time to time identified
by radical groups with the employers, especially when industrial
strife reached its peak in Eastern Australia in the great strikes of
the 1890's. It was this belief which lay at the root of the formation
of a political labour party intended to capture the machinery of
government and to use it on behalf of labour. That, however,
came late in Australian labour history and was preceded by the
industrial trade-union movement.

The unions formed in the first thirty years of this period were
craft associations on English lines. The lead in their foundations
was taken by skilled workers, and their concern was not to attack
the existing economic system but by collective bargaining within
that system to get and protect better conditions of work and pay.
Their aims can be summed up as the eight-hour day, improved
acts to regulate conditions of work in factory and mine, the defence
and improvement of wage rates, and the exclusion from the colonies of cheap coloured labour.

Until the late 1880's their growth was strong and they suffered
few setbacks. In the course of particular struggles they sought
greater strength in amalgamation, spreading far beyond the boundaries of any one colony. By 1890 such federal unions as the Amalgamated Miners' Association, the Federated Seamen's Union of
Australasia, and the Amalgamated Shearers' Union linked the workers of Australia and New Zealand in strong, well-organised association. This expansion was accompanied by a growing habit of
coöperation between the unions of different industries. Spasmodic
coöperation, as in the Eight-Hours Labor League, can be traced
back into the gold decade, but in the 'seventies and 'eighties the
unions built up a permanent machinery of coöperation in their
Trades and Labour Councils and Trades Halls, and in their Intercolonial Congresses.

The employers replied with employers' associations, which in turn stimulated still closer coöperation among the unions. The employers' associations grew by a similar process of federation, so that on the eve of the industrial strife of the 1890's the unions faced a Victorian Employers' Union, a New South Wales Employers' Union, and a Federal Council of the Pastoralists' Unions of the various colonies.

This parallel organisation marked the approach to industrial war. The unions had won many piecemeal victories in the thirty years before 1890. So long as they continued to win such victories, serious criticism of the economic system did not gain many followers. But during the 1880's it was becoming evident that such victories would not easily continue. The employers were growing uneasy about their precarious economic outlook. A world-wide fall of prices began in the 1870's. Its effects on wages were cushioned in Australia until the 1880's because of a continuing prosperity maintained by heavy public borrowing and by the development of areas previously undeveloped. Refrigeration which gave Australian meat and later fruit an English market; new discoveries of gold, copper, silver, lead, and zinc at Mount Morgan in Queensland, Broken Hill in New South Wales, Zeehan and Mount Lyell in Tasmania,[7] Kalgoorlie and Coolgardie in Western Australia; the expansion of both agriculture and pasture in New South Wales; and, in all the colonies, heavy government spending on railway construction, concealed from most people the deterioration of their economic prospects. Investments from England and the colonies continued throughout the 1880's to pour into the

---

[7] Tasmania's slow and painful recovery from its economic stagnation during the 'fifties and 'sixties had begun in the 'seventies with the discovery of tin and zinc and with the cultivation of potatoes. But recovery remained slow until the latter half of the 'eighties, when silver and lead mines at Zeehan and gold and copper mines at Mount Lyell were discovered and when refrigeration made possible the export of apples to Britain. But Tasmania (the new name replaced Van Diemen's Land in 1855) never regained the position it had held in the first half of the century. The northern colony of Queensland quickly eclipsed it in population and trade in the 'sixties; and Western Australia did likewise during the new gold era of the 'nineties. Nevertheless, the emphasis upon Australia's economic and constitutional developments has obscured the earlier decades when Hobart had more than rivalled Sydney in such matters as schools, learned societies, publishing, and the theatre. By 1860, Hobart was the Dublin of Australia; but Tasmanian cultural history still awaits its historian.

banks, land and building societies, and government loans. But the price of Australia's staple, wool, began to fall in 1886, and by 1893 fetched little more than half the 1885 price. Copper, silver, and cattle prices fell likewise. These things prepared the employers to attack wage rates, and, together with various local signs of the instability of an unsecured prosperity, checked at length the spate of loans. The loan-fed land boom broke in 1891 with a series of failures of land and finance companies in Melbourne and Sydney and with many banks suspending payments.

The threatened industrial war had already broken out. The unions were doomed to be defeated, for depression made concession within the economic system impossible and provided the employers with large reserves of unemployed labourers to replace those on strike. The employers understood their advantage: "Never before," wrote one of them in July, 1890, "has such an opportunity to test the relative strength of labour and capital arisen."

CHAPTER V

The Commonwealth, 1901-1939

BY L. F. FITZHARDING

THE CENTENARY celebrations of 1888 fitly mark the peak of the period of carefree expansion and the assimilation of the men and capital brought by the gold rushes. It was a period of great achievement, but the cost also had been great, and had been met largely from loan money. The period which followed, extending roughly from 1890 to 1914, was one of less exuberance but of great social and intellectual importance. Modern Australian ways of thought took shape in the 'nineties. The period opened with a series of acute financial crises and a number of industrial disturbances which brought an unprecedented bitterness into employer-employee relationships. Men were forced to reëxamine the very foundations of the national life and economy so long casually accepted. They became more aware, too, of the contrasts underlying the appearance of prosperity: of the squalor of city slums and the hardship and poverty of the bushworker and small "selector." Gradually, a new set of values emerged, and Australia gained a new consciousness of herself as a nation and a new social philosophy which was the characteristic expression of her nationhood. This process, in which a newborn literature and art played their parts, found expression in politics in the formation and rise of the Labour Party, and in the federation of the six States into a single Commonwealth, speaking with one voice on matters of national concern, while leaving the authority of the States undiminished in a wide range of local affairs.

Victoria had received the greatest share of overseas investments and was to some degree the centre for reinvestment in the other colonies. Land values had risen to astronomical heights and become

the subject of frenzied speculation. In 1890, when export prices
had already begun to fall, failures in the Argentine and the consequent collapse of an important London financial house led to
panic on the London market. The flow of funds for investment in
Victoria ceased suddenly. Industrial unrest, drought, and rising
unemployment aggravated the position. The climax came in April,
1893, when the Commercial Bank, one of the greatest in Victoria,
closed its doors. The hasty proclamation of a five-days bank holiday by the Government only intensified the panic, and all but
one of the Victorian banks were forced into reconstruction. In
Sydney there was a run on the banks, but the Government, by
prompt and firm action, averted the worst effects of the crash, and
gradually confidence returned. Victoria lost, temporarily, its financial leadership and sank into a ten-years lethargy. New South Wales
had more resilience, because it had a larger reserve of undeveloped
resources, but the psychological shock was very great. The thinking
of a generation was coloured by the bank crashes of 'ninety-three,
as was that of a later generation by the depression of the 'thirties.

The depression was followed by a drought: in ten years the
number of sheep fell from 97,881,221 to 70,602,995. Two things
helped to restore production and, in spite of falling prices, to maintain the country's trade. Following a number of small rushes, the
discovery of the Coolgardie gold field in Western Australia in
1893, and of the "golden mile" at Kalgoorlie the following year,
led to a reënactment of the atmosphere and scenes of the classic
gold rushes in the vast waterless deserts of Western Australia.
Fortunes were made and lost, even more by speculation than by
prospecting. The output was very large, and rose steadily through
the first decade of the twentieth century, putting Australia once
again among the world's leading gold-producers. The other factor,
less spectacular but no less significant, was the work of William
James Farrer (1845–1906), at first singlehanded and then with the
collaboration of governments and experts all over the world, in
the scientific breeding of drought- and rust-resisting wheats. It
was largely a result of his experiments that by 1900 a million acres
had been added to the wheat area and three million bushels to
the crop. This expansion continued until 1917, when both area
and production reached a peak.

ALFRED DEAKIN
1856–1919

WILLIAM MORRIS HUGHES

The contraction of spending and the fall of prices were accompanied by the first large-scale labour troubles in Australia. While these affected especially the maritime and pastoral industries and the silver-lead mines at Broken Hill, their significance extended far beyond these industries, which, as both sides recognised, were merely the chosen battlegrounds for a trial of strength between capital and labour. Both sides had recently organised on inter-colonial lines. During the years of prosperity, unionism had become well established in the skilled trades, and had won many concessions. In the 'eighties the miners formed an intercolonial organisation under the leadership of William Guthrie Spence (1846–1926), who soon afterward organised the seminomadic bush-workers into what was to become the Australian Workers' Union, for many years the most powerful union in Australia. The greater number of these men were more or less unskilled: many were small selectors who eked out a living by seasonal work, or the flotsam and jetsam of the failure of the free-selection movement to find, for the diggers, a living on their own land as the gold rushes receded. Among these men the new type of unionism, with its gospel of "mateship" and a "fair go" for all, spread like a bushfire.

The issue, as both sides clearly saw, was whether labour, through its organisations, was to have any share in the control of industry, in bad times as well as good. Whatever the actual pretexts, the real fight centred around freedom of contract as opposed to the closed shop and collective bargaining by the union for its members. In each campaign the unions, in spite of a spirited and sometimes bitter struggle, were decisively defeated. In every State, the government came out openly on the side of the employers. Police and military were called out; strike leaders were arrested under obsolete statutes and given long gaol sentences. In spite of this, there was relatively little violence. The strikers were not revolutionaries, and the disturbances were confined to the industrial field. The unions were completely crushed, and the gains of previous years were all swept away. Freedom of contract seemed secured for years.

A few of the more idealistic and theoretical of the workers followed the socialist journalist William Lane (1861–1917) to found a New Australia more to their liking in Paraguay. Other labour leaders, more practical, turned to politics. The employers had won, they argued, because the state had thrown its weight in on their side. The answer was to organise politically and secure control of the state for the workers, or at least gain sufficient voice to ensure its neutrality. From the failure of the great strikes the Australian Labour Party was born. Its appearance was opportune. Politics in the Eastern States were passing through a period of stagnation. There were no big figures—Sir Henry Parkes was no longer an effective force. The parties fought over dead issues: principle was second to place. Into this atmosphere the Labour Party brought a breeze of earnestness, a contact with social and economic realities. New ideas were stirring. Henry George had visited Australia in 1889, and had a considerable following. The writings of Bellamy and Morris were read and discussed. There were even small groups of disciples of Karl Marx.

Labour's entry into politics was spectacular in its success, at least on the surface. In 1891, the year after a great maritime strike, thirty-six endorsed Labour candidates were elected to the Parliament of New South Wales. The Party split, however, on the tariff question, and their influence was nullified. In 1893 a reorganised Labour Party came to the fore. Winning fewer seats, it was much more coherently organised and disciplined, and held the balance of power and made and unmade governments for the rest of the decade. The essential feature of the new organisation was the control exercised over members individually by caucus, and collectively by the Annual Conference of the Party. Controlling whatever government was in power from the cross-benches, exacting "support in return for concessions," first from the genial and rotund Sir George Houston Reid (1845–1918) and then, when he would go no further, from the bluff protectionist Sir William John Lyne (1844–1913), without themselves accepting any share of office, they were instrumental in placing a whole series of measures improving the status of the workers in various branches of industry on the statute book. While most successful in New South Wales, Labour pursued similar tactics in the other States.

What the Labour Party was to the worker, the Federal movement was to the younger men of the middle and professional classes. The federation of the colonies had often been discussed, and an abortive attempt had been made, with the Federal Council

of Australasia, in 1884. This had been more or less academic discussion by officials: now the question was taken to the people and
became one of moral as well as political fervour. A report on Australian defence by a British expert in 1889 caused a considerable stir.
Moreover, the financial depression emphasised the folly of six
States each surrounding itself with a tariff wall against the products
of the others. A Convention in 1891, attended by the leading statesmen of all the colonies, produced a draft constitution, which was
substantially that finally adopted. For a time it seemed that the
draft would be engulfed in the abyss of apathy into which earlier
schemes had fallen. In New South Wales the Free Trade Party
attacked the scheme violently. The rising Labour Party viewed it
with suspicion as a red herring to distract attention from social
reform. Inter-State jealousy played its part, and Parliaments, beset
by financial and industrial crises, showed no enthusiasm.

The deadlock was broken by an appeal direct to the people.
The Australian Natives' Association (a body combining friendly-
society and political activities) sponsored a new procedure, by
which the State Parliaments would all pass acts providing for
direct election by the people of delegates to a special Convention,
which should draw up a constitution to be submitted by referendum to all the people of each State. The new proposal was taken
up with enthusiasm. Federation Leagues were formed throughout
the country, and leaders like Sir Edmund Barton (1849–1920)
and Alfred Deakin (1856–1918) threw their energies into the campaign. After some delay the necessary legislation was passed and
the Convention met in 1897. The earlier draft was taken as a
basis, though many alterations were made. The main problem was
to reconcile the insistence of the larger States on the supremacy of
the House of Representatives (elected on a population basis) with
the desire of the small States for equal rights for the Senate (in
which all States are equally represented) even in regard to money
bills. There were other cross-currents among the delegates—personal and party as well as State. A clause, introduced almost as an
afterthought, gave the Commonwealth power with respect to "conciliation and arbitration for the prevention and settlement of
industrial disputes extending beyond the limits of any one State."
Originally intended to apply to the maritime and pastoral indus-

tries, and the like, the workers in which migrated, in the course of their occupation, over State boundaries, this clause was to assume a much wider importance.

The Constitution finally agreed on was referred to the people in June, 1898. There were large majorities for its adoption in Victoria, Tasmania, and South Australia. In New South Wales there was a majority, but it fell short of the figure fixed by the State Parliament as necessary. Reid, who earned himself the sobriquet of "Yes-No" by supporting the idea of federation while criticising the draft constitution severely, saw which way the tide of public opinion was running and convened a conference of premiers at which he obtained some concessions to New South Wales, including the location of the capital in that State. The amended proposals were resubmitted and carried by increased majorities in all States. Western Australia did not hold a referendum, but joined the other States before the proclamation of federation.

The Commonwealth was proclaimed on January 1, 1901. The first cabinet, led by Barton, with Deakin as his chief lieutenant, has been described as a "team of captains." It included six former State premiers; and few men but Barton, who concealed beneath his apparent indolence great ability and powers of leadership, could have held together such strong and politically incompatible personalities as Sir John Forrest (1847–1918), former explorer and for ten years undisputed ruler of Western Australia, and the fiery radical lawyer Charles Cameron Kingston (1850–1908), under whose dominance South Australia, in the same period, had become the most politically progressive of the colonies.

In the early Federal Parliaments the lines of party division were not clear. Technically, the Government and the Opposition (led by Reid) were divided on the fiscal question. The Protectionists included a strong group of radical liberals, while the Free-Traders were predominantly conservative, but there were exceptions on both sides. The Labour Party formed a compact and highly organised minority, its members agreeing to differ on the fiscal question but remaining united on all else. Its leader, John Christian Watson (1867–1941), like most of his followers still a young man, was a shrewd, tactful, and conciliatory politician. He had been chairman of the Sydney Trades and Labour Council and one of the original organizers of the Party in New South Wales. Throughout the first fifteen years of the Commonwealth, Labour, with a few brief exceptions, either held the balance of power or was itself in office. But much of its policy was common to the more progressive wing of the Protectionists, and it is frequently difficult to assign credit for any particular measure to one party or the other. The general tendency was to continue and extend into the Commonwealth sphere the social policies—the "socialism without dogma"—of the 'nineties, and to give concrete form to the ardent, if somewhat narrow, nationalism which had brought the Commonwealth into being.

The first Parliament was largely concerned with creating the machinery of Federal administration, and with the great questions of tariff and immigration policy. On the fiscal question the result was a compromise which lasted till 1908: a tariff which, though protective, was far short of the demands of Victorian manufacturers, and which would also bring in the revenue necessary to run the Commonwealth and compensate the States for the loss of their customs revenue. For this purpose the Commonwealth was committed to pay more than three-quarters of its revenues from customs and excise for ten years. There was general agreement on the exclusion of all coloured races, and on the repatriation of the Pacific Islanders employed in the Queensland sugar-cane fields.

Barton resigned in 1903 to take a seat on the High Court, a body analogous to the United States Supreme Court, to which was entrusted the task of interpreting the Constitution and holding the balance even between the Commonwealth and States. The Court was at first rather conservative in its influence and, guided mainly by judgements of United States Chief Justice Marshall, as for example *McCulloch v. Maryland,* a vigilant guardian of State rights. Later a different school of interpretation made its appearance, and for a time, from 1921, was predominant. The Court, through its interpretations, has played a large part, not always recognised, in shaping the forms of Australian life.

In the second Parliament, Deakin, a liberal Victorian Protectionist, succeeded Barton as Prime Minister and shifted the emphasis to social questions. This brought out the lack of real unity in the older parties. Deakin and many of his followers were in

sympathy with much of Labour's programme, though disliking
their methods and organisation, but the Protectionists included,
also, representatives of the big Melbourne manufacturers and confirmed conservatives like Forrest. The Free-Traders, under Reid,
though essentially conservative, had no coherent policy. Deakin
once aptly described Reid's policy as a "necklace of negatives," and
his election campaigns tended to revolve around an animal, generally believed to be a figment of his imagination, called the "socialistic tiger."

The question of arbitration had already caused some trouble
under Barton. Revived by Deakin, it caused a break with the
Labour Party over the inclusion of state employees, such as railway workers. Deakin resigned and for a short time Labour held
office with Protectionist support: then the conservative wing of
the Protectionists joined Reid to form a coalition government.
This too was short-lived, and was succeeded in 1905 by the second
Deakin administration, in which liberal elements predominated
and which was to hold office for the next three years.

With Labour support, Deakin launched a vigorous policy of
higher protection to be linked with machinery to ensure that
benefits should be passed on in wages, imperial preference, national defence, old-age pensions, and the control of trusts and
monopolies. Much of his legislation, however, including that implementing the "new protection," was declared invalid by the
High Court. Yet this government did much to consolidate the
organisation of federation and to set the lines of further development. Even its failures were significant, as showing that the Commonwealth was fast reaching the limits of the powers allowed it
by the Constitution. No less important was the conversion of the
Labour Party to protection, and although the "new protection"
was rejected by the High Court, the doctrine that industry had
an obligation to pay "a fair and reasonable wage" based "on the
normal needs of the average employee regarded as a human being
living in a civilised community," formulated by Mr. Justice Henry
Bournes Higgins (1851–1928), was applied by him as President of
the Commonwealth Court of Conciliation and Arbitration, established in 1906, to an ever-widening field of industries, and came
to be adopted also in one form or another by the State tribunals.

By 1908 most of the ground common to Labour and the Protectionists had been covered, and Labour was growing tired of maintaining in office a party which actually formed a small minority of the House. A direct challenge was issued to the Government, and a new Labour administration took office under the dour but inflexibly honest Andrew Fisher (1862–1926), seconded by the mercurial and combative little Welshman William Morris Hughes (b. 1864).

This was soon followed by a fusion of the anti-Labour parties, with the result that a somewhat bewildered Deakin found himself head of a government whose chief supporters were "the whole of my opponents since Federation." These manoeuvrings failed to inspire confidence in the electors, and a general election in 1910 returned Labour with a clear majority in both Houses.

The years 1910 to 1913 were years of general prosperity. Export prices were good; production, especially of wheat, was increasing; and the net immigration was the greatest on record. Against this background the Labour Government, led by Fisher, was able to round off and extend the social legislation of its predecessors. There was no violent change of policy, though the emphasis and methods might be different. The organisation of defence, the Navigation Act regulating conditions on coastal vessels, the extension of old-age pensions, and the granting of maternity bonuses followed, with slight differences, the lines already laid down. The taking over of the issue of notes by the Commonwealth aroused more opposition. Still more distinctively Labour were the establishment of the Commonwealth Bank and the imposition of a Federal land tax, long urged by the picturesque Canadian-born, American-trained King O'Malley. The Bank was designed to secure for the people as a whole a share in the profits of general banking and at the same time to serve some of the purposes of a central bank. Under the autocratic control of the Governor, Sir Denison Samuel King Miller (1860–1923), it soon repaid the loan of £5,000 from the Treasury which formed its original capital, and was making large profits. It played an important part in financing the War of 1914–1918. In 1924 it was reorganised to make it more definitely a central bank, and was put under a board. The land tax was intended, in the first instance, to compel subdivision of large estates held as sheep stations and so to promote closer settlement. It was levied on the unimproved value of land exceeding £5,000, and may reflect in part the early influence of Henry George on the Labour Party. Not particularly successful in promoting closer settlement, it proved during the war a useful source of revenue, and has been retained by succeeding governments ever since.

Like the Deakin Government, Labour found itself hampered by the Constitution in attempts to control monopolies and to regulate industrial conditions. In 1911 and 1913, attempts were made to obtain greater powers by referendum, but both attempts were defeated.

The States showed in general the same trend as the Commonwealth. In all, Labour parties evolved from centre parties to the official opposition while their opponents were forced into union: in every State but Victoria a Labour Government had held office by 1914. In New South Wales a Labour administration had, since 1910, embarked on a series of experiments in state ownership of industry. Even in Victoria, the most conservative of the States, the character of Australian development had given rise to large-scale experiments in "state socialism" in the form of irrigation and land-settlement schemes, transport and public utility boards, and so on. It was realised by all parties that in Australia, with its wide areas and relatively low fertility, development must involve a large degree of government action.

By the end of its term, the Labour Party realised that it had reached the limit of progress possible under the Constitution as it stood. Amendment had been twice refused. It would seem that, even if the war had not intervened, the epoch that began in the 'nineties had worked itself out.

The outbreak of war in August, 1914, came in the middle of a general election brought about by a deadlock between the Senate, where Labour still commanded a majority, and the House of Representatives, where since 1913 a Liberal Government existed precariously by the Speaker's casting vote. Both sides declared in favour of wholehearted participation in the war: Andrew Fisher pledged "our last man and our last shilling," while his lieutenant, William Morris Hughes, was to prove the most fervent and dynamic of war administrators.

Australia at once placed her new and efficient, though as yet untried, navy under the British Admiralty, and offered to raise and equip an expeditionary force. Of the military history of 1914–1918 there is no need to speak in detail here. Australian forces served at Gallipoli, in Palestine, and on the Western Front, and achieved a reputation for dash and enterprise in the field, as well as for a certain disregard of the niceties of military discipline at other times. More than 60,000 Australian soldiers were killed, and the total casualties were about 320,000. These are approximately the same as the casualties of the United States, though the total population of Australia did not reach 5,000,000 till 1918.

Internally the war involved great changes, many of which were to prove permanent. The Commonwealth very early assumed responsibility for handling all loans on behalf of the States. Until this time, borrowing had been left almost entirely to the States. The war forced the Commonwealth to enter the money market on a large scale: £92,000,000 were raised in Britain, and £188,465,000 locally. In 1915, the Commonwealth, previously dependent almost wholly on indirect taxation, imposed an income tax. This was followed by succession, amusement, and war-profits taxes.

As the war progressed, more and more spheres of economic activity were brought under Commonwealth control. The ordinary limitations of the Constitution were suspended, the High Court giving a wide interpretation to the defence power, which was held to cover, for instance, the control of the price of bread. The base-metals industry, which was largely under German control, was forcibly reorganised in Australian hands. The main export industries were all brought under boards which regulated their marketing: the entire output of wool and wheat, and of some other products, was purchased by Great Britain. In 1916, faced with grave difficulties in lifting the wool and wheat crops, Hughes, on his own initiative, purchased a number of ships in London and established the Commonwealth Line, which, after performing valuable service during the war, later fell into difficult times in common with other shipping enterprises and was finally sold in 1928. Price control, though attempted, was only moderately successful: during the war years the wholesale price index rose 68.5 per cent, and the cost of food and groceries 46.6 per cent.

Wartime conditions brought industrial unrest, culminating in a widespread strike in the transport and associated industries in New South Wales, in 1917, which was soon broken but left a legacy of bitterness. The Arbitration Court, restricted by a series of High Court judgements, was quite unable to provide the requisite elasticity of adjustment. Special tribunals were sometimes resorted to, notably with respect to the coal-mining industry, and the prestige of the Arbitration Court was seriously lowered. An element of theoretical extremism made its appearance. The I.W.W., though numerically insignificant, attained considerable importance. Its doctrines of violence and class warfare gave a focus for the growing dissatisfaction with the achievements and the older system of arbitration and amelioration.

In 1916 Hughes, who had succeeded Fisher as Prime Minister, returned from a visit to England and the Western Front convinced that the voluntary system could not supply enough recruits to maintain the Australian forces at strength. A section of his party, including several ministers, were strongly opposed on principle to conscription for overseas service. Hughes put the question at a referendum, and in spite of an intensive campaign in which the full resources of the press and the opposition supported him, conscription was rejected. Intense feeling was aroused on both sides: few questions have provoked such passionate cleavage in the nation. Hughes, William Arthur Holman (1871–1934), the Premier of New South Wales, W. G. Spence, and a number of other notable figures were expelled from the Labour Party. Hardly any man who had played a leading part in the Party from 1891 till 1914 remained, and a period of somewhat groping readjustment followed. Distrust of political leaders, always present, was intensified. The old nationalism was replaced in part by a theoretical internationalism, but largely by an ostrich-like isolationism. Both were expressed in the demand for a negotiated peace made by a party congress at Perth in 1918. Theoretical socialism gained somewhat more weight in party councils, and in 1921 the objectives were made more explicitly socialist. Harassed by the loss of its accustomed leaders on the one side and by the activities of extremist minorities on the other, lacking strong leadership or clear-cut policy, Federal Labour sank back to a decade of political impotence while it strove, painfully, slowly, and not altogether with success to reëstablish its identity and restore its lost self-confidence.

But this was in the future. Expelled with a small "rump" for a following, Hughes retained office, and, after a brief experiment with a National Labour Party, joined with the opposition to form a new party, the Nationalists. As their leader he retained office throughout the war, without any marked change of policy. Representing Australia at the Peace Conference, he vigorously pressed her claim to German New Guinea and to a share of reparations payments, and resisted the Japanese proposal to write a declaration of racial equality into the Covenant of the League of Nations.

Hughes remained in office till 1923, but was increasingly subject to criticism from his own party. His autocratic manner and the resolute way in which, under the War Precautions Act, he had "governed Australia with a fountain pen," had made him many enemies: his radical background and associations were disliked by his new associates. The Country Party, a new factor in Australian politics representing the larger rural interests, which made its first appearance in 1919 and gained considerably at an election at the end of 1922, refused to work with him. In February, 1923, he was succeeded by Stanley Melbourne Bruce (b. 1883), a scion of a Melbourne importing house, educated at Cambridge, who had entered politics in 1919 after a distinguished record with the British Army. Bruce formed a coalition with the Country Party, whose leader, Sir Earle Christmas Grafton Page (b. 1880), a surgeon with wide interests and a long association with the rich and partly undeveloped Clarence River district in northern New South Wales, became Treasurer and Deputy Prime Minister. This coalition remained in power till 1929.

In many ways the early 'twenties mark the beginning of a new epoch in Australian history. Prior to 1914, Australia was still predominantly a primary producing country. Her people, even those who dwelt (as more than half had always done) in cities, were still close to pioneering conditions. In the 'twenties, secondary industry, fostered by the war and sheltered by increasing tariff protection, took an ever greater place in the national economy. The steel industry and its subsidiaries were firmly established. More and more the factory replaced the farm as the normal setting of Austra-

lian life. Even in the country, the automobile and the telephone
wrought a revolution which is not yet complete. Road transport
became a major industry. The number of cars increased from
136,848 to 656,314, and the number of telephone instruments from
4.41 per hundred inhabitants to 8.8. The ubiquity of motor cars
led to a demand for better roads, and long strips of bitumen or concrete replaced dirt tracks or gravel roads throughout the length
and breadth of the country. Radio and civil aviation were beginning: the series of great pioneer flights began with that of Sir
Ross Macpherson (1892–1922) and Sir Keith Macpherson Smith
(1890–) from England in 1919 and culminated in the transpacific
flight of Charles Edward Kingsford Smith (1897–1938) in 1928.

The 'twenties were, like the 'eighties, a period of consolidation.
Yet, in spite of high prices, of reckless immigration propaganda,
and of a great increase in the volume of public works and public
borrowing, there was an undertone of misgiving. Geographers
expressed doubt whether Australia's resources were really unlimited, and suggested that the limits had nearly been reached. Economists were concerned about the spiral by which protective tariffs
led to higher prices which were reflected by the Arbitration Court
in higher wages, thus forming the ground for an application for a
further tariff increase. But while prices continued high and loan
money flowed easily, these murmurs remained unheeded.

The slogan of the period was "men, money, and markets." The
men were to be provided by various immigration schemes supplemented by a strong Development and Migration Commission to
examine the resources of the country and the Council of Scientific
and Industrial Research to aid their exploitation. The money was
provided by a borrowing policy which increased the public debt
of the continent, exclusive of war debt, from £443,000,000 to more
than £980,000,000 in nine years. But, as time went on, the emphasis
shifted more and more to markets. The war had familiarised primary producers with organised marketing, and the difficulty of
competing in world markets with their costs increased by protection led them to look more and more to the government for assistance. Typical is the Paterson butter scheme of 1926, by which a
voluntary levy on all butter produced helped to subsidise exports,
the cost being borne by the home consumer.

In Australia, as elsewhere, the postwar years saw a wave of fiscal nationalism. The tariff of 1921 applied a more systematic protection than any of its predecessors, and was made more elastic to meet fluctuations in overseas conditions. An expert body, the Tariff Board, was set up to advise the Government and examine all claims for assistance. Protection, however, failed to bring satisfaction to the growing class of city artisans. There was doubt whether real wages were keeping pace with the general prosperity, and a belief in some quarters that the arbitration system prevented them from doing so. A vocal minority fanned unrest and advocated direct action. Some unions played State and Federal jurisdictions against one another. There was a serious seamen's strike in 1925, and, when the period of prosperity was coming to an end, attempts to scale down wages produced a prolonged strike and some violence in the timber industry (1929) and in the coal fields.

The amendment of the Constitution was discussed intermittently throughout the decade. In 1921 a constitutional convention was promised, but it never was held, and in 1929 a Royal Commission produced a comprehensive report. The main development of the period was in the technique of combined Commonwealth-State action. Typical was the River Murray Agreement, which set up a Commission representing the Commonwealth and the three States bordering the Murray to carry out a large-scale scheme of water conservation. Irrigation projects were also carried out by individual States. Another pattern was that of the Main Roads Agreement, by which the Commonwealth provided money for roads of national importance, the work being carried out by the States, for the war had placed the Commonwealth in a position of financial superiority over the States which it was reluctant to abandon. Under the Financial Agreement of 1928 the Commonwealth took over responsibility for the debts of the States, and all future borrowings were to be controlled by a Loan Council representing all the Australian governments.

In 1927 the Commonwealth Parliament moved into its own capital at Canberra. Since federation, it had occupied temporary quarters in Melbourne. Canberra had been selected as the site in 1908, a competition, won by the Chicago architect Walter Burley Griffin (1876–1937), had been held for the plan, and preliminary work was begun in 1912. Interrupted by the war, construction had been resumed with vigour afterwards. At first much criticised, the "bush capital," in spite of setbacks of depression and war, has come to play a steadily increasing part in the national life.

In 1929 the storm clouds were already gathering on the economic horizon when Bruce was defeated on the question of withdrawing the Commonwealth from the field of arbitration. In the ensuing election, Labour, which had greatly improved its position in 1928 and, under the active leadership of James Henry Scullin (b. 1876), had proved a very effective Opposition, secured a substantial majority, though the Senate remained hostile. During the decade, Labour had held office for greater or less periods in every State: it now took office again in the Commonwealth.

The record of the Bruce-Page Government must be judged in the light of world trends in the 'twenties. So judged, its achievement was considerable, though unspectacular. Bruce, too aloof to become a popular figure, though he was unrivalled as a Parliamentary leader, was later to find a more congenial milieu and do his best work as Australian High Commissioner in London.

The new Government had scarcely taken office when the storm broke. A catastrophic fall in export prices (in 1930 they barely topped 50 per cent of the 1928 level) and at the same time a sudden stoppage of loan money were reflected in disastrously widespread unemployment. The trouble was diagnosed as mainly financial. A special emergency tariff severely restricted imports. At a conference with the State premiers, the Government secured agreement on a drastic policy of deflation: an all-round reduction of wages, salaries, and interest by roughly 20 per cent. This was associated with substantial reductions in government expenditure and public works and increased taxation, designed to balance budgets. Already some relief had been given to primary producers by the devaluation of the Australian pound by 30 per cent in terms of sterling, on the initiative of one of the private banks.

The Premiers' Plan gave rise to severe criticism among the Government's supporters, but the moderate section prevailed and the plan was put into operation by all the governments except that of New South Wales, where the Labour Premier, John Thomas Lang (b. 1876), had a rival plan, involving nonpayment of interest on bonds and reduction of all official salaries to a maximum of £500 p.a. This precipitated a constitutional crisis. The Commonwealth paid the interest in default and garnisheed the amount from the State Treasury. Lang was dismissed by the State Governor and went out in an aura of martyrdom. His action had done much to disrupt his party, both in State and Federal politics.

The Scullin Government, which had to face the full brunt of the storm, fell apart from internal dissensions. Edward Granville Theodore (b. 1884), the strong man of the team and an extremely able, if radical, financier, was temporarily removed from the stage by charges of corruption arising from some actions when he was Premier of Queensland. The gentle and sensitive Scullin, broken in health by strain and overwork, returned from a visit to London to find a growing rift between the financially orthodox and the radical sections of his cabinet. He soon lost office to Joseph Aloysius Lyons (1879–1939), a former schoolmaster and Premier of Tasmania, who bolted the Labour Party to head a new conservative grouping, the United Australia Party, into which the Nationalists merged. Lyons was no profound statesman, but a very astute manager whose personal charm, large family, and likeness (eagerly seized by caricaturists) to a koala bear endeared him alike to the public and his colleagues. He remained in office, either alone or in coalition with the Country Party, until his death early in 1939, shortly before the outbreak of the war, the approach of which clouded his last months.

The depression of the 'thirties, like that of the 'nineties, produced a heightened self-awareness, one symptom of which was a renewed interest in Australian literature and a number of attempts to establish a local publishing industry. But while the effect of the 'nineties had been to turn men's minds toward internal problems, that of the 'thirties was rather, in the long run, to direct attention to international relations. The depression had brought home forcibly the dependence of Australia on her foreign trade, just when a wave of restriction and economic nationalism was sweeping over the world. That Australia herself had met the depression by a prohibitive tariff and an exchange depreciation which, with sterling also depreciated, made foreign buying almost impossible, did nothing to improve the popularity of her goods. Even wool was threatened by substitutes. At the same time, the menace of Japan was looming larger in Asia, and the peace of Europe was becoming more precarious year by year. The 'thirties were dominated by a search for markets and for security. They were marked by a gradual emergence of self-consciousness of Australian nationalism in a troubled world, and a series of attempts, fumbling but nonetheless significant, to discover Australia's place in the world and to evolve a national policy.

The process began with the Ottawa Agreement of 1932, which promised Australia a protected market, especially for those products of specialist intensive agriculture which had been developed during the 'twenties—dried fruits, dairy produce, and sugar—in return for a promise to revise the tariff and make no increases except on the recommendation of the Tariff Board.

The Ottawa Agreement was frankly an emergency measure; it gave no help in the long-range problem of finding fresh markets abroad; and it did not assist Australia's wool, the market for which, under the influence of autarchic national policies and exchange difficulties, was shrinking ominously. In May, 1934, the Prime Minister said: "In the past, Australia has concentrated on Empire markets, but it must now seek an expansion of foreign trade. There is an ever-increasing tendency for countries to confine their purchases to countries which buy from them. Australia will do the same." A Department of Commerce had been established in 1933, and Trade Commissioners were appointed to Tokio, Shanghai, Batavia, Cairo, and Wellington. (Commissioners had already been appointed to New York and Ottawa.) Soon afterward, a series of negotiations was commenced for reciprocal trade treaties, and a special portfolio of Minister for Trade Treaties was created in 1935. Treaties were concluded with Belgium, France, and Czechoslovakia, and the new intermediate tariff was extended under the most-favoured-nations clause to a number of other countries.

Out of these bilateral negotiations arose, in 1936, the "Trade Diversion" episode. Protracted negotiations with Japan had failed to produce agreement. A new policy was announced as a bargaining weapon, designed to increase exports, expand local secondary industry, and increase employment. By a system of quotas, import licenses, and increased duties a series of imports from Japan and the United States were virtually prohibited—notably, cotton and artificial silk piece goods and motor chassis. The immediate result was to provoke a Japanese embargo on wool and to antagonise the United States. The motives appear to have been complex, but the chief one seems to have been a desire to impress the British Government in order to secure favourable terms when the Ottawa Agreement should expire in 1938. The policy was very strongly criticised in Australia, and was soon completely discredited.

In Australia as elsewhere, questions of defence became increasingly dominant as the 'thirties went on. The activities of Japan in China and her withdrawal from the League of Nations caused growing anxiety, even though the significance of the Manchuria "episode" was not at first realised. In spite of an exchange of "goodwill missions" in 1934, suspicion of Japan was increased by her commercial tactics and her withdrawal from the London Naval Conference of 1935.

In 1935 the question of the application of sanctions to Italy provided the first major Parliamentary debate ever held on foreign issues. The practical effect was nil, but the clarification of attitudes was interesting. The Government based the case for sanctions not on the principle of collective security, but on loyalty to Britain. Neutrality would be tantamount to secession. They also tried, rather unconvincingly, to distinguish sanctions from war, and on this issue the veteran Hughes left the Cabinet—to be restored a few weeks later when the fuss had subsided. The Labour Party united in opposing sanctions, some from genuine pacifist conviction, others from an isolationist attitude to wars in which Australia was not obviously and directly concerned.

The debate served to bring into sharp focus the defence issue. It revealed clearly that, both materially and psychologically, Australia was unprepared for any crisis involving the threat of war. There was general agreement on the need for a considerable strengthening of defence. Two main theories were held. That of the Government, envisaging coöperation with Great Britain by means of an expeditionary force as the main objective, called for concentration mainly on the army; the other, of which John Curtin (1885–1945), who had succeeded Scullin as Leader of the Labour Party, was spokesman, envisaged the defence of Australian territory as the first, if not the only, objective, and urged that the available funds should be expended on the air force and navy as defensive arms. The election of 1937 decisively endorsed the Government's policy, and increasing sums were set aside for defence in each of the following years, as the symptoms in Europe grew more ominous. The complacency of the 'twenties and the depression of the 'thirties had left much leeway to make up, and the Munich crisis found the country still far from ready for war. The impression made in Australia was profound, but the Government's policy remained, in Lyons' words "tune in to Britain," and there was a general reaction of relief that war was averted.

For the same reasons, attempts were made from time to time to appease Japan, though suspicion of that country's intentions was rapidly deepening. Australia was becoming increasingly conscious at last of the threat from her "near north," as is shown, for instance, by the somewhat naïve proposals for a Pacific pact put forward by Lyons at the Imperial Conference of 1937, and by the growing interest in the work of such unofficial bodies as the Institute of Pacific Relations.

After September, 1938, the imminence of war overshadowed every other issue. All that remained was to make the best possible use of what time remained. When Germany invaded Poland in September, 1939, there was no debate and no one was surprised by the official announcement that, since Great Britain was at war, Australia was at war also.

Part Three:

CONSTITUTIONAL AND
POLITICAL DEVELOPMENT

CHAPTER VI

*The Constitution and Its Problems**

BY KENNETH HAMILTON BAILEY

O N NEW YEAR'S DAY, 1901, with the union in a federal Commonwealth of the six self-governing British colonies, Australia became a nation, and not merely a continent. The new federal constitution drew its formal legal validity from its existence as an Act of the Parliament of the United Kingdom. In substance, it was the product of Australian social forces, Australian thought and action. Its deepest roots were a realisation that intercolonial trade rivalries ("the barbarism of borderism") menaced the prosperity of all, and a desire to exercise, through union, a more effective influence on international policy in the Southwest Pacific. It had taken shape in Australia in the 'nineties as a result of convention debates, parliamentary proceedings, and popular votes and campaigns.

The Constitution: Origins and Outlines.—More fortunate than the Philadelphia Convention, the fathers of the Australian constitution were able to take guidance from federalism in contemporary working practice. Not only was the United States model before them, but the Swiss and the Canadian as well. After close study, their preference went for the United States pattern. The choice lay deeper than such familiar names as Senate and House of Representatives. The basic principle of the Australian division of powers—that the federation has only its expressly enumerated powers, the general residuary powers remaining with the states—comes straight from the Constitution of the United States. Further, though a full century of industrial and social change lay between

---

* This chapter was written before Professor Bailey's appointment as Commonwealth Solicitor-General.

the two constitutions, no one can read the two lists of federal
powers without being struck by the relatively large amount of
similarity, the relatively small area of divergence. The commerce
power of the Commonwealth, for instance, is identical in substance
with that of the United States. The Senate, representing each state
equally, was likewise American in inspiration, though the method
of direct election was not adopted in the United States until 1913.

But the fathers of Australian federation did not make the mistake of trying to transplant into Australian politics the American
federal system in its entirety. They followed Canada, for instance,
in applying to the federal government the British system of a parliamentary executive, and not the presidential system. This choice
was natural. The British system had long been in operation in all
the Australian colonies and they preferred the pattern they knew.
The choice of parliamentary or "responsible" or Cabinet government involved, also, on practical grounds, another departure from
American practice. The Australian Senate, for instance, was placed
in a position of legal inferiority to the House of Representatives
in matters of finance, and generally in the event of a deadlock
between the Houses.

The British model was followed again in the absence from the
Australian constitution of any general Bill of Rights. Individual
freedom and the basic human rights were to be protected, as in
Britain, not *against* but *by* the legislature. The constitution is to
that extent based on parliamentary, not on people's, sovereignty.
This has naturally facilitated the exercise of regulatory powers
over individual rights both of personality and of property, in
obedience to the rising tide in favour of social control which has
operated in Australia as in other democratic communities.

In the group of express powers of the Commonwealth Parliament which have no counterpart in the list for Congress in the
Constitution of the United States, the power to make laws with
respect to conciliation and arbitration for the prevention and
settlement of interstate industrial disputes has probably had the
most striking effect on Australian economic and political life. The
presence of this power in the constitution grew out of distinctive
local experience—serious and prolonged strikes in the 'nineties in
the shearing and maritime industries, where workers went from one

colony to another and when nothing but Australia-wide action, for which no instrumentalities existed, could have been effective.

The financial adjustment between federation and states was another original feature of the constitution, embodying a hard-won compromise that is known unflatteringly to Australian history as the "Braddon blot." Customs and excise became exclusive federal powers. That was natural. But customs and excise had provided the main revenues of the federating colonies. The new federation must obviously be compelled to make available for the states a substantial proportion of its revenue from these sources, or state finances would be ruined. But what would be the initial cost of the new federal government? And how rapid would be its expansion? Out of stubborn bargaining, a ten-year solution emerged. The Commonwealth was to refund to each state, for the first ten years, in the ratio of tax collected, three-fourths of customs and excise receipts. Thereafter the Commonwealth Parliament itself would decide what Commonwealth-state financial relations should be. The Commonwealth Parliament was also (by Section 96 of the Constitution) authorised to grant financial assistance to any state on such conditions as the Parliament thought fit. As Alfred Deakin (1856–1919) later said, federation left the states bound, financially, to the chariot wheels of the Commonwealth.

If the basic features of the Australian federal structure came from the United States pattern, with a parliamentary executive as in Canada, it was Switzerland which supplied the inspiration, in the shape of the popular referendum, for the method of amending the Australian constitution. Amendments could be initiated in the federal Parliament only, and would become effective only if approved at a referendum by a majority of the electors voting, and also by a majority in a majority of the states. This device was hailed by observers at the time not only as consonant with the spirit of democracy that pervades the constitution as a whole (e.g., in the provision for triennial Parliaments), but also as promising a simpler and more effective amending process than any of the other contemporary federations.

The Australian Machinery of Government.—State constitutions in Australia, as in the United States, are not derived from the constitution of the federation. Some departments of the former colonial administrations were transferred at once to the Commonwealth, e.g., posts and telegraphs, defence, and quarantine. Other state functions would pass to the Commonwealth as the federation gradually occupied the fields assigned to it. Otherwise the state machinery continued to function just as before, with the new federal institutions superimposed upon it.

Each state, in 1900, had a bicameral Parliament with a Legislative Council (upper house) elected on a property franchise, except in New South Wales and Queensland, which had a nominee House. The former has since been made subject to indirect election. The latter was abolished in 1917. The five remaining Legislative Councils are all, in practice, powerful bodies, exercising a markedly conservative influence upon state legislative programmes.

For all practical purposes the state legislatures already enjoyed, in 1900, autonomy vis-à-vis the Parliament of the United Kingdom. The state executive, on the British Cabinet system, was responsible to the local legislature. Formally, the head of the state administration was a governor appointed from Westminster. But in 1900 he was already, save in the most exceptional matters, in the position of a constitutional monarch, obliged by convention, like the king himself, to act upon the advice of his ministers, and not ordinarily subject to direction from London. Since 1900 his approximation to the position of the king has become steadily closer.

Local government in all the states was British in broad pattern, and largely in terminology. But the powers of local bodies were meagre and relatively unimportant, and have remained so. Education and police, for example, have traditionally been functions in Australia of the state, not of the municipality. The reason is to be found partly in the traditional paternalism of government in Australia, partly in the artificial character of local boundaries, partly in the problems of great distances and of settlement radiating from a few seaboard centres. Local government has always been one of the weak spots in Australian political organisation.

The observer from abroad of Australia's institutions is often surprised by the greatness of the land area and the smallness of the population. Australia has roughly the same area as the continental United States. The distance west by rail from Canberra to Perth (Western Australia) is comparable with that from Washington, D.C., to San Francisco. From Canberra north to Cairns (Queensland) is half as far again as Washington is from New Orleans. Even today, however, there are only six states, and there are fewer people in all Australia than in Greater New York. The House of Representatives has only seventy-four members, the Senate only thirty-six: six from each state. New South Wales with twenty-eight seats, and Victoria with twenty, dominate the House of Representatives.

The governor-general, even more emphatically than the governor of a state, stands in the same relation to his ministers as the king does to his in Britain. Since 1930, the governor-general has been appointed on the advice of the Cabinet in Australia. He represents the king, not the British Government, which maintains for that purpose a high commissioner in Canberra.

The judicial machinery of the Commonwealth is based fundamentally on that of the United States, with a federal supreme court called the High Court of Australia. But this High Court also acts as a common court of appeal from the supreme courts of the states. The parallel here is with Canada.

Unlike the Canadian constitution, however, the constitution of Australia greatly restricts the competence of the Judicial Committee of the Privy Council to determine appeals from the High Court in constitutional cases. This has had an important influence upon constitutional development in Australia. By Section 74 of the Constitution, the Privy Council cannot entertain an appeal from a decision of the High Court on any question concerning the limits *inter se* of the constitutional powers of the Commonwealth and a state, unless the High Court itself, for special reasons, certifies that the question should be determined by the Privy Council (which the High Court has done, only once, in 1914). These *inter se* questions include the overwhelming majority of all Australian constitutional questions. Even in other matters there is no appeal from a decision of the High Court except by the special leave of the Privy Council, which in practice is rarely given. The rôle of the Privy Council in Australian constitutional development has therefore been relatively slight. The interpretation of the constitution has, for the most part, taken place in Australia and at the hands of an Australian tribunal.

The Problems of the Constitution.—Federalism in Australia is subject to the defects of federation everywhere. Sixty years ago, Albert Venn Dicey, basing his views primarily on the experience of the United States and Switzerland, analysed the drawbacks of a federal constitution in terms that subsequent experience has only served to confirm. Federalism, said Dicey, means weak government; it means conservatism; it means legalism. Weak government, because of the division of powers between the federation and its component states; conservatism, because federal written constitutions are proverbially hard to change; legalism, because of the principle of judicial review, and because any substantial political question tends to raise issues not merely of policy but of constitutional power. Nevertheless, federalism, like everything else human, possesses the merits of its defects. It does, after all, offer a technique for the government of large areas in which regional sentiment is too strong or too diverse for complete political unity. The drawbacks, as Dicey analysed them, are also safeguards. "Weak government" also means scope for regional autonomy and social experimentation; "conservatism" and "legalism" mean security for minority rights.

In appraising the success or failure of a federal constitution, the existence of two broadly distinct though complementary approaches to the problems of federation should also be kept in mind. Some thinkers regard the essence of a federal system as being the continued exercise by the component states of autonomous powers of a substantial and significant character. They therefore tend to deprecate as unfederal any extension of federal powers, even by interpretation, which would substantially diminish the sphere of operation of the states. Other thinkers, however, follow Dicey in emphasising that the dominant purpose of federation is to create a nation: a nation for defined purposes only, but nevertheless a nation: a political organisation not indeed characterised by *unity*, but nevertheless by *union*. Thinkers of this second school, on their part, deprecate any attempt to curtail, by reference to any assumed ambit of state powers, the action of the federation in exercising, in accordance with the constitution, the national authority.

In the brief course of Australian history the Commonwealth has grown in function and in authority, in a sense at the expense of the states, to a degree and in directions never contemplated in 1900.

Few Australians today would say, however, that the constitution had failed, or that the problem of tomorrow should be to undo the nation-building that has taken place. Most Australians would say emphatically, on the contrary, that the constitution has enabled Australia to solve the outstanding problems of her national life, and achieve the main objects of federation.

The industrial development which has been the prominent feature of Australia's economic history has taken place in pursuance of the Commonwealth's tariff policy. Immigration has been regulated, both by way of encouragement and by way of restriction, in accordance with the community's strong desire to maintain its British traditions and to avoid the mixture of races which has produced social conflicts elsewhere. In two world wars, the Commonwealth has found in the "defence" power sufficiently wide and flexible support for a highly organised, not to say total, war effort. Australia has taken her place as a nation, not only in British Commonwealth affairs, but in international relations and in international organisation generally.

Nevertheless, the constitution does have its problems, in plenty. Fundamentally, they are problems in adjusting a nineteenth-century constitution, much of whose contents echoed still earlier ideas derived directly from the Constitution of the United States, to the changing needs of a twentieth-century industrial democracy. When the federation was established, the Australian economy was not basically very different from that of the United States in 1787. But the industrialisation and urbanisation of Australia has proceeded apace, stimulated not only by the two world wars, but also by the world depression in the interval. Questions of employment and unemployment, of production and distribution, of industrial relations, have all taken on a national aspect that none foresaw in 1900.

Two basic elements in Australian political thought, underlying, or rather, perhaps, overlaying, party divergences, have at one and the same time created constitutional problems and also given an impetus toward constitutional adjustment. One is the much greater willingness of the Australian electorate, compared with the American, to accept and even to demand positive governmental policies of social and economic control. This tendency may be seen most clearly, perhaps, in the creation of agencies, both state and federal, for the regulation of industrial relations. The same tendency can be seen also in repeated efforts to stabilise the major primary industries, both in war and in peace, by means of organised marketing under public authorities and by the provision of home-consumption prices to cushion the impact of precarious marketing conditions abroad.

The second of the basic Australian political ideas is that in common fairness the governmental resources of Australia ought to be so far shared that the citizen is enabled to participate more or less equally, irrespective of the particular state to which he belongs, in the burdens and advantages of citizenship. These considerations have had a marked effect in the financial relations between the Commonwealth and the states and in the sphere of social services.

To give effect to these two basic elements in Australian political thinking has called for bold governmental experiment and some constitutional change. So also has the adjustment of the constitution to the twentieth-century industrialisation of Australia. The instruments of solving these problems of the constitution are broadly two: development by interpretation, in the ordinary course of the judicial review of legislation; and resort to the formal processes of constitutional amendment, strictly so-called.

Perhaps, however, it is a mistake to concentrate overmuch on these two formal instruments of constitutional adjustment. Under a constitution by which the sum total of governmental powers is, broadly speaking, divided between Commonwealth and states, a tremendous amount can be accomplished by means of coöperation between them. Much has indeed been accomplished by this means in Australia. Take the control of civil aviation, for example. This is incontestably a field in which a uniform legislative and administrative code is required. The constitution as it stands permits the Commonwealth to carry out Australian obligations under international aviation agreements. This is under the external-affairs power. Outside the agreements, however, the Commonwealth can deal only with interstate and overseas aviation. Intrastate operations are exclusively a state field. The problem has been solved, in practice, by the states' willingness to bring the Commonwealth's code into operation within their own boundaries.

Similar kinds of mutual aid have been found effective in fields such as health and marketing. A meeting of the Commonwealth and state governments in the form of a premiers' conference has almost become an extraconstitutional institution in Australia, primarily with the object of bringing about common action. But the great difficulty about this technique is admirably expressed in John Adams's aphorism: "It is hard to make thirteen clocks strike all at once."

In Australia, indeed, there are no more than seven governments; but there are actually thirteen Houses of Parliament, and an adverse vote in a single Legislative Council may nullify the most promising programme of Commonwealth-state coöperation. Civil aviation is a good example in this regard also. It took nearly twenty years to bring about common action, even in so uncontroversial a matter. Here, indeed, is another of the problems of the Australian constitution.

Change by Interpretation: the Courts.—Because there is no Bill of Rights in the Commonwealth constitution, the rôle of judicial review has been narrower and less spectacular than in the United States. It is through the great indefinable generalisations about the process of liberty of expression, of the protection of life, liberty, and property, that the judiciary has exercised its most powerful influence on American public law. These slogans are absent from the Australian constitution. On the other hand, in contrast with the Canadian constitution, the result of the exclusion from the Privy Council of the majority of constitutional cases has been that the interpretation of the constitution has naturally been closer to what Holmes called the "felt necessities of the time" in Australia itself.

Until the end of the First World War the High Court adopted a general principle of interpretation which was definitely restrictive of the Commonwealth. This principle was that a power given to the Commonwealth should be so interpreted, if possible, as not to permit the Commonwealth to enter, by way of one of its powers, upon fields that were left, under other powers, to the states. The Commonwealth's express powers with respect to excise, for example, were interpreted as not including licencing fees in general, though, in English legislation before 1900, "excises" did ordinarily include charges of this kind. The reason was that the wider meaning would allow the Commonwealth to encroach on the field of the regulation of professions and callings, which otherwise would be left to the states, e.g., as intrastate trade and commerce. Similarly limiting decisions were given as to the Commonwealth's powers with respect to corporations and taxation. The American doctrine of the "immunity of instrumentalities," likewise followed by the High Court in these years, is in one sense merely a special application of this federal principle.

In 1920, however, the High Court, after some changes in personnel, laid down an entirely different principle for the interpretation of Commonwealth powers. This was distinctively national in emphasis. An express grant to the Commonwealth should be given its full ordinary natural meaning, and not be artificially restricted by reference to its possible effect upon the powers left to the states. Otherwise its positive intention to establish a nation for the purposes set out in the constitution would be frustrated. As well cut down the express gifts in a will by reference to the assumed content of the residuary estate.

The adoption of this new principle of interpretation was chiefly due to the efforts of Isaac Alfred Isaacs (b. 1855), who as Attorney-General of Victoria had been a leading member of the Conventions of 1897–1898, and, after federation, became successively Commonwealth Attorney-General, Justice of the High Court, 1906, Chief Justice, 1929, and Governor-General, 1931. The decision of 1920 (the Engineers' case) has been several times challenged but decisively reaffirmed, and may now be regarded as settled. As usual with judicial decisions, its full effect has been disclosed only as individual cases of its application occur.

The decision in the Engineers' case itself asserted the authority of the Commonwealth Court of Conciliation and Arbitration to make awards binding on the employees in state industrial undertakings (including railways). A later application of the same principle of interpretation, with potentially even more far-reaching consequences, was the decision that the Commonwealth Parliament could give effect to the International Civil Aviation Convention, even though in doing so it dealt with subjects otherwise exclusively within state powers.

The same approach can be found in several decisions on the financial powers of the Commonwealth. Thus in 1926 the High Court held that the Commonwealth Parliament, in providing funds under Section 96 to assist the states in the construction of main roads, could lay down conditions as to the type of road to be constructed. Resolute use of the method thus endorsed could easily subordinate state activities to Commonwealth policy, even in matters otherwise exclusively of state concern, in any instance where the states required, or could be induced to accept, financial help.

The high-water mark of Section 96 was reached during the Second World War. State income tax varied widely in severity from one state to another. The constitution, however, forbids Commonwealth taxation to discriminate between states. Even at the worst pinch of the war, therefore, the Commonwealth was unable directly to equalise the burden of taxation by taking up the slack in the less heavily taxed states. Determined to raise more revenue from income tax, the Commonwealth imposed tax on a uniform basis, at a level so high as virtually to exclude the states, but at the same time offered to each state a grant roughly equivalent to its own previous income-tax collections, on condition that it abstain from imposing a tax on incomes. This uniform tax plan received general public support and was upheld by the High Court. The complaining states contended, but in vain, that so wide an application of Section 96 was inconsistent with the very basis of a federal constitution.

Except for the early and temporary adoption of the federal principle as the basis for a restrictive interpretation of Commonwealth powers, the High Court has, on the whole, and wherever alternative views were possible, adopted interpretations that have made for the extension of Commonwealth authority. For example, the industrial powers, limited and indirect though they are, have nevertheless been interpreted widely enough, within their scope, to bring the majority of Australian wage-earners within the awards of the Commonwealth Court of Conciliation and Arbitration. Superficially, at any rate, the commerce power has been an exception to the general rule. The High Court has not yet followed the Supreme Court of the United States in bringing within federal power related intrastate transactions and related productive operations. The power over interstate commerce, therefore, has not yet served the Commonwealth as a foundation for the range of industrial economic and social control which the same form of words has supported in the United States. But constitutions are more than forms of words. In Australia the constitution operates upon different economic conditions. With only six states in so large an area, interstate trade does not occupy anything like so large an area of the nation's economic life as it does in the United States, and is not so closely integrated with other parts of the economy.

Organised marketing plans, both Commonwealth and state, have encountered a serious constitutional obstacle in the categorical declaration in Section 92 that interstate trade and commerce shall be "absolutely free." The prohibition is as impressive as it is sonorous. Free from what? From duties of customs and other financial imposts? From discriminatory regulations of all kinds? From all forms of governmental control? The problem has many times vexed the courts, including the Privy Council. The inclusion of interstate road transport in state measures for coördinating road and rail transport within the state has been upheld. So has the inclusion of the interstate movement of produce or stock in state regulations directed at safeguarding public health. But the Privy Council has invalidated, as applied to interstate transactions, the simplest form of ensuring a home-consumption price for primary products, viz., a law prohibiting interstate carriage of produce except in pursuance of a licence which requires compliance with prescribed export quotas, thus forcing the surplus off the domestic market.

The fate of schemes under which a centralised marketing agency compulsorily acquires the whole of a commodity and markets it for the benefit of the producers is still uncertain. A non-Labour Government in 1937 and a Labour Government in 1946 sought by way of referendum to secure the exclusion of marketing plans from the operation of Section 92. Neither attempt succeeded. So strong, however, is the demand, among primary producers especially, for regulated marketing and a controlled home-consumption price that the struggle to find some line of reconciliation with Section 92 still goes on. The courts, as already indicated, have left the governments substantial latitude.

Change by Formal Amendment: the Referendum.—Almost from the outset, proposals for amending the constitution have been under discussion in the Commonwealth Parliament. An alteration requires absolute majorities in both Houses followed by an approving majority vote, at a referendum, not only in Australia as a whole but also in a majority of states. There being only six states, as many are needed for a majority as for a two-thirds majority—a stringent requirement.

The referendum has not fulfilled anticipations as a method of effecting constitutional change. The Australian voter has proved unexpectedly conservative. Referendums have been held on ten occasions—in 1906, 1910, 1911, 1913, 1919, 1926, 1928, 1937, 1944, and 1946. Only on four occasions—1906, 1910, 1928, and 1946— has a proposed alteration been approved by the required majorities, and two of these were on minor matters. In addition, government bills for constitutional alterations have on five occasions passed one or both Houses, but have not been submitted to popular vote. A number of private members' proposals have also been introduced. The total number of bills for constitutional alterations is fifty-eight—i.e., more than an average of one per year.

The main objectives of change have been the extension of federal powers in commerce and industry and the settlement on a more permanent basis of the financial relations between the Commonwealth and the states. The latter objective was substantially attained in 1928, when an amendment was approved validating a general financial agreement between Commonwealth and states. Attempts at the former have failed again and again—before the First World War, between the wars, and at the close of the Second World War.

The main dynamic for constitutional change has come from the Australian Labour Party. Representative basically of the trade-union movement, the Labour Party has had a platform which announces socialisation as its political objective. But this has been the long-term programme. In actual working practice, Labour has been empirical and gradualist, concentrating on the improvement of industrial conditions and the extension of social services.

On the constitutional side the picture has been much the same. The platform has been "unification"—the radical transformation of the federation into a unitary system of government, with subordinate provincial councils replacing the present coördinate legislatures of the states. In practice, however, Labour proposals for constitutional change have never gone so far. They have selected more limited objectives. The nearest that a Labour Government ever came to a formally unificatory amendment was in 1930, when it was proposed to give to the Commonwealth Parliament the power to amend the constitution without resort to a referendum. This proposal was negatived by a non-Labour majority in the Senate, and was never submitted to the people.

The natural thing for any reforming movement in Australia is to press for federal control: otherwise the problem must be attacked on six different fronts, through the several states. The natural line for Labour has therefore been to urge the extension of the Commonwealth's limited industrial and commercial powers. The general argument is that customs duties, trading, and conditions of employment are all so interdependent, and react so powerfully each upon the other, that they should all be placed under the same control. Since the Commonwealth already—and necessarily—controls the customs, it follows that all the other powers should similarly be vested in the Commonwealth.

The Labour Party has by no means stood alone in pressing for constitutional change. The logic of Australia's industrial development, the demand for national action in war and in the face of economic depression, have made themselves felt on all sides of politics. Proposals for extended Commonwealth powers in commerce and industry have been put forward by non-Labour as well as by Labour governments.

These considerations may at first sight make apparently inexplicable the repeated failure of governments to obtain popular approval at referendums for extended national powers. The explanation is to be found along three main lines. In the first place, it is exceedingly difficult in practice to keep the abstract question of whether the Commonwealth should have a particular power clearly separate in the voter's mind from the logically quite different, concrete question whether he would favour the particular kind of exercise of the power which is contemplated by the government that at the moment is seeking to amend the constitution. The

employer may in practice be unwilling to concede to a Labour
Government in the Commonwealth the power to fix hours of
labour. The employee may be just as unwilling to concede it to
a non-Labour Government. Questions of constitutional power
become inextricably confused with questions of legislative policy.
Constitutional change becomes interwoven with party politics.
Parties in opposition urge the rejection of amendments not easy
to distinguish from some which they had themselves proposed
when in office—and, of course, vice versa.

Second, antagonism to central control has been, and remains,
a powerful element in all questions of constitutional change, especially among the people of the outlying and less populous primary-
producing states: Queensland, South Australia, Western Australia, and Tasmania. This is natural, and is found in all federations.
Regionalism is all the stronger in a huge country like Australia,
in which, moreover, the art of decentralised administration has
not yet been fully learnt. Tasmania, Queensland, and South Australia have seldom given an affirmative vote at a referendum.

The result, third, of these interacting factors of party politics
and regional sentiment is a most complex criss-cross of opinions,
in which there is always much scope for the simple maxim of caution—"when in doubt, vote No."

In the latter half of the Second World War the Curtin and
Chifley Labour governments, under the energetic stimulus of Dr.
H. V. Evatt, Attorney-General and Minister for External Affairs,
commenced a more vigorous and sustained drive for constitutional
change than Australia has ever known. The circumstances were
undoubtedly favourable. On the one hand, under the unified
national leadership and direction of the Commonwealth—made
possible by an extensive judicial interpretation of the defence
power—Australia was putting forth something very like a total
war effort. On the other hand, the declared war aims of the United
Nations included postwar reconstruction at home on a generous
scale; nothing less, in fact, than to establish a new order, in which
the people could achieve the Four Freedoms, in particular freedom from want and freedom from fear. For such purposes the
existing division of powers between Commonwealth and states,
with limited and divided national authority in the vital spheres of

production, commerce, and employment, could scarcely provide a sufficient constitutional basis.

In October, 1942, not long after the tide of war in the Pacific had turned in favour of the United Nations, Dr. Evatt introduced into the House of Representatives a bill to modernise the "horse and buggy" constitution of 1900, by giving the Commonwealth Parliament full power to make laws "for carrying into effect the the war aims and objects of Australia as one of the United Nations, including the attainment of economic security and social justice in the postwar world, and for the purpose of postwar reconstruction." A list of specific subject matters was added, by way of illustration merely.

The breathtaking boldness of this move caused some reaction, particularly in the state legislatures. The Government invited comment and criticism, and summoned to a Constitutional Convention at Canberra in November, 1942, representatives of both Government and Opposition in the Parliament of each state, as well as of the Commonwealth. Such a body had no legal authority, but it met, in the Prime Minister's words, as an "advisory council of the whole nation."

Labour governments were in office in four of the states (but not in Victoria and South Australia) as well as in the Commonwealth. As a result of previous debates in the states, however, much opposition was expressed to the Commonwealth's plan. Eventually a compromise was reached. The Government would not proceed with its plan for holding a wartime referendum. On their part, the state premiers would do their utmost to ensure the immediate passage through their respective Parliaments of a bill in common form referring to the Commonwealth until the expiration of five years after the cessation of hostilities of fourteen subject-matters selected as desirable for the purposes of postwar reconstruction. By virtue of a special provision in the constitution—Section 51 (xxxvii)—the Commonwealth Parliament has power to make laws with respect to any matters so referred by the Parliament of a state.

The plan broke down. New South Wales and Queensland promptly referred all the matters in the agreed form. South Australia and Western Australia referred some of the matters, but in substantially altered form. Tasmania passed no bill at all. Victoria referred all the matters, but only on the condition that all other states did the same—a condition which of course was not fulfilled.

In 1944 the Commonwealth Government carried through both Houses a bill embodying the main features of the Convention plan. The fourteen powers, en bloc, until five years after the cessation of hostilities, in order to permit of sufficient national authority, even when the defence power shrank to peacetime limits, were to handle the difficult tasks of unwinding the war effort and organising the transition from war to peace. The list provided, among other things, for increased Commonwealth powers over employment and unemployment; production and distribution; profiteering and prices; trusts, combines, and monopolies; national works; national health; and family allowances. In addition, three safeguards were added to the fourteen powers—guarantees of freedom of expression and of religion, and a restriction on delegated legislation. It was by far the most comprehensive measure of constitutional change that the Australian people had ever had to consider.

The bill was not approved at the referendum. There were affirmative majorities in two states only (South Australia and Western Australia). The over-all majority was also negative. From the point of view of the future, the most important thing perhaps was the general recognition that the constitution as it stands is outmoded, and that early extension of national powers is needed.

The results of a further referendum in 1946 suggest that this recognition is gaining ground. There were three separate proposals for new Commonwealth authority with respect to (1) the provision of certain social services; (2) the organised marketing of primary products, without restriction from Section 92; and (3) the terms and conditions of employment (but not so as to authorise industrial conscription). The first of these proposals was carried. A majority of electors voting approved the other two as well; but there were majorities in three states only, so that the second and third proposals were rejected. Queensland, South Australia, and Tasmania returned adverse majorities.

Looking ahead, the greatest problem of the Australian constitution still seems to be how to adjust the division of powers to the requirements of an advanced industrial democracy. Experience has shown how precarious is the popular referendum as an instrument for this purpose. Yet the logic of Australia's industrial and commercial development cannot in the long run be denied. If Australia's future course is reasonably smooth, the adjustments will no doubt be made empirically, piecemeal, aided perhaps by improved techniques of preparation for referendums which would help to lift constitutional change out of party politics; aided perhaps also by improved techniques of administration, which would allay regional fears of "remote control." There are some who see Australia's future constitution in terms of a unitary but decentralised organisation, in which the present six states will be replaced by perhaps eighteen or twenty provinces. Such a solution, however rational, implies so great a departure from the nation's historic system as to be difficult to envisage in the immediate future. A return to emergency conditions, economic or military, might so far break up established patterns of thought as to make possible entirely new structures. The past few years have at least shaken the people's confidence that the present constitution is satisfactory as it stands.

CHAPTER VII

Australian Party Politics

BY ROSS GOLLAN

THERE ARE three major parties in Australian politics: the Australian Labour Party (more often called Labour, or the A.L.P.), the Liberal Party, and the Country Party. Of the three, Labour has the longest history and it goes back only to the early 1890's. The Liberal Party's genesis traces to a fusion, in self-defence against the A.L.P., of previously harshly opposed free trade and protectionist parliamentarians in 1909. Since 1909 the fusion has had several names. The Country Party arrived on the federal stage just after the First World War.

This lack of party continuity springs from the fact that political causes which stirred prefederation Australia failed or were fulfilled with the epochs which produced them. The first great Australian political fight was for full self-government, in place of British Colonial Office administration, of the individual colonies from which have sprung the six states of federal Australia. Even in New South Wales, oldest of the Australian colonies, the fight was not completely won till the 1850's. Through most of its course it was led by William Charles Wentworth, earliest of Australia's greater politicians, orator, lawyer, journalist, explorer, squatter, and autocrat. Behind Wentworth, for the fight's duration, stood almost every Australian, adoptive or native-born. Won, the fight left behind it no material for an enduring party credo. Wentworth quickly turned, in mob opinion, from democracy's champion to symbol of a privileged squatter class. He neither had, nor needed, a political heir.

In the second half of the nineteenth century there were two great, and not dissociated, Australian political issues. One was federation. The other was protection versus free trade. On the principle of federation there was little basic disagreement. On how the principle should be practised, there was much. The piecemeal development of Australia had endowed the separate colonies with divergent local economies which would be unpredictably, and perhaps intolerably, affected by a common political control. For instance, of the two largest colonies, Victoria was protectionist; New South Wales, less vehemently, held free-trade views which might not be able to survive federation. (They did not.)

Yet it was a New South Wales free-trader who struck out the spark from which the federal lamp was permanently kindled. In 1889, military experts demanded central control as a prerequisite of adequate Australian defence. In a speech on October 24 of that year, Sir Henry Parkes, the seventy-four-year-old Premier of New South Wales, called on Australians everywhere to link hands, establish an Australian parliament, and form themselves into a nation. The cockney oratory of Parkes, immigrant, former Chartist, radical opportunist, mighty educationist, and as bad a poet as ever put out a printed book of verse, could control almost anything except his extraordinary aspirates and, in this matter, his own parliament. His speech led to a national federal convention of 1891 which drafted a federal constitution acceptable to most of Australia, but not to the parliament of New South Wales. Parkes lost his Premiership and died five years before others, notably his fellow New South Welshman, Sir Edmund Barton, and Alfred Deakin, noblest Victorian of them all, perfected his federal work.

The other late nineteenth-century Australian political issue was still unresolved when the Commonwealth came into official being on January 1, 1901. Protection in Australia was the synthetic product of a journalist of genius, David Syme, who saw it as the means of preventing the economic collapse of his home colony, Victoria, at the end of the gold-rush boom. In Victoria, protection played the part Syme predicted, placing him in a position of local authority which let him make and break Victorian colonial ministries at whim. Colonies richer in exportable products looked at the Victorian experiment across colonial boundaries studded with customs houses. It seemed that tariff policy would be the chief permanent party demarcation in the new federal parliament. No other living issue seemed in prospect. And, for responsible government in the British tradition, an Opposition was as necessary as a Government.

This anticipation overlooked two facts. One was that once the federal parliament began to commit Australia to high tariffism, growth of tariff-sheltered industries would create political pressure groups too powerful to be defied by the most enthusiastic of would-be free-trade parties. The other was the imminent rise to major federal parliamentary standing of the Labour Party. The rise was least foreseen by Labour itself, which had thrown its influence against federation on the ground that the Commonwealth constitution was designed to hamstring political radicalism.

But the anticipation proved true enough of the first Commonwealth parliament. A moderately protectionist Government, led by Barton with Deakin as his chief of staff, was glowered at across the parliamentary tables by a revenue-tariff (i.e., free-trade) Opposition. Labour, a midget party of sixteen out of seventy-five in the House of Representatives, had to leave its members free to vote as they chose on fiscal issues; otherwise it would have lost some of its members. Australia found itself quickly committed to a policy of protectionism. For the rest, the first parliament wrote into the virgin statute book measures ("White Australia," for example) which the public demanded from all parties, and provided such of the necessary working machinery of government as had been left by the constitution for parliamentary enactment. No clear pattern was provided of the shape of party things to come.

Things were different in the second parliament, elected in December, 1903. Barton, possessor of all qualities needed by a great political leader except the power of sustaining his own interest in his own leadership, had retired from the Prime Ministership to the High Court bench. Deakin, Prime Minister in his stead, met a new House of Representatives in which Labour, now twenty-three members strong, held the balance of power. Labour could keep Deakin in the Prime Ministership while it pleased. It could, when and if it chose, substitute for him the Leader of the Opposition, George Reid, witty, opportunist, fat, and able. It might even, on sufferance, become a government itself.

The third contingency soon eventuated. An issue which brought into conflict Deakin's reverence for the spirit of the federal compact and Labour's demands for statutory arbitration blew up in the House. Deakin was defeated, and on April 27, 1904, John Christian Watson was sworn in as Australia's first Labour Prime Minister. Watson lives in Australian political history only by reason of this priority. His right-hand man in this first Labour Government was very different—William Morris Hughes, of whom more anon.

Labour's Cabinet was predestined to last no longer than it took the other two parties to hammer out a fiscal truce and find a parliamentary opportunity for uniting against Watson. On August 18, 1904, Reid became Prime Minister, to fall in his turn when his incautious nostalgia for free trade gave Deakin reasonable cause for withdrawing a grudged support which had never contained the possibility of sustained alliance. Deakin resumed the Prime Ministership in July, 1905, and held office to November, 1908.

In several respects it was the most remarkable Prime Ministerial period in Australian history. Deakin never possessed a party majority in the House of Representatives; from the 1906 elections on, he was, in fact, leading the smallest party of three. That he could remain Prime Minister was in part due to the substantial radicalism that underlay his protectionism. Labour, as he leaned on its support with increasing heaviness, had the satisfaction of knowing that he was implementing parts of its policy it would then have had no chance of implementing on its own account. But in part, too, Deakin's success was one of mind over matter, of political character over parliamentary numbers. Time enough having passed since his death in 1919 to permit his career to be seen in better perspective than those of most of his successors, he seems bound to continue to rank among the really great men of Australian history.

First, though not necessarily foremost, because of his personal contribution to the actual creation of the Commonwealth. He was the man behind the scenes in the final, touchy, intercolonial negotiations which brought federation. If he had preferred the more public rôle, the negotiations might easily have broken down.

Second, because of his legislative spadework as Barton's chief of staff in the first parliament. Traces of that spadework are perhaps hard to find beneath the present structure of Australian government. But part of Deakin's monument is the fact that the foundations created by the spadework continue sound.

Third, because of his permanent contributions to the common philosophy of Australian political parties. One of those contributions was "the new protection," frequently reaffirmed as Labour's tariff policy, powerful in the fiscal thought of parties opposing Labour, i.e., a protection specifically planned to assist and force Australian industries to improve the Australian living standard. This was originally one of Deakin's concepts. To another may be traced most of what has proved enduring and practicable in Australia's program of self-defence.

Fourth, because of his deep influence, direct and indirect, on the outlooks of his successors. Hughes, talking "White Australia" and its Pacific perils against Woodrow Wilson at the Paris Peace Conference, continued one Deakin tradition. Curtin, in London in 1944, defined Australian views on the equality and interdependence of the nations of the British Commonwealth in almost exactly the same way as Deakin had defined them, also in London, thirty-seven years before.

First traces of a breakdown in health which was eventually to force Deakin's political retirement were observable in 1908. They possibly account for his temporary loss of the Prime Ministership in that year. Labour had another taste of office, for six months. Watson had retired from the leadership, and the new Prime Minister was a Queenslander, Andrew Fisher, whose caution was preferred by his party to the stormy brilliance of Hughes, who still ranked as Labour's No. 2 man. Inevitable as was the Labour Government's fall on June 1, 1909, its term in office had rightly been regarded on both sides of parliament, not as a negligible 1904 type of episode, but as a portent for the elections of 1910, preventing all possibility of future working arrangements between Deakin and Labour. Deakin, succeeding Labour for a last and brief term as Prime Minister, for the first time led a party with a clear parliamentary majority. It was a party formed by the fusion of all non-Labour elements of the then parliament, and from it traces, in direct descent, the Liberal Party of today. It was created over the dead body of free trade.

The 1910 federal elections were the first in which only two sides were in the field. Labour won, and Fisher began his second Prime Ministership with forty-two supporters in the House of seventy-five. With that safe majority he could and did go ahead with legislation more comprehensive than any previous government had attempted. His more radical measures were, in the main, akin to Deakin's, and one of the tragicomedies of that parliament was the sight of Deakin, as Leader of the Opposition, trying to counter Labour arguments that were his own brain-grandchildren.

Labour today most cherishes from the 1910–1913 parliament the memory of the Acts establishing old-age pensions and the Commonwealth Bank, which, by a further Act of 1945, was eventually to be given plenary powers over the entire Australian banking structure. Historical accuracy adds that the scheme for the Commonwealth Bank was forced on an unwilling ministry by a junta of its supporters.

The 1913 elections produced one of the prettiest political deadlocks in the Australian record. Deakin had retired from the leadership of the Liberal Party. His successor, Joseph Cook, distinguished chiefly by industry from the average parliamentarian of the time, had a House of Representatives majority so small that his government, replacing Fisher's, was perpetually dependent on the casting vote of the Speaker. This was bad for Cook; but there was worse. Labour controlled the Senate. Under Australian conventions of executive government, the Senate could not unseat a Cabinet. But it could impede and reject legislation without which the Cabinet could not govern. By straight left in the Senate and right hook in the House, Labour did everything possible to force Cook from office.

In 1914, having already made minor Australian political history by being the first Australian non-Labour Prime Minister to have begun his parliamentary career as a Labour man (he had successors in this respect in Hughes and Lyons; his own break with the Labour machine occurred in prefederal days in New South Wales), Cook made more and bigger history. He became the first (and, so far, the only) Prime Minister to obtain a double dissolution. This is a constitutional expedient especially designed to solve a deadlock. A government whose proposals for legislation have repeatedly been rejected by the Senate can ask the Governor-General for a dissolution of both Houses. If dissolution is granted, Senators, who normally sit for six-year terms, half of their number retiring alternately each three years, all face the electors simultaneously with the House of Representatives, the idea being that elections thus held will return two Houses in agreement about what the electors really want on the issues originally in dispute.

It was bold play rather than bonny play. The election campaign quickly set against Cook. The First World War broke out in the middle of the campaign. Patriotism became an election issue. And Fisher's one really memorable recorded phrase was itself enough to ensure Labour's return: "Should the worst happen, we will stand by the Mother Country to help and defend her to the last man and the last shilling." Labour again became the government and its majorities were overwhelming both in the House of Representatives and in the Senate.

Fisher stood the nerve-biting strain of war administration for a year only. October, 1915, saw his resignation as Prime Minister. In his stead came Hughes. For fourteen years Labour, fearful, perhaps prophetically, of his brilliance, had held Hughes down to its No. 2 parliamentary place. Now it faced a vacancy which he, and no one else, could fill for it. He had come out of an early manhood of immigrant vicissitudes to be one of the chief architects of parliamentary Labour, first in New South Wales and then in the Commonwealth. In Labour's years of struggle, he was its principal tactician and incomparably its ablest debater. Now he was its leader, its Prime Minister. In little more than a year he was to break with Labour.

The story was short and simple. Gleefully using dictatorial wartime powers, Hughes brought new vigour into Australia's administration. He went on a mission to London and made a great mark; for a time he attracted Lord Northcliffe's vagrant fancy as a just possible alternative to Asquith as British War Prime Minister. He came back to Australia believing that conscription for overseas service (conscription for home service existed, and by Labour's own peacetime insistence) was necessary to reinforce troops already sent by Australia to the war. He submitted the question to a referendum of electors, which decided against such conscription. Nonparliamentary industrial labour was on the no-conscription side. Even before the referendum the Parliamentary Labour Party was split wide open on the issue. After the referendum a meeting of the Party showed that the breach was permanent. Hughes walked out, taking with him enough supporters to give backing for the tactics which installed him, early in 1917, as leader of a National Government, chiefly drawn from former political opponents (including Cook). That Government commanded in parliament a majority enhanced by bitter general elections in the same year.

The conscription split had been temporarily embarrassing for Hughes. It was calamitous for Labour, which took ten years to climb back to respectable parliamentary numbers. Its only real satisfaction in that decade was the Prime Ministerial fall of Hughes. That, however, did not come until early 1923. In the interval the National Party, incorporating the Liberal Party and conscriptionist former Labourites, had carried everything before it. Hughes had corralled for the party most of the returned-soldier vote. There at first appeared no great significance in the advent, in the 1919–1922 parliament, of a new third party, the Country Party, catering for the sectional interests of primary producers, and critical, therefore, of some aspects of the tariff, but in other matters a blood brother of Nationalism.

As that parliament wore on, however, Country Party members showed mounting hostility toward Hughes. The 1922 elections produced an unexpected result. Labour was still far away from real prospect of power. But the Country Party had achieved a key position. Without support from it, the Nationalist Party would not have a clear majority in the House. Gone were the valiant days when Deakin could govern as leader of the weakest party in three. Coalition was the obvious solution. The Country Party was unprepared to join the Nationalists while Hughes remained Prime Minister. If the Nationalists had been completely and solidly behind Hughes, the Country Party's stand might have been resisted. But there were sections of the party in which no wartime happenings had abated prewar hostility to Hughes. Hughes accepted the inevitable.

Early in 1923 the Prime Ministership was assumed by a political dualism. The titular holder was a Nationalist, Stanley Melbourne Bruce, a young Victorian who had been only five years in parliament before achieving its highest office. Associated with Bruce and equal in authority, if not in title, was the Country Party leader, Dr. Earle Page.

The Bruce-Page Government held office through six years and three parliaments. And it was Hughes who brought it down. At the elections of 1928, Labour achieved numbers enough to make it a parliamentary Opposition with which to reckon. In 1929 Bruce attempted to repeal Commonwealth industrial arbitration legislation in order to make the regulation of wages and conditions in industry a matter entirely for the state parliaments. So many Australian voters without party affiliations worked under industrial awards of the Commonwealth that the proposal brought about the most bitter public controversy since conscription. Hughes moved a vital amendment to Bruce's proposal and whipped up enough allies among nominal supporters of the Government to bring about the Government's defeat by one vote.

Labour enthusiastically voted with Hughes. An election was precipitated. Hughes's obvious hope that he and his supporters would hold the new parliament's balance of power was frustrated. Labour, under the leadership of James Scullin, achieved a smashing electoral triumph which was soon to prove, for itself, a smashing political disaster.

Scullin, with two former state Premiers, E. G. Theodore (Queensland) and Joseph Lyons (Tasmania), among his chief lieutenants, had been a notably able Leader of the Opposition. As Prime Minister he ran into twin blizzards: the world depression, and a Senate emphatically hostile to Labour. The Senate position might have been, but was not, dealt with early in the Government's life by quick strokes to force a double dissolution. The depression was another matter and one involving special problems for a Labour Government. Labour had talked, hard, of itself as a party of radical finance. But the Australian economic structure was in a mess which could be cleaned up only by orthodox economies of a type anathema to the Labour left, or by new financial legislation of a kind which had no chance with the Senate. Discussion of much that happened in the Scullin Government's life would involve subjective comment on contemporary politics that is outside the scope of this book. In the end the desperate Government had to count on opposition support to get through parliament measures temporarily reducing the Australian standard of living.

Meanwhile its supporters had split three ways. One section, under Lyons, was to coalesce with the Nationalists to form the United Australia Party. Another renounced Scullin's leadership and attached itself to the then New South Wales Premier, J. T. Lang, who had declared himself against the Scullin financial proposals. On this New South Wales section's motion on a minor matter, the House of Representatives finally brought the Scullin Government down.

The resultant 1931 elections proved such a landslide against Labour that the United Australia Party was, for the next parliament, able to provide its own majority without Country Party support. Lyons was Prime Minister, and when, in 1934 and 1937, election figures made coalition with the Country Party necessary, Page once more shared the reins of government.

Meantime, Labour was trying to rebuild. It took nearly six years to heal the breach between federal Labour and the New South Wales section. Any breach would have been damaging, but this one was critical, for New South Wales returns more than a third of the members of the House of Representatives, and the New South Wales public was showing, at successive state elections, that it would give a majority in no sphere to a party dominated by Lang. The final peacemaker was John Curtin, who in 1935 followed Scullin as leader of the federal Labour opposition.

In 1939 Lyons' death in office caused a sudden political transformation. Hughes, who just failed to obtain party election to the Prime Ministership, would on this occasion have been acceptable to Page and the Country Party. R. G. Menzies, the United Australia Party choice, was not, but he was chosen. Menzies, as Prime Minister, had to work parliament on the assumption that the Country Party was not prepared to go to the length of helping in his defeat on the floor of the House. Under the pressure of the Second World War a coalition was eventually devised, but relations between Menzies and some of his supporters remained uneasy.

At the 1940 elections Labour was a hair's breadth from complete success once again. Dr. H. V. Evatt's act in stepping down from the High Court bench to enter politics on the Labour side had influenced the New South Wales middle-class voters toward Labour. The Party made gains in the key state, which were just offset by a couple of surprise results elsewhere. Real control of the new House of Representatives lay with a couple of independents whose views were unascertainable. All that the Government could do was to stay in office and hope for the best. By mid-1941 its position had become critical. In the faint hope of remedying things, a change of Prime Ministers was made, Menzies stepping down in favour of the new Country Party leader, A. W. Fadden. Six weeks later the Fadden Government was defeated on its budget, both independents voting with Labour.

Curtin, Labour journalist and until then comparatively little known outside his own party, was the new Prime Minister. Within three months of taking office his government was faced, by reason of Pearl Harbour and its consequences, with the gravest emergency of Australia's existence. In measures to achieve a maximum Australian war effort he had coöperation from the Opposition reciprocating that which he had himself given on war matters as Opposition Leader. Major credit in the public mind for what was done inevitably attached to him. The 1943 election result, returning forty-nine Labour members and two Labour-supporting independents, the largest majority in federal history, was, in essence, a vote of confidence in Curtin as war leader. After the elections his health rapidly failed. He died in 1945 and was succeeded by J. B. Chifley, his closest political associate and friend. At the 1946 elections the Chifley Government's majority was very handsome, but some of the Curtin-won ground was lost.

The fact that a running narrative of Australian political history contains little reference to clash between rival parties over essential principle is significant. Until now there has been little such clash. Essential principle would find itself rather lonely at normal Australian elections.

In theory there is a fundamental difference in basic philosophy between Labour and the two opposing parties. Labour has a socialist objective, to which its parliamentary representatives are formally pledged. Both Liberal (in 1944 the former United Australia Party and some other non-Labour groups merged into a new Liberal Party) and Country parties stand for reasonably free enterprise in a not excessively controlled society.

Constitutional restrictions on the Commonwealth Government's trading powers have so far, however, made the socialist objective something academic in federal affairs. Whether removal of such restrictions would lead to any serious attempt to implement the objective is one of the great question marks of Australian politics. So far,

Labour governments in the states, despite their constitutional freedom in the matter, have shown practically no eagerness for socialism. Where they have done so, they have usually met electoral disaster. The restrictions on the Commonwealth will remain until the electors agree to a referendum removing them. At referenda, Australia normally votes "No."

In practice, the approach of any Australian government to any major issue of its day has been decided less by its party politics than by the advice of officials and experts who are retained in office irrespective of change of governments. If the issue has serious election significance, the approach, inevitably, is that thought most likely to appeal to the minority of "swing voters," who really decide whether a government will survive or fall. More than 40 per cent of voters unshakably vote Labour; more than 40 per cent, equally unshakably, vote for the other parties. It is to the comparatively small residue of voters who make up their minds from election to election that the elaborate apparatus of Australian campaigns is directed.

Before the campaign, parties preselect their candidates. Labour preselection is a very serious business. There have been and will be exceptions, but the permanent expulsion from the Labour Party of any member who opposes a preselected Labour candidate is a rule usually rigidly enforced. Other parties vary in preselection practice, but attempt nothing approximating Labour antiheresy rules.

The campaign proper opens with a policy speech by each party leader. These days, each policy speech is broadcast over a national network. The tendency, except with the Liberals, is to dispense with the formality of delivering it at a public meeting. Until recently, matter contained in a policy speech was assumed to indicate the specific matters on which a mandate for government in the next parliament was sought. Labour's latter-day tendency has been to recite past achievements in government and ask for a blank cheque.

Elections are normally held every three years, simultaneously throughout the Commonwealth. The whole House and eighteen out of thirty-six Senators face the voters. Single-member electorates, at present seventy-five all told, return the personnel of the House of Representatives. Senators represent states and are elected by the whole of each state, voting as a single electorate. An increase in numbers is likely in the near future.

Voting is compulsory, on a basis of adult suffrage and by ballot. The compulsory-voting provision first operated in 1925. It results in a much bigger proportionate poll than previously, but has increased the percentage of informal votes and is not considered to have been of particular advantage to either side in politics. Adult suffrage has applied since federation and in some colonies votes had earlier been given to women.

The Australian colonies led the world in providing the secret ballot for electors, but the idea of the ballot came from overseas. On House of Representatives ballot papers of today, names of all candidates appear in alphabetical order without indication of party affiliation. It is obligatory to number the whole list of candidates in the order of the elector's preference, so that the preference system of counting the results can be fully applied.

On the Senate ballot paper, candidates are grouped according to their party. The order in which they appear across the width of the paper is decided by lot. This is to prevent repetition of tactics successfully practised at one election in the 'thirties, when, to take advantage of the tendency of uninformed voters to vote straight down the Senate paper, New South Wales Labour under Lang selected a team of candidates whose names all began with "A." Application of the preference system to Senate voting has come to mean that a party either has all or none of its candidates for each individual state returned to the Senate. As a result, non-Labour parties will for the three years beginning July 1, 1947, have, in all, only three Senators out of thirty-six. In the past Labour has had even worse underrepresentation.

The House of Representatives count completed, the party leader with a House majority can set about selecting his Cabinet, at present of nineteen members. If his majority is of his own party and that party is not Labour, he makes his own choice, restricted only by the fact that each member must be drawn from one or other of the Houses of Parliament. If he is to head a coalition government, he needs, by convention, to obtain the assent of the leader of the subsidiary party to the Cabinet personnel he is choosing from that party. With Labour, the position is different. The party leader does not pick the personnel of his Cabinet, which instead is selected for him by ballot of the Caucus, i.e., a full meeting of the Parliamentary

Labour Party. If dissatisfied with a minister so chosen, his only remedy is to dismiss the minister and make the dismissal an issue on which he is prepared to stake his leadership. Critics of the way Caucus works assert that this is one of three ways in which the Caucus system challenges the continued existence of responsible government. The other two are the policy of deciding on public issues in Caucus before they reach parliament and the requirement that Caucus members, irrespective of personal conviction, must vote in parliament in accordance with Caucus majority decision on matters declared vital by the leader of the party.

CHAPTER VIII

Public Administration and Its Problems

BY F. A. BLAND

THE OUTSTANDING characteristic of public administration in Australia is addiction to centralisation. The most intractable problems arise from the effects of this policy upon efforts to preserve the substance of popular government. It is proposed to examine four features of the Australian system as illustrating this text, and to suggest that the substance of popular government is impaired (1) by the absence of any comprehensive system of local government, (2) by the overly free use of statutory corporations to manage government businesses and other activities, (3) by the attitude of a highly organised public service, and (4) by the general approach to politics and administration in Australia.

Few will be found to deny that good government is no substitute for self-government. Hardly anyone, however, evinces any concern that the Australian political and administrative structure affords scant opportunity for training people in the art of self-government. Indeed, with all the nation's reputation for social experiments, there is a singular indifference to social and political theories. It can be argued that the needs of a people thinly spread over a vast island continent possessing unusual physical features and unevenly distributed resources defy the adoption of a system based upon a theoretically desirable distribution of functions between the several levels of government. It may be that the circumstances of the first fifty years cultivated habits of reliance upon the government that inevitably influenced the later preference for centralised control rather than for local or individual initiative. Be that as it may, nowhere in the British Commonwealth is local government so rudimentary as in Australia, nor do local institutions and local opinion exercise so little influence on the central organs of politics and administration.

If the plans of the Imperial Government in 1842 had been accepted, the later course of events might have been very different. The proposals were resented, however, because they explicitly stated that training in local government should be regarded as a prerequisite to the assumption of the status of responsible government. Their rejection reacted upon the colonial parliaments when later they found it imperative to create local institutions and to organise such services as schools and roads, police and gaols, water and light, as well as machinery for ensuring easy access to land, mines, rivers, and forests.

It has been made clear already that the Colonial Office in London was hampered by the absence of a clear-cut policy with regard to the Australian settlement. And there were other difficulties, including the need to rebuild a staff disbanded after the loss of the American colonies, the preoccupation of the home government with the domestic reactions to the French Revolution and the Napoleonic Wars during the first thirty years of the settlement; and especially the distance, measured in time, that separated London from Sydney—a distance so great that nearly a year might elapse between the despatch of a communication and the receipt of a reply. Added to these was the extent to which officials had to depend upon the written word of the governors to convey the meaning of situations for which there was little precedent to guide London officials.

Between 1801 and 1854, colonial affairs were administered by a Secretary of State for War *and* the Colonies. Thereafter, a separate Colonial Office was created, and when Dominion affairs became important after 1925, they were detached from the colonies and entrusted to a separate Secretary of State for the Dominions. Landmarks in Australian development included the Charter of Justice, 1823 (4 Geo. IV, cap. 96), which provided the first restraint upon the sole powers of the governors, and the Second Charter of Justice, 1828 (9 Geo. IV, cap. 83), which set up an executive council to advise the governor. In 1842 a partly elective and partly nominee legislative council (5 and 6 Victoria, cap. 76) was the prelude to responsible government granted by the Australian Colonies Government Act, 1850. The new constitutions became operative in New South Wales and Victoria in 1855, in South Australia and Tasmania in 1856, in Queensland in 1859, and in Western Australia in 1890. Finally, the Commonwealth of Australia was established as a federal system in 1901 by the Imperial Act of 1900, which, however, unlike the British North America Act for the Dominion of Canada (1867), embodied provisions for its local alteration without recourse to the parliament at Westminster.

Before Governor Phillip relinquished office in 1792, the original ideas of a penal settlement had been modified. Its dual use for convicts and as a colony created endless administrative complications for later governors. So far as it was a prison camp, authoritarian rule was natural. The governor combined in his person all the civil functions of lawmaker, judge, and administrator, as well as those of defence and police. So far as it was a colony welcoming free settlers, such powers were an affront to the instincts of Englishmen. These issues did not at once become significant, for the immediate problem was to feed, clothe, and employ the convicts, and so to do this as to facilitate their rehabilitation. Crops had to be sown, supplies obtained, roads and buildings constructed, and order maintained. Apart from some officials, there was no recourse but to convict material. Phillip as early as 1789 used the best-behaved of the convicts as a police force, which later developed into a local constabulary, although this resulted in friction with the military and the free settlers. The convicts were classified on arrival. Suitable men were reserved for government employment and fed and clothed from the public store. They were used to cultivate government farms, to construct roads and bridges, to erect public and other buildings, and to do work in the public offices, or in the domestic households of officials. The rest were assigned to settlers, military and civil, who were required to maintain them; or else they were given tickets of leave, especially if they had means to support themselves. But the underlying feature was government paternalism.

Under Macquarie's rule (1810–1821) the policy of convict regeneration and emancipist encouragement carried paternalism to new levels. But it also brought criticism from London about expecting the British taxpayer to meet all the costs of his public works, while it fostered locally the habit of reliance upon the government. On the other hand, Macquarie's attitude to education presents another side to this picture. He encouraged the erection of schools by subsidising local effort, and impressed upon the heads of families their duty to see that their children went to school.

The education problem well illustrates the absence of a clear-cut policy in the Colonial Office. Phillip's instructions (April 25, 1787) required him to use all proper methods to enforce "a due observance of religion and good order," and in 1790 these instructions were amplified. He was told that "in marking out each township, 400 acres should be set aside for the maintenance of a clergyman, and 200 acres for the maintenance of a schoolmaster." But only one chaplain was sent out with the First Fleet in 1788, and no schoolmaster. Some assistance was supplied by the London Missionary Society (formed 1795), but the first trained teacher was not sent out until 1809, and it was only when the second was appointed in 1812 that the Colonial Office assumed responsibility for his modest stipend of £100 a year.

One further illustration of conflicting aims is provided by the administration of justice. A military detachment had been sent out to control the convicts, but the practices of the officers and men, instead of fortifying the authority of the early governors, did much to undermine their prestige. Crime and civil disorder were dealt with by a court whose methods were akin to those of a court martial. Constitutionally, it was a vice-admiralty court established by Letters Patent of May 5, 1787, in pursuance of the provisions of 24 Geo. III, cap. 56, and consequent Orders in Council. The court was presided over by a judge-advocate (who until 1809 had no legal qualifications), with a panel of military and naval officers. This again was an affront to the rights of free settlers, and the arbitrary practices of the court led to vigorous demands for the introduction of trial by jury and the recognition of civil rights. No civil element, however, entered into the administration of justice until the reforms of 1823 and 1828, which also established a hierarchy of courts modelled on the English system.

When Macquarie left the settlement in 1822 he had increased its area from 2,000 to 120,000 square miles, and the population had grown from 8,000 to 30,000 under his regime. The governor's official staff had been correspondingly augmented, and among the senior officials appointed and paid from London there were a lieutenant-governor, a chief justice, a colonial secretary, a principal colonial surgeon, a surveyor-general, and, after 1824, an archdeacon responsible for churches and schools. Many free settlers had become wealthy, there was a prosperous merchant group, and many of the emancipists were flourishing in the professions. Between the free settlers and the emancipists there was a deep social cleavage, and its consequences long persisted. For example, in 1849, when the establishment of Sydney University was before the legislative council, Dr. William Bland was proposed as one of the first senators of the university council. Objection was successfully taken to his nomination because he had arrived in the colony as a convict twenty-five years earlier.

The division between the emancipists and the exclusionists not merely complicated local administration, but also hampered all proposals for constitutional reform. Until after Macquarie's departure the preponderance of convicts prevented anything in the nature of representative institutions. Thereafter the propriety of allowing emancipists to hold elected offices became the main issue in all suggestions for creating municipal or colonial representative bodies.

It will be remembered that municipal reform was delayed in England until 1835, and the desirability of adapting the new system to the needs of the colony did not become important until after that time. There were many proposals for tying municipal institutions into schemes for representative government, but they were wrecked by local opposition. The various governors had to be content with special agencies created ad hoc for such services as they wished to devolve upon the localities. For example, markets were launched by the governor in 1806, were later controlled by magistrates, but finally, in 1839, passed to the care of elected market commissioners, where they languished for twenty years. Roads were constructed by the government, which sought some return for their use by appointing trustees to collect prescribed tolls (1810). A new move was made in 1833 when a local act (2 Will. IV, cap. 12) sought with little success to define roads that should be maintained at the expense of the inhabitants of a parish. From time to time further steps were taken to try to enforce local responsibility, but by 1848 the roads passed to another ad hoc commission, thence to the state public works department in 1858, while in 1924 main roads became the care of a statutory government board. A similar development marks the provision of water and sewage schemes, for which the ad hoc authority predominates throughout the Commonwealth.

Even the growth of the government of metropolitan cities in Australia is marked by vicissitudes of government control. For example, Adelaide, the capital of South Australia, was incorporated in 1840, but the management of its affairs was transferred to a government department in 1843 and to a government commission between 1849 and 1852, when it reverted to popular control. Sydney's corporation, created in 1842, was superseded by a government commission in 1852; it was restored in 1857. The justification of the state authorities for this action was maladministration and ineffective discharge of statutory functions. The councils, however, complained of insufficient municipal resources, and sought financial assistance from the central government as an alternative to imposing higher rates. This issue is still unsettled.

The Imperial Act of 1842 (5 and 6 Vic., cap. 76) which conceded representative government also embodied the faith of the home authorities in the importance of municipal institutions. The governor was directed to incorporate district councils whose members were to be elected by local ratepayers. The size of the councils varied from eight where the population was less than 7,000 to twenty-one where it was 20,000 or more. Powers and duties embraced those usually committed to local bodies, and included responsibility for half of the cost of the much-disputed maintenance of police and gaols, as well as for education. The management of the police and gaols, however, remained with the central government, which was empowered to levy upon the district councils for their share. These levies were enforceable by distress warrants upon the property of officers and councillors.

The obligation to meet half the cost of police in itself made the measure unpopular, but its implications aroused the most bitter opposition from the new legislative council. Other provisions were attacked as indicating the home authorities' ignorance of local conditions. For example, the total population of New South Wales, including what is now Victoria and Queensland, was then only 130,000, thinly distributed over wide areas which included large tracts of Crown lands. The produce of even a high municipal rate would have been insufficient to finance the services committed to the district councils. (It might be noted that one hundred years later, there are in New South Wales only two cities outside the metropolis of Sydney with populations of more than 20,000, nine with more than 10,000, and five with more than 7,000.)

Governor Gipps did his best. He was fortified by his Canadian experience and firmly believed in the desirability of local government. He chided the citizens for their persistence in applying for government funds for local purposes, pointing out that he had no criterion by which he could measure the validity of their demands. But "let the people of each county, parish, or township spend their own money, and they will spend no more of it than is necessary, and they will spend it, too, more satisfactorily than it is possible for the government to spend it for them." The appeal was fruitless. General principles were less convincing than the specific schemes. Opposed by the legislative council and sabotaged in the localities, the scheme maintained a paper existence for about two decades and was then abandoned.

When the Australian Colonies Act of 1850 was being considered, the Committee on Trade and Plantations of the Privy Council prepared a statesmanlike report (April 4, 1849) which not only argued cogently the need for local government, but wisely suggested that half the proceeds from the sale of Crown lands should be allocated to the district councils. This would have provided finance for local improvements over an indefinite period and might have altered the whole course of Australian development. The suggestions were contemptuously rejected by the legislative council, which saw in it fresh indications of Imperial dictation and an unwarranted intrusion into the management by the colonists of their own affairs. The weighty pastoralist representation in the council is not without significance in appraising the reasons for the rejection. But subsequent responsible ministers were equally averse from adopting the suggestion, since the revenue derived from the sale of Crown lands has always relieved the state from the necessity of increasing the volume of taxation.

Ratepayers, on the other hand, evinced little desire to foster the creation of municipal institutions, since this would have involved their meeting from their own pockets an expenditure which they found it comparatively easy to extract from state treasuries. In New South Wales, for example, their obstruction to compulsory incorporation of rural areas persisted until 1906, when the Local Government Act of that year introduced a general scheme of local government, but on a far less comprehensive plan than that imposed by the Imperial Act of 1842.

In America, local institutions sprang naturally from the reasons for launching most of the settlements. In Australia, they have been created for reasons of administrative convenience rather than from any well-founded understanding of their place in an effective scheme of popular government. In all the state parliaments the prestige of governments has depended mainly on their readiness to dispense financial largesse for constructing public works throughout the electorates. Thus there developed the "roads and bridges member of parliament," who conceived it to be his duty to match his support of Cabinets by the extent of the local works he could extract from them. Even now, when members belong to disciplined parties instead of revolving around political personalities, the situation has scarcely changed. On the other hand, there has never been any attempt to reëxamine the principles rejected in 1849. The circumstances of Australian physical features and natural resources demanded far more than a casual distribution of functions as between state and local authorities. Merely to devolve duties without regard for the financial capacity of the localities was to create onerous burdens and foment dissatisfaction. The experience of all the states confirms this view.

By the 1870's all the states other than New South Wales had incorporated both urban and rural local councils; but in states like Queensland and Western Australia the result was merely to clutter the administrative structure with a series of ineffective authorities. For example, in Queensland the Local Government Act of 1878 created shires for the administration of sparsely settled rural areas, but in 1879 these were replaced by seventy-four divisional boards, each composed of nine members elected from three ridings, to administer a total area of 660,000 square miles. In Western Australia eleven local authorities administer areas larger than the State of Tasmania, and two others are larger than the State of Victoria. Such a structure is local government only in name, and merely relieves the central government from the care of minor domestic matters.

While the restricted functions of local governmental authorities have afforded little opportunity for training in administrative responsibility and have encouraged reliance upon the central government, the widespread use in Australia of the statutory corporation has contributed to the same result. Throughout the last quarter of the nineteenth century, population was rapidly increasing and the local authorities were in a chronic state of financial distress. It was impossible for them to meet new demands without a complete recasting of state-local financial relations. This the state governments were unwilling to undertake. But since demands had to be satisfied, recourse was had to the statutory corporation for managing such services as water supply, sewerage, and roads, and was gradually extended to cover the operation of abattoirs, fire protection, irrigation, pastures protection, main roads, hospitals, electricity, harbours, housing, and some aspects of public health. For some of these statutory corporations a loose connection with local government is maintained by the election of some members of the governing boards, but in most instances the boards are appointed by the state cabinets to which they owe varying degrees of responsibility. Adequate finance for the corporations is provided by giving them special rating powers, or by assigning specific revenues (e.g., the Main Roads Board receives the proceeds of motor taxation) or by special government endowment. The effect again is to withdraw responsibility from the locality and to vest it in a central governmental authority.

The statutory corporation had also been used to administer governmental business enterprises. State railways may be taken as an illustration. In the late 1840's, Australia felt a slight impact of the railway-building boom that surged through the Old World. Franchises were granted to private companies, but the fever of the gold rushes carried away both staffs and workmen and the companies were unable to proceed. The governments stepped into the place of the companies and undertook both construction and management of the new enterprises. But direct government operation opened the door to political interference.

In New South Wales the veteran statesman Sir Henry Parkes decided to relieve ministers of the political and administrative pressures which government operation encountered, by creating in 1888 a board of expert commissioners whose day-to-day administration should be removed from political interference. The government still controlled the provision of capital funds and the annual budget, and influenced the letting of contracts, but otherwise it left management to the commissioners. The desirability of constructing new lines was left to the decision of the government, which, however, had first to obtain a report from a parliamentary public works committee upon the suitability of the routes, the capital cost, the likely revenue, and so forth.

The use of the government corporation, as it is known in America, for operating business enterprises has become widespread in Australia. Its composition and powers vary. Generally, it consists of a board of three experts; occasionally, room is found for the representation of interests, but seldom of employee interests. Tenure varies from five to seven years, and staggered terms are not common. The bipartisan board often found in the United States is absent, although appointments not unconnected with political views are becoming common.

Early experience of the working of the corporations led to attempts to enhance the independence of the board of directors. In some cases, almost complete financial autonomy was conceded; in others, the autonomy was limited to excluding the corporation budget from the annual appropriation acts of parliament. In almost all instances, the corporations are removed from the jurisdiction of public service commissions with respect to the recruitment and control of staffs. This was the general situation until after the First World War. Thereafter, party politics, especially in the industrial states, developed a bitterness because parties tended to confront each other from platforms which were based upon opposite conceptions of the nature and purpose of government. In this atmosphere, it was realised that political parties could not ignore the extent to which the statutory corporations might affect political objectives. Political appointments to the boards of directors began to be made, while reorganisations of the structure of the corporations allowed for the intrusion of covert influence where overt action might arouse public resentment. The tendency, therefore, in those states in which militant unionism controls political labour parties is to bring the activities of the corporations under direct ministerial control. This is an instance where the self-interest of labour pressure-groups shelters under the respectable mantle of austere political theory.

In spite of the sixty years of experimentation with the statutory corporation, there has been little political examination of their implications. Independence was sought for the corporations to ensure efficient administration, continuity of policy, and stability in finance. Without besmirching the integrity of conventional government departments, it was generally conceded that the ordinary processes of public offices were inappropriate for the successful management of business undertakings. A change of ministers inevitably affects policy and this reacts upon management, staffing, and finance. Since this cannot but be inimical to business success, escape is sought in an independent agency. But such independence is inconsistent with the political theory of ministerial responsibility and accountability to parliament and the electors. Financial independence cuts across the doctrine of an all-embracing annual budget. Staff control involves the repudiation of a common public personnel policy.

It may be that Australian political theory will have to accommodate itself to the stubborn realities if the government wishes to operate businesses. But little thought is given to such suggestions as those of the Webbs in their *Constitution for the Socialist Commonwealth of Great Britain,* or to the English or American varieties of parliamentary standing committees. Meanwhile the situation is one of drift, although governments are showing increasing inclination to extend the scope and diversity of governmental ownership and operation.

The statutory corporation has also been used in the specific field of personnel management. The assumption of responsible government meant the transfer of the public service to the control of the states. The English reforms of 1853–1855 aroused some slight interest and Victoria led the way with attempts to secure a merit system, which took comprehensive shape in 1883. It fell to New South Wales, however, in 1895 to provide the model which has been adopted by all governments in Australia. Its Public Service Act enshrined the principles of open competition, of age limits for admission and retirement, of standard grading and classification, and of systems for fixing remuneration. The care of these things was committed to an independent public service commission of three members with seven years' tenure and eligibility for reappointment. The commission was also entrusted with the supervision and control of office organisation and equipment. Later developments have been in the direction of strengthening the prestige of the commissions by according their members life tenure of office. The public service commissions in the several states and the Commonwealth now discharge the functions which in England are committed to civil service commissioners and the establishments branch at the Treasury, or, in America, to civil service commissions and efficiency or classification bureaus.

The characteristic feature of recruitment policy is the appointment of juniors straight from school to the lowest classified grade, followed by advancement up the grade by annual increments. This inevitably entails inbreeding which is only partly corrected by making promotion beyond certain levels contingent upon passing internal examinations. Professional and technical positions, however, are usually filled by competitive oral tests based on proved qualifications. Until after the First World War, this method of recruitment was rigidly followed. It was then found that officials so recruited were not equal to the new tasks demanded at the higher levels of administration. This led, first, to encouraging officials to take university courses, and later, particularly in the Commonwealth service, to the selection of a limited number of university graduates for clerical and administrative divisions. Even so, no systematic distinction is made between routine and administrative positions, nor is there any positive belief in the value of university training as a qualification for administrative duties. No one denies that this training is indispensable for most professional positions, but administration is not yet recognised as a profession.

The First World War was also responsible for a marked change in the attitudes of staff associations to public service commissions. The traditional acceptance of their decisions prescribing conditions of work and rates of remuneration was replaced by an aggressive demand for prior consultation and joint determination. Stimulated by the pressure of rising costs of living upon standard salaries, and envious of the ease with which industrial workers had their rates of pay adjusted by arbitration courts, the black-coated members of the public service turned to politics to secure the substitution of the arbitration courts for public service commissions for salary fixation. Although this meant weakening the authority of the commissions in their most vital part, the governments acquiesced in the demands of the staff associations, and arbitration courts now provide an alternative method for determining salaries. The application of a common scale to groups of employees has lessened the importance of efficiency and merit and has measurably increased the cost of government.

The suitability of industrial arbitration courts has been questioned in informed circles, and proposals have been made for creating special arbitration tribunals to handle public service suits. But only in the Commonwealth public service has this plan been followed. Even there, however, disparities are revealed between judgements of the special arbitrator and the public service commission regarding adequate remuneration, similar to those which are experienced in the states where the ordinary courts operate.

In still another field did the war destroy established public service conventions. It had always been accepted that official neutrality in politics was a condition precedent to permanence of tenure. There had never been in Australian experience anything akin to the American scheme of spoils to the victors, nor did the Australian system of parliamentary government lend itself to rotation of office. The campaigns that preceded admission to the arbitration court for salary fixation whetted the appetite for politics, while the emergence of labour on the government benches in New South Wales, just before the war, opened to some officials the vision of advantages that might follow from political friendships.

Thereupon was fanned an agitation to concede full citizen rights to public servants. Narrowly interpreted, this meant the right to contest seats in parliament without prior resignation from the public service. Little thought was given to the problem of whether the obligations of public servants were compatible with active participation in politics, or whether the public might come to question the impartiality and integrity of officials who openly avowed partizanship on the political platform. Almost without discussion the New South Wales constitution was amended in 1916 to permit officials to contest elections without prior resignation. Successful candidates cannot sit in parliament and still remain in the public service, but defeated candidates resume duties at the conclusion of the campaign. Again the lead of New South Wales has been followed by the other states, and during the last decade all except Tasmania have conceded the demands of public servants to allow them to choose politics as an alternative career to the public service. Most administrators agree that public service politicians are not merely an embarrassment in the public offices, but that they herald the change to a politicalised public service.

A counterpart of this development is the growing inclination of public service unions and staff associations to affiliate with the trades and labour councils, the industrial organisation of the political Labour parties. Where the public has seemed indifferent to the emergence of political public servants, it has become apprehensive and critical of group affiliations, especially when that action has been taken by state schoolteachers and the state police. They feel that this step conclusively discards the principle of official impartiality and aligns the public service as a whole with the labour unions in any conflict with the general public. These developments are of too recent a character for their full effects to be appraised. There has been nothing as yet in Australia corresponding to the British Trades Disputes Act[1] of 1927 which restricted public service unionism to internal action and prohibited affiliation with external groups. It is conceivable that, if officials had to choose between security of tenure and a political career, they would prefer security. But the growth of a politically active public service numerically strong enough to hold governments to ransom sets fresh limits to popular control.

The issue raised by the rapid growth in the scope, content, and complexity of modern government is whether this development is compatible with the retention of popular control. The essence of popular government is found in the ability of the people to force those who wield power to use it according to popular wishes. The substance of popular government has been lost if the machinery of government is ineffective for that purpose. Parliamentary machinery was devised mainly to provide political controls. Little has been done to ensure administrative controls. Yet today administration

---

[1] Editor's note: This Act, passed by a Conservative Government, was repealed by the Labour Government in 1946.

is all-important and all-pervasive. The threats to individual rights and liberties come far more from officious and arbitrary administration than from arbitrary legislation. Again, in older countries, the protective methods of parliament against arbitrary rule were superimposed upon well-defined and clearly understood local institutions. Even in the newer world of America, the vigour of the early local authorities left their impress upon later constitutional and administrative developments. In Australia, local institutions provide little counterweight against the central authorities. They did not grow as in other countries; they have been made, and their operation is mechanical rather than spontaneous. The Commonwealth has, therefore, a far less effective cushion against aggressive centralism than exists in Britain or America.

Space forbids more than a summary statement of current trends in politics and administration. General Smuts's assertion that parliament is becoming of less and less importance finds ready acceptance in Australia. Sessions are short and few; debate languishes ... rigid party discipline; and the enactment of party measures ... gone conclusion, save where upper houses are not elected on ... franchise. Furthermore, the task of lawmaking is passing ... more to officials through their power to make regulations. ... merely fill out details of acts of parliament; they assume ... ive form through their use to remedy omissions and to ... ion to government intentions. The high-water mark of ... was reached during the war, when from a single Na... ty Act there stemmed during the first nine months of ...,523 regulations and orders. There is also a growing ... remove from the scrutiny of the courts the content of ... ulations, as well as for officials to be clothed with judicial ... determine conflicts which arise from the interpretation ... upon regulations which the officials themselves have framed.

The expansion of governmental functions, too, makes it extremely difficult, if not impossible, for ministers to maintain any effective control over the discretionary powers conferred upon officials, and there is even a tendency to invest officials with administrative independence akin to that associated with judicial independence. Policy declaration by officials is a novel development and fundamentally affects the doctrine of ministerial responsibility.

Furthermore, the administrative processes are applied uniformly throughout each political area, and when this is done directly by locally stationed central officials, it is accompanied by all the disabilities that directions from a remote administrative centre entail. People in far-distant localities feel impotent in their dealings with the central authorities, and are involved in heavy costs in time and money when they have to travel to the capital cities to seek redress of their grievances.

Still another aspect of centralised administration is revealed by the ever-accumulating tasks that are being assumed by Australian governments. Decisions must often be made without sufficient consideration of the implications of policy or administration. The people who have to put up with these decisions tend to grow resentful, to doubt official competence, and to incline to passive resistance. If decisions offend powerful interests, they are openly challenged. Successful challenge tends to bring the law into disrepute, to put a premium on lawlessness, and to undermine the foundations of th democratic processes. These and other comparable develop have all been intensified by the war, but they have only throw relief the defects of the normal political and administrativ ture in Australia.

Proposals abound for recasting that structure in order to the substance of popular government. Not the least i such a redistribution of powers and functions as wil local government is taken into full partnership, and, added responsibilities, be able to relieve the central a the mass of detail that now overwhelms them. So long, the central governments believe in their omniscience competence they only succeed in reducing people to a fe impotence and exasperation.

CHAPTER IX

Foreign Policy

BY SIR FREDERICK EGGLESTON

Australia is a democracy with a way of life and political ideas practically identical with those of the United States or of Britain and other Western democracies. But she is a small nation in an alien sea. New Zealand is the only neighbour with a similar outlook. At one time the isolation of these countries protected them, but such protection cannot be permanent in a contracting world. In the southeast of the continent of Asia live half the human race. In the archipelagoes of the Pacific lie innumerable islands, some of great richness, many inhabited by undeveloped and primitive peoples unable to take care of themselves in a j gle world. If these islands were dominated by a strong hostile power, the defence of Australia and New Zealand would be difficult without aid from outside.

The foreign policy of Australia must, therefore, be concerned with the problems which arise from this situation. The strategic factors upon which her existence depend are as follows:

1) Australia has a population of little more than seven millions.

2) She is so isolated that at first sight her value to other nations in world strategy is not apparent.

3) The approaches to Australia from crowded Asia are through the archipelagoes of islands which provide many bases for attack.

4) The distribution of the small population over the large area raises difficult problems of defence.

These factors are geopolitical in character. Their impact has been inescapable and it can never be completely overcome. The main cause of difficulty is the small population in relation to the area to be defended. Now, although Australia could hold about three or four times her present numbers, a population of thirty millions would not altogether relieve the strategic difficulties because of climatic conditions. One-third of Australia has a rainfall of less than ten inches, and another third a rainfall of between ten and twenty inches, most of the latter in the tropics. In this area, population must always be exceedingly sparse. The desert area separates the eastern settlements from those of the southwest, and the latter have the strategic characteristics of an island.

A population of thirty millions would certainly ease the position somewhat, but the increase of population possible in any relevant period will make no sensible difference to the present problems. The Australian rate of increase has been as great on the average as that of the United States. If we take American experience as valid, an increase of two per cent per annum is the maximum possible, and this will not bring Australia to thirty millions for ninety years. Asiatic immigration would not diminish the strategic problems. It might mean more rapid increase, but only if the standards of the immigrants remained at their present low level. Oriental peoples betray an obstinate determination to retain their communal habits, culture, and standards. Thus, their loyalty in the event of a struggle is doubtful, and they might well be a liability rather than an asset from the point of view of defence.

Australians historically have shown an increasing awareness of these factors and the possibilities involved in them. At first, they felt safe as a part of the British Empire. Later, the power of the British to guarantee security in every part of the globe declined, while differences of interest developed which required impartial and independent consideration. Finally, the device of Dominion status, voluntary coöperation within a group under the British Crown, was adopted. The story of this development in relation to the various external problems with which Australia came into contact is of some interest.[1]

After the loss of the American colonies, there was a gradual re-orientation of British ideas. The boon of self-government was freely bestowed. British policy in relation to self-governing areas may be expressed in three formulae:

[1] For a short account of Australia's foreign relations till 1921, see *Cambridge History of the British Empire*, Vol. VII, chap. xxviii.

1) The British Government should remain solely responsible for foreign policy throughout the Empire. This was categorically asserted by Asquith at the Imperial Conference of 1911, but his excessive emphasis seems to have indicated a lack of conviction.[2]

2) The British Government would be responsible for the defence of the Empire as a whole; this would take the form of naval defence. Local defence would be the responsibility of the respective colonies.[3]

3) It was contemplated that the colonies would supply the products of the soil and would take in return British manufactures.

This last remnant of the old mercantilist system, which still remains in many British minds, proved the least stable of all these concepts. Some colonies adopted a protective tariff in the 'seventies, and an effective system came into being in Australia shortly after the federation was established. Australia was always ready to give Britain preference and joined wholeheartedly in the Ottawa system, though it is very doubtful whether it was to her advantage. Her own adventures in external trade policy have not been particularly fortunate. The trade-diversion policy of 1936 which gave advantages to Britain and placed trade with the United States and Japan (countries which wanted to sell and would not buy) under licence achieved a maximum of irritation with a minimum of benefit.

The history of British colonial relations shows a relaxation of the other two principles mentioned above, with ever-increasing acceleration. Up to the time Australian federation was accomplished in 1901, it was, of course, difficult for six different colonies to adopt a national point of view and a common external policy. But the movement for federation arose in part from the pressure of world movements and in particular the colonial policy of Germany. The threatened intrusion of European powers into the Pacific in the 'eighties led to a clamour in Australia that Great Britain should annex all the islands surrounding Australia. Though this was refused, Queensland planted the British flag in Papua, the part of New Guinea nearest to Australia, and forced its annexation by Great Britain,[4] and when, after some fifteen years of debate, the

---

[2] See *Cambridge History of the British Empire*, Vol. VII, p. 536.

[3] Despatch No. 64 of 1863 Victorian Parliamentary Papers 1862/3 IV 1379.

[4] See *Cambridge History of the British Empire*, Vol. VII, p. 529.

Commonwealth was established, Papua was taken over as an Australian dependency in 1906.

This shows, I suggest, that Australia has always been sensitive to foreign politics. The contingent sent to the Sudan in 1886 and the troops sent to South Africa in 1899-1901 may be ascribed either to the same consciousness of her dependence on world events or to an uncritical loyalty to the British Crown, but at any rate they brought the Australian people at a very early stage of their national existence into touch with world movements. As a result, in the first decade of the Commonwealth an active defence policy was inaugurated, the two chief elements of which were compulsory military training and the establishment of an Australian navy. The justification for these was put specifically on the ground that Australia was a sparsely settled continent within a short distance of the most densely populated areas in the world, that she enjoyed the institutions of democracy, and high living standards, and that these would be impossible unless she could protect her shores from invasion or infiltration.

When she created her defence organisation, she frankly sought the advice of British experts and adopted a system in which coöperation in Empire defence would be facilitated. There was some lifting of the eyebrows by naval officers at the idea of an Australian navy, though some of the most eminent naval strategists, such as Admiral Tryon[5] and Lord Fisher,[6] agreed with the policy. The Australian protagonists were aware of the principle of concentration in naval strategy, but they were not inclined to accept it as an absolute dogma and they well knew that with military and naval resources they could draw attention more effectively to Australian needs. Throughout the whole of the history of Australian foreign policy, we find the consistent formulation of a view of Australian interests by Australian experts, within the framework of Imperial coöperation.

The view that Australia showed a weak sense of nationhood because she did not adopt a completely independent position is, of course, nonsense. It ignores the factors in her strategic situation to which I have drawn attention: her isolation and the contraction of the world owing to new inventions. In these circumstances, the Australian policy of coöperation was dictated by common sense. The

---

[5] P. Fitzgerald, *Life of Sir George Tryon*, p. 235.
[6] Lord Fisher, *Memoirs*, p. 192.

cry of Laurier at Imperial conferences—"Do not call us to your councils lest we be made responsible for your policy"—had no echo in Australia. Australians have never felt that coöperation meant subservience. Canada has always existed within the orbit of a mighty power. This great power, of course, conducted its own policy for the defence of the North American continent.

It is not suggested that the principles of coöperation between Australia and Britain were always satisfactory and logically consistent. Whitehall was aloof and disinclined to be confidential. Australia, more through mental laziness than subservience, was rather inclined to accept the advice of British staff than that of independent-minded officers who were always present in her establishment. It remains an anomaly that up to the outbreak of the Second World War, the navy and air arms were commanded by British officers, and the chief staff officer of the army was on occasion selected in Whitehall.

Dominion status was not heard of before the First World War, and on its outbreak Australia accepted the fact that she was at war and should take part in it. The extent of her contribution she determined herself, and her participation was fully and freely given. When her forces left her shores, the units almost invariably remained intact under Australian generals and staffs, but they moved as part of the British armies under British army generals. This coöperation was regarded as entirely satisfactory by both sides. At one time, after Gallipoli, public opinion in Britain was nervous lest the failure should be resented, but the defeat was regarded in Australia as the fortune of war. The strategy of Gallipoli has been condemned by most Australian military experts, but there was no recrimination.

At the Peace Conference of Paris, Australia came into contact with world problems as a whole, and with a new status. She was given a separate position at the Conference, took part as a full member in all discussions, signed the peace treaty, and became an independent member of the League of Nations. On the other hand, with the other Dominions, she attended the meetings of the British Empire delegation. The duality of Australian opinion is shown by the fact that the Australian Cabinet passed a resolution adverse to separate status, but W. M. Hughes, the Prime Minister, ignored it.[7]

---

[7] Commonwealth Debates, 1 Oct. 1920, XCIV, p. 5817.

The issues in which Australia was most interested at Paris were reparations, the League of Nations, and the disposition of the German colonies. Her connexion with the first was due to the accident that Hughes, being a fierce protagonist of a hard peace, was made Vice-Chairman of the Reparations Commission. Her interest in the German colonies adjacent to Australia, the German New Guinea group, was much closer. Clemenceau placed the subject of the disposition of German colonies early in the agenda in the hope that the Dominions would go for complete annexation, and they snapped the bait. The British delegation strongly opposed the solution of annexation. The mandate system was forced by the preponderant influences at the Conference, Britain and the United States, on the claimants for German territory—a most desirable result. Australia accepted the League of Nations wholeheartedly at the Conference, but one significant incident at the discussions affected her. Japan attempted to secure an affirmation of racial equality in the Covenant. Australia voted against it in a minority, but President Wilson ruled that for so dangerous a proposition unanimity was required. The incident was significant for the future. A declaration of racial equality was in reality harmless so long as it was understood that it did not prevent a country from controlling the composition of its population. Japan would probably have accepted this qualification.

The status occupied by Japan at the Conference was, of course, due to the fact that she had been an ally of Britain for some years and had joined in the war against Germany from the first. This move was due to her calculation that the spoils from a defeated Germany would be relatively easy to obtain. These included the islands of Micronesia, which brought her halfway to Australia and immensely improved her strategic position if, at any time, she might want to pursue a career of extended conquest. This deal was arranged between Japan and Great Britain, and the feeling of Australia was shown by the fact that Mr. Hughes was blamed by his party for agreeing to it. To what extent he was actually responsible has never been determined.[8]

Japan, however, proved herself a useful ally and joined the League of Nations, and though Australia retained her consciousness of the approach of Japan, she relied on a League policy for a

[8] Commonwealth Parliament Debates, LXXXIX, 12419–12607.

progressive settlement of international problems. It was believed that the disarmament agreements which had been made at Washington in 1921–1922 would protect Australia from the large-scale aggression from which she might suffer. Only a few persons suggested that even if disarmament à la Washington might, as was thought, reduce the vulnerability of the Imperial powers in the Pacific, it would prevent them from helping China if she were attacked. As a result of the Washington treaties, Australian armaments were reduced, her battleships scrapped. Later, compulsory military training was dropped. Australia faithfully attended the League meetings at Geneva, accepted the mandate for German New Guinea, and took part in all the movements made to develop League activity and strengthen its powers. She made no very distinctive contributions, but I think it is correct to say that she would have gone further than Britain in the support of proposals such as the Protocol. The ambiguous attitude of British statesmen during this period is very largely responsible for the lack of progress in the solution of League problems.

The failure of the Disarmament Conferences disappointed those in Australia who were deeply anxious for the success of the League. Australia was less disappointed at the failure of the Economic Conference, though students realised that the success of the League depended on the two questions of disarmament and economic development.

Australia entered into the mandate for New Guinea and, with minor exceptions, secured the commendation of the Mandate Commission. She applied similar safeguards for the protection of the natives in her colony of Papua. She did not fortify these territories; fortification was prohibited for New Guinea by the mandate terms, but, in any event, large-scale fortifications were beyond her power and would, of course, have been unnecessary in the crisis if the strategic bastions of the Pacific, Manila and Singapore, had held.

The Manchurian incident was the critical blow at the system which Australians imagined had been established at Geneva and Washington. Some people blamed Australia for influencing Britain not to impose sanctions on Japan. I do not believe that there is a shred of evidence to support this criticism; the legend seems to have arisen from the habits of the so-called analytical expert who sees on the board a move which might be considered likely and then speculates on whether it was made, speedily creating the impression that it did occur. It should have been obvious to everyone that in the circumstances economic sanctions would mean war and that the British fleet with no base east of Suez could not, without outside assistance, wage a war successfully against Japan, which had five bases in the vicinity.

This led to the view that the League of Nations system was defective and needed strengthening and that unless it were strengthened its feeble powers were more a menace to peace than a safeguard. A further step in the dialectic led to the conclusion that defences in the Pacific must be strengthened, and an examination of the Singapore thesis was made. Some experts in Australia came to the conclusion that an attack by Japan on a large scale would only come if Britain were involved in Europe, and in that case Singapore could not be reinforced and might be lost as a bulwark of British interests in the Pacific. It was urged that Australian defence policy should be reorganised with this in view.

When Australian military critics became more insistent, the old dualism in Australian policy reasserted itself. The Australian government paid deference to British experts. Sir Maurice Hankey (later Lord Hankey) was sent out from Britain to give assurances and the dissident officials were discomfited. Though urged by John Curtin, then leader of the Labour opposition, to put their main effort in the air arm, little that was effective was done. As Lyons attended the Imperial Conference of 1937 when confidential discussions on defence took place, it must be assumed that Australian policy followed the advice then given.

When the Pacific war broke out, the course of events confirmed the fears that were held by Australian experts that concentration on more insistent problems by Britain and on internal problems by the United States would leave both unprepared if Japan made an attack in the Pacific. Singapore, the buttress on which Australia was asked to rely, fell and any expectations that Japan could be delayed in the Philippines or the Indies were speedily dissipated. The whole of the vast area and riches of these islands came under Japanese control. The old German New Guinea was occupied and only Papua remained in British hands. Australia expected invasion and, even if that were not in the Japanese plan for the time being, a strong power in control of the islands occupied by Japan would always have Australia at her mercy.

This long course of historical development has built up over the geopolitical factors, mentioned at the beginning of this chapter, a series of strategical problems, to meet which an Australian foreign policy must be devised. The main factors in Pacific strategy are, I suggest, as follows:

1) China and the crowded populations of Southeast Asia form gigantic masses of man power, with ancient cultures but imperfectly developed, living in extreme poverty, conscious of new ideas but unable to realise them without aid. They will be explosive if their position is not improved, while the world will benefit if it is.

2) The area contains a large number of communities of small or medium population in varying stages of political development, from primitive tribes to decadent kingdoms and empires, none of them able to defend themselves in an unordered world.

3) The state of Japan was, before the war, politically stable, industrially developed, and at a high pitch of military organisation. She is now defeated, but could build up her power and morale as quickly as Germany did after the last war, if permitted to do so.

4) Several Western empires have interests in the area. Russia holds a Pacific seaboard to her empire, but the other powers control the congeries of small communities in Malaya and the Indies and other islands. The only political unity possessed by these people is due to the rule of these Western empires.

These features of the Pacific area were laid bare by the war. The rapid conquest by Japan showed the strategic instability of the area, and the reconquest showed the superior strength of the Western powers, particularly the United States, when it could be exerted. Such a reconquest, however, does not of itself restore stability to this area. If the Western powers recede from their zones of force, Japan could come again and repeat her performance. This strategic situation will remain until other Asiatic powers, particularly China, attain the same degree of economic and political stability as Japan. Of course, if Japan were permanently put out of action, it is possible that another might take her place. I do not think this likely. The future depends, if power politics is not to be mitigated, upon the agreement of the great powers, particularly Russia, Great Britain, and the United States.

Another conclusion may be deduced from the war. The Western empires were unable to protect their possessions in the islands from the first Japanese onslaught. The Pacific was reconquered, mainly by a campaign magnificently conceived strategically by the United States staffs. There have been few successes more spectacular in the history of warfare. The essential bases from which this reconquest was started were Australia and New Zealand. If these had been taken by Japan, reconquest would have been much more difficult, if, indeed, possible. Island bases alone would have been insufficient. Therefore, although Australians are deeply grateful for the protection they received, they are also conscious of the fact that Australia has a strategic importance that was not previously recognised. This importance arises partly from its proximity to the strategic centre of gravity and partly from the fact that it is a food-producing and -exporting country, has considerable industrial development and plenty of room. Crowded India, with greater proximity to the centre of conflict, was not, on the whole, so good a base.

Australia, therefore, is a small or middle power faced with difficult strategic problems and has to formulate her policy accordingly. Small nations unable to assure their own security have two courses open to them: to seek friends and make alliances, or to seek a solution for the problems of power in an international scheme. Many small nations have a geographical situation which makes them important to larger nations. Many have affinities with larger powers in race or in way of life. Factors such as these dictate the choice of friends.

Australia, as we have seen, has some value but not a great deal from her geographic position. She is within the British Commonwealth and is in the freemasonry of democratic communities. But Australian strategic problems are unique and require the most careful watchfulness. Great powers, however friendly, are not apt to understand the special problems of their smaller friends. Nor do alliances of this kind necessarily build up a satisfactory world order. They cannot give that security which is necessary for development and welfare. These considerations have induced Australia to espouse heartily the cause of international security through world organisation, and she has therefore become a member of the United Nations.

Her fight against the Dumbarton Oaks draft, conducted with ability by the Minister for External Affairs, Dr. H. V. Evatt, was due to the fact that the veto virtually rendered the five great powers independent of the world organisation, and, as wars arise from the rivalry of great powers, it provides no means of avoiding wars. But Australia recognises that the United Nations does afford a forum for world opinion and negotiation. Within it, international institutions can slowly be built up and a security scheme developed. So long, therefore, as the United Nations functions, Australian foreign policy will be framed to work through it to strengthen the principles which are designed to promote peace and to develop a system of world security.

The future foreign policy of Australia will, therefore, have to be worked out through a new international instrument. Although the factors on which that policy must be based have long existed, they have been revealed in an unexpected form by the events of the war. Australian policy will thus have to make a new departure in which the old formulae will be inapt. The following suggestions on policy are, therefore, speculative and personal.

Australia's policy will be dominated by two main interests: (1) the establishment of an adequate scheme of world security; and (2) the political and economic stability of the Pacific area.

It is not suggested, of course, that Australia will not be concerned with every great question that comes before the United Nations, but the political and economic stability of the Pacific area is of primary importance to Australia, as I shall show.

It is not possible to describe here in detail the security provisions of the Charter, or draw attention to the implications involved, many of which are imperfectly understood. We must realise that no security scheme is established by the Charter, but has to be created through the machinery set up. This machinery will be based on a set of agreements, made by the members of the organisation with the Security Council, by which forces and facilities will be made available. When the scheme is formulated, it will be the dominant factor in the situation. It will be necessary, therefore, for Australia to scrutinise carefully what is put forward by the Military Staff Committee and see that it contains the means of achieving protection. It is not worth while to speculate at this particular stage what form the scheme would take and what Australia should ask for. The following matters, however, seem important.

1) The general plan of security should recognise regional considerations. The Pacific should be treated as a region, and the strategic problems for the area should be the foundation for the scheme. It is recognised that world peace is one problem, but special strategic problems exist in each area and there is a chance that, if the survey is on too wide lines, the special problems of one area will be overlooked. It is only too likely that the Atlantic will engross the attention of the great powers, to the exclusion of the Pacific. At any rate, it will be the function of Australia to keep the Pacific in the world focus.

2) Australia is vitally concerned in the accomplishment of a real scheme of international security. If the attempt fails, the chance of avoiding a third world war is small. The difficulties are obvious, but if sound strategic principles are put into operation it should be possible to evolve a scheme by which aggression can be foiled. This will involve the selection of bases from which international forces can operate. It will be the preoccupation of the Australian government to see that this is worked out on lines suitable to the Pacific area.

3) Australia's attitude toward the demand for bases by the United States is thus involved. Bases required for the international security scheme should be held not individually, but internationally, or by trustees for the United Nations. If no security scheme is agreed to, however, national bases will have to be created. Personally, I do not think that security can be obtained in this way; for if one nation claims bases, others will retaliate. Nations will then have to form alliances and it is hoped that bases can be used on reciprocal terms by Australia and her Allies.

4) An international scheme of security involves mutual contributions from all members. Australia is ready to make hers, though many parts of the Pacific will be unable to do so for some time. The scheme will, I believe, take the form of a regulation and limitation of armaments. It cannot allow for the unlimited growth of the armaments of any one power. It should develop some kind of international force so disposed as to meet possible aggression.

5) In her policy within the United Nations, Australia will recognise that her interests are identical with those of New Zealand, and, in accordance with the Australia–New Zealand pact, will consult and concert policy with her. She will act as a member of the British Commonwealth and will probably be regarded as a leader for that group in the Pacific area. She will cultivate friendship with other Pacific powers and especially with the United States.

But security is not enough. A security scheme is at best a mere barrier against aggression, and if the forces of disunity or distortion in the world are great enough they will break down any barrier. The most urgent problem of Australian foreign policy today is the political instability of the area to the north. The political consequences of this instability are full of danger which is insufficiently recognised. Very few countries in the Pacific are politically or economically stable. China, with its ancient—all too ancient—civilisation, is in a relatively early stage of economic development and has many political problems to solve. If she had had the stability of a Western state, Japan could have made no impression on her. Other nations like Siam, though they had achieved some economic development by their own effort, could not hold their own against Japan. In the other parts of the area, there are communities in all stages of growth from primitive tribes to small principalities and decadent empires. In all, the standard of living is pitifully low—the lowest in the world.

As we have seen, the whole of the insular area and some of Southeast Asia is held by Western empires. These empires were not able to hold their possessions against the first onslaught by Japan, but they have supplied the arms and military resources by which they were reconquered from Japan. They have given their possessions the only integration, the only semblance of political unity, they have shown. The war has, of course, altered the situation. These peoples demand something more than they have been given in the past. The empires have been in a strict sense commercial empires, supplying goods for world markets, organising for that purpose the labour of the indigenous peoples. This has raised standards, but not by much. Such an export economy is itself unstable.

Great changes in the area are, therefore, inevitable, and whatever they are, Australia will be affected. She is interested in the economic development and industrialisation of China and the countries of Southeast Asia. With each rise in their standards and their purchasing power, Australia will gain. But the dilemma of security and progress affects all these movements. Economic development and political stability cannot be achieved until there is an effective security scheme, and there cannot be an effective security scheme unless these countries can contribute to it and are politically and economically equipped to do so.

The problem is, of course, far more urgent in the archipelagoes, the area covered by the Western empires. There are, of course, nations like Burma and the Philippines which are achieving self-government, either within or outside their present regimes. What should be asked of them is that they should join the United Nations, accept its obligations, and contribute their share to security. But it is clear that many primitive peoples have no present capacity for self-government. The natives of New Guinea, for instance, have no semblance of political structure at all, no leaders or institutions. Village elders settle what is needed for order. A village will speak a different language from that of another five miles off. These primitive peoples are scattered throughout the whole area, side by side with more developed but still illiterate peoples.

Political integration is also affected by the mixture of races. This can be understood from the fact that there are forty-eight different races in the Netherlands East Indies Empire. There are four distinct races in Java alone, and seventy-eight petty princes or rajahs. In British Malaysia there are 2,800,000 Chinese, 2,700,000 Malays, and 1,000,000 Indians. To say that these empires can be vacated by their present holders without any constructive provisions to meet these problems is to talk without meaning. Such a step would throw the area into chaos. These people are not less apt to tyrannise or exploit their fellows than imperial powers. Even though their aims have been mainly commercial, the imperial powers have prevented much exploitation and have created worthwhile development. Java now supports 70,000,000 people. How many would it support if Dutch organisation and efficiency were absent?

The danger to Australia from chaos in the area immediately to the north can hardly be overestimated. The security scheme of the

United Nations must depend on the ability of its members to contribute to the scheme and support it. If the area is vacated, we shall at best have a series of copra republics that would need to be supported and could make little contribution. They would, nevertheless, occupy important areas which produce valuable strategic materials and would thus be the lure and the prey of an aggressive power.

It is Australia's view that the system of trusteeship under the United Nations Charter will enable the requisite order to be established and the necessary tutelage given. It is not suggested for a moment that all dependent territories should be put under trusteeship, still less those which are emerging into a regime of self-government or which have existing political organisations of some strength. Trusteeship, however, appears to be required for those which are unable to look after themselves or which, by reason of a mixture of races, do not form communities in the social sense. Australia would, I believe, prefer individual trusteeship to international government. The experience of condominiums has been unfortunate.

The objective of trusteeship should be the education, political training, and economic advancement of the indigenous peoples, and Australia would have preferred that there should be some form of account by all colonial powers for their dependent territories. It is a pity also that the question of bases should obtrude and frustrate the trust conception. There is no reason at all why a base should not exist in trustee territory, no reason why its existence should affect the relation between the trustee and the dependent peoples. The old mandate areas were in effect demilitarised, and that was a very good thing. There seems already to be a demand for trusteeship on account of strategic advantages to be gained from the possession of the trust area. A concession to this feeling would be fatal.

Territories should emerge from trusteeship when they are able to defend themselves or contribute to a system of international security. It would be a pity if they severed themselves entirely from the regime of the trusteeship power; but if they demand this, it should be on condition that they become members of the United Nations.

Australia is very much in favour of regional groupings such as that which has been established in the Caribbean Commission. Knowledge should be pooled; there should be coöperation in services, research, and development. But it is not considered that such a policy would render trusteeship unnecessary.

What is required for the rest of the nations of the Pacific is economic development, and the utmost use of the machinery of the Economic and Social Council should be made for this. The series of economic and financial organisations which have been established—the International Fund, the International Bank, the Food and Agriculture Organisation, the International Labour Organisation, and others—should be linked with the Economic and Social Council and assist it to carry out the economic advancement of undeveloped countries. This will take several forms; most Asiatic countries need a great deal of primary development. China requires roads, railways, river control, electric installations, and communications of all kinds. But China also requires a considerable amount of industrialisation to use her enormous man power. China is only the most important example in the Pacific. In more backward countries what is required is primary development, mainly roads and communications, agricultural training, and experiment.

Such a policy is a long-range policy and will take many generations to realise. It will involve large investment by the countries with capital, and that investment will be at some risk, but if it can be made effective, it will mean much to the world and not least to the surplus-exporting countries whose production cannot now be absorbed at home. It will be a difficult process, but the point is that immediately it begins it will give many people a vested interest in peace and security. In a busy concentration on welfare, ideas of war may be sublimated. On the other hand, unless a workable scheme of security exists, such a programme will be impossible.

A policy on these lines appears to me to be implicit in the actions of Australia at San Francisco in relation to security, trusteeship, and the Economic and Social Council. It is a policy which will present many difficulties and, perhaps, dangers. But it is a creative policy, one which should excite the imagination and attract the interest of all Australians.

Part Four:

ECONOMIC AND SOCIAL DEVELOPMENT

CHAPTER X

The Growth of the Australian Economy

BY HERBERT BURTON

ECONOMIC development in Australia has been very much as might have been expected in a colony of British settlement undertaken at the end of the eighteenth century in a sparsely occupied continent. The settlement of central and western Canada took place over the same period. In both colonies the rights of the native inhabitants received scant recognition, their land was appropriated to produce commodities for exchange, and overseas trade bulked large in the colonial economy. Extensive use of land preceded intensive use, the soil was ruthlessly exploited, but finally, as the end of the frontier was reached, conservation had to be practised, and the economy developed diversity and maturity.

In each colony the circumstances of its foundation and history introduced particular variations. The penal purpose of the original settlement in New South Wales led to an attempt to create a subsistence economy of peasant proprietors, artisans, and shopkeepers, for some thirty years or more. Australian geography, the needs of Yorkshire woollen manufacturers, and the search by British capitalists for profitable investments changed British policy to one of pastoral development. The success of pastoral development put an end to penal settlement. The gold discoveries of the 1850's struck a blow at the dominance of pastoralism. Their influence in Australian history was as profound as that of the Civil War in the economic history of the United States. The large influx of capital and population led to a more intensive use of land, and to greater development of industry. To the end of the nineteenth century, however, and even until the great slump of 1929, the Australian economy remained primarily colonial. Development depended mainly on import of capital, a high proportion of production was for export, Australian manufacturing was mainly sheltered, and trade was oriented mainly on Britain. The present century has seen a great growth in maturity of the Australian economy, and the colonial characteristics are rapidly disappearing. But the Australian economy still remains closely integrated into the pattern of world trade and susceptible to its fluctuations.

The period to 1821 was dominated by the British policy that New South Wales was first and foremost a penal station. Individuals and officials, like Captain Arthur Phillip (1738–1814), the first governor, may have had visions of a new Britain in the southern seas, but the attitude of the Colonial Office was more prosaic. It was not concerned with acquiring a continent, but with disposing of convicts—and as cheaply as possible. To save expense the colony was to become self-sufficient in foodstuffs as soon as possible, while it was hoped that it might also produce some commodities to exchange for indispensable imports. Convicts as they served their terms were to be settled on small farms; soldiers, officials, and free settlers could be granted somewhat larger holdings. Until the convicts were "out of their time," they were employed on government farms or on public works.

But the problem of making the little colony self-sufficient in food supplies was not simple. The coastal strip of New South Wales was unsuitable for grain production, and several times in the first five years the colony was on the verge of starvation when harvests failed through flood or drought. From time to time during the first thirty years it was necessary to import grain, but in 1818 the problem was solved. The crossing of the Blue Mountains (1813) opened up the more reliable wheat lands on the western slopes of the Divide, but the main relief came from the settlement of Tasmania, which began in 1803. The valleys of the Derwent and Tamar gave easy access to the best agricultural land in the little island; within fifteen years Tasmania was exporting wheat freely to the mainland, and all danger of famine was past. By 1802 the increase of flocks and herds was sufficient to allow free slaughtering of animals for food, and from that time on fresh meat was abundant and cheap.

Meanwhile, Captain John Macarthur (1767–1834), of the New South Wales Corps, by his experiments in growing fine wool had demonstrated the possibility of producing wool for export. He obtained the first large grant of land (5,000 acres) for wool production in 1805, and from then until 1831 large grants could be obtained by capitalists, usually at the rate of one acre for each pound of capital. Until 1810 the economy was a mixed one, with public and private enterprise fairly evenly balanced. Convicts were assigned to private employers who were responsible for their keep but who were able to exploit their labour. The government also ran farms and a retail store, and bought grain and meat from settlers at a high fixed price. Thus did they provide for the needs of the garrison, the officials, and the convicts. The object of relieving the British Government of all expense for the establishment was not achieved, for until 1821 private settlers were never numerous enough to take all the convicts off the hands of the colonial governor, and the balance had to be employed on public works which though useful were not commercially profitable.

This was particularly so under Macquarie, Governor from 1810 to 1821, and the most outstanding of all Australian governors. In the twenty-two years to 1810 only some 12,000 convicts were sent to Australia; between 1810 and 1821 Macquarie received 22,000 convicts. Since thousands of these were left on Macquarie's hands, he used them to construct roads, bridges, wharves, and public buildings for the development of the colony. His attitude was Australian rather than British; he was not so much concerned with the pocket of the British taxpayer as with the future of Australia. This eventually led to his recall, but he prepared the way for the subsequent expansion.

Already under Macquarie the settlers of New South Wales were turning to sheep-raising, for which the country was more suitable than for agriculture until railways brought cheap transport to the midwestern plains. The export of wool in 1820 was only about 175,000 lbs., a mere drop in the bucket of English imports of about 30,000,000 lbs. After 1821, however, free settlers with capital came at the rate of nearly a thousand a year, mainly to grow wool. In addition, the first big British pastoral companies began operations: the Australian Agricultural Company and the Van Diemen's

Land Company (each with a capital of £1,000,000), in 1826. This import of capital led to the first pronounced boom in prices for Australian stock, but a slump followed upon the English crisis of 1826. The slump occurred later in Australia because sailing ships took six to nine months on the voyage. So rapid, however, was the expansion of wool-growing that convicts were no longer able to provide a sufficient labour force. It was shortage of labour in the Australian economy that caused land grants to be replaced by land sales in 1831, and the use of land revenue to subsidise the immigration of "free" labourers.

Edward Gibbon Wakefield (1796–1862) was mainly responsible for the adoption of the new policy, advocated in *A Letter from Sydney* (1829), which, though written in a London gaol, showed a sound grasp of the Australian situation. The funds from land sales were used mainly to provide low fares to Australia, for otherwise immigrants naturally preferred the vastly shorter and cheaper passage to America. Australia remained an attractive field for British capital through the 'thirties, especially as the English usury laws (making 5 per cent the legal maximum rate of interest) were relaxed in New South Wales in 1834. Australian banks were floated in London to finance this investment, and the years 1838–1840 saw a boom in land sales and immigration. Then came the slump; wool prices fell heavily in Britain, and remained low until 1851. This checked the import of capital from Britain, land sales fell off, and immigration was affected as a result. Only in South Australia (founded in 1836 as a free colony) was there any marked economic progress in the 'forties, following upon rich finds of copper in 1843.

In spite of adversity the pastoral industry continued to expand, and to dominate the Australian scene. From 1821 to 1851, the sheep on Australian pastures increased from fewer than 500,000 to 17,450,000. By 1851 Australia had become the chief exporter of wool to the world's market; her export had expanded from about 175,000 lbs. in 1821 to 2,500,000 lbs. in 1831, and 38,000,000 in 1851. The pastoral industry had provided most of the land revenue which brought some 100,000 "'assisted" immigrants to Australia between 1832 and 1851, at a time when immigration was indispensable for economic progress. Pastoralism provided the bulk of Australian exports, and directly or indirectly provided more em-

ployment than any other branch of the economy. Agriculture was
limited to the provision of local needs; manufacture was entirely
of a sheltered nature; mining was limited to the production of
copper for export and of coal for local use; transport was primitive,
and the other service occupations were little developed. In such
an economy wool was not only king but virtually an absolute monarch. Population grew from 35,500 in 1821 to 438,000 in 1851.
Transportation of convicts to New South Wales stopped in 1840,
and to Tasmania in 1852. The pastoral industry had transformed
Australia from a penal station into a colony of free settlement.

The gold discoveries of 1851 and the next few years brought
about a revolution in the Australian economic scene. In the 'fifties,
gold-mining produced more wealth and gave more employment
than the pastoral industry. As the yield of gold declined, pastoralism regained first place, but it never recovered its former predominance. From being absolute it became a constitutional monarch,
set about with rivals with growing claims. Between 1851 and 1860
Australia produced nearly £106,000,000 in gold, of which more
than £80,000,000 was exported. These finds attracted hundreds of
thousands of immigrants, and population almost trebled between
1850 and 1860. In no other decade has immigration reached such
proportions, and never again was it to exercise so important an
influence in population growth. Down to 1860 roughly three-
quarters of the growth in population was by immigration; since
1860 roughly three-quarters has been due to natural increase. The
gold discoveries made it possible for the Australian population to
grow rapidly by means of natural increase, and decreased the need
for schemes of assisted immigration. In fact, as the frontiers of
land settlement were reached in the older colonies, such schemes
were discontinued in response to opposition from organised wage-
earners. By 1890 only Queensland and Western Australia, the two
pioneer states, were still subsidising immigration.

The gold finds of the 'fifties also exerted a dynamic effect upon
world prices and prosperity. In Australia they set on foot a rise in
prices that brought a revival of prosperity to every colony. They stimulated economic recovery in Britain by making a significant addition to the gold reserves of her banking system. Between 1851 and
1860 Australia produced more than 40 per cent of the world's gold,

and exercised a decisive influence on world prices and prosperity. Although she was to produce even more gold (£142,000,000) between 1901 and 1910, it did not have the same importance, for by that time South Africa had become the chief producer and Australia supplied only 18 per cent of world output. The yields of gold declined decade by decade after 1860, until the rich fields of Western Australia sent them soaring again after 1890; since that date at least three-quarters of Australian gold has come from the western state.

Other minerals added their quota to Australia's production of wealth in this period. In Tasmania, tin was discovered at Mount Bischoff in 1871, and copper at Mount Lyell in 1884. Mount Morgan in Queensland proved prolific in gold (1882), and also rich in copper. These copper finds were welcome, as the South Australian mines were petering out. But the richest find of all in this period was of the silver-lead-zinc ores of Broken Hill (1883), which still continues to be the chief source of industrial base metals for Australia. Yet in spite of these finds mining did not regain the relative position which it had in the 'fifties, and the chief development in the production of industrial minerals was to come after 1900.

Gold and population brought self-government to all the colonies except Western Australia between 1855 and 1860. It was gold that finally brought population and self-government to the western state in 1890. The economic importance of this constitutional advance was that it gave the colonies control over their own Crown lands and revenue, and enabled them to borrow overseas on the security of these assets.

One of the main essentials for economic development was the provision of cheaper and speedier transport for the inland areas. The coaching firm of Cobb & Co., started on the Bendigo diggings in 1853 by four Americans, provided a service of the first importance for mails, passengers, and light freight. These services spread through the three eastern states, and reached their zenith about 1870; then they declined before the advance of the railway, and the automobile gave the *coup de grâce*. The last coach route closed in 1924 in south-western Queensland.

For heavy freights, railways were needed, and the states began to build and operate these services; private enterprise preferred quicker and richer returns. The railway mileage grew at an accelerated pace, until the disastrous slump of the 'nineties temporarily checked the expansion. From 215 miles in 1860 the figure grew to 994 in 1870, 3,675 in 1880, 9,757 in 1890, and 12,995 in 1900. By then about half the present railway mileage had been built, and the eastern capital cities had all been connected by 1888. The value of this achievement was marred by the adoption of different gauges: only Melbourne and Adelaide had no break of gauge between them.

As railway mileage grew, so did the public debt. From £30,000,000 in 1871 (£18 per head), it grew to £155,000,000 in 1891 (£48 per head), and to £213,000,000 in 1901 (£56 per head). The greater part of the money was spent on railways, and other means of communication such as telegraphs and submarine cables. Though the debt was large, almost all the expenditure was for useful enterprises which, if not always directly profitable, at least increased the productive capacity of the country. In normal times the burden of debt service was not heavy, but besides the public borrowing there was a heavy influx of private capital from Britain, particularly between 1878 and 1891. Much of this money went into speculation in mining shares and real estate, and was responsible for unhealthy boom conditions in the 'eighties, particularly in Melbourne. The crash came in 1892 after the fall of prices for wool, metals, and wheat, and Australia suffered the worst banking crisis in her history in April and May, 1893. To the end of the century economic conditions remained adverse. It was difficult to raise overseas loans, business was depressed, and despite the attraction of the western gold fields Australia as a whole lost people by emigration. To cap it all, a series of disastrous droughts occurred, reducing the number of sheep from 106,400,000 in 1891 to 53,700,000 in 1902.

Though the century ended in economic gloom, great progress had been made since 1860 in agriculture, dairying, and even in manufacturing, as well as in the pastoral industry. The progress in agriculture was the outcome of several factors in conjunction. The Australian farmer, like the American, was fertile in devising machines because of the relatively high level of wages. In 1843 John Ridley (1806–1887) in South Australia invented a "stripper" for harvesting wheat; further improvements followed, and in 1888 Hugh Victor McKay (1865–1926) in Victoria began the manufacture of harvesters in Australia. Other men, such as Robert Bowyer

Smith of South Australia, enabled the new settler to get a crop from partly cleared land by means of the "stump-jump" plough (1876). After 1865 the railways began to provide cheap transport to the ports, and so the typical Australian wheat-farm developed on large-scale lines, with an average size of 750 to 1,000 acres. By 1866 an overseas export trade in grain was begun from South Australia, to be followed soon from Victoria.

Another factor that played a part in this development was land legislation, which gave the crop-farmer access to lands formerly monopolised by the "squatters." As gold yields declined and diggers looked for alternative occupations, many turned to farming. But the best arable areas were mostly locked up in grazing leases, often for many years. Manhood suffrage soon broke that stranglehold, and Sir John Robertson (1816–1891) in New South Wales passed the first Selection Act in 1861. This enabled small settlers to buy up 320 acres at £1 per acre, anywhere on Crown land. The other states all adopted similar legislation, and as a result the next thirty years saw a great extension of cultivation, particularly in South Australia and Victoria, where railways were rapidly built to the wheat areas. The Selection Acts were badly abused, particularly in New South Wales, and amendments had to be devised to prevent fraud and evasion. But they began the liberal land legislation which aimed at making land available for cultivation and for dairying, as well as for grazing purposes. That they had a part in promoting the spread of cultivation cannot be denied. Table 1 shows the growth of the area

TABLE 1

Year	N.S.W.	Vic.	Qld.	S. Aust.	W. Aust.	Tas.	Total
1861..	246,000	387,000	3,000	359,000	25,000	153,000	1,174,000
1891..	853,000	2,032,000	225,000	2,094,000	70,000	157,000	5,430,000
1901..	2,447,000	3,114,000	457,000	2,370,000	201,000	224,000	8,814,000

under crop in this period (in acres). Most of this cultivated area was in wheat; other crops were grown only for local consumption, except sugar, which was grown in Queensland from 1862 and was providing an export trade by 1875.

But wheat-farmers met with serious trouble after 1880, owing to the continuous cropping of their land. Australian soils are naturally deficient in phosphates, and their fertility was soon exhausted. Professor Custance at Roseworthy Agricultural College (1879) in South Australia pointed to the need for using superphosphate of lime, and by 1900 it was coming into use on wheat farms. Rust and smut were also a scourge for the wheat-farmer, and here the work of William James Farrer (1845–1906) was invaluable in providing strains of wheat which would resist these diseases and give the best results in the Australian environment. Farrer was one of the great pioneers in plant breeding. Thus mechanisation, liberal land legislation, railways, science, and education all played their part in developing the Australian wheat industry. By 1900 wheat and flour contributed about 5 per cent of the value of Australian exports.

The introduction of refrigeration after 1880 made possible the development of two other important export industries, dairying and meat-raising. Until then, both were restricted by the size of the local market. Although population grew from 1,146,000 in 1861 to 3,765,000 in 1900, this did not give these industries scope for expansion similar to that in agriculture or wool production. The work of James Harrison (1815–1893) and Thomas Sutcliffe Mort (1816–1878) was of first-rate importance in the successful development of commercial refrigeration, and so by 1900 butter and frozen meat were making significant contributions to the value of Australia's exports.

Meanwhile, manufacturing industry had also begun to enter into competition with imported goods, again mainly as a result of agitation by unemployed miners looking for new jobs. As early as 1866 Victoria began to give tariff protection to the manufacture of textiles and leather goods, clothing, and boots and shoes. The main development of the metal industries took place in New South Wales, which had much superior sources of black coal. The growth of manufacturing was such that by 1891 industrial workers were as numerous as rural workers (each 30.7 per cent of the total), whereas in 1871 there had been 44 rural to 26.5 industrial workers. The slump of the 'nineties hit industrial production severely, however, and the figures for 1901 showed primary producers in the ascendant once again (see table 3 below).

Thus in the period from 1851 to 1901, helped by the stimulus of the gold discoveries, the Australian economy gained in diversity and strength. Population and production grew rapidly, in spite of the setback caused by the slump of the 'nineties. Table 2 shows the trends from 1871. At the end of the century the pastoral industry was still making the chief contribution to the national income, but it no longer occupied a position of solitary eminence.

TABLE 2

	1871	1881	1891	1901
Population....................	1,701,000	2,307,000	3,241,000	3,825,000
Value of material production....	£47,000,000	71,000,000	96,000,000	115,000,000

The federation of the Australian states into the Commonwealth in 1900 was indispensable to the development of the Australian economy. Intercolonial tariffs were hindering the development of manufacturing, and the breaking down of these barriers helped industrial development. National policy concentrated on the provision of opportunities for employment by promoting both closer settlement and manufacturing. The liberal land legislation of the states was supplemented by the Commonwealth, which sought to break up big holdings by a graduated land-tax (1910) and acquired land for soldier settlement after the war of 1914–1918. Even without this deliberate policy it could have been expected that agriculture, dairying, and small farming would grow at the expense of the area given over to grazing. This in fact is what has happened. It might have been expected also that manufacturing would grow even faster than agriculture. But the Commonwealth was not content to let things work themselves out in this fashion; it accelerated the process by a policy of substantial tariff protection from 1908 onward. As a result there has been a further change in the balance of the Australian economy in the present century. The pastoral industry has continued to grow slowly but to lose ground relatively; agriculture has grown more rapidly, though relatively it has also lost some ground. The chief advances have been in dairying, manufacture, and the service occupations. Some of these changes are revealed by table 3, showing the percentage distribution of breadwinners.

This table brings out very clearly the *relative* decline in the proportion of the population engaged in material production, and the rapid growth of the service occupations from 29.5 per cent of total breadwinners in 1871 to 42.4 per cent in 1933. This has been a familiar phenomenon in countries where productivity per head has been increasing, and shows that Australia is among the countries with a relatively high level of technical development. It is notably true in agriculture and the pastoral industry, and although the

TABLE 3

Occupation	1871	1881	1891	1901	1911	1921	1933
Professional..........	5.1	5.5	6.2	6.8	7.3	8.7	9.2
Domestic service.....	11.6	12.2	11.6	12.2	10.1	9.1	8.7
Commercial..........	8.1	9.2	12.2	13.6	14.5	15.3	16.4
Transport...........	3.8	4.5	6.8	7.4	8.0	9.0	8.1
Industrial...........	26.5	29.4	30.7	26.1	28.4	31.2	31.5
Primary.............	44.0	38.2	30.7	32.5	30.4	25.8	24.0
Independent........	0.9	1.0	1.8	1.4	1.3	0.9	2.1
	100.0	100.0	100.0	100.0	100.0	100.0	100.0

actual numbers engaged in primary production increased from 536,-000 in 1901 to 657,000 in 1933, they encountered a setback between 1911 and 1921 (609,000 to 605,000), during the period of accelerated industrial development of the First World War. But while the numbers engaged in primary production over the period 1901–1933 increased by less than 23 per cent, the value of primary production doubled, and the volume more than doubled.

The progress of the individual rural industries can be summarily indicated by the figures of production at selected dates (see table 4).

TABLE 4

Year	Cattle	Sheep	Wool (lbs.)	Meat exports (lbs.)	Butter (lbs.)
1900...	8,640,000	70,600,000	472,643,000	163,063,000	114,380,000
1921...	14,440,000	86,120,000	762,105,000	234,535,000	267,070,000
1938...	12,862,000	111,060,000	1,023,000,000	496,000,000	456,000,000

Year	Crop area (acres)	Wheat (bushels)	Sugar (tons)	Dried fruits (cwts.)	Wine (gallons)
1900...	8,814,000	48,353,000	112,000	49,000	5,121,000
1921...	15,070,000	145,874,000	182,500	305,000	11,014,000
1938...	23,500,000	187,256,000	810,000	1,860,000	20,430,000

These figures show clearly that production increased much more rapidly than the numbers of livestock or the area under crop, and give some indication of the increasing productivity. In the nineteenth century the average weight of the fleece had doubled between 1840 and 1880 (from 2¼ to 5½ lbs.), and it almost doubled again by 1938. Increasing yields in agriculture and dairying also helped the rapid expansion of production, though some of the increase was also the result of schemes for raising prices in the local market. Since 1916 the expansion of the dried-fruit industry has been aided by the raising of local prices under the protection of a tariff duty; further assistance came from Imperial preference in 1925 and a wine-export bounty in 1930. Thus Australian and British consumers have subsidised the industry, which exports about 80 per cent of its output of dried fruit. A similar marketing scheme for raising the local price was introduced for butter in 1926, and in 1932 Britain granted a preference. In 1926 about one-third of butter production was exported; by 1938 the proportion exceeded one-half. So, too, with sugar production; rapid expansion has been helped by an embargo on imports plus a fairly high domestic price, and more than half the output is "dumped" overseas. Thus the more rapid expansion of the intensive rural industries, while it would no doubt have occurred in any event, has been accelerated by national policy.

One branch of primary production showed no increase in the value of its contribution to material production in the period 1900–1938. The average annual value of minerals fell slowly, in the first three decades, from £24,000,000 to £21,000,000. This fall was due almost entirely to declining gold yields, and was arrested by the great rise in the price of gold which took place after 1932. There was a marked revival in gold-mining, but it did not regain the place it occupied in the first decade of the century, when it accounted for nearly 60 per cent of the value of mineral production. Most important to mining since the turn of the century has been the increased production of industrial minerals—coal, lead, zinc, ironstone, copper, and tin. By 1938 these contributed more than half of the total value of mineral production and provided the essential basis of an expanding industrial economy. After 1939, war caused a sharp expansion in the production of industrial minerals. Although the number of miners employed fell from 66,000 to 49,000 by 1942, the decline was almost entirely in gold-mining. The intrinsic importance of mining is clearly not to be judged merely by the numbers it employs or the money value of mineral production.

Great as were the increases in most fields of primary production, these have all been exceeded in the present century by the progress in manufacturing. This is perhaps best brought out by the average annual figures of recorded production at two different periods (see table 5). The figures do not include the service occupations, and are

TABLE 5

Field of production	1907—1911		1935—1939	
	Annual value of production (£m)	Percentage of total	Annual value of production (£m)	Percentage of total
Agricultural...................	37.4	21.3	81.1	18.7
Pastoral......................	52.0	29.7	91.4	21.0
Dairying, poultry, and beekeeping.................	17.6	10.0	52.0	12.0
Forestry and fisheries..........	4.7	2.7	12.7	2.9
Mining......................	24.3	14.0	27.2	6.3
Manufacturing...............	39.0	22.3	169.6	39.1
Totals.................	175.0	100.0	434.0	100.0

therefore not to be confused with national income, which rose from £315,000,000 in 1914–1915 to £814,000,000 in 1937–1938.

The effect of the war from 1939 on was to increase sharply the importance of manufacturing in the Australian economy. In 1942–1943, factories contributed £352,000,000 in the total recorded production of £630,000,000, or 56 per cent, while national income rose to £1,228,000,000. National income rose further to £1,283,000,000 in 1943–1944.

The rapid growth of manufacture was not only the result of reaching the "end of the frontier" of extensive land settlement. From 1908 onward, tariff policy aimed at fostering factory development. Industries in competition with imported goods went ahead, especially textiles, clothing, food-processing, and agricultural implements. Important steps were taken when the refining of copper ores was begun at Port Kembla in 1909, and of zinc ores at Risdon (Tasmania) in 1920. In the meantime, the Broken Hill Proprietary Co., Ltd., Australia's biggest industrial corporation, had taken a step of fundamental importance. It built at Newcastle (New South Wales) a modern steel-works which began production in 1915 and has since provided the materials for a network of subsidiary metal-

working enterprises. During the First World War the new steel industry proved most valuable for the munitions industry and for
railway construction, but the Commonwealth depended on Britain
for artillery, heavy munitions, and machinery. Industrial development was greatly stimulated by the interruption of overseas trade,
though the actual numbers employed fell during the war. In 1921
the new war industries received tariff protection, and development
continued under the cover of substantial duties, which were raised
further in 1930 as a result of the depression.

Important advances took place during this period in the metal
and machinery trades, particularly in motor assembly and body-
building, and in the rubber and tyre industries. Industry suffered a
severe setback in the depression, and factory employment fell from
452,000 in 1929 to 337,000 in 1932. Then a rapid recovery took
place, and by 1936 manufacturing had passed all previous levels of
employment and output, and went on to higher levels each year.
This recovery was helped by several factors. The depreciation of the
currency gave added protection, for although duties against British
goods were reduced in 1933 to compensate for exchange depreciation, this did not apply to foreign goods. The level of money wages
was considerably reduced between 1929 and 1933 (20 per cent),
through adjustment to cost of living and a 10 per cent cut in real
wages (1931). Though the cut in real wages was fully restored by
1937, *nominal* wages had not recovered to their previous level by
1939. Adversity also stimulated efficiency, and there was a significant
increase in the size of the business unit, particularly after 1939. In
1933, factories employing more than 100 workers accounted for less
than 43 per cent of industrial workers; by 1943 the proportion had
risen to 61 per cent.

The outbreak of war in 1939 found Australian industry far
stronger than in 1914, and in a position to meet most military needs.
There was no manufacture of aero or automobile engines, but automobile assembly and body-building were well developed. Production of airplanes was developed, and artillery and munitions of all
kinds were produced in quantity. Ship-building was pushed ahead,
but the Commonwealth had to depend primarily on America and
Britain for shipping services, tanks, aircraft, and heavy equipment
such as tractors and bulldozers. The impact of the war on Australian

industry is seen in the rise of factory employment from 565,000 to 759,000 workers between 1939 and 1943. Nearly all this increase came from the chemical industries (20,000 to 54,000) and the metal and machinery group (178,000 to 328,000), while between 1936 and 1944 steel-making capacity was more than doubled. But although manufacturing has made such advances, it should be noted that down to 1939 it contributed little to export trade. Its average contribution for the ten years to 1939 was only 5 per cent, whereas the pastoral industry provided 48 per cent, agriculture 24, mining 12.5, dairying 9.5, and forestry and fisheries 1 per cent. During the war its contribution increased sharply, but it should not be too readily assumed that this will be maintained in peacetime. The expansion of export trade in manufactured goods may be expected to be a slow business, since the size of the Australian market hampers the adoption of mass-production methods.

Another sphere in which the Australian economy has been reaching toward maturity is finance. Until 1929 Australia continued to borrow heavily overseas. In 1914 about two-thirds of the public debt had been raised overseas, but the establishment of the Commonwealth Bank (1912) greatly helped the rise of a local bond market. It played an active part in raising loan issues during the war of 1914–1918, and by 1930 nearly one-half the public debt of £1,100,000,000 was held in Australia. By 1940 the overseas debt had declined to 44 per cent of the total (£1,340 m.) and was beginning to be redeemed. Australia has also raised the greater part of her industrial issues in this period, though some import of capital has continued. Though the war has more than doubled the public debt of Australia, the overseas debt has been further reduced, and now amounts to only about one-fifth of the total.

Another sign of growing maturity has been the long-term decline in the colonial character of the Australian economy. Though Britain still remains the chief market for Australian goods, and also the main source of imports, this dependence on the Mother Country is clearly decreasing. In the five years 1893–1897 Britain took 69 per cent of Australian exports, other British countries 9 per cent, and foreign countries 22 per cent. But in the five years before the war Britain's share was only 52 per cent, and that of foreign countries, 35.5. Although the Ottawa system worked against this long-term tendency, it cannot permanently check the movement toward decreased reliance upon the British market. A similar tendency is at work in the Australian import trade, where Britain's share of the Australian market over the same period has fallen from 70 to 45 per cent while the share of foreign countries has grown from 19 to 40 per cent. This process may be expected to continue in future as the Australian economy grows in strength.

Public policy has played an increasingly important part in economic development since 1900. Besides helping industry by tariffs and subsidies, the Commonwealth has supplemented the efforts of the states to promote intensive farming by schemes for water conservation and irrigation. The chief projects since 1900 have been the Mundaring Weir (Western Australia), which brought water to the Kalgoorlie gold fields in 1902, the Burrinjuck Dam on the Murrumbidgee (New South Wales) in 1913, and the Hume Weir (1936) on the upper Murray. The Murray itself has been controlled by a series of locks as a result of the River Murray Agreement (1914), and in Queensland the Dawson River has been used to irrigate the main cotton-growing area. By 1938 the irrigated farming area in Australia was nearly 900,000 acres. Part of the policy of closer settlement has been the provision of improved transport services. Railways doubled in length between 1900 and 1925, to reach a figure of 26,000 miles, one of the main projects being the transcontinental railway completed in 1917. After 1925 there was little more railway-building, owing to the competition of automobile and air transport. By 1939 there were 28,000 miles of railway, but road-building had been going on much more actively since 1926, the expenditure of the states being supplemented by a subsidy from the Commonwealth of an equal amount. The war brought a further sharp increase in mileage of "made" roads and also in aviation facilities, but it did nothing for the railways beyond overtaxing their services.

The expenditure on development was not confined to public works, but also extended to subsidising immigration in periods of expansion. When, in 1901, the policy of excluding coloured races was adopted, it was felt that such measures had to be justified by a positive policy of encouraging white immigration. Between 1902 and 1906 there was a net emigration owing to a depression, but the tide turned in 1907 and a shortage of labour occurred. By 1912 all

states were again subsidising migration from Britain, and in the
years 1911–1913 there was a net gain of 230,000 immigrants. War
interrupted this policy, but it was actively resumed in 1922 when
Britain passed the Empire Settlement Act to assist emigration to the
Dominions. In 1925 Britain and the Commonwealth coöperated in
a scheme to settle 450,000 British in Australia within ten years, but
the slump caused its abandonment in 1929. During the depression
Australia again lost population by emigration, and the subsequent
gains by immigration down to 1940 were small (see table 6). The

TABLE 6

Year	Population	Growth	Net immigration	Percentage ratio of immigration to growth
1900.........	3,765,000	....	....	....
1910.........	4,425,000	660,000	40,000	6
1920.........	5,411,000	986,000	208,000	21
1930.........	6,501,000	1,090,000	314,000	29
1940.........	7,069,000	568,000	32,000	6

slow growth of population in the last decade is not peculiar to Australia, but the experience of the present century, thus far, suggests
that it would be unwise to expect a great deal from immigration in
the future growth of the population.

While public policy has been trying to accelerate the economic
development and the peopling of Australia, it has also been striving
to mitigate and control economic fluctuations.

The steps taken to reduce inequality of incomes might be considered part of this policy, though they were taken in response to a
demand for social justice rather than as a result of economic theory.
Social services have been expanded; the funds are mainly provided
by taxation that has become steeply progressive. Minimum wages
aim at providing a guaranteed subsistence, while social services and
pensions help to redistribute income. Between 1913 and 1939 *public*
expenditure on health and pensions increased from 19 to 97 shillings per head, and on education between 1901 and 1939 *public* expenditure increased from £4 to nearly £13 per head annually. Much
of this development has resulted from the strength of organised
labour.

But the main steps toward controlling fluctuations have been taken in the field of public borrowing and budget expenditure. Between 1907 and 1914, and again between 1920 and 1929, public authorities borrowed freely to promote development. In the 'twenties, uneasiness began to develop lest this policy of "everyone for himself" might accentuate economic ups and downs. Accordingly, in 1927 a financial agreement between the Commonwealth and the states set up the Loan Council, which should fix the amount of public loans each year and allot the funds between the various claimants. Soon afterward the slump of 1929 occurred, and national income fell from £768,000,000 to £528,000,000 in 1932. In an effort to counter the depression the Commonwealth and the states agreed upon the Premiers' Plan of 1931, which sought to balance budgets and promote recovery by reducing costs. Although the policy had deflationary features, it also aimed at recovery by exchange depreciation (1931) and by expansion of central bank credit to finance budget deficits and public works. This policy of maintaining employment and stability was then continued, so far as it was compatible with maintaining the overseas exchange rate unchanged. The Commonwealth Bank Act of 1945 has now given the Commonwealth Government power to determine banking and financial policy. This is the culmination of a steady evolution over the last twenty years, and is in accordance with the report of the Royal Commission on the Monetary and Banking Systems (1937). We may regard it as one more indication of growing maturity or of movement toward a planned economy in Australia.

CHAPTER XI

Australia and the World Economy

BY E. RONALD WALKER

THE WORLD ECONOMY against which Australia's development must be studied is limited in time to the era since the American Revolution. It is the world economy that grew from the flowering of free enterprise and the progressive mechanisation of industry and agriculture; from the displacement of mercantilism by the free market; from the establishment of the gold standard and an international currency system; from the achievement of sufficient political security to permit the development of international investment on a large scale. It is a world economy that appears, since 1914, to have begun to disintegrate again, into a number of politico-regional groups, walled off from each other by trade barriers, foreign-exchange controls, and restrictions on migration. Each group is held together by political ties, economic interdependence, and some common social philosophies. This economic disintegration has been represented as but an aspect of the breakdown of the international political order of the nineteenth century.

At the present time, when the reëstablishment of a stable international political order appears to be the most urgent task confronting humanity, there is a natural tendency to assume that this requires also the reëstablishment of a world economy, integrated as before through trade and financial relationships, and free from discriminatory restrictions. At the same time there are powerful forces in every country whose weight will be thrown in the direction of narrower, more easily controllable, markets. Australia's uneasiness over the probable American interpretation of "postwar international economic collaboration," as envisaged in the original lend-lease agreements and subsequent declarations, is symptomatic of this problem.

International trade in the relatively free world economy was broadly of two types, namely, exchange of radically different commodities between regions that were clearly economically complementary to each other, and exchange of a wide range of commodities between countries whose economic structures were not fundamentally dissimilar. The inevitability and desirability of the former type is more readily recognised. It is illustrated by "north-south trade"—the exchange of tropical products against the products of temperate zones; and by the trade relations between mature industrial countries and countries specialising in bulk production of foodstuffs and raw materials—the latter consisting both of newly settled countries and of industrially backward regions of the Old World.

But a surprisingly large part of the world's trade has consisted of the exchange of partly fabricated materials and finished manufactures between industrially mature countries. This second type of trade is based on differences (often small) in relative costs of production, differences in quality, or reputation and traditional consumer preference for products of a certain region. It is trade of this type that has presented the greatest challenge to economic theory.

Yet a fundamentally similar phenomenon is presented inside every mature industrial country. While there may be regional specialisation within each country, there is also diffusion of the manufacture of similar goods throughout the country, and, in the absence of monopolistic agreements, manufacturers' markets overlap so that different regions exchange almost identical goods. That the same sort of trade should be carried on across national frontiers is not inherently surprising, provided the frontiers do not themselves constitute serious obstacles to commerce. This was the essence of the system of world markets, with free convertibility of currencies, relatively low customs duties, and the absence of quantitative restrictions on trade.

Australian trade has hitherto been predominantly of the former type—the exchange of her primary products for manufactures and some tropical products. But as the population has expanded, and with the assistance of tariff protection, her own manufactures have developed to a stage of self-sufficiency in many lines. Now, as Australian steel begins to find a market in England, Australia's trade is beginning to contain items of the second type—the exchange of similar products between industrially mature countries. When this stage is reached, however, there is a strong temptation to seek self-sufficiency in still more manufactures, even if this involves a gradual withdrawal from the world economy.

Australia's participation in the world economy was initially through the United Kingdom, and British influence upon her trade has remained predominant. It was natural for British goods to accompany the British men and women who came to Australia in British ships, bringing British capital with them, and for the Australian colonies to spend in Great Britain a major part of loans floated there for developmental projects such as railway construction. Similarly, Britain was the natural market for Australian exports and encouraged the development of those products, such as wool, that met Britain's own needs for raw materials. As the network of world trade grew in extent and complexity, Australia's commercial relations became more diversified, though for long England still served as an entrepôt for much Australian merchandise that was eventually consumed in other countries.

Although the main economic task confronting the penal colony of New South Wales at first was to attain some degree of self-sufficiency, and to live off the land, it seemed only natural to hope that, as in the American colonies, some staple products would be discovered which could be exported in exchange for the necessary imports. The first commodity to be exported was coal. A small amount was loaded on a ship sailing to India in 1797; and a shipment was made to the Cape of Good Hope in 1801. But the development of mining was slow until after the middle of the nineteenth century, when the establishment of railways and the visits of steamships provided a regular market. The few local products exported in 1820 were carried in a single ship of 300 tons; and it was not until the 'thirties that the wool trade was firmly established, though the first commercial export was made in 1821, when the population of the colony was still only 35,500.

The Bank of New South Wales had opened in 1817, and the Bank of Australia in 1826. The prospect of higher interest rates, allowed in Van Diemen's Land in 1830 and in New South Wales in 1834, encouraged the establishment of several other banks in the 'thirties, at the time of Australia's first trade boom. This ended in 1841–1843, when Australia had her first trade crisis, provoked by the fall in British prices (wool, which sold at two shillings per pound in 1836, fell to one shilling and a penny in 1843) and by the interruption of British investment following England's financial difficulties of 1839. Wool remained the staple export, and by 1845 Australia had become the chief source of supplies for the British woollen industry. The 'forties saw the beginning of copper exports, and the first ship-ment of wheat, from South Australia; but Australia as a whole did not attain self-sufficiency in wheat until 1880, or a large export trade until the twentieth century. The first major gold discoveries in 1851 provided a spectacular competitor for wool, and gave a rapid impe-tus to immigration. Gold production and exportation carried Aus-tralia through the period of the American and British financial crises of 1857, so that they made little impact on the economic life of the colonies; but the petering out of this first gold rush fathered the development of protection for manufacturing industries in Victoria in 1864.

Wool continued to dominate the scene, but the 'eighties saw a gradual diversification of exports, along with heavy importations of capital and a land boom. There were expanding exports of copper, tin, silver, lead, and coal; and gold was still significant. In 1878 the first refrigerated cargo of Australian meat and butter reached Eng-land, opening up an important new line of trade. Australia had exported canned meat to the British Admiralty as early as 1843, and this product began to be known to the general public in Britain in the late 'sixties. Refrigeration was to stimulate not only the meat and butter trade, but also, later, a trade in fresh apples and pears. Exports of hides, skins, leather, and tallow also increased. Of this trade three-fourths was with the United Kingdom, one-twelfth with other British possessions, and only one-sixth with foreign countries. The establishment of French and German shipping lines in the 'eighties promised a wider diffusion of commercial contacts, but the economic link with the Mother Country was still extremely strong.

The crisis of 1893, ushered in by a fall in the prices of wool and wheat, and by temporary suspension of British lending, provided striking evidence of the vulnerability of the type of economy that Australia was developing—a vulnerability that was again demonstrated in 1929. The business and borrowing cycle ran somewhat as follows: Good prices for exports created good business conditions in the colonies, and buoyant public finances. The colonies became an attractive field for British investment, both in Australian pastoral and commercial undertakings and in colonial government stock. Some of this new money would be spent in the United Kingdom for capital equipment; the rest would go to swell the sterling balances of the Australian banks, which would take advantage of their improved liquidity to expand their advances in Australia. The proceeds from exports would also strengthen the sterling balances of the banks and provide a basis for further credit expansion. High incomes and prices in the colonies in due course attracted a flood of imports, which tended to run down the banks' sterling balances, except so far as further borrowing and continued good seasons and prices replenished them. A collapse of export prices or a suspension of oversea borrowing would lead not only to an immediate contraction of income and expenditures in Australia, but also to a sharp fall in the sterling balances of the Australian banks. This decline in their liquidity would lead to a contraction of credit, thereby reinforcing the initial decline in incomes and expenditure. The ensuing depression contained at least some of the seeds of recovery, for the decline in expenditure would check the flow of imports and ease the strain on the banks' sterling balances. Recovery would be hastened by any improvement in export prices or any new factors encouraging British investment. Gold discoveries in Western Australia assisted the recovery from the depression of the 'nineties, and were followed later by renewed importation of capital.

Federation brought, for the first time, an Australian trade policy in place of the diverse fiscal policies of the six Australian colonies. Overseas trade, along with defence, immigration, and external affairs, was among the subjects of legislation reserved to the Commonwealth Parliament. The protectionist policy of Victoria, in conflict with the low-tariff policy of the other states, had been described as "the lion in the path" of federation; but before long the Commonwealth found itself committed to protection as a settled national policy. The First World War strengthened the protectionist sentiment, not only by establishing some new manufactures, but also by emphasising the importance of industrial development in

relation to defence. Heavy immigration in the 'twenties lent support to the popular belief that expansion of manufactures was necessary to employ Australia's growing population. The depression
of the 'thirties necessitated a profound adjustment in the balance of
trade; overseas borrowing virtually ceased, and the prices of exports
fell severely in relation to import prices. Increased tariffs were
among the methods used to effect the necessary reduction in imports, and with recovery there was a substantial replacement of
imports by new Australian manufactures.

The depression had a more spectacular effect upon the world
economy, because less expected, than the war of 1914–1918. For
Australia, as for other countries relying heavily on international
trade, it concentrated attention on the disadvantages of dependence
upon world markets, and the possible embarrassments arising from
adherence to international monetary standards. It created an intellectual climate basically different from that in which countries
had struggled, in the immediate postwar years, to restore the gold
standard and to curb the inflationary potential of the credit system.

On the eve of the depression, Australia's exports amounted to
about one-third of the value of recorded production and provided
about one-fourth of her total national income. Her trade was now
more widely diffused than at the time of the crisis of 1893. The
United Kingdom was absorbing only about 45 per cent of Australia's exports, British possessions about 10 per cent, and foreign
countries about 45 per cent. The decline in Britain's share was
partly illusory, since it was due in part to the growth of direct buying of wool by European countries which had previously bought
Australian wool from Britain. More than 40 per cent of Britain's
merino wool imports was still reëxported. Australia's chief wool
markets, after Britain, were France, Germany, Belgium, the United
States, and Italy. Her wheat was going mostly to Britain, India,
Italy, Japan, Egypt, South Africa, and France. Beef was exported
mostly to the United Kingdom, Belgium, Germany, the Philippines,
and Egypt. A little mutton went to Canada, the Malay States, and
the United States, but most, again, to Britain. Italy rivalled Britain
as a customer for hides, with Germany and the United States also
in the picture. Thus Australia's markets were predominantly British
and European.

Australia's imports were still drawn mainly from the United Kingdom, but the growth of American industry and the industrialisation of Japan had produced a progressive diversification of Australia's sources of supply for manufactured goods. With the United States she had a consistently adverse balance of trade, and the dollars to cover her excess of imports from that country came from her favourable balance of trade with the rest of the world.

Financially, Australia was still closely linked with Britain. Apart from commercial investments in Australia, British investors had subscribed heavily to loans floated in London by the Commonwealth and state governments, especially in the period after 1920, when Australia was trying to link immigration with the importation of capital for development. During the 'twenties the governments were spending at the rate of £40,000,000 per annum or more on "loan works," and three-fourths of this money was raised in London, the rest in Australia. Loans were floated in New York for £47,000,000 (about $200,000,000), but these represented only 4 per cent of the national debt and 8 per cent of the external public debt in 1928–1929. On the eve of the depression the Australian government had been busy for some time examining projects for further developmental expenditures under an agreement with the United Kingdom government, which was prepared to pay a large part of the interest on developmental loans, provided that an appropriate number of immigrants was absorbed.

When Australia had reorganised the Commonwealth Bank into a central bank in 1924, she had turned to the Bank of England for advice; and as the financial outlook became precarious in 1930 it was natural to seek advice from the same source. Sir Otto Niemeyer visited Australia to consult with the government on the best methods of handling the situation created by a sharp fall in wool and wheat prices, and the virtual closing of the London money market to new Australian loans. Sir Otto's analysis of the situation was in terms of conventional financial principles, and ended with the observation that "in recent years Australian standards have been pushed too high relatively to Australian productivity and to general world conditions and tendencies; costs must come down." Britain had not yet encountered her own financial crisis, nor had Lord Keynes's *Treatise on Money* yet burst upon a startled world. Aus-

tralian political leaders were confronted by the dilemma of either
running counter to the international principles of sound finance,
or imposing on the Australian people a policy of deflation and wage
reductions.

In their first panic, the states and Commonwealth governments
agreed to balance all budgets, to raise no more loans overseas, and
to restrict loan expenditure from domestic sources to such works as
promised to yield revenue to cover the service of the debt. Most
academic economists advocated a simultaneous reduction in wages,
depreciation of the exchange rate, and expansion of central bank
credit to prevent further contraction of bank advances. The Commonwealth Arbitration Court implemented the first proposal; the
Bank of New South Wales broke away from the other banks and
implemented the second; and the inability of the governments to
balance their budgets implemented the third, to the discomfort of
the orthodox-minded Commonwealth Bank, which discounted their
treasury bills only under protest. The government also took direct
steps to "correct" the balance of trade by raising the tariff and imposing prohibitions and quantitative restrictions on luxury imports. Under the Premiers' Plan of 1931, all government salaries,
as well as rents and interest rates, were reduced, and the internal
public debt was converted to lower rates of interest, mostly on a
voluntary basis.

Throughout the whole period there were two outstanding issues
affecting Australia's attitude toward the world economy. One centred upon the Commonwealth's determination to meet all external
debt charges; and when the Labour Government of New South
Wales chose to default rather than impose the sacrifices which the
Premiers' Plan entailed for the wage- and salary-earner, the Commonwealth assumed responsibility for the service of the debt and
attached the state's revenues. This policy was endorsed by the state
electorate in the ensuing polls. The other issue was the extent to
which a relatively stable exchange rate should be maintained, as a
basis for participation in the world economy. Some sections of
opinion favoured deliberate exchange depreciation as an alternative to the deflationary features of the Premiers' Plan, even if
such a policy should involve Australia's virtual withdrawal from
the world economy.

The solution finally adopted was a curious but significant compromise. In January, 1931, with Britain still in gold, the freeing of the Australian exchange rate carried the London rate to £A131 to £stg100; when Britain left gold, the rate was officially pegged at £A125 to £stg100, and held there throughout all the vicissitudes of sterling. Thus the Australian pound was in fact depreciated still further in terms of all gold currencies, including the United States dollar, but the degree of depreciation was determined by the position of sterling in the world economy, rather than by the Australian balance of payments with the outside world.

Throughout the economic disturbances of the 'thirties and the accompanying growth of international political insecurity, Australia's economic links with the Mother Country were strengthened. She participated in the Ottawa Agreements, receiving greater preference in British markets and giving in exchange not only preferential tariff rates to Britain, but also access for British manufacturers to the Australian Tariff Board when particular applications for protection were being considered. In 1936 she introduced a new trade-diversion policy under which an import licencing system on a wide range of goods was expected to divert purchases from foreign countries (especially from Japan and the United States) to the United Kingdom, as well as perhaps lending some additional protection to Australian manufacturing industries. This policy, which brought prompt retaliation from America and Japan, was abandoned in 1938, although a quota system was retained for automobile chassis from countries other than the United Kingdom.

In the period from the depths of the depression (1932) to the outbreak of war there was considerable development of manufactures in replacement of predepression imports. The depression had produced an apparently permanent shift in the conditions affecting the degree of industrial self-sufficiency. In the first place, the abandonment of the policy of borrowing overseas at a rate equivalent to about 5 per cent per annum of the national income implied doing without imports to that extent. Secondly, the comparatively greater fall in export prices as compared with import prices implied a decline in the advantage to be gained by specialising in export production of raw materials and foodstuffs for exchange against imported manufactures; in other words, in view of the deterioration of the terms on which international trade could be conducted, it was to Australia's advantage to produce a larger proportion of her requirements of manufactured goods. Thirdly, the continued growth of population and the gradual maturing of technical competence were diminishing Australia's relative disadvantage as a manufacturing country. Consequently, on the eve of the Second World War the value of output of manufactures was almost double the value in 1919; and more than a third of Australian breadwinners were employed in factories and construction industries. Imports were valued at £99,000,000 sterling in 1938–1939, as compared with £143,000,000 sterling in 1928–1929 (about $385,000,000 as compared with $675,000,000 at the exchange rates ruling in each year). The primary industries were increasingly concerned over the problem of markets, while the conception of national development had come to be increasingly associated with so-called secondary industries.

During the war, overseas trade and external financial transactions were brought under strict control, as in all belligerent countries. All foreign-exchange dealings were supervised by the Commonwealth Bank, and all commercial imports came to be under licence, while a substantial part of the total import trade, especially after the entry of Japan, consisted of goods secured from the United States and Canada under lend-lease and mutual aid. The export trade was conducted largely by the government, which acquired all wool, wheat, and several other crops, and the export surplus of meat, dairy products, and most minerals, for sale to the United Kingdom under exclusive contracts. Later reverse lend-lease to the United States also rose to a huge figure (£A223,000,000 by December, 1944, as compared with lend-lease imports of £A303,000,000 up to January, 1945). The abnormal nature of wartime trade is illustrated by the fact that imports of civilian goods were stabilised at about £80,000,000 sterling, or four-fifths the prewar level (money values, which included a large element of price inflation), while imports of war supplies in 1943–1944 were about £130,000,000 sterling. Imports of civil goods from the United Kingdom had fallen to 53 per cent of the prewar figure, and from the United States had risen to 177 per cent of prewar. India, too, had grown in importance as a source of imports. Of war supplies imported in 1943–1944, about 60 per cent came from the United States and only 25 per cent from the

United Kingdom. One consequence of the war, which may be of lasting significance, was that many Australian importers who previously had looked primarily to Britain as a source of supply had to establish contacts with American firms; and many American manufacturers were introduced to Australian customers for the first time.

Of special significance, too, was Australia's wartime experience in trying to plan her trade as a whole, as contrasted with the peacetime development of protectionist measures designed to assist particular industries. Australia had not succeeded, by the end of the war, in fully integrating her export controls with the regulation of imports, since exports and imports were still managed by separate government departments, under different ministers. But the war had demonstrated, far more convincingly than any economist's textbook, the true nature of international trade, as the exchange of easily produced goods for those that would be costly in terms of productive resources if made within the country. And the planning of trade, from the viewpoint of a common national goal, was no longer an unfamiliar notion.

The end of the war found protectionist sentiment more strongly entrenched than ever. Australia's industrial war effort had been impressive, covering a wide range of weapons, machinery, and explosives. The foundation had been laid, behind the tariff wall, by the development of steel, metal manufactures, textiles, and chemicals. The achievements of Australia's secondary industries were a source of national pride almost as great as the deeds of her fighting men, if not greater. They had bred a technological self-confidence— a sometimes exaggerated belief that Australia could make almost anything. With Australian steel now the cheapest in the world (so far as the simpler forms were concerned), it was natural to expect that the postwar period would bring a further wave of industrial development, even if the heavy-metal industries themselves must contract to a peacetime pattern. Moreover, the Australian Labour Government, which had weathered the storm of the Pacific war, was pledged to a postwar policy of full employment; and in view of the relatively small numbers of workers needed for rural industries, and the uncertainties of their world markets, the retention of wartime advances in manufacturing seemed an essential part of a full-employment programme. If the peacetime home market could not support all the manufactures that had sprung up to meet the needs of war, some of them, at least, would find markets overseas. Australian industries and the government were thinking, as early as 1944, of an export trade in manufactured goods after the war.

The full implications of such aspirations were probably not widely understood. In the Ministry of Post-War Reconstruction, the Secondary Industries Commission and the Rural Reconstruction Commission may have worked side by side, but not hand in hand. There was little evidence, in the latter months of the war, of a plan for the future development of the national economy as a whole, against the background of a world economy which clearly expected Australia to continue buying manufactured goods and selling raw materials and foodstuffs.

Mr. Colin Clark, in his *Economics of 1960,* had predicted that the terms of trade would swing so far in favour of raw materials and foodstuffs after the war that Australia, if she chose, could raise her standards of living appreciably by concentrating on primary production for export, importing more of her manufactured goods, and transferring her displaced workers into tertiary production, that is, the service trades, which must expand with increasing prosperity. But Mr. Clark's predictions rested on the assumption of a rapid industrialisation of the Far East, and in any event were not congenial to the mental attitudes developed by Australia's wartime industrial achievements.

Public opinion was more concerned over the extent to which Australia's liberty of action in the field of industrial development might be restricted by political pressures from the great powers. In particular, manufacturers were uneasy over the possible implications of Article VII of the Mutual Aid Agreement, which bound Australia to consult with other participants upon measures to reduce tariffs and other trade barriers.

In the various international discussions of postwar international economic collaboration, Australian government representatives consistently pressed the view that "the objectives of the Atlantic Charter can best be attained by attaching primary and indeed supreme importance to the adoption of measures to promote full employment, and increased production and consumption of goods. . . . The maintenance of a high level of employment throughout the world would undoubtedly have a beneficial effect in increasing trade, production and consumption, and so in preventing recourse to methods associated with extreme economic nationalism" (Dr. H. V. Evatt, Minister for External Affairs, announcing Australia's Mutual Aid Agreement with Canada, in 1943). This sustained campaign led to the inclusion, in virtually every international instrument, even in the United Nations Charter itself, of a reference to the desirability of achieving full employment, and it undoubtedly helped to mobilise a body of opinion that will influence economic policy in many countries. Up to the time of writing, however, Australia had failed to win the support of the great powers for a special international agreement to promote full employment; and the government had been correspondingly lukewarm toward the Bretton Woods proposals and toward any general scaling down of tariffs, though it eventually joined in the former and, at Geneva, entered into negotiations looking toward the latter.

Australia's future rôle in the world economy, however, may depend less on the present aspirations of her manufacturers than on the success achieved by the great powers in political and economic collaboration among themselves. Australia still has very strong sentimental and economic ties with Britain. Every element of international political insecurity in the postwar world will not only encourage Australian efforts toward self-sufficiency, but also concentrate her external trade upon Britain and the Empire. On the other hand, if Britain must buy her security and stability at the cost of her "imperial trading system," as Americans call it, Australia would probably conform to the general policy of the Empire.

CHAPTER XII

Primary Industries in the Economy

BY J. G. CRAWFORD

UNTIL 1930 the story of Australia's primary industries was one of development and expansion. In the early nineteenth century, agriculture for the subsistence of the colonies was fostered, and the gold discoveries in the middle decades greatly encouraged local agriculture. Wool, the first industry to develop significantly for export, was the mainstay of Australia's overseas economic relations until the period 1880–1930, during which there was a general expansion and development of agricultural industries for export markets. Closer settlement became the established policy of Australian governments—a policy which reached its peak in the last decade of the period. Both for soldiers and for immigrants, settlement on Crown lands and on resumed and subdivided estates was greatly stimulated. The full effect on production was experienced in the 'thirties, a decade of great difficulty for Australian primary industries.

Throughout the period of development, land was relatively plentiful. The time had not yet arrived, in spite of several disastrous droughts and at least two economic depressions (the 'nineties and the early 'twenties), to worry overmuch about the limits set by physical factors: soils, climate, and topography; or the economic factors: capital supply and markets. The high prices after the First World War obscured the warning signs; and even the phrase "men, money, and markets," used by Mr. S. M. Bruce as Prime Minister in 1926, was so interpreted that, given the men and capital, Australia's land resources could be safely developed without worrying about markets. Had not these always followed production? At least so it seemed until the events of 1930 to 1939 necessitated a general stocktaking.

The estimate was not limited in interest and concern to primary producers. It was no longer true that the Australian economy "rode on the sheep's back"; nevertheless, Australia's capacity to import depended predominantly on successful exports of its agricultural and pastoral products. Within Australia the majority of incomes came from nonrural occupations; yet none was safe from the repercussions of fluctuations in the prices and volume of primary exports. So-called scarcity economics (e.g., production control to raise prices) made some headway, but certain new ideas, such as the "marriage of health and agriculture," also struggled for recognition. That the fortunes of agriculture were bound up with prosperous industrial communities at home and abroad was not yet fully recognised. "Full employment" as a slogan belonged to the next decade.

While producers and governments worried about ways and means of introducing economic stability into the rural economy, they also began to realise that not all the primary industries were the last word in efficiency (despite important technological advances and a very high output per man engaged), that marginal areas must be contracted, and, not least important, that physical limits were very real, requiring a new emphasis on conservation rather than exploitation of limited resources.

The war period produced problems of its own, but it also demonstrated how important were higher levels of living for the welfare of primary producers. The end of the war with its great food shortages immediately posed again all the questions raised in 1918 and answered then so optimistically in Australia. There is more concern about policies of soldier settlement this time, but many are now asking, Why the caution? A new period of expansion for primary production is surely indicated? The answer is likely to lie in moderate expansion within the limits set by measurable factors: physical resources and long-term market prospects, but with greater recognition of the fact that Australia must carefully conserve its usable land and pay more attention to the efficiency of its farm practices.

In any country the capacity of farmers to produce is determined mainly by the quality and quantity of their physical resources, the methods of farming in general use (especially in relation to farm size), and a number of factors, usually summed up as economic, which are on the whole beyond the control of farmers.

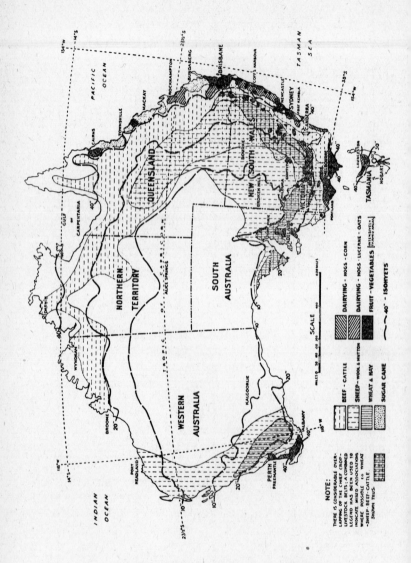

Fig. 1—The chief crop and livestock belts of Australia.

The importance of geographic limits on the development of Australia's primary industry has been indicated in chapter 1 by Professor J. Macdonald Holmes. The influence of rainfall, water supply, latitude, and topography is summed up in the land-use map (see p. 8). The use of the land, with its remarkable and necessary emphasis on settlement on coastal and adjacent areas, can be explained logically and in a manner which in no major sense reflects adversely on the historical achievements of a young nation.

Rainfall is the predominant influence. Average annual rainfall is the first control, but no less important are seasonal incidence and reliability. Considered in relation to temperatures, topography, and soil type, the character of rainfall clearly determines the pattern of settlement. The pattern set by physical controls may be modified. For example, irrigation may offset low rainfall (but not soil factors), as in the Murray River basin, the only important irrigation area in Australia. Improved communications and special crop varieties have pushed agriculture into the 10–15-inch rainfall belt in the southeast and southwest, the marginal areas referred to later.

To some degree, too, public policy can offset economic limits. Thus tropical agriculture with white labour in Queensland, especially sugar production, has been developed because the Australian community as a whole is prepared to meet the economic cost. In the future, the development of the northern areas of Western Australia as well as of the Northern Territory may proceed on a similar basis.

Land-use controls are thus not limited to physical factors. Institutional factors are also important. Other public activities which have influenced the pattern of settlement include land-settlement laws which have undoubtedly facilitated the development of agriculture at the expense of large-scale grazing in the safer rainfall areas. Yet most of these public policies are in line with the possibilities of production which are presented by natural resources and market outlets rather than defiant of the limits imposed by natural and economic forces.

The combination of various forces is pictured in charts 1 and 2 and in the land-use map. They illustrate the relative importance of the major groups of industries, the general trend of development in

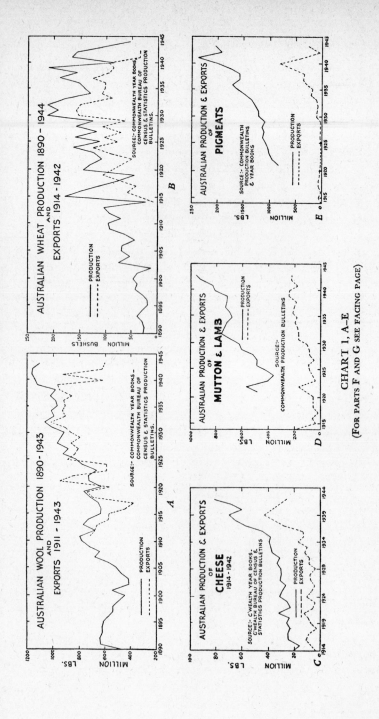

CHART 1, A–E

(FOR PARTS F AND G SEE FACING PAGE)

the production of several commodities, and the great significance of export trade in many instances. It will be seen that in terms of net value of production (roughly the income at the farm available for owners, workers, and creditors) the order of importance is pastoral (mainly wool, beef and sheep meats), agricultural (wheat and fruits), and dairying (butter and milk). In employment terms, however, dairying is more important than the pastoral group, though

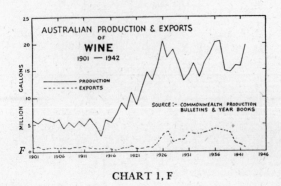

CHART 1, F

CHART 1, G

the basis of classification, which excludes mixed farming as a group, is somewhat deceptive in this respect. The most closely settled areas are in the irrigation settlements in three states along the Murray River and three of its tributaries—the Murrumbidgee River in New South Wales and the Goulburn and Loddon rivers in Victoria.

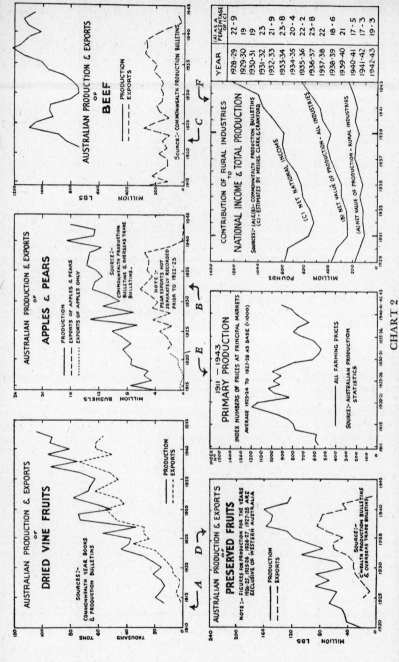

CHART 2

For the most part the future development of farming must take the form of more intensive treatment of areas already settled in the east, the southeast, and the southwest. This will mean in some industries an increase in the ratio of capital to land, the latter hitherto being the "extensive" factor.[1] Development within these physical controls will, however, be determined principally by economic conditions. Australian production is substantially greater than the needs of the local population, so that the living standards of farmers are closely bound up with their ability to maintain and develop overseas markets at satisfactory prices. This was the essence of the problem of the prewar decade and the major factor in the stock-taking which was begun in that period and is not yet completed.

If this chapter seems to deal mainly with problems experienced and policies evolved in the prewar decade (1930–1939), it is because it was in this period that a new rural policy became necessary. This decade, opened by the Great Depression, brought an end to the policy of continuous expansion by new settlement. Australian experience in the 'thirties was not unique: it was much the same as that of Canada and the United States. Market restrictions and low prices were apparently the results of the depression, but the depression was far from being the whole story. Accordingly, it is important to look at the picture closely, as the present trend in policies, though not devoid of the expansionist attitude which prevailed before the 'thirties, is markedly influenced by the experience of the ten years in question.

In 1939 the economy had, for the most part, recovered from depression levels. Even so, in the rural sector there was ample evidence of maladjustment which had not been overcome by the legislative measures adopted as a result of the depression. It was apparent that the rural economy was not able, without increased government aid,

---

[1] Australian agriculture is extensive, i.e., commercial, based on holdings which are large in land size compared with European standards. Unfortunately, statistical data are inadequate: the only figures available refer to the average size of all alienated holdings in use, whether for market gardening or huge pastoral stations or ranches. The typical size in each industry is not available, and caution should be exercised in comparing averages for all holdings. Thus the average size in Victoria is 560 acres, compared with 8,050 acres in Queensland, the latter figure reflecting very large grazing holdings in the semiarid southwest and the tropical cattle stations of the centre and north. (See *Commonwealth Yearbook*, 1941, p. 532.)

to maintain all the farmers and farm workers (about 550,000 on some 250,000 holdings) at living standards broadly comparable with those of urban dwellers. In crude statistical terms, farm bread-winners were about 21 per cent of the total breadwinners in the decade ending in 1939, but their share of the national income averaged only 17–18 per cent and fluctuated widely. In real terms, it was evident that better facilities for education, higher housing standards, wider recreational opportunities, and more abundant social services were available to the urban dweller than to farm dwellers. Some rural industries fared better than others. The general descending order of prosperity was probably grazing, agriculture (including orcharding), and dairying.

There were the usual direct evidences of instability throughout the rural economy. Average prices received for farm products declined in the ten-year period ending in 1938–1939, compared with the level for the previous decade (see chart 2E), but there was no commensurate fall in costs, even over the decade. Perhaps the clearest symptom of a difficult situation was an increase in rural indebtedness of 20–25 per cent between 1927 and 1939, in spite of substantial progress in some states with debt-adjustment programmes.

Behind the symptoms of maladjustment lay the causes, which were more serious and persistent than the immediate cause, the Great Depression. They were to be found in the decreased rate of growth in European and Western Hemisphere populations; tariff protection in European countries striving for self-sufficiency; low living standards in Asia, where markets were negligible in spite of large populations; and mass "underemployment" in Britain and the United States, where many were continually underfed and poorly clothed, whereas other millions suffered in peak unemployment periods. Not least disturbing was the revelation in Australia itself of the importance of the general level of employment and incomes for the farmers' home market. The average annual consumption of beef per person in Australia increased from 93 lbs. in 1931–1932, a year of high unemployment, to 140 lbs. in 1938–1939. The equivalent change in butter consumption was from 28.9 lbs. to 33.9 lbs. Exports rose in the same period, and it was observed that in the more prosperous years the consumer both abroad and at home was able and willing to pay more reasonable prices to the farmer.

While the conditions of demand for the farm products were unfavourable in themselves, they became the more difficult because ability to supply products reached its peak in the same decade. A glance at the accompanying charts will show that for some primary industries the decade marked a period of development appreciably greater than anything that had taken place previously. For the most part it reflected the intense settlement activity of the 'twenties. Also important were the development of new and improved pastures (e.g., clovers in the southeast) and more efficient methods of production. Slaughtering rose substantially, butter output advanced from 300,000,000 lbs. to 430,000,000 lbs., and the output of citrus fruit increased from 4,000,000 to 5,000,000 bu.

Besides a greater volume of production because of expanding acreage and, to a lesser extent, intensification of production, the output per man was continuously increasing. This phenomenon has been more marked for the primary industries as a whole than in the output per area or animal unit. Increased productivity per man in the twenty-five years ending in 1940–1941, as estimated by Miss B. Appleton, was 60–70 per cent for all primary industries, with somewhat less than average for pastoral, and up to 100 per cent for agricultural pursuits, basing the calculations on moving averages of indices of annual production and permanent lands engaged in primary industries. These figures reflect more efficient utilisation of labour and, more especially, the marked growth of mechanisation of farming. Under these conditions and in the face of restricted markets, primary industries have not offered employment commensurate with increasing output. Whereas actual numbers engaged in farming increased from 450,000 to 550,000, or 22 per cent from 1911 to 1933, farm output increased by 50 per cent in the same period. Farm employment in this period declined in relative importance, from 25 per cent of the total breadwinners in 1911 to about 20 per cent in 1939. The usual concomitants of economic progress were evident: fewer people were required to feed a given population and nonrural employment increased in relative importance. Hence export market restrictions assumed special importance, threatening a need for transferring resources from primary to nonprimary industries at a faster rate than could be managed without economic distress among rural populations. (See chart 3.)

1.

PERCENTAGE DISTRIBUTION OF AUSTRALIAN BREADWINNERS BETWEEN VARIOUS TYPES OF INDUSTRIES. (CENSUS 1933)

OTHER ACTIVITIES

RURAL TRANSPORT 3

RURAL INDUSTRIES

DIRECT PROCESSING OF RURAL PRODUCTS

21

2

33 SECONDARY INDUSTRIES

41

5

OTHER BREADWINNERS

SOURCE:- RURAL RECONSTRUCTION COMMISSION – FIRST REPORT

2.

APPROXIMATE DISTRIBUTION OF FARM & FORREST BREADWINNERS AMONG SPECIFIC TYPES OF INDUSTRY (CENSUS 1933)

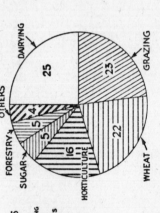

DAIRYING

OTHERS

FORESTRY

SUGAR

25

4

5

5

16

HORTICULTURE

22

WHEAT

23

GRAZING

SOURCE:- RURAL RECONSTRUCTION COMMISSION – FIRST REPORT

3.

NET VALUE OF PRODUCTION FOR ALL RECORDED INDUSTRIES: AUSTRALIA

(NOTE:- DEPRECIATION & MAINTENANCE COSTS HAVE NOT BEEN DEDUCTED)

AVERAGE FOR FIVE YEAR PERIOD ENDED 1940-41

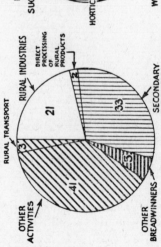

AGRICULTURE

PASTORAL

12·6

18·5

7·8 DAIRYING

1·6 POULTRY & BEE-FARMING

6·6

MINING

FORESTRY

FACTORIES

50

TRAPPING & FISHERIES

SOURCE:- PRODUCTION BULLETINS, &, COMMONWEALTH BUREAU OF CENSUS & STATISTICS

CHART 3

Although born of reaction to world economic depression, the Ottawa Agreement of 1932 proved more than a defence against insecurity for Australian exports; it has, in fact, assisted the expansion of the fruit industries, especially for canning, drying, and winemaking. Under the Agreement, Australia gained preferential advantages in the United Kingdom for meat, dairying, and fruit and wine industries. The last group, though small in total importance, probably benefited most, having secured preferences also in the Dominions of Canada and New Zealand, and would now be placed in a difficult position should preference be modified substantially. Preference was not unimportant for the other commodities and did assist in softening the sharp edge of depression. Wool and wheat are so dependent on non-Empire markets that preference (even though secured for wheat) could not be an important factor. Moreover, the main wool-producers for the British market are the Dominions themselves. On the whole, even if preferential tariffs were to be continued, Australia must look elsewhere than the United Kingdom for any great expansion of its markets, except for gains that will result if a full-employment policy is effectively sustained.

Besides entering the Ottawa Agreement, Australia depreciated its rate of exchange on London, thus affording relief to primary producers, who now received £125 Australian for every £100 sterling.

Special attention was paid to home markets because of the low prices ruling in export markets. Two price schemes had come into being before 1930, but they were greatly extended after that date. The usual policy was, behind an appropriate import tariff, to fix home consumption prices at a level rather higher than the ruling export prices, so that the average return to producers would give a more reasonable return in relation to average costs of production. Such an arrangement had been made, first, for the sugar industry, and similar arrangements followed for dairy produce, dried vine fruits, and wheat. The schemes were not without difficulties. The tendency was for the improved prices to attract new producers into the industry and to encourage existing producers to expand their output, thus raising the ratio of exports (at the lower prices) to the relatively fixed levels of home consumption. Consequently the possibility of production control was seriously considered. However, because of the lack of constitutional power over production by the

Commonwealth and the difficulty of securing agreement among the states, little was achieved except in wartime, when Commonwealth defence powers were adequate for the purpose.

Constitutional difficulties were met also in establishing home consumption prices. Neither the Commonwealth nor the states can legislate against free trade in commodities between states, and Commonwealth legislative efforts to do so were successfully challenged. In spite of this, the schemes for butter and dried vine fruits have continued successfully on a voluntary basis. The constitutional basis of the wheat scheme has been rather different and it has not been challenged.

Apart from the forms of assistance outlined above, both Commonwealth and state governments made available substantial sums to primary producers, much of which went to wheat-growers. A comprehensive scheme of debt adjustment was introduced in 1934, the Commonwealth providing funds (£9,500,000 up to 1942–1943) for states to use under legislation designed to meet the needs of each state.

Besides direct financial assistance by way of bounties to the wheat industry, steps were taken by the states, with Commonwealth aid, to reduce wheat-growing in marginal areas. These areas were mainly in the semiarid belt of unreliable rainfall and soil-drifting.

The Second World War intervened before the various policies of the 'thirties could be tested for their long-run soundness. Whether sound or not, they were piecemeal reactions to the pressure of events; there had yet to be evolved a coherent national policy. It was recognised that marketing legislation, debt adjustment, reconstruction of marginal areas, and provision of rural amenities should fit into a national pattern. Not least encouraging was the wider understanding that conservation of soil, water, timber, and natural pastures was vital to the future stability of Australian primary industries. To the need for conservation was added a recognition that the results of technical and economic research could be more effectively applied in the interests of greater efficiency. Research by state departments and by the Commonwealth Council for Scientific and Industrial Research (the largest single research agency in the Commonwealth) was producing results in experimental stations and laboratories but not sufficiently on farms, primarily for lack of adequate extension services and sometimes for lack of appropriate economic assistance to farmers.

All these were recognised as important elements in agricultural policy, but many doubted their adequacy as a permanent solution of the problems of rural economy. Preferences, exchange depreciation, and two price schemes assisted all industries in some degree, and dairying perhaps the most, with wool benefiting only from exchange depreciation. Conservation and research to promote increased competitive efficiency were essential, but would any of these measures prevent a decline in primary production in the absence of expanding markets based on growing populations, freer world trade, and higher levels of employment and income? The advent of war temporarily lessened the urgency of the question. Nevertheless, there was a general, though frequently reluctant, admission that an Australian agricultural policy must be formulated within the framework of measurable physical resources, on the one hand, and manifest (if not always measurable) economic forces, on the other.

There was also a recognition that rural policy was no longer a matter of independent and separate actions by the six states and the Commonwealth. Under the Constitution the latter controlled exports and had established export marketing boards, but did not control domestic marketing. The states had powers over production and over most phases of marketing within their borders. In the face of prevailing conditions, and in the light of the division of constitutional powers, machinery for coöperation between Commonwealth and state was imperative, and the formation of the Australian Agricultural Council, in December, 1934, was a decided advance.

The Council is a permanent organisation which has functioned continuously since its formation. It comprises the Commonwealth Minister for Commerce and Agriculture and the Minister for Agriculture in each state. Its functions are wide enough to cover all phases of rural policy.[2] The Council is assisted by a permanent Standing Committee on Agriculture which consists of the permanent heads of the state departments of agriculture and of representatives of the Commonwealth departments concerned with the agenda. The Council and the Standing Committee have done a

[2]For a detailed statement of functions, see *Official Yearbook of the Commonwealth of Australia*, 1941, p. 472.

great deal to coördinate the legislative, administrative, and research activities of the Commonwealth and the states. The success of the machinery in securing wartime coöperation was a hopeful augury for its now-accepted rôle in the formulation and administration of a national rural policy.

The war brought a number of important changes in Australian agriculture, particularly after the entry of Japan. In the earlier years a number of industries, including canned fruits, apples, pears, eggs, and meat, were adversely affected by export shipping restrictions. Wool would have suffered heavily but for the United Kingdom contract to purchase the entire clip for the duration of the war and one year after at a price higher than prewar levels.

With the extension of the war to the Pacific, there were large special demands for foodstuffs for the Australian and Allied services, and the acreage under crops of intensive cultivation was increased heavily. The acreage under potatoes and other vegetables rose from 215,000 acres in 1938–1939 to 476,000 acres in 1944–1945. Production of eggs increased from a prewar average of about 60,-000,000 dozen to 105,000,000 dozen, and the output of pig meats increased from 87,000 tons in 1938–1939 to 130,000 in 1944. Acreage under flax expanded from a prewar figure of about 2,000 acres up to 60,000 acres in 1944–1945. Processing (canning and dehydration) of meat and vegetables made phenomenal advances in comparison with prewar levels.

Increases in production were attained in spite of heavy depletion of the rural labour force amounting to 25–30 per cent of the prewar figures. The reason for the success in stimulating production lay mainly in the Commonwealth policy of issuing contracts for a great part of the required production and of providing guaranteed prices for other commodities. This action was supported by the announcement of production goals for the major primary products, these goals being allocated between states and, in some instances, local producing areas. The organisation of production was assisted by district war agricultural committees, which were financed by the Commonwealth and controlled by state departments of agriculture.

In view of the over-all shortage of labour in rural industries during the war and the heavy expansion achieved, it is hardly surprising that production of some other commodities declined, owing to shortage of fertiliser (used extensively by most Australian primary industries), shortage of labour, and, to some degree, shortages of machinery and materials. Because of the scarcity of resources it was necessary to establish priorities for labour and fertiliser, and this also militated against production in certain industries. Moreover, for a time the heavy surpluses of wheat, wine, apples, and pears brought these commodities within the category of restricted production.

One of the heaviest declines in production occurred in the wheat industry, where 14,300,000 acres were sown in 1938–1939 and only 7,900,000 acres in 1943–1944. Despite heavy subsidies to price, the dairying industry also declined, mainly because of successive bad seasons. It was affected also by competition for resources from crops for which high wartime prices were being paid. The sugar industry declined in production from 820,000 tons in 1938–1939 to 507,000 tons in 1943–1944, owing principally to shortage of fertiliser and harvesting labour. Other industries which declined were tobacco, cotton, barley, and maize. In all the major industries the shortage of labour has meant that arrears of farm maintenance accumulated, thus handicapping their competitive position in the postwar period.

The cessation of hostilities sharply emphasised the matter of future policy for some industries. Those producing only for the home market (e.g., potatoes and other vegetables) faced immediate contraction with the decline of service demands. For others the question was less urgent (except in terms of soldier settlement), since long-term contracts with the United Kingdom covered exportable surpluses up to June, 1948, for eggs, dairy produce, and meats. For dried fruits the market was assured at least for a similar period; for wheat the short-term view was similarly reassuring for the producer who was encouraged to produce the maximum in 1946.

While the stress throughout the war was on production for war needs, certain pointers for future policy received remarkable emphasis. It was clear that consumers, enjoying high incomes, were anxious to purchase more and better foodstuffs—and did so when supplies were plentiful. On the other hand, there was a striking warning to Australia of the dangers of wasting resources. Bad seasons culminated in 1944–1945 in drought and dust-storms—signifying wasting soils, often through overstocking and inadequate water conservation. The loss of 20,000,000–30,000,000 sheep was a blow to the war effort, and it was more—a sharp reminder to Australians that their land-use policy required review.

Finally, it may be noted that the stress of war gave emphasis to methods resulting in increased output per man. It is doubtful whether agriculture, which has become more and more mechanised, can reabsorb directly on farms all the labour force lost during the war without a greater increase in markets than is anticipated. In any event, the extension of wage regulation to an increasing number of rural industries may further limit the possibilities for direct farm employment. This has been the experience of the dairy-industry wage award. The fact is not an argument against awards, but rather suggests the need for developing employment opportunities off the farms, including the service occupations which are important to farming activities.

There are important signs—in actual legislation as well as in public statements—that future policy is to be based on active international collaboration to promote an expanding world economy, as well as on the need to conserve and utilise Australia's limited natural resources more efficiently. In effect this means a policy of moderate expansion of production tempered by a more careful assessment of physical and economic forces than was evident before 1930.

Australia has given ample evidence at various international assemblies, beginning with the League of Nations Assembly in 1935, of her belief that primary producers and consumers have a common interest in policies designed to promote higher levels of employment and living. Prosperous economies in the United Kingdom and in the United States are particularly vital to Australia's export industries. The economic development of so-called backward areas is likewise important, as is a prosperous home market. It is in regard to the latter that one of the major dilemmas in Australian rural policy threatens to arise. Domestically, effective full-employment policies are likely to be associated with higher industrial and rural wages, with consequent direct and indirect effects on the cost-structure of primary industries. In these circumstances the competitive position of export industries will be made worse unless measures to make primary industry more efficient are successful and, at the same time, employment policies abroad are favourable to prices somewhat higher than the prewar levels.

A successful rural policy requires more than the prosecution of general employment policies, important though they are. There is an increased awareness of the importance of research and extension work, the latter service having been particularly inadequate before the war. All branches of research are being expanded, but three in particular should be mentioned. The first is a Wool Research Trust Account into which the Commonwealth Government pays funds—matching pound for pound a wool tax paid by growers and used mainly for publicity—to foster all phases of research into the wool industry. The Government contribution, some £300,000 per annum, will, it is hoped, by facilitating large-scale research, enable wool to compete with its many synthetic rivals.

The second development is in agricultural economics, hitherto markedly neglected. The Bureau of Agricultural Economics, with the aid of state departments, will help to fill the gap. Its functions, on a much more modest scale, are broadly comparable with those of the United States Bureau of Agriculture. Not the least important of its tasks, from the viewpoint of administrators and farmers, is the issuing of annual economic-outlook statements based on its investigations of economic factors in each industry. The third development, following hard on successful work in the State of New South Wales and the recent droughts, is the establishment of a joint Commonwealth and states Soil Conservation Service.

On the side of economic security it is already evident that, in spite of constitutional difficulties, efforts will be made to stabilise prices and farm incomes. The various two-price schemes already established will not be lightly abandoned, and a new price stabilisation scheme is being established for the wheat industry. A minimum price will be maintained by paying into a reserve fund a part of any excess of actual export prices over the guaranteed price. The reserve will be supplemented by Commonwealth Government funds as necessary. Production control will be exercised if unmanageable surpluses threaten. For wool—an industry in which large surpluses have accumulated—a British Commonwealth disposal scheme will operate under, and a floor will be placed under, auction prices each season.

There is a danger, recognised but not yet resolved, in all the price-control measures. If they are fixed solely to ensure high incomes, the incentive to greater efficiency is weakened and thereby defeats efforts in other directions.

Direct measures to promote rural welfare are under consideration. Although farming may have advantages as a way of life, in practice they are greatly reduced (except in very closely settled areas) by inadequate amenities. Even with parity in incomes, problems of distance and sparseness of settlement make it difficult, except as part of a national policy, to provide adequate health and educational services, housing, and recreational opportunities.

All these matters have received varying degrees of expression in the war service land-settlement policies. There must be economic prospects for the industries to be expanded—a matter which the Bureau of Agricultural Economics is required to investigate. The Bureau, in its analyses of land-settlement proposals, must also ensure that the level of farming efficiency gives promise of being equal to, or better than, the average efficiency ruling in the industries concerned. Subject to these tests, efforts must be made to ensure for the settler opportunities for a comfortable living.

All told, there are signs of a coherent national rural policy as contrasted with the admittedly *ad hoc* miscellany of policy items of the prewar period. The newer policy may be outlined as follows:

I. Objectives
   1. To raise and make more secure the levels of living enjoyed by those dependent on primary industries.
   2. To conserve and use agricultural resources in a way that recognises the change from exploitation to careful development and sound husbandry.

II. Content of Policy
   1. A general economic policy—domestic and international—which will give the primary industries a basis for further development.
   2. Measures to conserve resources.
   3. Efforts by legislation, research, and educational services to promote more efficient farm practices so as to reduce costs per unit of output.
   4. Measures to promote the stabilisation and security of farm income.
   5. Action designed directly to promote farm living standards.

This summary of recent and likely policy developments is admittedly a rationalisation. It is the author's interpretation of the nation's reaction to the recent history of its agricultural development. Conflicts are evident and dilemmas many. It is reasonable to argue, however, that a national policy is developing which combines hopefulness for the future with the realism imposed by the experience of the 'thirties. The Australian economy is a mature economy in the sense that secondary and tertiary forms of employment have increased in importance relative to primary industries. Secondary industries will almost certainly play a larger part in export than hitherto. Nevertheless, it is to efficient primary industries that the country will continue to look for the principal means of importing capital goods and specialist consumers' articles of the kind associated with a general economic policy directed to full development and employment of the nation's resources.

CHAPTER XIII

Secondary Industries in the Economy

BY BRIAN FITZPATRICK

GREAT FAMILY FORTUNES in Australia, reflecting the time of the exploitation of the chief sources of wealth, have usually been gained from primary production and merchandising, not from manufacturing, and with few exceptions were established in the nineteenth century. There is no Australian equivalent of Carnegie or Nuffield, and because it is capital held overseas, and not local accumulations, that commands the most profitable investment fields in manufacturing, it is unlikely now that there ever will be. Correspondingly, at whatever tempo the wartime industrial revolution in Australia may proceed, the lion's share of the direct gains from metals-processing and -finishing, industrial chemicals, rubber, motor-vehicle and aircraft manufacture, and ship-building is likely to enrich chiefly absentee investors.

The manufacturing industries were large enough, even before the Second World War, to make up nearly half of the value of all production. But they had contributed less than a third, just after the First World War, and earlier still, when the century began, only a fifth of the total value of production. Industrialisation, this comparison would suggest, is a phenomenon of recent years; the fact is that by the time the national economy was strong enough to stand the weight of heavy industry and the light industry which it feeds, overseas owners of patents, techniques, and capital were in a position to edge all but a minority of the local enterprisers out of the rising second storey, except as managers, where they predominate.

Australia's traditional rôle has been that of a primary producer, with a small population depending to an exceptional degree on

[204]

international trade, especially with Great Britain. This phase resulted, in the nineteenth century, in flocks of sheep such as no man had dreamed of, unrivalled new types of merino, and the subdivision of most of the usable land among families engaged in pastoral (and incidentally in mining and mercantile) pursuits. Long before the end of the century Australia was supplying more than half of all wool imports by woollens-manufacturing countries, and a greater proportion of the world's fine wool. Wool-growing, with profitable side lines of gold- and base-metals mining, and importing, for the sons of the shepherd kings, made up most of the small Australian quota of millionaires of the Century of the Uncommon Man. Economic development since then has been mainly, though by no means exclusively, the work of governments using capital borrowed from overseas small investors for the reticulation of railway, water supply, and industrial power, and of managers of Australian branch enterprises of overseas corporations.

The romance of "glittering prizes," so far as it attaches to Australian economic development, belongs for the most part to the past and to the pastures. There are no more James Tysons (1823–1898) to scoop up several million pounds from their stock runs after starting at £30 a year as pannikin bosses or working overseers; or Sir Samuel McCaugheys (1835–1919) to give £300,000 to one Australian university, £250,000 to another, an equal sum to the Presbyterian Church, and £600,000 for the schooling of soldiers' children. No twentieth-century "immense Australian"— a resentful phrase of one hundred twenty years ago—owns the equivalent in manufacturing plant of McCaughey's sheep principalities. His four stations on the Darling alone, in the far western part of New South Wales, once stretched 280 miles along the riverbank. A road 127 miles long ran across nothing but his paddocks. One of his fences extended for 90 miles in a straight line. The McCaughey stations sheared a million sheep a year.

Large accumulations by individuals were not characteristic even of the pastoral industry, in which British banking and agency companies were extremely important from the 1860's; or the mining industries, where, also, overseas interests soon bought into or took over the richest of the gold, copper, silver-lead, tin, and zinc mines. But sometimes local owners retained and improved upon their holdings in association with capitalists in England and America. Sir Clive Baillieu, for example, comes of a family notable for its place among the "hillionaires" who made fortunes out of Broken Hill silver-lead after 1885. He was made president of the Federation of British Industries, after many years in London as a director of a score of companies within the British nonferrous metallurgical ring, including the ruling Anglo-Australian group, which has its headquarters in Collins House, Melbourne.

Richard Gardiner Casey, who has served as Treasurer of the Commonwealth, Australian Minister at Washington, United Kingdom Minister of State in the Middle East, and Governor of Bengal, comes of an Australian family which likewise established itself at strategic points of the nineteenth-century economic structure. His father (1846–1919), of the same name, was chairman of the Mount Morgan Gold Mining Company, which worked a "hill of gold" in Queensland; chairman of Goldsbrough, Mort and Company in Melbourne, one of the great wool-broking firms of the world; and of the Electrolytic Refining and Smelting Company of Australia, Sydney, processing metals at Port Kembla, New South Wales. (Incidentally, it was William Knox D'Arcy, one of a small syndicate that developed Mount Morgan, who first exploited Mesopotamian oil.)

An English family whose Australian founder was Edward Knox (1819–1898) has been prominent for more than a hundred years in control of the solitary Australian large-scale exporter of capital— the Colonial Sugar Refining Company, which, with funds exceeding £15,000,000, has a monopoly of sugar-refining in Australia and New Zealand, owns great plantations in Fiji, and ranks second only to the Broken Hill Proprietary Company (steel) in industrial capital in Australia.

The Colonial Sugar Refining Company laid the foundations of its vast consumer-goods manufacture in 1842, when Edward Knox I started the Australasian Sugar Company, with plant and capital backing from England, at Canterbury near Sydney, to refine raw sugar from the Philippines "under the present improved process by steam." There were only a hundred thousand free people in New South Wales then, but they drank four times as much tea per person as their English contemporaries, which made a good prospect for the sugar company. (Further, "of Spirits, to a great extent drunk in water, and with refined Sugar," Edward Knox advertised, "the excess is greater." The foundation was made at a time when little sugar cane was grown in Australia and none at all in Queensland, the tropical state which is the locality of most of the cane farms today. In that respect sugar manufacture differed historically from the domestic character of nineteenth-century manufacturing.

There sprang up small local flour mills and breweries in the Australian "earlies," and even the germ of a textile industry (which did not develop much during more than a century). Such enterprises were associated directly with the products of the fields and pastures. With the increase in farming and in population about the middle of the nineteenth century, they were enlarged, and included the manufacture of farm implements, meat-preserving, and fellmongering. Up to and after the end of the century, secondary industry still had this domestic stamp. Victoria, in 1888, representatively, had only fifteen factories employing more than a hundred hands, five treating animal and vegetable matter, four making clothing, and two working metals. In the two principal colonies, Victoria and New South Wales, manufactures and commerce together employed only a sixth to a fifth of the breadwinners in the last forty years of the nineteenth century (compared with two-fifths today, in factory employment alone). Some of these nineteenth-century enterprises survive and have reached substantial dimensions, notably Sydney's 110-year-old brewing firm, which usually holds sixth place in capital ranking of all manufacturing concerns; the Sydney gas-supply firm, nearly as old and only a little more highly capitalised; the Victorian beer combine; and the H. C. McKay farm-implement manufacturing company, formidable in Australia even to International Harvester. But modern industrialised Australia did not really grow from these.

Nor did it have its origin in the gold-mining companies which soon after the first discoveries in Victoria and New South Wales in 1851 took over the fields from the individual diggers. Victoria alone produced substantially more gold than California in the 'fifties, though the Californian discovery of 1849 was the first great strike of modern times. Western Australia, forty years later, easily surpassed the earlier Victorian record. Mount Morgan in Queensland, producer from 1886 of "the richest native gold hitherto found," paid about £4,400,000 in dividends before the end of the century. And today a group of Anglo-Australian gold-mining companies, capitalised at many millions of pounds, control most gold production of Australia and the neighbouring Pacific Islands. But gold veins soon run out and the gold towns die with them.

The modern industrial structure is to be traced not from gold but from silver, from "the greatest silver mine in the world" as the Broken Hill Proprietary Company in 1935 described its original mine, which yielded fabulous quantities of silver and lead after 1886. When this company, now the owner of the Australian steel monopoly, was formed to mine silver and lead in 1885, a young blacksmith, A. W. Cox, played euchre with George McCulloch to decide whether he should pay McCulloch £150 or £120 for a fourteenth share. (McCulloch was the manager of the Mount Gipps sheep run, on whose property the Broken Hill lode was found in 1883 by a boundary rider. Another item of interest about Mount Gipps is that Sydney Kidman, the cattle king, once worked there for ten shillings a week.) It scarcely matters who won; Cox's share was worth £640,000 within three years.

This rich company, in which British capitalists soon held an 80 per cent share, produced nothing but base metals from the earth and immense dividends until 1915, when it blew in its first blast furnace at Newcastle, New South Wales. There was already a small iron industry of long standing in the same state, smelting local ores. But the Broken Hill Proprietary Company used and uses the seemingly inexhaustible South Australian ores, two-thirds iron, which it leased originally in 1901 for fluxing materials for its smelters. Industrialisation began in earnest in Australia when the Company switched from silver to steel during the First World War; it became established in a wide range of capital-goods industries in the 1920's, and since 1939, under the stimulus of war needs, has gone ahead too fast for official statisticians to keep pace. However, the figures given in the Commonwealth *Production Bulletin,* even for 1941–1942, comparable as far back as 1907, show a remarkable contrast with those of earlier years.

By 1942 there were 733,609 Australian factory workers, of whom 58.3 per cent were employed in establishments of more than 100 hands—the Commonwealth statistician clings to this archaic ceiling while factories employing 5,000 and 10,000 rise around him. This proportion was half again as great as that of thirty years before, and the difference is not a fair measure of the progress of private manufactures, for government railway and tramway workshops, now employing about 15 per cent of all workers in larger factories, employed three times that percentage of the whole before the days of the Broken Hill Proprietary Company. For the same reason the doubling between 1907 or 1912 and 1942 of the percentage of metalworkers on all factory workers represents an understatement of the growth of metals manufacture in importance. There were 428,127 metal-workers in 1942, when they were 58.3 per cent of all factory workers, compared with 47,060 (19 per cent) in 1907 and 66,472 (20.3 per cent) in 1912. But nearly a third of the metal-workers, before the establishment of the Company, were employed in government workshops, and though such workships greatly expanded between the earlier dates and the later, by 1942 only one-eighth of metal-workers were employed by the government.

War, especially after 1942, when Australia became the principal Allied base in the Pacific, caused vast changes in the economy, including a redistribution of balances of employment, plant, power, and access to raw materials among the industrial groups. It is not possible at this stage to survey profitably the nature and extent of the redistribution or to estimate its possible permanent effects. But, using again the measuring rod of employment, which is as indicative as any other, it is worth noting some of the more marked wartime effects on the five main areas of manufacture.

The easy leader—industrial metals, machines, implements, conveyances—increased its share from 31.8 to 38 per cent between 1937–1938 and 1941–1942, the latter being an earlier date than the drastic reconstruction of the national economy under government war organisation of industry. The important clothing industry had nearly half as great a volume of employment as the metal factories in 1937–1938, but less than a third four years later, and its share of the employment total fell from 15.3 to 12.2 per cent. Textiles, advancing rapidly in importance through the 1930's as a new area for comparatively large capital interest, did little better than hold its place. The food, drink, and tobacco group, which like the textiles and clothing industries had to supply hundreds of thousands of

Allied servicemen's requirements in addition to the (much rationed) local market, was getting by in 1942 with 13.1 per cent, as compared with 14.6 per cent in 1937–1938. The chemicals group nearly doubled its proportion, from 3.4 to 6.5.

A comparison over a longer period, as between the investment in nonbanking public companies at the beginning of the First World War and of the Second, gives striking evidence of the secular shift of economic emphasis. Investment in 1914 in public companies engaged in the pastoral industry and in gold, coal, and base-metals mining amounted to one-half of all investment in nonbanking companies. In 1940 it was less than one-fifth. Investment in manufacturing in 1914 was one-fifth, in 1940 one-half, of the entire investment. Moreover, the larger business unit had markedly improved its position: nearly three times as many companies, each with shareholders' funds (paid-up capital plus undistributed profits) of more than £1,000,000, operated in 1940 as in 1914, and their proportion of total investment had moved up from 41.5 to 70 per cent. Of twenty-seven million-pound companies operating in 1914, ten were pastoral (wool-broking, stock and station agency, etc.); six, base-metals mining; five, shipping; one, railway; and only five, manufacturing (two breweries, two gas companies, and the Colonial Sugar Refining Company). But the 1940 list of million-pound concerns shows scores of manufacturing companies, including half-a-dozen metals-processing and many fabricating firms, three chemicals manufacturers, even a couple of textiles manufacturers, and a variety of rubber, paper, oil, and power companies, besides several consumer-goods manufacturers.

Whereas in preindustrial 1914, gold-mining, wool-broking, and base-metals mining, in that order, easily led other industrial and business groups in capital ranking, in 1940 the metals industries were far ahead of all other nonbanking businesses, and manufacturing as a whole was a repository of substantially more investment than other production and distribution, even though retail trading, in which few public companies engaged in 1914, by 1940 accounted for an investment equivalent to £26,000,000.

The Australian manufacturing structure, much of it built according to the advice of expert technicians on loan from overseas and equipped with the latest in plant and equipment, was set up behind a protective tariff wall. But the use of natural resources which are rich in certain limited fields, and the advantage of circumstances, like the delay in the industrialisation of the neighbour Dominion of New Zealand, the two wars, and the Second World War's heritage of devastation and need for the industrial reëquipment of Australia's "near north" (i.e., the Far East), have brought a hopeful prospect to the new industries—the prospect of substantial exports. Before the Second World War, manufactured goods were a tiny item, about 4 per cent, in the relatively great export trade of Australia. But now at least two of the main monopolised industries announce that they are ready to compete on even terms with the older industrialised countries for the trade of the "near north" and even more distant markets. The industries are steel and glass, the second of which is controlled by Australian Consolidated Industries, the result of mergers carried out over a quarter of a century. The glass monopoly has the peculiarity of being capitalised almost exclusively by resident Australians and New Zealanders.

In this it differs from the majority of greater Australian companies, except for the large brewing companies (which have long been firmly established on a state basis of division of sales territory), the paper companies, most of the food-packers, and some of the textile firms. The metals industries, both ferrous and nonferrous, are intimately connected with great British holding companies in very complex ways, and through one of the great subsidiaries of the Broken Hill Proprietary Company some Australian steel is manufactured with the help of American Armco capital. Similarly the Australian tie-up with New York in nonferrous metals is, through London, a close one. The Ford Company and General Motors, of the three large American manufacturers in the field, divide the Australian motors manufacture. General Motors has taken over a local enterprise and has allowed a small amount of local capital. Dunlop's and Goodyear share the rubber manufacture with Olympic, a lively and competent Australian competitor, bidding successfully for part of the market. Industrial chemicals in Australia are almost wholly the province of Imperial Chemical Industries. Its Australian and New Zealand branch, with some local capital, is closely connected with the steel monopoly through two-way shareholdings and interlocking directorates. The great pastoral companies, still a large factor in Australian economy, are predominantly British enterprises. Some of them, and a few of the major banks, are firmly built into the intricate system of vertical and horizontal trusts and the cartels, which includes the most profitable manufactures, the long-established shipping combine, and the principal coal mines. The ruling combine of the Broken Hill Proprietary Company commands about a third of all capital invested in Australian manufactures on the public-company level of organisation. Much of this capital is British—exactly how much it is impossible to determine.

However, in spite of the importance of overseas capitalisation of most of the principal manufactures of Australia, government enterprises play a greater productive rôle than in most other industrialised countries. The State Electricity Commission of Victoria, supplying most industrial and domestic power and lighting to the second industrial state, is more highly capitalised, and a greater earner, than any private industrial enterprise. It has its main seat in a Commission town, Yallourn (from two aboriginal words meaning "brown" and "fire"), on the brown coal fields a hundred miles from Melbourne, where it generates power. As a "decentralised" undertaking, it is a rare example. Even after the number in government munition factories had been substantially reduced, between August, 1943, and May, 1945, there still remained 79,000 workers, one-tenth of the whole factory force. In May, 1945, persons in government employ were as many as 521,300 (August, 1943, peak of 546,900; July, 1939, 405,000), compared with 1,916,100 privately employed.

New South Wales has two manufacturing centres outside the capital, Sydney, namely, Newcastle and Port Kembla. South Australia has one, Whyalla. All are ports, all important centres of manufacture, all predominantly (in the case of Whyalla wholly) "B.H.P." towns. For the rest, manufacturing is concentrated in Sydney and Mebourne, but there has been some significant growth of industry in the capitals of South Australia and Queensland also. New South Wales, with 44 per cent of the factory production (in 1940) and nearly all the good black coal, and Victoria, with 33 per cent, began the war as the manufacturing centres of Australia, and the wartime organisation of industry did not detract from their preëminence. The dispersal of factories to provincial towns was not large enough to seriously affect the traditional concentration.

CHAPTER XIV

Tertiary Industries in the Economy

BY COLIN CLARK*

IN AUSTRALIA, as in other countries, it is being realised that tertiary industries have been absorbing an increasing share of the working population and, in fact, form the only body of industries which is likely to expand appreciably in future. With increasing productivity of labour in secondary industries, the proportion of working population engaged in them is unlikely to expand, and in some countries (e.g., the United States and Great Britain) has already passed its peak and begun to decline, as the percentage engaged in primary industry did many years earlier.

The percentage of population engaged in tertiary industries is closely correlated with the level of real national income per head. In other words, service industries as a whole become important when the community is wealthy enough to demand them. Some (e.g., building and transport) are necessary in all countries, rich or poor. Others (e.g., the cinema) could not be described as essential, but when incorporated in the accepted standard of living they become conventional necessities satisfying a definite need. A last group of services, mostly of the luxury type, is probably the last to appear in response to a rise in real income: transactions in which customers pay for atmosphere, extra attention, and personal services.

The Australian level of real income per capita is well up in the scale from an international point of view, and the percentage of working population engaged in tertiary industries is correspondingly high. The proportions engaged in transport, communication, commerce, and finance are particularly high in relation to other

* Mr. Clark wishes it stated that R. H. Fields, B. Com., of the Queensland Bureau of Industry, is to be taken as joint author of this chapter.

countries for which information is available. It is difficult to do more than describe many of the tertiary industries concerning which little besides employment information is available. For the most part, what follows is an analysis of the results of the 1933 census, which is out of date but probably is better than a distorted wartime picture, though it should be kept in mind that the 1933 census was itself distorted in some degree by the depression.

Primary industry is fairly well defined, as is secondary industry, once a decision is made regarding building and construction—which is generally excluded from secondary industry. All other industries are classified as tertiary. The group therefore covers a heterogeneous collection of industries. The main types are building and construction; transport; commerce and finance, including all wholesaling and retailing, banking, and insurance; government administration, together with all the professions, health, education, religion, and law; and the group of personal service industries, comprising hotels, boarding houses, laundries, sports and recreation, and private domestic service.

The growth of the main industrial groups in Australia since 1901 is shown in table 1, so far as they can be sorted out from census rec-

TABLE 1
DISTRIBUTION OF PERSONS IN INDUSTRY

Industry	Working population			
	Census of 1901	Census of 1911	Census of 1921	Census of 1933
Primary (except mining)........	408,211	415,121	476,163	551,102
Mining......................	118,149	101,519	62,167	68,436
Manufacturing................	294,349	384,991	484,385	605,708
Building and construction.......	117,942	136,539	168,959	209,962
Transport and communication...	133,820	175,076	241,676	272,502
Property and finance...........	31,426	30,695	43,759	55,571
Commerce....................	179,085	233,835	301,591	391,619
Public administration, professions, and entertainment......	124,648	133,252	186,370	241,399
Personal and domestic..........	193,047	194,184	204,537	239,295
Totals....................	1,600,677	1,805,212	2,169,607	2,635,594

ords. The working population includes employers, those working on their own account, employees, and unemployed; but it excludes those whose grade of employment was not applicable (mainly pensioners who before 1933 were coded to their previous industry) and workers not receiving remuneration. The "undefined industrial workers" group in 1901, 1911, and 1921, and the "labourers, industry undefined," in 1933 have been distributed among the manufacturing, building and construction, and transport and communication groups. The estimated distribution was 40 per cent to the "grade not applicable" group and 30 per cent to each of the other two.

The figures have been reduced to a percentage basis in table 2.

TABLE 2

DISTRIBUTION OF PERSONS IN INDUSTRY BY PERCENTAGE

Industry	Percentage of working population			
	Census of 1901	Census of 1911	Census of 1921	Census of 1933
Primary (except mining)	25.5	23.0	21.9	20.9
Mining	7.4	5.6	2.9	2.6
Manufacturing	18.4	21.3	22.3	23.0
Building and construction	7.4	7.6	7.8	8.0
Transport and communication	8.4	9.7	11.2	10.3
Property and finance	1.9	1.7	2.0	2.1
Commerce	11.2	12.9	13.9	14.8
Public administration, professions, and entertainment	7.8	7.4	8.6	9.2
Personal and domestic	12.0	10.8	9.4	9.1
Totals	100.0	100.0	100.0	100.0

All but the first three groups are tertiary industries. The percentage of total working population engaged in these industries has risen progressively from 48.7 per cent in 1901 to 50.1, 52.9, and 53.5 per cent in 1911, 1921, and 1933, respectively. Inspection of the subdivisions of the tertiary group in the table shows that there has been a fairly regular rise except in the personal and domestic group, which has fallen regularly. The low figure for transport in 1933 was due to less shipping in port on census night. The numbers recorded for males in shipping were about 9,000 below the 1921 total for males.

Some of the tertiary industries have employed predominantly female labour in the past. This is obvious in view of the occupations included—nurses, teachers, waitresses, and domestic servants. As shown in table 2, 53.5 per cent of all employment in 1933 was in the tertiary industries; the figure for males was only 48 per cent, whereas 73 per cent of females found work in these groups. As tertiary industries expand and offer greater employment opportunities, they will be called on to provide more jobs for males. That this has happened up to the present is shown by the fact that in 1901 only 43 per cent of males but 71 per cent of females were engaged in tertiary industries. The increase in male employment was mainly in building, transport, commerce, and entertainment, whereas public administration and personal domestic service continued to absorb more females than males.

The extent to which the tertiary group is likely to expand in future is illustrated by table 3. The figures are derived from data

TABLE 3

Estimated Distribution in Queensland by 1965

Industrial group	Numbers of workers	Percentage of total
Agriculture and pastoral...............................	134,000	23
Mining and manufacturing............................	105,800	18
Building and construction.............................	47,300	8
Transport and communication........................	51,200	9
Commerce and finance................................	95,600	17
Other services.......................................	143,400	25
Totals...	577,300	100

from a family-budget survey held in Queensland in 1939–1940 which allow us to calculate the amounts of different goods and services likely to be demanded at different income levels. By making estimates of the future level of income it was possible to estimate the likely demand and hence employment (allowing for greater efficiency and shorter hours) in the main secondary and tertiary industries. Most of the advance in the tertiary group is expected to come in the boarding-house, café, and hotel trades, and through increased demand for holidays and recreation as a result of the higher incomes expected for primary produce. The Australian picture should not be markedly different from the estimate for Queensland, though there would be somewhat more in manufacturing and fewer in primary occupations.

Data on the numbers engaged in tertiary industries in each of the states is shown in table 4 (see p. 218), based on the 1933 census. A quasi-census of civilians was taken in June, 1943, along with the issue of ration books, but the distribution of employment among industrial groups was too distorted by call-up and mobilisation for war to be of much value in indicating the status of Australian tertiary industries. For convenience the absolute figures are accompanied by the percentage of total breadwinners in the state. The "not applicable" grade and workers receiving no remuneration have not been removed from these figures, as was done in previous tables, but the numbers of these groups involved in tertiary industries are small and the figures serve for comparison. The "labourer, industry undefined" group has been allocated as in the preceding tables.

The percentage figures show a marked uniformity as between states. Comparisons of average real income by states are not available, but we would not expect differences large enough to cause great variation in living standards. The South Australian figure is higher than would perhaps be expected, but it is a wealthy state. The figure for Western Australia is high compared with the Queensland figure because its isolation makes it more difficult than in the Eastern States to satisfy the needs of tertiary industry. Tasmania suffers because the population is not sufficient to support a city of the size required to provide a full range of services, and therefore is dependent in some degree on Sydney and Melbourne.

The building and construction group has been combined in the table because of the adjustment to the "labourer, industry undefined" group in the 1933 census. The total conceals a high building figure in New South Wales and a low one in Queensland, which, however, had a high construction figure. New South Wales was apparently building more houses at that time, but the low figure for Queensland probably reflects the smaller number of man-weeks of labour needed to build a timber house there, compared with the brick houses of other states.

The transport and communication group covers transport by rail, road, water, and air, and postal and telephone services. It is fairly evenly spread among the states, though it is somewhat lower in Victoria and Tasmania because of their smaller size.

The relative importance of the various transport services can be judged from the number engaged in the main individual transport industries, as shown by the 1933 census, before adjustment of the

TABLE 4
EMPLOYMENT IN TERTIARY INDUSTRY GROUPS BY STATES, JUNE, 1933

Group	Number engaged							Percentage of working population						
	New South Wales	Victoria	Queensland	South Australia	Western Australia	Tasmania	Australia*	New South Wales	Victoria	Q'ns-land	South Australia	West'n Australia	Tasmania	Australia*
Building and construction	86,331	57,139	28,693	17,825	13,779	5,861	210,290	8.4	7.5	7.4	7.6	7.4	6.9	7.2
Transport and communication	110,642	68,215	41,476	24,734	19,211	8,148	273,098	10.8	8.9	10.6	10.6	10.3	9.5	10.7
Property and finance	21,053	17,876	6,681	4,738	3,768	1,373	55,624	2.1	2.3	1.7	2.0	2.0	1.6	2.1
Commerce	151,209	118,519	48,670	38,284	26,610	10,817	394,473	14.7	15.4	12.6	16.4	14.2	12.6	14.6
Total	172,262	136,395	55,351	43,022	30,378	12,190	450,097	16.8	17.7	14.3	18.4	16.2	14.2	16.7
Public administration	9,670	5,837	3,483	1,889	2,010	604	24,271	0.9	0.8	0.9	0.8	1.1	0.7	0.9
Defence	2,891	2,168	331	112	133	96	5,780	0.3	0.3	0.1	0.1	0.1	0.1	0.2
Law and order	9,629	6,190	2,912	1,679	1,322	727	22,575	0.9	0.8	0.7	0.7	0.7	0.9	0.8
Religion, etc.	5,217	4,495	2,190	1,456	1,187	507	15,135	0.5	0.6	0.6	0.6	0.6	0.6	0.6
Health	21,434	15,253	8,160	4,600	3,722	1,712	55,018	2.1	1.9	2.1	2.0	2.0	2.0	2.0
Education	21,467	15,946	7,734	5,112	3,791	1,913	56,081	2.1	2.1	2.0	2.2	2.0	2.2	2.1
Other professional	22,643	14,153	7,592	3,844	4,086	936	53,360	2.2	1.8	1.8	1.6	2.2	1.1	2.0
Total	92,951	64,042	32,402	18,692	16,251	6,495	232,212	9.0	8.3	8.2	8.0	8.7	7.6	8.6
Entertainment, etc.	9,857	7,462	3,207	1,535	1,505	651	24,250	1.0	1.0	0.8	0.7	0.8	0.8	0.9
Personal and domestic service	90,994	69,365	34,324	22,598	16,534	7,824	242,378	8.9	9.0	8.8	9.7	8.8	9.2	9.0
Grand total	563,037	402,618	195,453	128,406	97,658	41,169	1,432,325	54.9	52.4	50.1	55.0	52.2	48.2	53.1

*The Australian figure includes the Northern Territory and the Australian Capital Territory and is therefore slightly larger than the total of the states.

"labourer, industry undefined" group. The figures in table 5 cover those engaged in service and maintenance only, and exclude construction and workshops.

TABLE 5

Transport service	Number engaged June, 1933
Railways	77,692
Tramways	15,733
Garages and taxis	15,286
Carrying and cartage	37,925
Motor cars and buses	4,541
Water transport (including harbour services, loading and unloading)	39,752
Communication	30,888

Air transport recorded only 349 employed in 1933, but by 1938–1939 the annual mileage flown had almost quadrupled.

Rail transport in Australia is likely to be adversely criticised by those who fail to understand the peculiar conditions under which it operates. Some who look at the different rail gauges in use, ranging from 3 ft. 6 in. in Queensland and Western Australia to 4 ft. 8½ in. in New South Wales and South Australia, and 5 ft. 3 in. in Victoria, may be inclined to dismiss them as inherently inefficient, but the figures do not support such a decision. Besides, it is not generally realised that, as most of the population is grouped along the coast, which is plentifully supplied with harbours, railways are subjected to intense competition from sea traffic. This is particularly true of heavy goods consigned for long distances, which generally go by sea. The railways are therefore deprived of much of the type of goods traffic which allows the American railways to operate at exceptionally low costs. The relative efficiency of railways is not easy to measure. Though charges are not based on cost over the particular section of line, when reduced to a measure of real cost they probably give the best indication of efficiency.

Table 6, from figures published in *Conditions of Economic Progress,* shows the real costs of railway transport in different countries in 1935, measured in man-hours per thousand ton-kilometers of goods transported. The relatively high Australian efficiency is surprising, considering the sparse population, the long distances, and the light loading. There is no doubt that the Australian railways have done a good job, and in the outlying states the narrow gauges have made it possible because they permit steeper gradients, sharper turns, smaller goods yards, and other factors in railway economy. Smaller mileages of wider-gauge line would not have opened up such vast areas.

TABLE 6

REAL COSTS OF RAILWAY TRANSPORT IN 1935

Country	Man-hours per 1,000 ton-km.
Australia	43
United States	13
Great Britain	64
France	59
Italy	85
Belgium	62
New Zealand	68
Denmark	40
Sweden	34
Germany	54

Road transport before the war was less developed than in some other countries, owing to the condition of the roads and the high price of petrol, but even so the railways were feeling the effects of road competition. The Australian ratio of cars to population was about one car registered for each twelve and a half persons, the total registered being 562,271 at the end of June, 1939. Including commercial vehicles (trucks, buses, and utility trucks) and motorcycles, the total of motor vehicles was 899,533.

The commerce group covers a tremendously wide range from hawking to departmental stores. It also includes advertising, debt collecting, and so on. It is difficult to obtain accurate measures of cost or efficiency for commerce, since few data are available.

The numbers engaged in retailing were not separated from those in wholesaling until 1943. As far as can be judged, the importance of wholesaling was being reduced before the war because of direct buying from manufacturers by large departmental and chain stores. There has not been a development of chain stores in Australia comparable to that in America, nor of coöperative enterprises as in England. A few large chains have branches in most towns, and in the capitals they are spreading through the suburbs. But neither the intensity of development nor the range of activities which have been "chained" has been so great as in some other countries. There is, however, scope for increased efficiency in dealing, such as accompanied the growth of the chain store in the United States and the co-operative in Great Britain, and already some efforts have been made by other types of firms to offset chain-store economies by joint buying.

The movement in efficiency of retailing over a period, as measured by its real cost, can be judged from the change in margins between retail and wholesale prices. These have been calculated for a specified assortment of foodstuffs covered by the Melbourne wholesale price index. When divided by an index of wage rates, the real costs of distribution are obtained. (See table 7.) The absolute figures are calculated in Australian pounds. The real cost shows a rapid

TABLE 7

Period	Gross distributors' margin, 1901 base	Index of wage rates, 1901 base	Real cost
1901—1904........	99.2	100.6	98.6
1905—1909........	102.0	104.8	97.5
1910—1914........	112.3	122.0	92.1
1915—1919........	120.4	148.8	81.0
1920—1924........	196.8	212.0	92.9
1925—1929........	193.2	228.8	84.5
1930—1934........	156.5	197.2	79.3
1935—1938........	165.7	202.0	82.1

decline until the early 'twenties, when it jumped back to slightly above its level of ten years before. The figure for the late 'thirties was still slightly above its lowest level during the First World War. In the United States, however, real costs of distribution fell 44 per cent between 1913 and 1938.

Government and local government administration and the services largely provided by the government, such as education and justice, are well distributed among the states. Although this indicates that there is not much disparity in the level of services, it is likely that the cost to outlying states with sparse populations is higher than in more thickly populated states. The figures shown in table 8 are by no means the total persons employed by the various governments. In Australia, quite apart from wartime controls, the various governments (federal, state, and local) operate many services, often in competition with private industry. Railways and tramways are almost entirely under public ownership, but in broadcasting, banking, insurance, and many other activities the government concerns form only part of the total. Government employees in these would be included in the census with their relevant industrial group, hence the figure shown in the table covers only general administration and services not covered by specific industrial codes.

The last group, "personal and domestic service," covers a diverse range of individual industries which cater to personal needs. Hotels, boarding houses, and cafés form a rather large part of this group. The hotels are mostly "tied" houses controlled by breweries, and, as might be expected, are run for profit rather than for the comfort and convenience of their patrons. They are designed for the consumption of the greatest quantity of beer in the shortest possible time—which, incidentally, provides the best conditions for drunkenness. This unfortunate situation has been created mainly by a regulation which was intended to promote temperance by limiting the number of hotels. As is usual with restricted entry, the influence of monopoly can be exerted to the full. Cafés in Australia are generally specialist concerns, not to be compared with the drugstore and counter-lunch facilities in the United States. Other industries in the group are hairdressing parlours and laundries, and are generally small establishments.

Whereas tertiary industries are distributed fairly evenly among the states, the regional spread of industrial groups within the states is very uneven. This is shown in table 8, as at June, 1933, giving percentages of the total in each industrial group living in metropolitan or provincial cities, or rural areas. Because of varying percentages of population in the capital cities and because there may be differences of definition between states, the last column gives a similar percentage spread for the population as a whole. The proportions of population in capital cities have continued to increase since then, and the process was speeded during the war. However, no later figures are available.

The table must be interpreted broadly, as we would not expect the services to be distributed strictly according to population. In all states, commerce and finance, and entertainment are concentrated in the capital cities, but all groups have a higher proportion in the capital than its share of population. In Queensland and Tasmania the provincial cities are well supplied on a population basis. In Queensland most of the provincial towns grew originally as ports, and the first railways were designed to serve the ports, not to direct all traffic to Brisbane. Although the New South Wales percentage of

TABLE 8

REGIONAL DISTRIBUTION OF TERTIARY EMPLOYMENT, JUNE, 1933

(Percentages)

Industry	Region	New South Wales	Victoria	Q'ns- land	South Aus- tralia	West- ern Aus- tralia	Tas- mania	Aus- tralia
Transport and communication.	Metropolitan	55	62	35	57	50	35	53
	Provincial city	23	11	30	14	14	29	22
	Rural	19	24	30	21	27	28	25
Commerce and finance.......	Metropolitan	67	72	52	76	71	43	66
	Provincial city	21	12	28	9	11	40	19
	Rural	12	16	20	15	18	17	15
Public administration and professional..............	Metropolitan	63	66	48	71	67	44	61
	Provincial city	21	12	25	9	10	34	19
	Rural	15	22	26	18	23	22	20
Entertainment, sport, and recreation...............	Metropolitan	70	80	55	79	79	61	71
	Provincial city	21	8	29	9	10	28	18
	Rural	9	10	15	10	10	11	11
Personal and domestic service.	Metropolitan	53	59	35	59	53	36	49
	Provincial city	24	12	26	10	14	32	21
	Rural	23	29	39	31	33	32	30
Total of above..........	Metropolitan	61	67	44	68	62	40	60
	Provincial city	22	12	27	11	12	35	19
	Rural	16	21	27	20	23	23	20
Total population of state.	Metropolitan	47	55	32	54	48	27	47
	Provincial city	22	11	21	9	10	25	17
	Rural	31	34	47	37	42	48	36

provincial city population is slightly higher than Queensland's, Newcastle accounts for most of it. In Tasmania, also, there is only one large city, Launceston, apart from the capital.

It is possible to show the actual spread of industrial groups within the states, but there is no measure of whether the provincial towns are provided with services to the full extent of the demand from their own inhabitants and those of the surrounding region. This can be gauged only by reference to employment per unit of regional income. So far as is known, no regional figures of employment in service industries in conjunction with national income for the regions are available outside Queensland. The Queensland figures of employment per million dollars of regional income, together with those of other countries for which the data were available, were given in an article by the author, "The Economic Functions of a City," published in *Econometrica*, April, 1945. The figures quoted for Queensland cities are given in table 9.

TABLE 9
EMPLOYMENT IN QUEENSLAND CITIES

Region	Population of largest city	Income of region	Commerce and finance	Government and education (exc. defence)	Private domestic services	Other service industries
			Number employed per million dollars			
Queensland....	....	$439,000,000	155	45	39	85
Gladstone......	5,000	6,000,000	75	36	25	56
Warwick.......	7,000	15,000,000	93	36	53	85
Gympie.......	8,000	15,000,000	129	53	38	65
Mackay.......	12,000	16,000,000	131	26	27	54
Bundaberg.....	13,000	12,000,000	106	46	37	66
Maryborough...	14,000	22,000,000	97	35	36	55
Cairns.........	15,000	26,000,000	120	35	29	73
Ipswich........	23,000	21,000,000	98	60	33	72
Toowoomba....	30,000	46,000,000	102	35	41	84
Townsville.....	31,000	54,000,000	108	43	38	75
Rockhampton..	35,000	37,000,000	114	35	43	82
Brisbane.......	335,000	169,000,000	229	52	40	103

There is no reason to believe that if figures were available for other Australian regions they would not fall into their correct place in such a table. The basis of comparison adopted above is the only logical basis which measures the level of services provided by a city for its region, considering the wealth of the region, i.e., the demand for services. Generally speaking, if employment is below the average for the state one may conclude that the main city is not large enough to supply the range of services provided for the state as a whole. Of course it may be true that even where employment is high, inefficiency may reduce the real level of services.

The figures indicate, in conjunction with American and British data, that a city needs a population of 100,000–200,000 before an adequate range of services can be provided. This means that in Australia only a few of the capital cities and Newcastle, New South Wales, are large enough at present to supply a full range of service industries. Until other regional centres are developed, many will have to depend on visits to the larger cities for their services or perhaps pay high prices in the small towns for inadequate service. Some separate service industries are well staffed in country areas. Some of these are to be expected; transport, for example, tends to collect in certain centres which usually are workshop centres as well as junctions. It appears, also, that the dry and thirsty west is relatively well provided with hotels. Although some mining towns have faded away when mining ceased, an interesting example of adaptation comes from Charters Towers (not shown in table 9), which became an important city while its mines were productive and has since developed as an educational and service centre.

CHAPTER XV

Banking, Finance, Fiscal Policy

BY S. J. BUTLIN

THE AUSTRALIAN banking system includes four types of banks: the Commonwealth (central) Bank, the commercial (or trading) banks, savings banks, and rural or agricultural banks. The Commonwealth Bank, publicly owned and controlled, operates as a central bank, with powers greatly increased and functions much extended during 1945. The trading banks carry on the usual commercial banking business and are privately owned and controlled. The most important of these are referred to as the great trading banks; there are three others which trade in Australia on a small scale.[1] Savings banks are operated by the Commonwealth and by the states of Victoria and South Australia; in Tasmania two trustee savings banks operate under state supervision. There are also a few agricultural banks, in each instance owned and controlled by a state, and concerned primarily with fixed-term loans for rural industry.

The small number of trading banks is associated with a high development of branch banking. The emergence of a unit bank system has never been a real possibility. Branches appeared very early; the first bank, that of New South Wales, commenced business in 1817 and the first branch (of another bank) appeared ten years later.

---

[1] The principal trading banks existing at the end of the war were Bank of New South Wales, Commercial Banking Company of Sydney, Union Bank of Australia, National Bank of Australasia, Bank of Australasia, English, Scottish and Australian Bank, Bank of Adelaide, and Queensland National Bank. As this note is made, postwar consolidations promise to reduce the total to seven. The others are Ballarat Banking Company, Bank of New Zealand, and Comptoir National d'Escompte de Paris. Before 1941 there was also a Yokohama Specie Bank.

A few so-called local banks appeared in the 1830's, but none survived the depression which developed in 1841. Later sporadic local banks were unable to compete with the metropolitan institutions, and, in the absence of strong opposition, branch banking steadily spread with the geographical extension of settlement in the nineteenth century.

Side by side with that growth went a process of amalgamation and concentration which was a more potent force in restricting the number of banks than was failure. Numbers reached their peak before the great bank smash of 1893, from which emerged a highly concentrated system, and there have been further amalgamations in the twentieth century. Attempts by foreign banks to extend their activities to Australia have never succeeded, mainly, it is said, because existing institutions have united to resist, and the offices of foreign banks which survive are not seriously concerned with domestic business. Three of the banks have head offices in England, but their main fields of operations are Australia and New Zealand, and several of those incorporated in Australia do business in New Zealand also.

A natural consequence of the high degree of concentration has been what economists call monopolistic competition. In Victoria the banks are formally organised as the Associated Banks, but everywhere there is a large degree of unanimity in major trends of policy and in terms of business. Competition survives within this framework, and agreement, tacit or otherwise, has not always lasted in periods of crisis, but aggressive competition does not exist and, in fact, except for short periods, has never existed in Australia. A further consequence is that each of the great trading banks operates in several states and thus all are subject to federal law, which covers banking extending beyond the limits of any one state. As might be expected, there is, apart from the impact of federal law and of the Commonwealth Bank, a unified Australian banking system in the sense that the same practice is observed everywhere and policy is determined by a few central offices which do not pursue independent and uncoördinated action. In that sense there has been a unified Australian system since the middle of the nineteenth century, that is, long before federation. It was a unity which owed little to state laws, which were divergent, but which in the mildness of their restrictions imposed no barrier to the trend.

The Commonwealth Bank was created by federal law in 1911. The more vocal of its sponsors, the "torpedo brigade" of the Labour majority of that time, under the leadership of colourful King O'Malley, thought of it as an aggressive competitor which would smash the "banking ring." But the first Governor, Denison Miller (1860–1923), had other views, and in any event the Bank became involved in the finance of the First World War to the exclusion of other questions; Labour did not again control the Federal Parliament until 1944. But 1911 became part of the Party's tradition, solidified by controversy in 1918 and thereafter, and by the bitter opposition to trading banks during the Great Depression. Although the 1945 legislation fell short of the nationalisation of banking which is one of the Party's official objectives, it derived from that tradition and owed some of its questionable features to the persistence of Labour's goal.

In 1924, after the central-bank fashion of the 'twenties, the Bruce-Page (non-Labour) Government legislated to make the Commonwealth Bank a central bank, much on the lines of what the Bank of England was supposed to be, and even copying the main points of its organisation. All the conventional weapons of a central bank armoury were provided, but no great change resulted. The Bank itself was sympathetic to private enterprise in banking, as were successive governments, except for the Scullin (Labour) administration of 1929–1931, which, however, being in a minority in the Senate, was unable to carry its banking legislation. More important was the fact that central banking cannot be transplanted so simply. Provisions for rediscounting bills and for open-market operations would necessarily have been mainly in government securities, and governments regularly raising new loans would have resisted action which would have affected the yield of government bonds and which in any event would not have been very effective in controlling bank lending.

The Great Depression made banking a subject of violent political controversy, but made little impact either on the attitude of the Bank to its central-banking functions or on its ability to exercise effective direction. It did, however, issue in a Royal Commission, whose otherwise modest proposals included a striking one, namely, that the trading banks should hold reserves with the Commonwealth Bank to an amount specified, without limit, by that Bank. These proposals, however, were talked out in public discussion in the years before the outbreak of war in 1939, without leading to any government action.

Wartime control of banking has followed the familiar pattern, but it may acquire permanent significance because the banking legislation of 1945 provides the machinery by which much of it may be maintained. This legislation empowers the Commonwealth Bank to continue exchange control, and "to determine the policy in relation to advances to be followed by the banks"; in a special form conditioned by wartime experience, the proposal for compulsory reserves variable without limit has been in effect adopted; banking in future requires government licencing. The Commonwealth Bank itself is reorganised and, under a governor who is responsible not to a board but to the government, is to add to orthodox central banking an actively competitive general banking department (this has existed since 1911 but has not competed with the trading banks) and departments for rural credits, mortgage loans, industrial finance, and housing loans, respectively. The Commonwealth Savings Bank comes explicitly under its control. To this remarkable centralisation of the organisation not merely of the Commonwealth Bank but of the whole banking system is added explicit political control, for the Bank is directed that it must give effect to government monetary banking policy as notified to it. It is unnecessary to comment on the degree of power which this places in the hands of the government, but perhaps it is necessary to point out that the powers can be used in various ways, or not at all, and that governments change.

The implications of the legislation, even in the short period, will not be clear until reconstruction programmes are defined and in process of being implemented. But some notion of what could happen may be gained by considering the legislation in relation to the equally marked trend toward the centralisation in the hands of the Commonwealth of high policy in public finance.

Australian governments derive their revenue from two major sources: taxation and the earnings of business undertakings. For the Commonwealth, taxation normally provided, before 1939, three-fourths of its total gross revenue; the Post Office has made consistent and increasing profits, whereas the federal railways have made small losses. For the states, taxation accounted for a little more than one-third of the total gross revenue, but this is explained by the large receipts from business enterprise, amounting in recent prewar years to almost one-half of the total revenue. But few state businesses show net profits (the railways have done well since 1939 because of war transport, but at the cost of severe depreciation of equipment), and collectively they have always been a source of net expenditure. Territorial revenue consistently yielded the states something less than 4 per cent of total receipts. The other significant source is Commonwealth payments to the states.

For the Commonwealth, the chief taxes have been income (personal and corporate), customs, excise, and sales tax, with minor amounts from land taxes and estate duties. From 1929 until the outbreak of war there was a marked trend away from taxes on income and property toward indirect taxation, although war finance under a Labour Government interrupted the movement. A similar trend was observable in the states, and for the same reason—the haphazard grasping after revenue in the depression years of the 'thirties. State taxation relied more heavily on income and property taxes, being excluded from all forms of customs and excise (the latter including sales tax). There are also miscellaneous state taxes on motors, liquor, and racing; stamp duties; and, for several states, lottery revenue.

The most striking trend in expenditures has been the growth of federal social-service commitments, especially since 1941, the Labour Government having won acceptance of the extension of wartime income tax to low-wage incomes by associating it with a National Welfare Fund. In pursuit of its policy, it has promised further extension of such expenditure in what was formerly the province of the states. In respect, therefore, to both taxation and expenditure, the future relation of Commonwealth and states remains to be determined. To a greater degree than the First World War, the Second World War disturbed what has always been an uneasy balance, and it is certain that the permanent increase in the financial importance of the Commonwealth will be much more marked, though it is no more than a continuation of the trend toward centralised finance which has dominated the financial relations of the Commonwealth and the states since 1900.

At the time of federation, customs and excise taxation became the exclusive right of the new Commonwealth, but, as this deprived the states of their main source of revenue, and the Commonwealth was not expected to have expensive functions, it was provided that three-fourths of this revenue should be paid to the states. In 1910, as the Constitution permitted, the Federal Parliament substituted per-capita payments by which the states received each year 25s. per head of population. Against this, the Commonwealth commenced to compete for taxes, first in the land tax in 1910, and in 1915 in income tax. After the First World War prolonged debate issued in the Financial Agreement of 1928. The states had wanted to recover exclusive tax fields, whereas the Commonwealth wished to abandon per-capita payments. As the Commonwealth Government had no need to offer compensation, the states had to acquiesce in the terms offered.

Besides providing for sinking funds, the Agreement covered an annual payment to the states for interest on debt, formal recognition of an existing Loan Council, and eventual federal liability for state debts as they then stood. In place of per-capita payments were substituted permanently fixed contributions, at the same level as per-capita payments in 1926–1927, toward interest on state debts. The Loan Council had been acting as an advisory body for some years. It consists of a representative of each of the seven governments, the Commonwealth having two votes and a casting vote. All borrowings after the Agreement are to be arranged by the Commonwealth under the direction of the Council, are to be covered by Commonwealth securities and on terms fixed by the Council, and are to be restricted in amount each year to limits determined by the Council. All governments have relied mainly on borrowing for capital expenditure, and until 1939, apart from a debt of less than one-fourth of the total, during the First World War, Australian public debt was characteristically for public works. Commonwealth defence loans are not subject to Council control, though they are reported to it. During the war, therefore, the work of the Council became largely formal. War loans dominated the situation, and state loans disappeared as, with intensification of the war, man-power and materials shortages made the prosecution of extensive public works impossible.

Even before the war, in its main function of controlling and co-ordinating borrowing, the Council had only moderate success. In the depression years of the early 'thirties it seemed to be exercising effective control and to have stopped what was apparently a loop-hole in the Agreement—the provision that a government might bor-row internally for temporary purposes beyond Loan Council limits. This would have covered deficits and similar depression loan needs, and on the surface the Council was successful in controlling bor-rowing even for these purposes. But the operative control was the scarcity of lenders. With recovery, a more serious gap in the Coun-cil's powers became apparent, for its power extends only to borrow-ing by governments, not to that by semigovernmental bodies such as municipal councils, water boards, and the like. There was no widening of the scope of local government and no greater initiative in local affairs—simply an intensification of the normal local activ-ities which would absorb the maximum number of unskilled men to the relief of state governments. The significance of the Agree-ment proved to lie less in the systematic coördination of borrowing through the Council than in the medium it provided for the imposi-tion of conservative financial policies on reluctant governments during the depression, and the severe limitation of the independ-ence of the states in directions which may mean a great deal to radical governments. At the same time, the extension of Common-wealth action into what were previously regarded as state fields, and the growth and systematisation of special grants to state govern-ments, have given the Commonwealth a marked degree of indirect influence over state policies.

Apart from payments made since 1927 under the Financial Agreement, the Commonwealth has made other transfers to the states, steadily expanding both in amount and range in the last twenty years. It is sometimes asserted on behalf of the Common-wealth that its expenditure for the relief of primary producers has operated to relieve state budgets by further amounts. There is some truth in this, since relief to primary producers was politically un-avoidable, but the states would not have spent so much as the Commonwealth, and most of the federal expenditure took the form of bounties, a field reserved by the Constitution for the Commonwealth.

Until 1929 the most important systematic federal subsidy to the states was for roads. In the depression years that followed, the Commonwealth enlarged the scope of grants-in-aid to provide payments for local public works, subsidies to metalliferous mining, forestry, and unemployment relief, to be expended by the states under prescribed conditions. The total payments were not great, but they are significant as marking an extension of federal activity into what were previously state responsibilities, accompanied by a measure of Commonwealth supervision, and inducing states to undertake expenditures of their own which they would not otherwise have made. "No community," as Professor W. K. Hancock says, "will allow its leaders to lock the door against a fairy godmother."

Since 1910 special grants have been made under Section 96 of the Constitution by which "the Parliament may grant financial assistance to any State on such terms and conditions as the Parliament thinks fit." Western Australia has received such grants from 1910, Tasmania from 1912, and South Australia from 1929; but until 1933, though the claims of these states were submitted from time to time to Royal Commissions and other bodies, there was little coordination between their respective reports and recommendations. The general assumption on which all these grants were made was that the states concerned were working under temporary difficulties, and needed merely temporary financial aid to tide them over. With the world depression, the problem of these states became acute and their talk of secession stirred the Commonwealth in 1933 to appoint the Commonwealth Grants Commission.

The Commission consists of three members with the duty of inquiring into and reporting on the claims made by any state for financial assistance under Section 96. It was intended that the Commission should be a continuing one so that a uniform policy might be established. In spite of short-term appointments of its members, it continues to operate and its recommendations have always been accepted by the Federal Government.

The three claimant states asking for grants have been Western Australia, Tasmania, and South Australia, which are dependent mainly on rural production and have large areas of useless territory and small populations. Originally, they based their claims on the adverse effects of federal policy, especially the tariff, but they have come to accept the basis adopted by the Commission. At first the Commission was inclined to accept the net adverse effect of federal policy as the measure of a grant, but this was found impossible to estimate. In the course of its investigation the Commission was impressed by the then deficits of the claimant states. It therefore modified its approach, making the budget position of the claimant as compared with that of the other states its first approximation to the need for a grant. In subsequent reports the Commission has come to recommend "grants on the basis of financial needs. . . . The grant should be sufficient to enable a State in difficulties to function at a standard not appreciably below that of other States."[2]

The achievement of the Commission has been its ability to offer a temporary solution which is acceptable to both parties; the Commonwealth is prepared to pay the amounts recommended by the Commission and the states to accept them. Not much more can be expected of any adjustment of federal finances than that it should be acceptable for a few years. But for the future there would seem to be more hope in an extension of a system of grants-in-aid, in place of the present special grants, in which the Commonwealth might encourage state expenditure in desired directions and in which the present claimant states might be helped to attain that "fair Australian standard" which the Commission takes as its ideal. Such an outcome seems likely, since uniform income taxation is to continue.

The occasion for uniform taxation was the need under the stress of war to raise the Commonwealth income tax to steeply progressive levels. An obstacle was the diversity of scales, concessions, and other conditions of state taxes to which the federal taxes were added. Even more important was the need to peg state revenues, to limit competition for labour and materials. Accordingly, having failed to secure consent of the states, the Commonwealth in 1942 passed legislation which had the effect of eliminating all state income taxes for the duration of the war and one year after a single federal tax took their place. The states receive annual compensation in payments equal to their average income-tax revenue in the first two war years. It was provided that claims for additional financial assistance should be heard by the Grants Commission. The legislation survived a

[2] Fifth *Report,* p. 8.

legal challenge as to its constitutionality, and worked smoothly. The states prospered because of swelling railway revenues and war-enforced cuts in expenditure. There were minor claims for further compensation, but they were of little importance. This policy has now been made permanent.

Like the Grants Commission, the Financial Agreement, and the Loan Council, the introduction of uniform taxation has only changed the form of the problems of financial relations, which are no more "solved" than they have been at any time since federation. The trend is more clearly than ever toward a decline in the political significance of the states, as the Commonwealth gains in importance. The drift to centralised finance is part of the general movement toward effective unification within a nominal federalism.

CHAPTER XVI

The Rôle of Labour

BY LLOYD ROSS

TWO FORMS OF SOCIETY clashed in the early days of Australian development: a settlement partly convict, partly free, in which men were demanding simple democratic rights, higher standards of living, and access to land; and a settlement which in effect extended to Australia the British struggle between the masses and the rising capitalists. The labour movement (a term here used to designate both the trade-union and political activities of the working class) in the Australian colonies had its intellectual roots in the varieties of thinking characteristic of the Chartists, the pioneer trade unionists, the Irish Republicans, the Owenites, and other British movements of that time. Early Australian trade unionism—for unionism preceded separate working-class political action—moved vaguely and indecisively both toward struggles for economic objectives and toward assisting more widely based struggles for political rights. Politically the pioneer trade unionists were, in effect, the working-class wing of that party, of whatever name, which was liberal in programme. The workers co-operated with the rest of the community, for example, in resisting transportation and in demanding self-government; and on their own part they formed societies which were either organisations to guarantee the members benefits in times of distress, or true trade unions, or a mixture of both.

Between 1833 and 1848 no less than eighteen unions appeared and carried on intermittently until about 1848. The membership varied from twenty-five to sixty. Local conditions such as rising prices, inability to go on the land, and fear of the competition of convict labour promoted organisation among the skilled artisans who had a monopoly position in the labour market. Basically these organisations are perhaps most accurately described as benefit societies, but their activities were often marked by trade-union characteristics. Local and temporary grievances brought together men in organisations that were modelled on English patterns. The personnel changed quickly because in this pioneer society men were rapidly moving through different occupations and even classes. Social and economic conditions were fluid and there were many avenues of escape from wage work. Only a small proportion of the 10,715 mechanics who were in the colony in 1841 were organised. There was no true place for permanent working-class organisation, but there was a rough continuity of demands because the grievances were enduring.

Furniture workers formed a union in 1833 which was probably the first true union. This club or society, as it was called, was admitted by one of its members to have been established for the maintenance of London piece-work prices, "to insure their tools from loss by fire, and assist the widows and orphans in distress"—a characteristic mixture of motives. In 1833, also, there is evidence of the formation of a "body of coopers," who, in collaboration with their brother tradesmen, held meetings to promote free immigration. In 1835 the typographical workers established a fighting union which lasted at least until 1844. In March, 1837, sailors engaged in whaling off the Australian coasts struck work to enforce a demand for an increase of pay from 3s. 6d. to 4s. a day. The shipowners replied that the demand would "materially retard the progressive advancement of our Colonial marine." Provoked by the economic sufferings of 1839, workers attempted to start a bakery—the "United Association of Sydney for the relief of the working classes." The Shipwrights' Benefit Society (which met in an inn called the Builders' Arms, as did the parent society in Great Britain) announced that they had £400 in their treasury and included as members "almost the whole of the useful class of men who reside in Sydney." An Australian Society of Compositors was formed in 1840 and promptly organised a strike in the offices of the Sydney *Herald*. The management retaliated by importing compositors from England. In January, 1840, the Phoenix Society of Tailors was formed. The building trades were organised. Other unions in existence, with dates of founding, were the Coachmakers' Benefit Society (1837), the Seamen's Benefit Society (1839), and a society of engineers (1840). The Sydney *Gazette* remarked, in 1840, that "The striking mania seems to be gaining ground in Australia." No working-class organisation established in this early period had a continuous existence after the 1850's.

It was not until the discovery of gold brought a rapid increase in population that stability and strength were gained by the unions. In the period after the gold rush the same combination of political and trade-union activity persisted. The revolt of the miners at Ballarat in 1854—the Eureka Stockade—led directly to political reforms and became the most popular tradition of the entire labour movement. The tradition of combining English theory and local aspirations is illustrated by the success of the campaign for the eight-hour day in 1856. A Welsh Chartist, James Stephens, found that building-workers in Sydney and Melbourne complained about the distress caused by working long hours in the heat of the Australian sun. He added Chartist theory to a simple local grievance, found an English liberal to coin the slogan "Eight Hours Work, Eight Hours Leisure, Eight Hours Sleep," and, taking advantage of the shortage of labour that existed in a new country, won an industrial struggle for shorter hours in a remarkably brief time. This victory stimulated the development of local unions and brought them quickly together in common committees. It led to the building of trades halls, the establishment of local trades and labour councils which coördinated all the unions, and even to the election of working-class candidates to Parliament.

Trade unionists were prominent politically in such organisations as reform and protection leagues, land leagues, and conventions. They also combined to intervene in support of labour legislation. Active trade unionists (for example, Charles J. Don) were actually elected to the colonial Parliament in the 1850's. However, their political activities were limited because they had to work at their trades during the day to support their families. Such payment as they got for their parliamentary activities came from their constituents. As an early trade unionist working among the miners pointed out, "With universal suffrage they must have class representation unless they had payment of members. . . . Without pay-

ment of members the miners could not be represented as miners."
When a group of men in the same occupation and with the same
grievances and aspirations were concentrated in one locality, there
was a strong tendency to try for political representation. In 1875
the trade unions combined to send Angus Cameron, the Secretary
of the Sydney Labour Council, to Parliament for West Sydney. He
was "probably the first member to receive financial support from
trade unionists." But he refused to carry out the wishes of the Council and lost trade-union support. The railway suburb of Redfern in
Sydney sent Cameron, supported by various unions, to the Legislative Assembly in the 'seventies, where he successfully introduced
amendments to the Railway Management Act.

Yet these pioneer labour parliamentarians were not, of course,
members of labour parties, or of any party, unless a liberal party
lent them some support. Indeed, they usually had a roving commission to assist any party that would introduce labour legislation. The
political activities of the unionists were usually spasmodic—a flurry
of activity at a particular election in support of a single candidate—
and there was no long-range political strategy. Lack of funds was
one obstacle.

The second all-Australian Trade Union Congress, held in 1884
(the first had been held in 1879), declared that, in order to obtain
better representation of the working classes in Parliament, "every
effort should be made to secure payment of members in those colonies that have not already adopted the principle." Although it
was argued in the Congress that payment in the colony of Victoria
had not helped to gain labour representation, the resolution was
passed by a large majority. Moreover, the Congress set up parliamentary committees to lobby in labour's interest. The mover of the
resolution declared that such committees had been established
for many years in England and had been successful in securing the
passage of many measures helpful to the working class. The committee was charged with supporting such measures as the extension
of protection to local industries, the repeal or amendment of the
Masters and Servants Act, the abolition of plural voting, and the
proper inspection of workshops, factories, boilers, and machinery.

Both the New South Wales and the Victorian committees presented reports to the third Congress, in 1885, indicating that Par-

liament had considered alteration of various legislation on the suggestion of the trade unionists. But the situation was not satisfactory. In November, 1885, the Victorian Trades Hall Council resolved that, "taking into consideration the fact that measures appertaining to the welfare of the working class have from time to time been shelved by the Legislature, this Council considers that the time has arrived when working-class representatives should be nominated to contest the constituencies." Three working-class candidates were nominated and endorsed in the following year by the Victorian Working Men's Political Association. The programme favoured anti-sweating legislation, anti-Chinese legislation, legalisation of the eight-hour day, single electorates, abolition of plural voting, a national scheme of irrigation, a national banking system, and a federation of the Australian colonies.

The fourth Trade Union Congress, in 1886, passed, with only one dissenting vote, a resolution asking for both labour representation in Parliament and payment of members. The former was considered impossible without the latter.

A complete survey of the situation reveals that unions were taking part only slowly and tentatively in political action. Some labour members were returned, but usually, as earlier, only in response to an unusual stimulus. However, both on the level of the thinking of union leaders, and on the level of practical work in electing candidates, it was obvious that the establishment of labour parties could not be far distant. The foundations had been laid.

Both liberal reform and easy toleration of labour's trade-union and political activity came to a dramatic end with the Great Depression and the resultant industrial disputes of the late 'eighties and the 'nineties.

In September, 1889, the marine officers formed an association. To obtain support for their demands on shipowners, the officers decided to affiliate as from March, 1890, with the Trades Hall of Melbourne. The shipowners promptly raised the objection that discipline would be difficult if seamen and officers were members of the same organisation. Their refusal to accept the affiliation of the officers precipitated a series of strikes and lockouts that lasted for five years. Numerous issues combined in one great struggle for power between capital and labour. Said the chairman of the Steamship

Owners' Association, "We are a united and compact body.... All the owners throughout Australia have signed a bond to stand by one another and do nothing unless a vote of all the members be taken." Replied the Labour Defence Committee, "It is the principle of unionism that is at stake." Australia was thereupon flooded by a wave of strikes which were eventually dissipated in the desert of defeat.

Unions heard the call of solidarity and responded, but were smashed. First the waterside workers, then the shearers, went to the assistance of the marine officers. The shearers, to be sure, seized this opportunity to try to win back their former status, which had been destroyed by the depression. They were beaten. Involved in this dispute was the vexed question of freedom of contract (the open shop), or the right of employers to hire whomever they pleased regardless of the union's wishes. When, after the first defeat, the employers reduced the shearers' wages and enforced freedom of contract, the shearers again revolted, only to be defeated once more in June, 1891. Members of the union executive were arrested and sentenced to gaol at hard labour for three years. A third time the shearers in Victoria and New South Wales resisted and again were beaten. An attempt of the Queensland shearers in 1894 to win recognition of the union failed also. The lead-miners at Broken Hill, New South Wales, conducted a series of disastrous strikes; so did the coal-miners.

But there were compensations for labour even in defeat. The strikes had demonstrated labour's solidarity. The Labour Defence Committee collected what were then large sums from Australian unions and the general public and received donations from English unions as well. In one three-month period the Committee distributed strike pay to 81,428 men whose union funds were exhausted. Barracks for homeless strikers were provided and meals were given at soup kitchens. A strike bulletin was issued daily. These expressions of solidarity constituted the most important lesson of the great conflicts—not the defeat on the immediate aims, but the victory in uniting men for a common purpose and a common struggle. The experience, indeed, is basic to any understanding of how labour, after what seemed to be a disastrous rout, could go on to establish political parties and newspapers.

The strikes were followed by a concentration of political activity, but the trade unions were determinedly rebuilt. There was a quickening of socialistic ideas. William Lane, the labour journalist of Queensland who did much to introduce Australian labour to socialism, wrote, in *The Worker,* that from the strike, as far as it had gone,

there are three great lessons to be learnt, the necessity for persistent organisation during times of peace, the necessity for merging the interests of any industrial union in the interests of the whole, and while neglecting none, to permit none to force the fighting till all are ready, and the necessity for political action as a solution of the individual difficulty, which really consists in the ownership by a few of the means by which alone the workers can work and live.

The New South Wales Labour Defence Committee reached a similar conclusion, concluding its final report thus:

Our organisation must become a means of education and constitutional power. Already it is half learnt. We have come out of conflict a united political labour party, destined amid all the hypocrisy of political life to brighten the lot of our children, if not our own lot. The rule that trade unionism must steer clear of politics was a golden rule when there was so much to be done within our present industrial environments. But that time . . . is drawing to an end, and ere we can radically improve the lot of the worker, we must secure a substantial representation in Parliament.

Labour in New South Wales led the way. In its first great attempt, in 1891, it won 36 seats, one-third of the total in the lower house of the state legislature. It was easier to win elections in those days. The electorates were small; the costs of running a campaign were slight and candidates were prepared to make heavy sacrifices to meet them; the old parties had no vast propaganda apparatus to be combated. A few canvassers going from door to door were able to reach most of the voters and at street-corner meetings Labour's case could be stated as effectively as that of the older parties. Politics were still in a fluid state. There were no great extremes of wealth and poverty, and no strong, inherited political loyalties. Moreover, at that time the desire for social reform was prevalent. The existing parties no longer satisfied the people. The time had come for a radical reshuffling of political allegiances. Labour rose to its opportunity, first in the states, then in the Commonwealth.

Labour fought the first federal election—that of 1900—on a platform of support for the adult franchise, old-age pensions, total exclusion of coloured and other races which were considered undesir-

able, and amendments to the Constitution to introduce the initiative and referendum and to solve the problem of possible deadlocks
between the two Houses. On fiscal questions all Labour candidates
were allowed a free hand. They could support protection or free
trade. Labour returned 8 of 36 members of the Senate and 16 out
of 75 in the House of Representatives. The anti-Labour interests
were divided between the Protectionists, led by Edmund Barton,
and the Free-Traders, led by George H. Reid. Labour supported the
Barton Ministry, which passed the so-called "White Australia" Act,
the universal franchise for federal elections, old-age pensions, and
a protective tariff. Labour's attitude was clearly expressed by the
Party leader in the Senate, "We are for sale and we will get the
auctioneer in and take care that he is the right man . . . I want to
show the Government what they have to do to secure our support."
It was the established Labour parliamentary policy of support in
return for concessions. When Barton retired to the High Court
Bench, the Prime Ministership and Labour support passed to Alfred Deakin, also a Protectionist. In the 1903 elections Labour won
25 seats in the House and 14 in the Senate. Deakin had 27 followers
in the House, the significant branch of the legislature, and Reid
and his free-traders 24. With Labour support, Deakin took office.

The outlines of Commonwealth policy had been sketched in by
the Barton Ministry, leaving a period of doubt. The next great
questions were certain to involve labour feelings intimately, since
labour was sure to advocate the application of principles hammered
out in the strike of the 'nineties. It was a period of political shuffling,
of marking time, until the two anti-Labour parties could settle their
tariff differences and take up the task of defending the conservative
interest as their principal business. When this happened Labour
would be placed in its proper position as the Official Opposition
and the alternative government.

The decisive issue proved to be the right of civil servants to approach the Federal Arbitration Court. Deakin opposed this and
Labour withdrew its support. William Morris Hughes, speaking
for Labour, declared that a man should not be a judge of his own
case and that therefore employees of governments, state and federal,
should have the right to appeal to an independent tribunal. On the
issue Deakin fell and Labour came to power.

With John C. Watson as Prime Minister, Labour held office from April 27 to August 17, 1904, the first Labour Ministry in Commonwealth history. This event, to which should be added distrust of Labour's "socialism" and the existence of serious industrial strife, led, in the words of Hughes, to the combination of the two anti-Labour parties to crush "this presumptuous and impious uprising of the hewers of wood and drawers of water." Labour was thereupon defeated in the House. This defeat foreshadowed the eventual solution of the conservative dilemma. In the succeeding election, Labour won additional seats, raising its totals to 27 in the House and 15 in the Senate. Although Labour was now the strongest single party in the House, it again supported Deakin until November, 1908. Senator George Pearce declared at that time, "Our party has kept the Deakin Government in office for nearly three years until dry rot has set in." On Deakin's fall, Labour, now headed by Andrew Fisher, again took office. After a little more than six months of this regime, the two anti-Labour parties arranged a permanent fusion and, in May, 1909, exerted their newly won power to defeat Labour, thereby clarifying the political situation.

Hitherto the working-class vote had been divided between Deakin and Labour, but when Deakin allied himself with the landowners and manufacturers whom previously he had denounced, the division of Labour's strength also came to an end. The electorate apparently felt that only an overweening desire for position and power could have united such bitter rivals. In 1910, therefore, Labour won 23 out of the 36 seats in the Senate and 42 out of 75 in the House. This gave Labour both power and office for the first time. With Fisher as Prime Minister, the Labour caucus elected a ministry composed of two miners, a wharf-labourer, a building-worker, a common labourer, a carpenter, a hatter, a compositor, an engine-driver, and a nonmanual labourer. Said Lord Bryce, "For the first time in history (apart from a movement of revolution) executive power passed legally from the hands of the so-called 'upper strata' to those of the hard-handed workers. Australia and the world saw a new kind of government of the people, by a class and for a class."

The principal legislation passed by the first Commonwealth Labour Government that had a majority in Parliament illustrates the mood of political Labour at that time. The establishment of an Australian navy and the introduction of compulsory military training were reflections of the growing nationalism and increasing independence of Great Britain. The establishment of a Commonwealth Bank was an expression of socialism and of a desire to control Australian financial development. Nationalism and socialism were the twin pillars of Labour thought. Labour, it can be said, brought back into Australian life the vigour, freshness, and progress that had been lost during the first decade of the century. And Labour owed much to the true socialists who moved in and out of the political organisation in accordance with the degree of their disquiet over the delay in introducing socialism. They acted as a channel of communication with ideas and events overseas, and gave stimulation to the Australian working-class movement, which was a mixture of land reformers, middle-class liberals, socialists, monetary enthusiasts, trade unionists, and high-tariff advocates.

The election of 1913 resulted in the anti-Labour party obtaining a majority of one vote in the House, while Labour won 3 new seats in the Senate, making a total of 29, to 7 held by the Government. When the Government provided a Speaker of the House, the members of the House were evenly divided, and Parliament thereupon became unworkable. A double dissolution—a simultaneous dissolution of both House and Senate—was granted on July 30, 1914. In the election that followed a few weeks later, Labour obtained a majority of 8 seats in the House and also won 30 of the 36 seats in the Senate. Andrew Fisher became Prime Minister once more. His Government was faced with the task of waging war.

The Labour leaders were stunned by the war. They had no specialist in foreign affairs among them. Indeed, they lacked an intellectual basis for an independent attitude in foreign affairs. The unions, for their part, were isolated from contacts abroad, absorbed in daily routine, saturated with craft outlooks which kept apart the different unions, full of satisfaction little distinguished from apathy because of recent social reforms. They, too, were bewildered by the sudden outbreak of general war. The Labour Party was, of course, liberal in method and social-democratic in purpose. Its attitude toward war was determined by its domestic outlook. The upshot was that both the Party and the unions supported the war with enthusiasm, if also without much knowledge.

Yet in contradiction to what might have been expected, meetings against war throughout Australia were broken up with official sanction, the Labour Government established a policy of censorship, suppression, and imprisonment which was as drastic as any in the world. Not merely were critical war books banned, but the authorities took the opportunity to interfere with labour papers and to ban a variety of well-known working-class books.

The very intensity of the attack on any groups or individuals who insisted on thinking for themselves forced the socialist minority both to clarify its ideas and to intensify its activities. In June, 1915, Frank Anstey, M.P., threatened to resign from the Party in order to criticise the Government's dedication to militarism. He opposed the War Precautions Act, the fount from which most of the restrictions flowed, and declared that nothing should deprive a British subject of the right of trial by jury. He insisted that the Labour Party was in existence primarily to carry out its platform "and not to be sidestepped, decoyed, or bullied into deserting its fundamental principles because of an accidental irruption." As the months passed and English publications began to filter through the censorship, and as the pacifists grew stronger in the knowledge that men like Snowden, Morel, and MacDonald in Britain, Luxemburg and Liebknecht in Germany, and Berger in America were opposing the war, doubts about the justification of the war were more freely spread, creating first apathy and then opposition.

The issue which precipitated a nation-wide public fight was conscription for overseas service. The proposal by the Government to institute this measure was defeated by referenda taken in 1916 and 1917. The campaigns waged over it split the Labour Party—indeed, the whole Australian community—from top to bottom, eventually causing the expulsion of many of the most experienced leaders (who were in favour of conscription) from the Party, including William Morris Hughes, who had succeeded Fisher as Labour Prime Minister in 1915. Because of this issue Labour lost office: Hughes managed to retain the Prime Ministership, though he was no longer the leader of the Labour Party. Eventually he fortified his anomalous position by joining the conservatives. This proved disastrous for political Labour in Commonwealth politics, for it was out of office from 1916 to 1929.

A wave of strikes came on the heels of the wrangle over conscription, reaching a climax in 1917. When the war ended, political Labour was taking a vote of its membership to determine whether or not it should withdraw its support from the war altogether. Labour was divided, in the process of disintegration within, and disowned without by the electors.

Though Labour had been nominally socialist from the beginning of its political career, it was not until the period of intensification of radicalism after the war that a socialist objective was clearly formulated. In 1921 Labour placed at the head of its Party platform as an objective, "Socialisation of industry, production, distribution, and exchange." The methods recommended to achieve this end were:

Constitutional utilisation of industrial and parliamentary machinery.

The organisation of workers along the lines of industry.

Nationalisation of banking and all principal industries.

The government of nationalised industries by boards upon which the workers in the industry and the community shall have representation.

The establishment of an elective Supreme Economic Council by all nationalised industries.

The setting up of Labour research and Labour information bureaus and of Labour educational institutions in which the workers shall be trained in the management of nationalised industries.

However, Labour was in a weak position in federal politics when this programme was authorised and for some years thereafter. By the time it had achieved office, times had changed and the radical impulse had somewhat waned.

On the eve of the Great Depression in 1929, James H. Scullin became Labour Prime Minister for the Commonwealth. Confronted with the intricate problems involved in governing the Australian economy under such conditions, Labour was unable to find satisfactory solutions. The trade unionists saw neither the justice of, nor the need for, lowering the standard of living. Ignoring the fall in the national income and the rôle of supply and demand under capitalism, the trade unionists argued in terms of a socialist state. Believing that purchasing power had been restricted by the banks, they called on the government to increase the issue of notes.

The Report of the Unemployment and Immigration Committee of the Australasian Council of Trade Unions declared that unemployment was inherent in the capitalist system, but it also expressed the belief that "the nature and the degree of unemployment are determinable to a considerable extent by factors within the present economic system that are controllable." So the Committee recommended the introduction of a federal scheme of unemployment insurance, protection to the point of prohibition against goods coming into Australia, provision against the export of raw materials that could be processed in any degree in Australia, nationalisation of banking, public works on the day-labour principle with preference for unionists, and settlement of unemployed workers on the land. The objective of the policy was to keep wages up.

The unions, however, were powerless against the combined opposition. The Labour movement was unable to reconcile in practice its conviction that capitalism was responsible for unemployment with the fact that a socialist revolution was utterly impracticable. Its thinking wobbled between two worlds, with the result that it really suffered the worst effects of both. Politically it fluctuated between resisting the plans for deflation advanced by non-Labour groups and attempting to popularise schemes for monetary expansion. The Party itself was divided over the issues; so control of the House did not work to the advantage of the Government. The Senate was hostile. The only possible course for the Government was either to accept the plans of the professional economists or resign and appeal the whole question to the people. Labour fatalistically drifted to defeat.

Labour officially accepted the so-called Premiers' Plan (evolved by professional economists and given political viability by the patronage of the premiers of the states), yet so great was the opposition of the Labour rank and file that Cabinet ministers in state governments who attempted to implement it were expelled from the Party. The Scullin Government was finally defeated in the House as the result of action taken by a dissident Labour group recruited from the members for New South Wales, where the most violent and forthright opposition to the Premiers' Plan had its greatest strength. In the ensuing election Labour was defeated. Joseph A. Lyons (1879–1939), who had been Treasurer in the Scullin Government but who in the hurly-burly of its disintegration had left the Party to be chosen as leader of the conservatives, became Prime Minister.

Two great crises had confronted federal Labour, a world war and a world depression. In both, Labour had been smashed by its own supporters and by the electorate. Scullin had neither the energy nor the self-confidence to restore the broken Party. Many Labour politicians had been expelled for implementing the Premiers' Plan; many of those who remained were tainted with support of deflationary measures.

When Scullin resigned the leadership in 1934, a little-known and untried figure, John Curtin of Western Australia, succeeded, mainly because he had consistently opposed the plan. To him fell the job of rebuilding the political strength of federal Labour. He turned out to be the most important figure in the history of the movement in this century. Curtin's story summarises the broad development of the movement in his time: left socialist and critic of the Labour Party in the first decade of the Commonwealth; antimilitarist and war-resister in the second decade; builder of the Party after disastrous defeat in the third and fourth decades; Labour Prime Minister and national leader in the Second World War. Under Curtin's benign influence internal quarrels were composed and splinter groups were brought back into the ranks. Then a slow movement took place, away from merely negative opposition to conservative proposals, toward a carefully considered programme of economic development and expansion.

International rather than domestic policy came suddenly to outweigh all other considerations. While there were, in the years before the Second World War, powerful groups in the trade unions which supported a policy of collective security, they were resisted by Curtin on the ground that Australia was powerless to resolve the problems of Europe. Curtin's conception of the great danger to Australia was that it might find itself involved in a Pacific war unprepared and unsupported. Knowing full well that the Australian people would not support defenceless isolation, he declared that overseas developments forced Australia to rely more and more upon its own resources and that therefore air power, founded on Australia's own industrial resources, offered the only feasible programme for defence. No one in Australia foresaw developments accurately, but Curtin was proved by events to have had the cleverest vision.

Curtin's native ability and his record for farseeing formulations of policy explain, in large measure, why he was able to take charge of the Government in September, 1941, while the Labour Party was a minority in the House, and why, furthermore, he was able to lead the Party to an overwhelming victory at the polls two years later.

So it happened that when the oft-predicted Pacific war came, Labour, after nine years out of office, was in a position to provide the leadership which Australia desperately needed. In executing the task entrusted to it, Labour recovered from the defeats of the First World War and the Great Depression.

It is difficult to point to wartime measures which were due exclusively to the action of Labour, but when emphasis is considered, the contribution of Labour is clear. The Curtin Government accelerated the conversion of industry from peacetime to wartime production, enforced "austerity" ways of living, conscripted men for production as well as war, enforced a truly Australian policy in war strategy, and gave drive and inspiration to the Australian effort that were tragically lacking in the period from the outbreak of war to the end of 1941.

When Curtin died in 1945, Joseph B. Chifley became Labour Prime Minister. Chifley had been Treasurer and Minister for Post-War Reconstruction. The general plan for reconstruction (see chap. xxviii) reflects his moderate views. However, the emphasis placed on full employment can be interpreted as a modern application of the long-range socialist determination to avoid the social consequences of another major depression; the change in the control of the Commonwealth Bank as a belated response to the demands of Labour during the Great Depression; and the rounding out of the social services as a revival of one of federal Labour's oldest aspirations. Nevertheless, one should not overlook the fact that among the rank and file there is substantial support for a programme of nationalisation which finds no direct expression in the plan; even if they pass by nationalisation, they will demand higher wages and shorter hours, regardless of technical economic considerations, as a reward for wartime efforts. It is unlikely that the Labour Government will have entirely smooth sailing in the postwar transition period.

The Australian Labour Party is both socialist and reformist, revolutionary and Fabian. The emphasis is constantly changing, depending on such influences as the current record of Labour governments, the existence or absence of industrial unrest annoying to the general public, the character of the interparty struggles (with which the history of the Party is peppered), and the prevailing national mood. At times the movement will insist on its policy of nationalisation; at other times it will be content with slow, fractional reforms. Disunity on theory often leads to division and breakaways, but because the Party is the only mass progressive movement in Australia, unity is always regained eventually. Since socialists are always active inside the movement, they keep socialistic ideas current in the Party. Labour has yet to implement its socialist program, but no prominent member of the Party dares to argue publicly that socialist theory and objectives should therefore be discarded. On the contrary, the movement continues to support experiments with socialistic legislation.

Any comprehensive history of Australian Labour must therefore comprise a study of the way in which the objectives of the Party have changed in response to the demands of the political scene. No labour party in any country has solved the problem of socialising industry by parliamentary means (though the Attlee Government in Great Britain is perhaps to show the way), but in no country has the socialist objective been more influential in the struggle for power between groups and individuals than it has been in Australia. Individuals have changed their views, not so much because of personal ambition, but because of the impact of practical problems. The trade-union leader, for example, emphasises the improvement of wages and conditions; as a politician he finds it necessary to consider carefully the views of those who are neither trade unionists nor members of the Party; as a Cabinet Minister he finds it obligatory to take into account the still wider national interest. Occasionally harmony is reached between the immediate needs of the socialists and the needs of Australia as a nation. The fact that this harmony, which was important to Labour's success during the Second World War, is often an historical accident suggests the difficult problems which arise when there are fundamental differences between the views and principles of Labour and the views of Australia as a nation of peoples with conflicting philosophies of society and government.

Labour has a tragic leaning toward political suicide, less in defeat than in victory, but it has an equal capacity for doggedness in adversity and therefore for eventual revival, as the record shows; a realistic sensitivity to the demand for reform and a tendency to fail to implement a socialist programme; a striking capacity for capable administration and a weakness for risking failure by allowing considerations of faction to determine appointments; on occasion a capacity to absorb the worthiest elements in the nation and on other occasions a weakness for acquiescing in demagogy and corruption, or simply mediocrity of personnel and policy.

The alternative confronting Labour in the postwar period is not so much between left and right as between the building of a Labour Party with programmes in harmony with national needs of tomorrow and a renewed drift toward the political doldrums, with power, perhaps, but without creative drive. There is little prospect that the Labour Party will form an alliance of any kind with the Communist Party, but the Communists hope to continue their influence on political Labour through their control of certain unions which are affiliated with the Labour Party. Unless the Communists succeed in capturing considerable influence by this indirect approach, it seems clear that the struggles between the opposing elements native to the Labour Party will be fought out within the traditional Labour limits. However the burgeoning issues are settled, it is certain that Labour will survive the difficulties of the postwar period only if it retains unity on a policy which is at once progressive, socialistic, and nationalistic. These are the traditional elements from which it has composed its programmes.

CHAPTER XVII

The Development of the Social Services

BY T. H. KEWLEY

THE NATURE of the Australian economy has determined an approach to the social services which is rather different from that taken in older countries. The expanding frontier made a Poor Law, such as that which developed in Great Britain, either unnecessary or inapplicable. In any event, social services of other types have been preferred.

Until recently the range of social services has not been wide. In the early twentieth century, interest centred around old-age pensions; later it shifted to maternity allowances as a means of relieving family costs and incidentally of encouraging the birth rate. These and similar experiments gained for Australia the reputation of being a pioneer worker in the social laboratory. Smugly satisfied with her achievements, Australia fell behind many other countries, and it was not until the depression of the early 'thirties that her complacency was disturbed. More recently the social services have been seen as a means of improving standards of living and have been extended to cover most of the vicissitudes of life and livelihood.

Commonwealth participation in the provision of social services was at first confined to old-age pensions (1909), invalid pensions (1910), and maternity allowances (1912). During the Second World War the Commonwealth widened its interests, and its activities were extended to include child endowment (1941), widows' pensions (1942), funeral benefits for invalid and old-age pensioners (1943), and sickness and unemployment benefits (1944). Some of these Commonwealth measures have superseded schemes which were already operating in one or more of the states. Others have provided for contingencies against which inadequate provision, or none at all, had been made by the states. In all instances the practice, unlike that in the United States, has been for the Commonwealth itself to undertake the administration as well as the financing of social services.

The only specific power relating to social services which is granted to the Commonwealth by the Constitution is one which deals with invalid and old-age pensions. (An extension of powers was obtained by referendum in 1946.) Other social services under consideration when the Constitution was being framed in the late 'nineties were regarded as being more appropriately left to the states. Some doubt was expressed at the time whether the Commonwealth, with its supposedly limited resources, would be able to finance old-age pensions. That doubt was dispelled in 1908, though at the expense of the financial security of the states, and the Commonwealth is now concerned, by some straining of its general powers (e.g., its appropriation power), to provide and administer a wide range of services. Not only were many new services introduced in the war years, but the rates of benefits already in operation before the war were increased. As a result, the annual expenditure by the Commonwealth on social services has been raised from less than £17,000,000, in 1938–1939, to an estimated amount of £80,000,000, or more than the total taxation revenue of the Commonwealth in 1938–1939.

In spite of the increasing activities of the Commonwealth, the states still provide a wide range of social services: education, housing, public health, hospitals, and maternal and child-welfare services. Their long-established institutions for the care of the infirm, the blind, the aged, and the insane are not likely to be duplicated or supplemented by Commonwealth action. Nor has the development of public social services rendered unimportant the work of voluntary charitable organisations. These form an integral part of the hospital systems of the states and play a traditional rôle in supplementing the public social services and pioneering new fields.

The following account is concerned primarily with the income-security services, i.e., those measures which are designed to maintain an income when earning power is lost (old age, invalidism, widowhood) or interrupted (unemployment, sickness), and to assist with expenditures arising at times of birth, death, and marriage. For all these the Commonwealth now assumes responsibility.

In the nineteenth century, voluntary organisations, many of which received Government subsidies, occupied the central position in the charitable relief systems of the several colonies. They conducted homes, refuges, and other institutions, providing "indoor" relief for virtually all types of social needs. They also granted "outdoor" relief, usually in kind, to the sick, the aged, and the infirm, and to widows and others who were destitute. The action taken by the colonial governments was conditioned mainly by the view that social provision by the state tended to undermine the thrift and self-reliance of the individual.

Before the end of the century the colonial governments were nevertheless forced by events to relieve the voluntary organisations of much of their work for the aged and infirm. The method they adopted was that of providing institutions, most of which were extremely unattractive and were conducted in such a manner as to discourage the individual from using them except as a last resort. Public reaction against this institutional or barracks system of caring for the aged, very like the reaction which had led earlier to the adoption of the boarding-out system for state wards, was an important factor in bringing about the enactment in New South Wales, in 1900, of legislation for old-age pensioners—the first of the modern income-security services.

The forces leading to the enactment of this measure, as with most of the later ones, were, however, complex. As early as 1896 an association was formed to popularise the idea of old-age pensions. Shortly afterward the Labour Party adopted the provision of old-age pensions as a plank in its platform. In the same year, an all-party committee of the New South Wales Legislative Assembly reported that the question was engaging the attention of prominent statesmen and others overseas, and asserted that the introduction of old-age pensions was both desirable and practicable. The immediate stimulus came four years later from the Labour Party, which held the balance of power in Parliament and kept a non-Labour Government in office in return for concessions.

The system introduced did not break any fresh ground. The Premier admitted that the legislation was a copy, with certain modifications, of laws which were operating in New Zealand. The Act proclaimed that "it is equitable that deserving persons who during the prime of life have helped to bear the public burdens of the Colony by the payment of taxes, and by opening up its resources by their labour and skill, should receive from the Colony a pension in their old age." This generous principle, which implied a system of universal pensions, was not fully observed, however, by the actual provisions of the Act, the most important of which limited the payment of pensions to those who could satisfy a means test.

Victoria introduced legislation on old-age pensions within a few weeks of New South Wales, and Queensland followed suit several years later. The pension systems in these three states were superseded by a Commonwealth-wide scheme which came into force in 1909.

The inclusion of the power to provide old-age pensions in the Commonwealth Constitution led to the inclusion of proposals to implement that power in the policies of both the Liberal and Labour parties in the Commonwealth Parliament. Even so, there was no precipitate action and the traditional British device was adopted of appointing a Royal Commission to examine the idea. Its report in 1906 was favourable, but budget difficulties seemed at that time insuperable, since the Commonwealth was temporarily required by the Constitution to pay over to the states three-fourths of the net receipts from customs and excise as well as all surplus revenue. These difficulties were partly overcome in 1908 by the passing of a Surplus Revenue Act, giving the Commonwealth greater control of its funds, and legislation was at last enacted for old-age pensions. The measure was introduced by the Liberal Party, but it was stimulated to action by the Labour Party, on whose support it relied if it was to remain in office.

The Commonwealth legislation closely followed the New South Wales scheme. Eligibility for pensions was provided for those who had resided in Australia for at least twenty-five years, who were of good character, and who were virtually without other resources. The nature of the pensions system has not since been changed in any essential, though the rate has been increased to accord with rising costs of living and with popular conceptions of what the pension should be.

The demand for invalid pensions was not so widespread as that for old-age pensions. Invalid pensions, based on a scheme which had been in force in New South Wales since 1907, were nevertheless provided at the last moment, as the Old Age Pensions Bill was being drafted. They became operative in 1910 on a Commonwealth-wide basis. The rates for invalid pensions are the same as those for old-age pensions. Before the passing of an amendment in 1942, total incapacity was an essential qualification. A further extension of the scheme in that year provided for the granting of an allowance both to the wife of an invalid pensioner and to her first child under sixteen years of age. No allowance is yet granted to the wives of old-age pensioners unless, of course, they are eligible for an old-age or invalid pension in their own right.

A Commonwealth scheme of widows' pensions was introduced in 1942. Before that, New South Wales and Victoria were the only states in which specific provision was made for widows. The other states did, however, grant some assistance to widows through their Child Welfare or Charitable Relief departments. Under the Commonwealth scheme, widows without children and under fifty years of age are not eligible for pensions. The term "widow" otherwise is generously interpreted and includes a "dependent female," i.e., a *de facto* widow, a deserted wife, a divorced woman who has not remarried, and a woman whose husband is in a hospital for the insane. The Government has expressly refused to regard as a widow a woman whose husband is in gaol.

These, then, are the services which are designed to maintain an income when earning power is lost through old age, invalidism, or the death of the breadwinner. Some 43,000 widows receive pensions, the total cost of which is more than £3,000,000 annually. The estimated cost of invalid and old-age pensions is about £27,000,000. Of persons in the eligible age groups, i.e., men over sixty-five years of age and women over sixty, some 270,000, or nearly every second person in those groups, receive a pension. Their large number accounts for the close attention which is given to old-age pensioners by members of Parliament, some of whom find it politically expedient to champion their cause.

Since the depression of the 'thirties attention has been focussed on measures designed to assist workers whose earnings are interrupted by sickness or unemployment. In the nineteenth century the measures taken for the relief of the unemployed were limited by two widely held beliefs: unemployment was regarded as a temporary incident which would disappear with better times; and it was assumed that many were unemployed through their own choice. No poor rate was levied, nor (except in Western Australia) were there any workhouses. During acute unemployment, governments made special grants to voluntary organisations for the relief of the families of the unemployed. But Government relief without work in return was exceptional. The customary method was to grant wages or rations in return for work specially provided by the Government.

In the early 'nineties a demand was made for remedying unemployment by granting free access to vacant Crown lands where groups could settle in "socialistic communities toiling for the common good and sharing in the common gains." This idea, popularised by William Lane, who was then arranging for his settlement of New Australia in Paraguay, was adopted only to a limited degree and did not prove successful.

The methods of relieving the unemployed adopted in the nineteenth century were continued in the twentieth. Except in Queensland, where a scheme of unemployment insurance was introduced in 1923, no new forms of responsibility were assumed by state governments until the depression of the 'thirties, when the task of relieving the great numbers of the unemployed had grown beyond the capacity of voluntary organisations. Special taxes were then imposed, and Government food relief systems were improvised.

The food relief systems have since continued in much the same form, though the demands made on them during the war years were small. It is probable that the recent Commonwealth scheme of unemployment benefits will have the effect of confining food relief to those who are unemployable. The state systems differ from that of the Commonwealth in that they are not regulated by Acts of Parliament. The value of the relief granted, which is usually in kind, has frequently been changed in accordance with ministerial instructions. Benefits provided under the Commonwealth system are in cash and—an unusual feature—they continue as long as the unemployment lasts.

The Commonwealth sickness benefits, also, may be granted for an indefinite period. If, however, permanent sickness develops, the beneficiary is transferred to the list of invalid pensioners. Unlike the unemployment benefit, no sickness-benefit schemes existed previously in the states. Some industrial awards provide for sick leave; and workmen's compensation laws cover industrial accidents. Apart from these, the main provision for cash payments in periods of sickness has been made voluntarily through Friendly Societies. Health insurance, including provisions for the payment of sickness benefits, was introduced by the Commonwealth Government in 1938, but was suspended before it came fully into operation.

Sickness and unemployment benefits form part of the National Welfare Scheme. The establishment of a National Welfare Fund, from which new social services are to be financed, was announced in February, 1943. This announcement was, in effect, a sugar coating to the pill of further increases in the income-tax rates, particularly in the lower-income groups, which were announced simultaneously. Only two services—a new form of maternity allowances and funeral benefits for invalid and old-age pensioners—came into operation on the establishment of the Fund. The estimated annual costs of these are £2,500,000 and £300,000, respectively. The payment of unemployment benefits (estimated to cost £2,000,000 annually for every 1 per cent of unemployment) and sickness benefits (estimated annual cost, £8,500,000) began in July, 1945. Hospital benefits (costing £4,400,000 annually) and pharmaceutical benefits, i.e., free medicines (costing £2,100,000 annually), are expected to operate later as part of the National Welfare Scheme. Other expenditures of the Commonwealth include those on an employment service and on subsidies for housing.

The measures making up the National Welfare Scheme, and the system of widows' pensions, were introduced by a Labour Government. They cannot, however, be credited solely to the Labour Party. Other forces played an important part in their introduction, not the least of these being the world-wide clamour for social security. Of the local influences the most important was that of the Commonwealth Parliamentary Committee on Social Security. This

Committee, composed of members of all parties and of both Houses of Parliament, was first established in 1941 by a non-Labour Government and has been continued by the Labour Government. Some of the subsequent legislation has followed its recommendations closely, and its members have been influential in a number of ways. It seems probable that much of the wartime social legislation would have been enacted, with perhaps less generosity and some differences (e.g., on a contributory basis), even if a non-Labour Government had been in power.

The Commonwealth now provides assistance with the expenses arising at times of birth, death, and marriage. A system of maternity allowances, introduced by a Labour Government, has been in operation since 1912. Amending legislation, in 1943, abolished the means test which had been imposed as an economy measure during the depression of the 'thirties, and also provided for the payment, besides the customary baby-bonus of between £5 and £7. 10s., of an allowance of 25s. a week for four weeks preceding, and four weeks following, the birth of a child.

The fear of being buried as paupers had induced many old-age pensioners to contribute small weekly sums to private mortuary funds to ensure for themselves a more dignified funeral. To banish this fear and to permit the pensioner to devote the whole of his pension to his maintenance, legislation was introduced by the Commonwealth in 1942 under which an allowance is paid toward the burial costs of invalid and old-age pensioners. There is no other system of government assistance toward the cost of burial. Some people, however, still make provision voluntarily through Friendly Societies.

There are various schemes whereby money may be borrowed for the purpose of building a home. The interest rates are usually moderate and there is liberal provision for the repayment of capital. There are no measures to help defray expenses arising at the time of marriage, but some assistance is granted toward the cost of maintaining children. A scheme of child endowment was introduced in New South Wales in 1927. This, the only state scheme, was superseded in 1941 by a Commonwealth-wide scheme. The Commonwealth plan now provides (at an annual cost of more than £18,000,000) for the payment to the mother of an endowment

of 7s. 6d. a week for each child, after the first, who is less than sixteen years of age.

The first child is assumed to be already provided for in the basic
wage, i.e., the lowest amount that can be paid to an unskilled
worker for a full week's work. In determining this wage, the Commonwealth Court of Conciliation and Arbitration has some regard
to the needs of a family of a certain size. In 1934 the Court adopted
a family unit of four. The Chief Judge of the Court stated, in 1941,
however, that the basic wage was then adequate only for the needs
of a family unit of three. About this time the Commonwealth Government announced its intention of introducing a scheme of child
endowment which would apply to each child after the first. The
Commonwealth endowment is not limited, as was the New South
Wales benefit, to those who receive no more than the basic wage
and whose family exceeds in number the unit provided for in that
wage. It is paid without respect to the income of the parents.

The Commonwealth has thus developed a system of social services which makes some provision for all the main vicissitudes of
life and livelihood. The system does not, however, provide for all
persons. With the exception of child endowment and maternity
allowances, the benefits are limited to those who can satisfy a means
test. The form of the means test varies with different services.
Both income and property are taken into account in determining
eligibility for invalid, old-age, and widows' pensions, and may
either lead to a reduction in the amount of the pension or dis-
qualify one for the benefit. For unemployment and sickness benefits, only income is taken into account. There is some evidence to
suggest that the means test has had the effect of increasing the
number of applicants for assistance from the Government. The
means test, however, has the support of the Labour Party, which
believes that it limits the benefits to those who most need them.

A feature of all the social services is that they have thus far been
noncontributory. Contributory systems have been proposed from
time to time and legislation for this purpose has twice been introduced in the Commonwealth Parliament by non-Labour governments. In 1928 the bill lapsed after the second reading speech. Ten
years later, legislation for health and pensions insurance was enacted and some of the administrative machinery was actually in

operation when the scheme was abandoned, partly because of the threatening world outlook. Non-Labour parties continue to advocate the adoption of the contributory principle in financing the social services, but opposition seems to be based primarily on the belief that the worker should not be required to pay directly for his social services.

The worker does, in fact, make a substantial contribution to the cost of the social services even though he is usually unaware of it. The relative contributions of different income groups cannot, however, be determined because of the complex manner in which the social services are financed. The money for child endowment comes partly from a pay-roll tax on employers. The National Welfare Fund, from which the newer social services are financed, consists of an annual grant from consolidated revenue of £30,000,000, or one-fourth of the proceeds from the income tax on individuals, whichever is the less. The remaining social services, also, are financed from consolidated revenue, a large proportion of which comes from the various forms of indirect taxation such as customs and excise duties and sales tax.

Amending legislation has now provided that, from January 1, 1946, all Commonwealth social services are to be financed from a single fund—the National Welfare Fund. A special tax on incomes, the proceeds from which are expected to total about £50,-000,000 in 1946–1947, is to be the main source of revenue for the Fund, into which is also to be paid the proceeds (about £11,000,000) from the pay-roll tax on employers. In 1946–1947 the deficiency between this revenue and the estimated expenditure of about £80,000,000 was to be met from the credit balance already in the National Welfare Fund. Later the deficiency will be met by a grant from consolidated revenue.

The social-service tax for single men with incomes of £3 or more a week, and for married men whose incomes are £7 a week or more, and who have children, is to be at the rate of 1s. 6d. to the pound. On lower incomes the rate decreases on a graduated scale.

The requirement that a direct contribution of this kind be made toward the cost of the social services has led to strong demands for the removal of the means test. As a consequence the Labour Party has appointed a private committee to report on the practicability of granting the demand. Meanwhile the Triennial Conference—the policy-making body—of the Labour Party has passed a resolution calling for gradual reduction of the means test.

The rates of the benefits are not uniform and are not related to subsistence needs. By far the most generous is that for old-age pensions, which in August, 1945, amounted to £1. 12s. 6d. a week. That they are not related to subsistence needs is all the more surprising in view of the tendency—at least before the depression of the 'thirties—to regard the Australian standard of living as something sacrosanct.

However, discussion of the Australian standard of living has centred around the system of wage fixation rather than around social services. Wages and working conditions are determined, for the most part, by industrial tribunals which derive their jurisdiction and power from statutory authority. The system of wage fixation is extremely complicated, and demands and suggestions for changes, both major and minor, are constantly being made. The system is neither simple nor immutable, but the basic principle of governmental responsibility for wage rates is rarely questioned. The system provides for both conciliation and arbitration. Four of the states have arbitration courts with state-wide jurisdiction, and three of these have also a system of subordinate tribunals of the wages-board type. In two of the states a system of wages boards alone operates. The most important and influential tribunal is the Commonwealth Court of Conciliation and Arbitration, which makes and interprets awards in industries with interstate ramifications. The awards are concerned with wages, hours, and working conditions, but the most important function of the tribunals, at least in the present context, is to determine the basic wage. This wage, which is the foundation of the entire wage system, is the lowest amount that may be paid to an unskilled worker for a full week's work. Margins or secondary wages, over and above the basic wage, are received by skilled or semiskilled workers to remunerate them for such skill or other qualifications as may be necessary for their work.

The notion underlying the basic wage had its origin in a judgement, in 1907, of the President of the Commonwealth Court of Conciliation and Arbitration, who was called upon to determine whether the wages paid in a certain industry were fair and reasonable. His determination purported to rest upon a calculation, based on the household budgets of nine families, of the cost of providing for the "normal needs of the average employee, regarded as a human being living in a civilised community." The amount necessary to provide for the "normal needs" of an unskilled worker at that time was declared to be £2. 2s. a week. It included provision for a wife and "about three children." The notion underlying this judgement has since influenced the determinations of both Commonwealth and state tribunals. But other factors are also taken into account in determining the basic wage. A Judge of the Commonwealth Court is reported to have said, in 1941, that "The dominant factor in fixing the basic wage was the economic or productivity factor, and the basic wage must be the highest that industry as a whole can pay. The needs of a family were only a guide in determining that wage, and were not an absolute guide."

The amount of the basic wage varies from time to time in accordance with changes in the retail prices of certain commodities. In August, 1945, it was £4. 18s. a week in Sydney. Single and married men receive the same rate, but the basic wage for women is only 54 per cent that for men. If the basic wage, as the Chief Judge of the Commonwealth Court stated in 1941, is sufficient only for the needs of a family unit of three, the amounts of the social-service benefits obviously have no relationship to subsistence needs. There has, in fact, been no significant demand that there should be such a relationship.

A demand is at present being made for greater uniformity among the benefits and, in particular, for an increase in the rates of widows' pensions to make them the same as those for old-age pensions. It is possible that this and other anomalies which have followed from the spasmodic development of the social services will be removed in the near future, for the Commonwealth Government has promised to introduce a bill to consolidate its diverse social legislation in a single act.

CHAPTER XVIII

The Social Structure of Australia

BY C. HARTLEY GRATTAN

THE EVOLUTION of Australia over a period of sixteen decades from a tiny, rather miserable penal colony planted on the edge of a continent about which the settlers were strikingly ignorant, to its present flourishing condition as a modern social-democratic community, is a remarkable example of man's creative powers. Development began slowly, suffered the ups and downs to which all societies are subject, spurting ahead on occasion, marking time almost as often, but resulting eventually in an almost magical transformation. Nations with longer histories have done far less.

The First Fleet brought out about 1,000 persons, including 529 male and 188 female convicts. Of the first settlers 7 out of 10 were therefore in bondage. Over them 209 marines stood guard. The Governor's staff consisted of 9 men, and 13 more were soon added. The rest of the small company consisted of 31 wives of marines, the wife of the clergyman, 24 children of marines, 17 children of convicts (born free, of course), and 2 servants. This made a total of 1,024—717 convicts and 307 free persons, of whom 232 manned the apparatus of government at various levels and 75 of whom were dependents either of members of the governing group or of the convicts. Plainly this was a highly anomalous society on any grounds, partaking more of the nature of a gaol community than of normal social life. The anomaly was neither accidental nor undesired. It was consciously planned. The intent of the government which had directed the enterprise was to found a gaol in a remote part of the world. The development of the colony in any other direction was hardly counted on very seriously at that time. Our interest is to discover how, by successive stages, a quite different society was nevertheless developed in Australia.

The thin edge of the wedge of fundamental change was inserted in the original instructions to the Governor. He was empowered to "emancipate and discharge from their servitude any of the convicts under your superintendence who shall, from their good conduct and disposition to industry, be deserving of favour." He was further empowered to "pass grants" of land to the emancipated convicts, of a specified size and under specified conditions. Moreover, under the date of August 20, 1789, the Governor was given further instructions on the terms of granting land to noncommissioned officers and "private men." On these foundations it was possible to build a system of production which, when strong enough, could burst the circumscribed bounds of the prison. On them a free society could be developed.

The wedge was driven deeper when, in 1792, the store-ship "Bellona" arrived in the colony with the first free settlers to come out. These consisted of six adult single men and a married man with his wife and five minor children. They had come on the promise of a free passage, free land, the assignment to them of convicts to labour under their direction, and other governmental assistance. They were the first of many assisted emigrants. The first-comers were poor—a farmer-fisherman, two farmers, a gardener, a baker, a millwright, and a blacksmith—but later, men of substance, claiming no assistance from the government for a passage, but a good deal otherwise, particularly in land and convict servants, would arrive and by virtue of their capital lay claim to large tracts of land. For many years the wealthy emigrant was much preferred by the local authorities, since he could give work to many convicts. But whatever the subsequent chances and changes, the fact remains that by 1792 there existed the opportunity to evolve a society partly bond and partly free, with an autocratic government designed to control the bond set over both. A struggle for power was in the making.

Not only would such a society naturally be riven by the gulf between bond and free, but it would also be riven by the almost inevitable distinction to be drawn between those who achieved freedom after having been in bondage and those who had always been free. Moreover, while a certain (but far from absolute) common condition was certain to obtain among the bond, the free would be divided not only vertically, so to speak, but also horizontally. As time passed, convicts of wealth were granted special privileges (as was the practice in England in those days), but they had very little effect on the condition of convicts in general. Among the free the situation was utterly different. The normal stratification into rich and poor soon developed, with the conflicts of interest associated with such a division, even though vis-à-vis the convict group, the free, of whatever background or economic condition, were a minority group. A society so variously constituted inevitably produced a shady half-world at its borders, which accounts for the fact that at a comparatively early date there developed in Sydney a slum area in which criminals, near-criminals, and other riffraff congregated.

How early in Australian history the social divisions developed is illustrated by the so-called Rum Rebellion which overturned Governor Bligh in 1808, exactly twenty years after the founding of the colony. The total population then was about 10,000. The rebellion was rooted in the opposition to government policy of a group of well-to-do free settlers who had set up a monopolistic economy which the government was trying to break up. A strong community of interest, arising from common participation in monopolistic practices, allied the military with the well-to-do free settlers. This gave the discontented ready access to the military power, the decisive power in the autocratically ruled colony. Governor Bligh, for his part, had the support of the free smallholders, who were victims of the system, for his policy, at the direction of the home authorities, was aimed at strengthening their position. Most of the smallholders, however, resided away from Sydney, the seat of government, and were entirely without influence over the military. Dr. H. V. Evatt offers the following economic interpretation of the rebellion: "it may be regarded as a contest between Bligh as the person chosen to execute a general policy which benefited the settlers and poorer classes and Macarthur as the representative of the rising trading and capitalist group, the money power, and the forces of combination and monopoly." Two further points should be made to round out the picture. The rebels were bitterly hostile to the emancipated convicts, especially if they supported Bligh, but the dubious petition to the military commander asking him to take over the government was signed, after the rebellion, by numerous persons from the shady periphery of society, in some instances under duress. All this within two decades of the first landing in the country!

The social conflict between free settlers and emancipists became exceptionally bitter during the administration of Bligh's successor, Colonel Lachlan Macquarie. The Governor's insistence that a man who had paid his debt to society should be granted all the privileges of a free man, including the right to dine at the Governor's table and be appointed to the magistracy, met with concerted opposition from the free men, called "exclusivists," "silver-tails," and so on. The quarrel played a large part in Macquarie's downfall, in spite of the fact that he was, on the whole, a creative public servant of the first order.

But Macquarie's regime was far more significant in another respect. He had administered the colony as a special kind of gaol in which free men were useful in proportion as they gave employment to convicts who otherwise would be a burden on the public purse. Macquarie consistently favoured moneyed emigrants, not working-class people. It was therefore more important to advance the interests of the emancipists than to conciliate the free, for emancipation represented the rather small element of rehabilitation in the whole sorry scheme of convict exile. This emphasis might have continued for many years had it not also been the time when the wool industry was getting established. Few people seemed to have realised that the wool industry would inevitably complete that disruption of the gaol pattern of society which was implicit from the beginning in certain of the Governor's powers, by providing at last a strong base for a free, self-supporting economy. Especially would this be true if the emigration of free people, including workmen, markedly increased, and if the number of native-born free increased as well. The wedge inserted in 1788, driven deeper in 1789, and again in 1792 would indeed be doing its inevitable work.

The most cursory examination of the census of New South Wales for 1841, prepared by Ralph Mansfield, and published in the same year, confirms all expectations. Mansfield states that the total population in 1821 was 29,783, and in 1841, 130,856. In 1821 the proportion of free to bond was 116 to 100; by 1841 it was 377 free to 100 bond. This in itself was enough to alter the whole tone of society. In 1840 transportation into New South Wales came to an end, ensuring that the predominance of the free would be ever more decisive. Also, the native-born free were increasing numerically if not proportionately. In 1821 they numbered 7,224; in 1841, 29,449, or two out of every ten persons. The tide of free emigration was strong. There is, however, some doubt about the quality of this emigration. Professor R. B. Madgwick is of the opinion that while they made a hard-working free labour force, they were deficient in moral and political ideals and were therefore too subservient to authority for the good of the country.

Mansfield's occupational analysis for 1841 was as follows:

Landed proprietors, merchants, bankers, and
  professional persons 4,477
Shopkeepers and other retail dealers 1,774
Mechanics and artificers 10,175
Shepherds and others caring for sheep 12,948
Gardeners, stockmen, and others employed
  in agriculture 16,670
Domestic servants 9,825
All other persons (females, children, convicts
  in government employment) 72,317

On the basis of this miscellany of figures and other relevant information, the structure of Australian society in 1841 can be outlined. The wool industry was already the basic wealth-producing industry of the colony. It was an industry in which substantial capital was necessary to make a start. The Australian frontier, in many respects different from the American, was thus a "big man's" frontier. The holders of broad acres were the dominant figures in the community, not only economically but politically. The middle group—or middle class—was small and rather precariously situated. Mansfield's classification of merchants, bankers, and professional persons with landed proprietors, thus placing them with the dominant group, seems as logical retrospectively as it undoubtedly seemed at the time. His category of shopkeepers and other retail dealers probably includes most of the true middle group. Its ideals were undoubtedly petty bourgeois and not, in the context of economic progress, at all disturbing to the upper group. The broad contrast was, therefore, between a wealthy landed group and the working class, which implies an oligarchical society.

The original working class had been the convicts. Their labour had laid the material bases of Australian life, both governmental projects like public buildings and roads, and works necessary to wool-growing under private enterprise. It was a cheap working force, docile for the most part, but by contemporary testimony dilatory and inefficient. It lacked an incentive to labour, for there was "nothing in it" save maintenance. In many important respects convict labour exhibited the characteristics of slave labour and had similar social significance. Labour laws, such as they were, reflected the relation of free master and convict servant. By 1841 the original labour force was definitely on the way out. It is interesting to note that the principal opposition to its abolition had come not from the government but from the landed proprietors, who cherished its cheapness and, possibly, its docility.

Free labour in Australia had to make its way in competition with convict labour. The latter set the standards of wages and conditions, and the laws applicable to convict servants were often invoked to control free workers as well. The results were unhappy, as one may learn from such books as Alexander Harris' reminiscences of the 1830's and 1840's, *Settlers and Convicts* (London, 1852). Under the circumstances, and with North America so much nearer, it is not surprising that the free labour force grew slowly and was recruited, as Madgwick contends, from inferior groups. The wonder is that it grew at all. But beginning in the 1820's it began to increase at a significant rate, rising toward a temporary peak about 1841, when Mansfield made his analysis.

The introduction of numerous free labourers into Australia was as significant for the future of the country as the introduction of free settlers to employ convicts had been. The free labourers, too, contributed to the break-up of the convict system. Abraham Lincoln's dictum that a nation cannot endure half slave and half free became operative. It was manifestly impossible to create an economically sound society in which a large part of the working class was bond, with very low standards of living, while another section was free but deeply and adversely influenced by the bond.

Though the campaign against transportation was conducted by the clergy and a miscellaneous group of humanitarian laymen mainly in moral terms, which were undoubtedly entirely relevant, the conscious or unconscious recognition of the fact that a free labour force must be universal in Australia, if the country was to be economically strong and politically sound, seems to have played its part. The abolition of transportation set the stage for an economy and a society in which all the participants were free—as freedom was understood in mid-nineteenth-century British countries.

The full development of the new situation was dramatically interrupted by the great gold rushes of the 1850's. Without them Australia might have continued to grow in wealth and population, but development would have been slow and the population never very numerous. The oligarchical tendencies would probably have been confirmed. Representative and even responsible government would not, it is likely, have worked in a thoroughly democratic fashion in the absence of strong pressure from below. It is difficult to see how that pressure could have been developed from the kind of working class an oligarchy would have tolerated. The gold rushes changed all that. Both in the short and the long run they had a democratic influence on Australian development.

The first effects of the rushes were as various as they were unsettling. Not only did they bring thousands of people into the country within a relatively brief time, but the immigrants were of a much higher quality than the early comers. The men of the rushes were motivated by the hope of quick fortune and therefore were of a type which took risks, struggled hard to overcome obstacles, both natural and man-made, and were disposed to protest injustices of any kind. The Eureka Rebellion vividly illustrates this phase. But it is well to keep in mind that every mass migration brings a mixed lot of individuals into a country. In any event, the newcomers not only reduced the convict remnant to an obscure position; they also accentuated the point that Australia was to be a country in which all men would be free.

Though the rushes temporarily turned Australian society upside down, they did not immediately transform the old economy. The first effect was to make it difficult to operate, owing to manpower shortages, but there were compensations in the expanded home markets in which high prices prevailed. Once the alluvial gold began to run out, which was relatively early in the decade, the problem was how to absorb the many newcomers who chose to remain. It was apparent that the pastoral economy could not possibly support so large a number; and it was also apparent that the pastoralists stood in the way of other uses of the land. The pastoral industry, indeed, found itself in a paradoxical position: it was still unquestionably the basic source of the national income, but it was an obstacle to new income-creating land industries. The struggle over the land therefore became acute in Australia at this time. The pastoral oligarchy was challenged, occasionally by "traitors" to their class. Earlier the pastoralists had conducted a long campaign against the Imperial authorities for the right to dispose of the land as they thought fit; now they had to contend against newcomers bent on an alternative use of the land they had so recently won.

In the larger view, however, the struggle over land was but one phase of a tremendous effort to develop the country. The foundations of modern Australia were being laid. Between 1860 and 1900 the population increased from 1,145,585 to 3,765,339, or about three times. The society which developed in those four decades in most respects followed the nineteenth-century pattern for colonies. Australia exported primary produce, mostly of pastoral origin in the beginning; though, as the years passed and technology allowed, larger quantities and more varieties of foodstuffs and industrial metals were exported. Australia imported manufactures, capital, and men. Under the expanding world economy of the period Australia could and did grow, though it was still at a disadvantage as compared with North America. Nevertheless, the results were reasonably satisfactory to capitalists, and astute or lucky men could rise in the world on the tide of economic progress. But as decades passed, the men at the bottom of the social pyramid developed an acute sense of frustration and injustice, which is reflected at the literary level in Tom Collins' *Such Is Life* and the sketches of Henry Lawson, and in romantic crime by the famous Kelly gang. It was a protest of the native-born.

The key to the situation is that, in spite of minor developments to the contrary, Australia still somehow remained a "big man's" country. Farming got under way so slowly and encountered so many technical obstacles that it did not play a rôle in Australian history comparable to its part in American history. When the workers turned to building-trade unions, as they did comparatively early, the largest and most powerful unions developed not in the skilled city trades or among factory workers but in mining, water-front occupations, and the pastoral industry. The latter development was remarkable in that the coming of trade unions to the land industries is ordinarily long delayed. It was not so in Australia. Equally pertinent is the fact that many workers in the pastoral industry, especially the shearers, were also struggling farmers who took on seasonal work to enable them to struggle a little longer. The unusual coalescence of interest between farmers, who are usually conservatives, and unionized landless workers clearly shows that Australia at that time, when the unions were gathering strength, was once more verging on an oligarchical social organisation. At the top were the big landholders, merchants, bankers, shipowners, and mining magnates. At the other extreme were the numerous men without property, or with property insufficiently productive to provide a good living. The middle class was still numerically small and politically and socially weak. It could hold place politically only by allying itself with one side or the other, and it usually chose the side of the big men or remained neutral. The Australian middle class has never been able to impose its values on the nation as the American middle class has done.

The division of Australian society in two radically opposed groups, even though the numerical majority of the people stayed on the side lines, was a portent of trouble. As long as the country was prosperous, serious trouble was averted. But when economic depression spurred the employers to resist trade-union demands, the crisis came. Vast and bitter strikes resulted; as the employers wielded the economic and political power, they won the battles.

At first glance it seemed to be an outright triumph for the oligarchical forces in Australian life. Unlike the working class before the gold-rush period, the labour group thereafter had shown fight but it had lost. But, as other writers in this book have made clear, victory was snatched from defeat by the workers' invasion of politics. Australia was thereupon launched on its career as a social democracy. It was the organisation of the workers for political action that made this possible. It was the distress of the liberal members of the middle class at the social cost of the great strikes and the kind of future the nation faced if the naked power of the employers went unchallenged that made it inevitable. For the record is clear: if the middle class had stood neutral in politics in the latter part of the nineteenth century, or had turned solidly to the support of the oligarchists, political labour would have had a far harder and longer struggle for power. Labour itself recognised this, for obviously it formulated its early election programmes to attract middle-class votes as well as those of its own normal followers. It was this discovery of common ground between the workers and the small, liberal middle class that gave the democratic forces in Australia their head. Between 1890 and the outbreak of the First World War they won a series of major victories. Not only in New South Wales, where labour's political tactics were hammered out, but in the federal sphere, the alliance, tacit or open, between labourites and liberal middle-class leaders, of whom Alfred Deakin is the most enduringly famous, changed the tone and condition of Australian life.

How deep the changes cut is a matter of opinion, for the fact remains that between 1916 and the Second World War labour had an unprofitable time politically, and the middle-class liberals in politics offered minimum assistance. The direction of social evolution was against experiments in social democracy and few were made. Rather, the emphasis was on the interests of producers, both farmers and factory-owners. The period was not uncreative from the larger point of view, but creation followed the canons of a fairly orthodox capitalism. The social democrats, for the most part, marked time, though they were not deprived of any important gains. What became apparent with reasonable clarity was that Australia, in spite of its world reputation, was a capitalist country far less tinctured by socialism than was popularly supposed. The Labour Party fiasco of 1929–1931 was occasioned at bottom by the Party's inability to establish a case for a policy of its own devising which was feasible under the terms and conditions of Australian capitalism. Income distribution followed a normally capitalist pattern, modified very slightly by wage awards under the Arbitration Court system and the social services. The contrasts of material condition inseparable from such a distribution of income were present in full measure. Slums, which had existed in the country from the earliest days, continued to exist; and so did the opportunities for luxurious living. But if the structure of Australian life was indisputably capitalist, its tone was now indisputably democratic. The spirit of the period 1890–1914 might wear an unattractive outward appearance, but it enjoyed a powerful inner life that guaranteed its eventual reëmergence.

In the perspective of history Australia is a creation of nineteenth-century world capitalism. The peculiarities of its history, attributable to purely local developments, have had a profound influence on the circumstances of life in the country. Perhaps the outstanding factor is the absence of a strong middle class able from its own strength to define a social ideal which is acceptable to the majority of the people. It has rarely, if at all, acted independently. Its characteristic rôle is that of a buffer between the contemporary group with oligarchical tendencies and the working class, favouring now one side, now the other, thus affecting the social balance, but not defining what it shall be. Since 1890 the social initiative has been passed between the working class, which seeks a social-democratic ideal, and the moneyed class and its allies, seeking to advance producer interests. The future of the country depends on the compromises between these two formidable groups, or the clashes which the absence of workable compromises may bring about.

Part Five:

CULTURAL ASPECTS

CHAPTER XIX

On Australian Culture

BY VANCE AND NETTIE PALMER

FROM THE BEGINNING Australian cultural life has had a tendency to base itself almost entirely on the British literary tradition, the inheritance of a single language and its great body of prose, poetry, and drama. The effect of this has been narrowing. It has inclined the average Australian to complacency about a Shakespeare he has never seen played and to a silent resistance to foreign influences and unfamiliar cultural forms. This reliance on the literary tradition has also, perhaps, given weight to academic exponents of culture at the expense of those of more creative mind. Whatever was lively, vigorous, and original in the community has had to assert itself against conservative forces.

And there has been no transplanting of large European communities to lend the uniform pattern of Australian life an interesting complexity. Many nationalities have contributed to the Australian population. There have been, over the last hundred years, freshets of immigration from the Scandinavian countries, from Germany, and from the Mediterranean; but these varied people have come as units and have been absorbed into the community. They have not preserved their ways of life, their traditional arts, seldom for long their language.

The Australian feeling has been against any kind of group segregation. So, though individual foreigners have contributed greatly to Australian culture (one thinks of the work in different fields of Leichhardt, Strzlecki, and Ferdinand von Müller), that culture has not been enriched by the European folk-imagination. Whatever original character it has attained has had to be evolved from within.

The Australian cultural task has been twofold: to keep the standards of an immature society at the levels of its tradition; and to inform them, wherever possible, with the spirit of the country. Civilisation cannot be truly effective if it depends too much on inherited forms. Australian growth was long hampered by unwillingness to recognise this truth.

Various factors were responsible, apart from the instinct of transplanted people to cling emotionally to familiar forms and ideas. Australia was settled by the eighteenth century—a century that had a fine sense of responsibility to the world it knew, but no disposition to encourage fresh, independent growth outside its borders. The eighteenth century was marked by readiness to carry its light to far corners, yet it had a stiffness of spirit, a disinclination to adapt itself to what it regarded as a barbaric new world. And there was uncertainty about the aims of colonisation. At first Australia was to be a penal settlement, where Britain's increasing number of convicts might, after their prison terms expired, support themselves by agriculture; then, when Macarthur's sheep-breeding experiments succeeded, the agricultural policy was changed to a pastoral one. This might seem to show some faculty for adaptation, but it acted only in simple bread-and-butter ways.

The spirit of the authoritarian century remained in Australia long after it had been superseded in Europe by the romantic revival. It persisted in ideas, verse, rhetoric, and architecture. It was plain in the general instinct of the official classes to resist the challenge of the new country. "No surrender to Rousseau and the wild," seemed to be their motto.

What Australia gained by the loyalty of its eighteenth-century pioneers to the civilisation they knew is definite. We have only to think of Captain Cook's experiments in dietetics, which helped to banish scurvy from long voyages; of Captain John Hunter's refined observation of terrestrial magnitude for the sake of subsequent navigation of the Australian route; of the careful charting and surveying done by Matthew Flinders and many other sailors. A tradition of civilised responsibility was established. But there was a negative side to the eighteenth century that became more apparent as the necessity of adaptation to the new country grew. Adaptation itself was distrusted as a breaking-down of standards.

Then, for the first half of the nineteenth century, government was mainly in the hands of temporary administrators who had little thought of anything but the need for making the country pay its way as a pastoral territory. And the pastoral policy was not favourable to settled living or cultural growth. Even in architecture there was little impulse to evolve a style suitable to the climate, or, rather, the varied climates. It is true that Governor Macquarie called on the skill of an architect from England—Greenway, a freedman—to design buildings that would lend some dignity to Sydney, the capital, but the result was a frugal version of some quiet corner of Georgian England. Any departure from the discretions of the Georgian scene got no further than Greenway's imagination, which, indeed, had luxuriated in the new setting. It is known, for instance, that he wanted to build a large mole and bridge into and across the harbour. But Macquarie would not consider such schemes and he got his fingers burnt even for what he had permitted when a commissioner arrived from England, about 1821, and with his footrule went over the plans for the expanding settlements at Port Jackson and Hobart.

It seems that Greenway in his designs (which included a public garden for the sake of botanists) had attempted something that is now called town planning. But town planning is not just a matter of visible surfaces. It is dependent on a clear view of a country's social and economic development and a will to build in harmony with that development. In the early Australia both were lacking.

In the 'thirties, however, there arrived a man who had definite ideas about the country's future and a determination to make it a Land of Promise for the people of other countries, particularly the crofters of his native land. John Dunmore Lang was a Scottish divine of robust character and active mind, and he soon made his influence felt. Crude and vigorous, he scattered his ideas broadcast and some of them germinated. Against the conception of a purely pastoral economy, feudal in essence, he set that of an agricultural democracy. He was active in bringing independent settlers—farmers, artisans, German vignerons—to Australia, and he encouraged them to absorb the spirit of the country and adapt themselves to its ways. His main aim was to create a solid, democratic society of small farmers and business men—if not a complete society, a powerful group that would counter the dominance of the pastoralists; but a subsidiary aim was to prepare the soil in which a popular, indigenous culture might take root.

For the names of townships that celebrated European battlefields he would substitute native names—Kurara, Muttaburra, Wollondilly—that were charged with the country's haunting strangeness and might evoke a particular emotion. Instead of a main street—usually a mere channel through which squatters' teams from the hinterland hauled wool to the coast—he would have an open square, like that of Spanish countries, where farmers could meet and exchange products and ideas.

The gold discoveries of 1852, however, played a more definite part than any human being in determining the future development of the country. In one decade the population not merely trebled but changed markedly in character. The newcomers were lusty adventurers from all parts of the world (though mainly from the British Isles) and when the gold petered out or could be mined only at deep levels they did not tamely accept the fact that most of the country was locked up in large holdings. There was vigorous political action and assertion of the democratic principles and egalitarian ideas that have since been a marked feature of Australian life and thought.

One result of this ferment was a greatly increased interest in education and a demand that, in its primary form, it should be freely available to everyone. In the 'seventies and 'eighties various legislatures introduced similar education acts, based on the belief that a democratic state should be responsible for the literacy of its citizens. Elementary education was to be compulsory, secular, and free. But the small schools scattered in thousands over the country were conceived only as bases. The work of popular culture was to be continued in mechanics institutes or schools of arts—community centres equipped with social halls and lending-libraries, sometimes with apparatus for technical instruction. The idea of such institutes did not originate in this period. In some towns, like Sydney and Brisbane, they had appeared before the gold boom. But the growth of ideas for institutional culture accounted for their rapid appearance in every township of a couple of hundred inhabitants. They were not a government responsibility like the primary schools, but they were usually subsidised, both directly and with grants of land for building. It is noteworthy, by the way, that toward the end of the century the influence of America was strong in Australia. In these libraries American popular writing was well represented: domestic novels, the sermons of Thomas DeWitt Talmage and Henry Ward Beecher, the social speculations of Edward Bellamy and Henry George.

In very small settlements, cultural impulses centred in the school. The Mutual Improvement Society, encouraged officially by educational authorities, was a monthly gathering of adults that often served a useful social function. For, after the local teacher had finished his stunt—a paper on Mr. Darwin's theories of evolution, perhaps—the meeting might resolve itself into an impromptu concert at which anonymous songs and ballads got a hearing. This oral literature, or pre-literature, the first attempt of the Australian community to express itself in its own terms about its own life, has never received much attention from Australian social students, and, except for fragmentary collections like A. B. Paterson's *Old Bush Songs* (1905), there is little record of it. Yet it showed a people gradually adapting themselves to the country they were coming to make their own. When conscious story-writers and balladists appeared, it provided them with a storehouse of material. Men like Henry Lawson and A. B. Paterson drew heavily upon it.

Literature in the formal sense had been hampered by the official attitude of detachment from the new country. What writing appeared in the cities was the work of cultivated men who were self-conscious and spiritually out of sympathy with their surroundings. Their personal detachment was accentuated by a pseudoclassical style, loaded with Latinisms and ornament, that remained in Australia as a sort of official language long after it had gone out of vogue in the country of its origin; and also, long after the Australian community (as can be seen from Sydney J. Baker's *The Australian Language*) had begun to coin new words and idiomatic phrases to express its own ways of thinking and feeling. Consequently, the early formal writings—essays, sketches, album verse—seems derivative and sterile.

On the contrary, the crude oral songs and ballads, though of no permanent literary value, had the seeds of new life in them. As the

folk-imagination of the American people played around legendary
figures like Paul Bunyan and Pecos Bill, so the Australian people
created myths about the bushrangers Ben Hall and Gardiner, or
conjured up mythical sheep stations like the Speewah, which was
a shearer's paradise. Thus by 1882, when J. F. Archibald, a journalist of genius, founded a weekly, the *Bulletin,* which was to give a
voice to the country, there were not merely a large number of story-
writers and verse-makers, but a potential audience with an appetite
for the imaginative rendering of its own life. Eventually the two
strands of Australian literary development—folk and formal—were
drawn together by men like A. G. Stephens, the critic, and Joseph
Furphy, the chronicler—men who revelled in the Australian idiom
and yet were well acquainted with "the best that has been said and
thought in the world."

In other fields the story of cultural development in Australia has
been similar—a struggle to make use of the universal inheritance by
assimilating not merely its form but its spirit. As with most new
countries, this often led to an exasperating conflict between what
was mature but infertile and what was crude but alive with growing
points. The development arising from the conflict was uneven, and
has often been affected by booms and depressions. When, for instance, Anthony Trollope visited Australia in 1871, he was impressed by the public library in Melbourne, which anyone could
enter and use at will; nothing of the kind existed then in London.
And literary institutes were being organised in all the small towns
of Australia. Yet the Munn-Pitt report of the Carnegie Corporation,
based on its survey in 1935, revealed that there had been no progressive development. City libraries were in a backward state and
country libraries had lost the original impetus that brought them
into being; they had become hardly more than "cemeteries of old
and forgotten books."

A similar unevenness could be noted in university development.
The flood of new wealth created by the gold discoveries resulted in
ambitious building, and impressive universities were established
in Sydney and Melbourne. Tiny though the classes were at first, they
were well articulated, especially in the humanities; and many of
the professors, graduates from abroad, wrote what were more than
textbooks on classic writers, on science, history, and law. Yet, except

in the sciences, it was a long time before the universities entered creatively into the life of the country. The older men did not train others to take up their work and adapt it to the needs of the community, and though Australian competence in the material sciences was taken for granted, it was customary to depend on experts from abroad for ideas and taste in the humanities. Consequently, most Australian creative writers are wholly or partly self-educated; and, conversely, few graduates of the universities have been authors of original work. But it must be said for the universities that they preserved a regard for learning and scholarship which, in a community growing steadily more commercial, might easily have been trodden under. The leading members of the professions have almost invariably come from the universities and have carried the influence of the humanities into public life. Alfred Deakin, an early Prime Minister, was more deeply interested in literature than in politics; Sir Samuel Griffith, first Chief Justice of the High Court, was a notable translator of Dante; Mr. Justice Higgins, who laid down the working principles of the Federal Court of Industrial Arbitration, lectured on Shakespeare and Greek poetry. Thus a tradition of culture was built up around the bar and judiciary that has affected the community as a whole.

Where cultural inadequacies have been pointed out, genuine attempts have been made to remedy them. The Carnegie Munn-Pitt report on libraries (1935) is an example. A free-library movement was organised soon after the report was issued. Its principal object was not to set up libraries or encourage their establishment by voluntary bodies but to persuade the state to develop ways and means to enable local governments (that is, municipal and shire councils) to establish them. It has had a powerful effect on the public and on governments, its most solid achievement being the New South Wales Library Act of 1939, of which it was the chief inspiration. The Act provides for the establishment of a library board and the subsidising of local libraries, and will probably be accepted as a model for the other states. The free-library movement has gained strength from the increased popular interest in books—an interest partly stimulated by the Army and Air Force Educational Services, which built up small, well-selected "box" libraries circulating to military units throughout the country.

A sober facing of facts, usually leading to action, has recently been the order of the day in most of Australia's concerns. The community is ready to take stock and reassess achievements. Phrases like that of Sir Hubert Wilkins, who said, as a scientist, that Australians were the "poorest rich people on earth," have made a deep impression.

The economic depression of 1930–1935 was perhaps the most direct influence in stimulating the critical mood. It led to a scrutiny of the Australian belief that not only a high standard of living but widespread security had been reached through labour laws and social legislation. The disillusioning 'thirties revealed that there was little to justify this belief. It was evident that, though Australia had been a pioneer in political fields (inventing the secret ballot) and in industrial legislation (a minimum wage based on the family unit), a stable society had not been created—much less a utopia. And some of the pioneering energy, quite marked when the mass of the people first took part in government, had run into the sand.

If Australians had failed in their main preoccupation of social planning, the newly awakened critical spirit was inclined to argue, what about the cultural side of life? Ever since the 'nineties, when artists like Streeton and Roberts had discovered a way of interpreting the Australian landscape through brilliant impressionism, complacency had prevailed in regard to the status of painting. Some solid bequests (like the Felton bequest in Melbourne) had enriched Australian galleries with a few indubitable Old World masterpieces. But the fashionable concentration of painting had led to conservatism—a resistance by established artists and their patrons to new trends that might work to their disadvantage. For painting again to assume vitality, a reëxamination of artistic values was necessary.

Architecture had never been a cause for pride, either aesthetically or in the capacity to adapt itself to the Australian background. Imitating, at a long distance, the styles (in themselves revivals) that careered across the face of nineteenth-century England, the pure lines of Georgian buildings, as in Greenway's first experiments, were soon followed by the Renaissance influence, carried out in stucco over brick and affecting many buildings of the suddenly wealthy 'fifties. Then the country was subjected to the effects of the revived Gothic, which was used not only for churches but, strangely, for academic and official buildings. These imitations of imitations were made easier in a century of commercial mass production, when it was possible to import superfluous decoration of poor design and materials. More than this: the habit of drawing all examples from other countries with different conditions and needs discouraged initiative in solving immediate, urgent problems. For instance, in the country it was necessary to have roofs that would catch the rain and at the same time be proof against bush fires. Designers took for granted that the solution of the problem was corrugated iron, and the widespread use of this hideous material on every kind of building in the smaller settlements has been a matter of astonishment to the visitor and a source of depression to the inhabitants.

But recently this hand-to-mouth policy has received not only destructive but practical criticism. New materials are being discovered and tried. The American architect Walter Burley Griffin, commissioned to carry out his winning design for Canberra, provided a stimulating influence. His emphasis was always on the need to experiment with materials and styles, building in conformity with the natural environment. Perhaps the most satisfactory of Australian buildings is the University of West Australia at Perth, a careful embodiment of past and present. The general outline of the building and the campanile are Spanish in style, but the chief hall, with its high, flat ceiling decorated in the aboriginal idiom, conforms with the colours and patterns that are inherent in the surrounding bush landscape.

In music the impulse to rely on what could be brought from overseas has been particularly strong and lasting. It was easy to take for granted that music, above all arts, depended on a background of long tradition, with immemorial folksongs—inevitably missing in a country established at the time of the Industrial Revolution. Therefore it was not until the 'nineties that serious attempts were made to organise an orchestra. Even then, there was no suggestion of a school of creative work arising from the conservatoriums of the capitals. Singers like Melba might be produced, but not composers. Sometimes the head of a conservatorium was a composer as well as teacher and administrator; sometimes a distinguished student escaped to Europe or America with a few unperformed compositions in his trunk. Original Australian music, however, seemed to lack not only opportunity and encouragement but a solid base. It was for this reason that a gifted composer, Henry Tate, in his challenging little book, *Australian Musical Possibilities,* suggested the idea of an Australian music inspired not by nonexistent ancestral folksongs but by the long, flattened scale of some of the Australian bird calls. The book has not had posterity, but there is more interest in such ideas today than when it was published in the 'twenties.

Musical creation is an activity that depends on hearing a variety of music. The musical life of Australia has been greatly enriched by the coming of radio. It has meant not only the daily presence of music (on all or most levels) but the development of permanent orchestras by the Australian Broadcasting Commission. These orchestras have risen to the challenge of famous visiting conductors, and have given the future of composers an air of reality—a reality emphasised by the fact that the Commission is compelled by regulation to broadcast a small percentage of Australian work.

Management of radio in Australia is conducted in a manner midway between that of Great Britain and that of the United States. There are two sets of stations: national and commercial. The Commission controlling the first shares the listeners' fees with the Postmaster-General's Department, which is responsible for the technical side of the service. The commercial stations are financed by advertisements. In spite of the Australian Broadcasting Commission's authoritative position, it has not yet settled on a policy in the arts that would mark it as a fixed cultural centre. There is always the temptation to compete for listeners with the commercial stations, and this sometimes leads to a lowering of standards. Yet it has helped to raise the musical taste of the general public to a high level, and has been the means of introducing many good performers and composers to the public. The hope that permanent orchestras, supported by state and municipal funds, will soon be established may stem from this influence.

The Commission, through its broadcasting of good plays, modern and classical, has helped to compensate for the lack of a living theatre. The theatre has never thrown down strong roots in Australia, though until recently the plays successful in London and New York were usually reproduced in Australian capitals by visiting companies. Such visits grew rarer as the cinema extended its hold, and the living theatre has been left mainly to amateur and semiamateur groups whose productions, however good, are seen by only a small public. The broadcasting of dramatic masterpieces, though it cannot substitute for the theatre, has helped to keep the theatrical tradition alive, and in the past few years there have been hints of a revival in the theatre itself. This is shown principally in the popularity of ballet. Choreographers and teachers (e.g., M. Borovansky and Mme Kirsova) who came to the country with Russian ballet companies have formed Australian groups and have awakened so great an interest in ballet production that it has become a distinct feature of Australian life.

These signs of cultural life are reënforced by the wartime growth of the Council for the Encouragement of Music and the Arts, a popular movement to stimulate artistic activity in the country and in factories. It hopes to widen the general response to art, and to increase public participation in it. This particular movement may be only a product of the war situation, but in many other quarters demands are being formulated for a better access to the cultures of the world, with an insistence that Australia is no longer too far away for such essential satisfactions.

Another recent development is the creation of a Literary Advisory Board, which has the responsibility of seeing that no work of outstanding merit shall go unpublished. In the past there was every chance of good work being kept from the light of day. Publishing had hardly reached the dimensions of a profession or industry, and was usually carried on as an adjunct of some bookseller's business. When good books were published they soon went out of print. It is a notable fact that when American troops first arrived in Australia and were anxious to read about the country as it appeared to its inhabitants there was hardly a book of major Australian interest available. Part of the Literary Advisory Board's function is to see that such a situation does not recur. It has a long-range policy of reviving all Australian books of acknowledged worth, a short-range one of sponsoring manuscripts of quality that have difficulty in finding publication. Besides, it can recommend the granting of fellowships to writers of proven ability who have definite literary projects in mind.

Magazines which appeal to the general public and are hospitable to new ideas are more numerous at present than they have been for many years. The *Australian Quarterly,* established in 1929, and closely associated with the A.I.P.S., is concerned chiefly with political affairs, but it also prints articles on cultural issues and, occasionally, critical essays on Australian writers. Devoted principally to literature, whether Australian or foreign, are such quarterlies as *Southerly,* the organ of the Sydney branch of the English Association; and *Meanjin Papers,* founded independently in Queensland but now published in Melbourne; and the occasional publications, the Communist *New Writing,* and *Angry Penguins,* originally an undergraduate effort at the University of Adelaide. The latter, together with its offshoot, *Angry Penguins Broadsides,* is an Australian equivalent of the "little magazine" given over to the experimental and the outré, a type common in Great Britain and the United States, with which, indeed, the Australian magazine has struck up alliances.

Max Dupain

PARLIAMENT HOUSE, CANBERRA

Australian National Publicity Association

THE UNIVERSITY, PERTH, WESTERN AUSTRALIA

Adastra Airways Proprietary, Ltd.

SYDNEY, N.S.W., FROM THE AIR

Max Dupain

AUSTRALIAN SMALL CITY: TOOWOOMBA, QUEENSLAND

CHAPTER XX

Literature

BY H. M. GREEN

THE DEVELOPMENT of Australian literature has two aspects: the gradual growth of the native at the expense of the overseas element and their fusion into something new; and the gradual attainment of absolute value. These do not necessarily coincide, and the two most notable Australian writers are far from being typically Australian. Today Australian literature is in its late adolescence; it has acquired certain marked characteristics, but they are by no means all-pervasive. It has also produced many writers of talent and two for whom genius may reasonably be claimed. Though its current output cannot compare with that of Great Britain or the United States, if the present rate of progress is maintained it may do so before long. Its history may be divided, for convenience, into four periods.

The earliest period was one of conflict—social, political, sectarian, journalistic, and with the soil—a conflict which was reflected in newspapers, pamphlets, memoirs, and explorers' journals. Together with this rough, vigorous literature of life there existed a thin and bookish "literature of exile" which covered virtually the rest of the literary field. In a few instances, however, native and overseas constituents in varying measures combined, and two of these instances deserve mention. The *Poems* (Melbourne, 1883)[1] of Charles Harpur (1813–1868) were based on actual observation by a man who was born in Australia and loved the bush, though he was unable to see it for himself or to describe it except in the phrases of Wordsworth, Shelley, and Tennyson.

[1] Dates given are of original publication. For notes on later editions see the Bibliography.

Still, Harpur's was a genuine though not a very large talent, and he blazed a track for a far more important poet, Kendall. About the same time, Robert Lowe, a young immigrant who played a part in local politics and afterward became a British Cabinet Minister, contrived, with the help of some not inconsiderable local talent, to produce in the *Atlas* (1845–1848) a newspaper whose sharp and amusing satires make it a landmark in Australian journalism.

The gold rushes, with their immense injection of life and energy in the 1850's, opened a second period, which later settled into a comparatively steady development along lines that had, for the most part, been laid down. In this period began the approaches to an Australian outlook. But the average Australian was still a transplanted Englishman. His point of view is reflected in *Geoffry Hamlyn* (London, 1859), whose author, Henry Kingsley (1830–1876), came out to Australia to look for gold, and after four years returned to England with a pile of manuscript. *Geoffry Hamlyn* glorifies the early squattocracy, which is seen as an overseas extension of the English county family. Nevertheless, there is something Australian about the atmosphere of the book and some of its minor characters. It is still interesting; and it opened up a new field of fiction and established its principal conventions.

Another transplanted Englishman was the melancholy and Byronic Adam Lindsay Gordon (1833–1870), whose writing, along with echoes and melodramatic doggerel, contains some poetry. The best of this is English in subject and tone, but Gordon helped to lay the foundation of the Australian ballad and was long accepted as the national poet of Australia. Henry Kendall (1839–1882), who was Australian-born, had a much better claim to the title in his day. A nature poet of somewhat the same type and with the same models as Harpur, he had greater sensitivity and creative imagination and was able to see what lay around him with his own eyes. The dominant characteristic of his poems is a gentle, contemplative melancholy.

The most important novelists of the period are Marcus Andrew Hislop Clarke (1846–1881) and "Rolf Boldrewood" (Thomas Alexander Browne, 1826–1915). Clarke produced the gloomy and powerful *For the Term of His Natural Life* (London and Melbourne, 1885). This is a tour de force, written under the influence of Dickens and Hugo, and it has their characteristic faults of sentimentalism and melodrama. But it has also some of their virtues, being vital and moving as well as noticeably individual. The nascent Australianism of the day was better represented, however, by Boldrewood, particularly in *Robbery under Arms* (London, 1888), a stirring tale of adventure and bushranging. To most of his principal characters England is still home; but the Dick and Jim in this book are the first Australians in fiction, and of their father Scott himself might have been proud.

At the end of the period appeared a magazine, the *Australian Critic,* which was edited by a group of Melbourne professors; its tone is not un-Australian, and it represents the academicism of the day at somewhere near its best.

In the third period, from about 1890, the literature of Australia became really Australian and also achieved something of world importance. The first was due mainly to the inspiration and guidance of the *Bulletin.* Aided by certain social and political developments, this weekly newspaper, by far the most striking and original that Australia has produced, subjected the young literature to a kind of forced draught. The *Bulletin* was founded by John Feltham Archibald (1856–1919), a man of highly original talent, who had the art of gathering other talents about him and of refining crude journalistic ore into small gold bars. Under Alfred George Stephens (1865–1933), its "Red Page" became the focus of Australian literature, especially for criticism. Stephens was a man of unusual reading, personality, and critical insight; some of the best of his work is contained in *The Red Pagan* (1904). After leaving the *Bulletin,* he brought out a critical review, the *Bookfellow,* of which a visiting American professor of journalism stated that in quality of matter and in forcefulness and virility he had not seen its equal anywhere. Two other good magazines were the *Lone Hand,* literary and popular, a child of the *Bulletin;* and the *Triad,* literary, artistic, and musical, an importation from New Zealand. All these papers, save the *Bulletin,* were relatively short-lived.

The literature produced under these circumstances was a literature of action, and of character as revealed by speech and action.

Though sometimes parochial and somewhat lacking in intellectual quality and background, it was fresh, vigorous, ultrademocratic, and extremely individual. Three writers emerge as best representing its three most important qualities. Henry Lawson (1869–1922) stands for what he called "mateship"; Joseph Furphy ("Tom Collins," 1843–1919) for self-assertive equalitarianism and independence of spirit; and Andrew Barton ("Banjo") Paterson (1864–1941) for easygoing carelessness and a spirit of happy-go-lucky adventure.

Lawson was popular as a balladist, but his short stories are most significant. In them he shows not merely understanding and sympathy (in his early work a little sentimentality) that reach beyond class and country, and an art that corresponds exactly with his material, but what an English critic has called "the faculty of bringing life to a focus, of making it typical."

Compared with Lawson, Furphy is deliberately parochial, but his vital energy puts Lawson in the shade—for a time. *Such Is Life* (Sydney, 1903), a huge and scattered panorama, is rich in character and incident. To Furphy only a particular class and country mattered. Everything else—Australian station-owners, imported Englishmen, Scotsmen, Irishmen, and other foreigners—was merely material for hard-hitting satire. There are long encyclopaedic soliloquies and sermonisings, heavy and pedantic; but the rest is simple, direct, and lifelike, and the whole book is pervaded with a strong and freakish sense of humour, with the intriguing personality of Furphy himself, and with his "offensive Australianism." The vitality floats it all along; and *Such Is Life* is widely regarded as a classic.

Paterson is the most important and the most characteristic of the Australian balladists. He owes something to Gordon and Kipling, and to the old bush songs, the poor relations of the folk ballads of older lands. Though he earned his living mainly as a city journalist, he was brought up in the country and spent his spare time there. In poetic expression Paterson was no great craftsman, but he has his moments of poetic vision, and his verses are saturated not only with the spirit of open-air Australianism but with a sardonic humour which Australians like to regard as their own.

Two other writers are in their age but not of it. "Henry Handel Richardson," who was born in Melbourne, left Australia at sixteen and lived in England until her death in 1946. Her *Fortunes of Richard Mahony* (London, 1930) is set in her native country, which she revisited in order to obtain authentic material. The book may be described as a study in pride and sensitiveness under friction and strain that bring about nervous and mental degeneration to the point of insanity. Like Hamlet and Meredith's Egoist, Mahony is a universal character and his death scene is among the most memorable in literature. Only the great world novelists have drawn life with such truth, sincerity, and insight as Henry Handel Richardson, and few have drawn it with greater power.

The second writer, Christopher Brennan (1870–1932), a scholar-poet, rooted in Latin and Greek classics, French symbolism, and the romantic philosophy of Germany, wove out of personal trial and disappointment a gloomy and brooding splendour, projecting it in giant shape upon the sky. Brennan's reading was immense, his intellect and personality overpowering, but will and temperament were at war in him, so that he read and dreamed instead of doing. His verse, heavy and often obscure, is sonorous and sometimes splendid. He can be compared only with the great poets.

The most notable of the intellectual poets of the period, after Brennan, is Bernard Patrick O'Dowd (1866–), prophet and preacher of "the new democracy," who represented its intellectual aspect, as Lawson and Collins represented it for the ordinary man. O'Dowd's verse, published in a series of booklets between 1903 and 1921, is sometimes dry and formal; yet it has a lyrical quality and shows a remarkable gift of gnomic imagery. Another intellectual is the philosopher-poet William Baylebridge (1883–1942), who, to vary the phrase of one of his critics, has made himself a poetic tartan but has cut it to his own measure. At their best, in *This Vital Flesh* (Sydney, 1939) and *Love Redeemed* (Sydney, 1934), his verses are lofty, dignified, and sonorous. Mary Gilmore (b. 1865) combines a simple, balladlike measure with a wisdom arising from wide and deep experience of life. Much of her best verse is contained in *The Passionate Heart* (Sydney, 1918). Hugh Raymond McCrae (b. 1876) is a rich and sensuous lyrist who contrives to inform stock types and situations with such intensity and colour that they create a fresh and vivid world of their own. His best poems were collected in *Satyrs and Sunlight* (London, 1928). John Shaw Neilson (1872–1942) is a poet of ecstasy who aspires continually after a beauty that is unattainable. His habitual mood is one of tender joy or tender pity, and he has written some warm and readily appealing ballads.

Of the novelists of the period, "Brent of Bin Bin," whose anonymity has been carefully preserved, published as late as 1928–1931 three novels dealing with the old station families, whom the writer loves this side of idolatry. The best of the three novels is the first, *Up the Country* (1928). They lack construction and their style is at times execrable, but they are classics of their kind. Miles Franklin (b. 1883), to whom has been ascribed at least a share in their authorship, has published, in *Old Blastus of Bandicoot* (London, 1931; Melbourne, 1932) and *All That Swagger* (Sydney, 1937), novels that deal with similar scenes, types, and incidents and have certain resemblances in manner. Finally, in a popular classic, *We of the Never Never* (London, 1908), Mrs. Aeneas Gunn (b. 1870) describes in fictionised form her experiences on a remote cattle station in the Northern Territory and the long and difficult journey to reach it.

Of the many capable short-story writers of the period only one can be mentioned. Arthur Hoey Davis ("Steele Rudd," 1868–1935) published, in *On Our Selection* (Sydney, 1909) and a number of successors, a series of highly original sketches of the life of the small, struggling Australian farmer and his family. These sketches are mere collections of incidents, crude but realistic, and filled with a rough humour that is actually a means of escape from a hard, drab life.

The first Australian playwright of significance, Thomas Louis Buvelot Esson (1879–1943), belongs to this period, and so does Australia's only essayist of world importance, Walter Logie Forbes Murdoch (b. 1874). Esson's plays are simple, direct, concise, romantic in spirit, but realistic in expression. Murdoch's essays, which might almost have been written in England, are the critical reflections of a cultivated mind, strong common sense, and an equally strong and sometimes sly sense of humour—with a touch of sermonising.

With the bursting of the boom that followed the First World War and the depression that came later, a new period set in: realistic, sophisticated, unillusioned. Writers began to look overseas for new ideas and methods, psychological analysis came into fashion, and there was a marked advance in construction and craftsmanship. At first almost everyone turned naturally to the novel, but there has lately been a remarkable efflorescence in verse and to a smaller degree in the short story; the wireless and the gramophone have, however, been almost fatal to the ballad.

The *Bulletin,* still Australia's principal literary paper, has helped greatly in the development of the novel, and several of the leading writers of the day have won its annual prize. These include most of the representatives of the Lawson-Furphy tradition; Katharine Susannah Prichard (b. 1884), Vance Palmer (b. 1885), Frank Davison (b. 1893), and Kylie Tennant (b. 1912). They practise a modernised version of the Australianism of the 'nineties, lacking its occasional tendency to parochialism and sentimentality, and possessing greater detachment and technical skill.

Katharine Prichard is the most notable Australian novelist after Henry Handel Richardson, and the most representative after Lawson. A widely read intellectual, she yet manages, as in *Working Bullocks* (London, 1926), to reveal, without psychological analysis, the minds of men and women who are, for the most part, inarticulate. Another of her best novels, *Coonardoo* (London, 1929), a tragedy set on a station in the far west, where the white life meets the black, is a prose symphony. Katharine Prichard inclines toward pattern rather than plot; her style is simple, colloquial, concise. With *The Roaring Nineties* (1946), a story of the gold fields of Western Australia, she has published the first of three volumes of what may be her masterpiece.

Kylie Tennant's general attitude, and in particular her sympathy with the worker, resembles Katharine Prichard's, but she makes the utmost of the comic aspects of tragedy, her novels lack construction, and her style is less closely knit. The best are *Tiburon* (Sydney, 1935) and *The Battlers* (London, 1941), which deal principally with the "traveller," the swagman, of the depression.

Wells of Beersheba (Sydney, 1933), by Frank Davison (1893), is a prose poem of the Light Horse in Palestine during the First

World War. His *Man Shy* (Sydney, 1932), a pastoral epic of untamable cattle in the mountains of northern Queensland, is actually an epic of freedom. Simple, lucid, unaffected, Davison's style yet suggests that it is the result of infinite pains.

Allied with these writers by reason of his directness, lack of psychological subtlety, and preference for ordinary types is Leonard Mann (b. 1895). The most characteristic of his novels is *Mountain Flat* (London, 1939); his *Flesh in Armour* (Melbourne, 1932) is the best of Australian novels of the First World War.

Palmer, and Davison also, link these writers with the psychologists. A self-conscious and restrained romanticist, Palmer is careful to avoid the defects of the age in which he was born. Like Katharine Prichard, he is a novelist of the ordinary man, but whereas her characters are objectively presented, his are not only shown from within but subjectively; so a certain similarity runs through their differences. Palmer is a conscientious artist, and no other Australian novelist is so fertile in images; the best of his novels are *Men Are Human* (London, 1930), and *The Passage* (London, 1930). From a historical point of view, the most important of the psychological novelists is Chester Francis Cobb (b. 1899), whose *Mr. Moffat* (London, 1925) introduced the stream-of-consciousness method into Australian fiction.

Certain other novelists are more important in themselves. Christina Stead (b. 1902), who now lives in New York, has talent, but seems unable to realise it completely. Her *Seven Poor Men of Sydney* (London, 1934) is a study, amorphous and rather morbid, yet fascinating, of Sydney's submerged or half-submerged, leftist intelligentsia. "Barnard Eldershaw" (Marjorie Barnard and Flora Eldershaw, both b. 1897) presents acute and sensitive observations of human, especially feminine idiosyncrasies, which are recorded with an ironic and sometimes gently malicious humour. Their first novel, *A House Is Built* (London, 1934), is simple and objective, but the later novels are modernistic in method. Eleanor Dark (b. 1901), whose psychological novels are marred by sentimentality and repetition of pattern, has produced in *The Timeless Land* (London and New York, 1941), which deals with the founding of Australia, a work of scholarship lit by the imagination. *Chosen People* (London, 1938), by Kenneth Mackenzie (b. 1913), is an accomplished essay in erotic social life, beautifully written, sometimes a little overwritten.

There are a number of satirists, including two of individuality and power. Brian Penton (b. 1904), in his long, closely packed *Landtakers* (Sydney, 1934) and *Inheritors* (London, 1936), is a debunker of the pioneers. "All these early settlers," says he, "were just slightly off their hinges," and, in fact, many of his characters are morbid to madness. In *Capricornia* (Sydney, 1943), another long and compact novel, by Alfred Xavier Herbert (b. 1892), characters and incidents are made to fit into a large design—to display, with indignant horror, the racial prejudice of the Northern Territory against the aboriginals and especially the mixed-bloods. The worlds created by these two authors are not human worlds but rather districts of hell; yet they are worlds, complete and self-consistent.

Other satires include the novels of the well-known artist Norman Lindsay (b. 1879). Chronologically he belongs to the previous period, but all his best work has appeared since 1930. Lindsay's principal subjects are sexual and religious taboos; crude, but bursting with life, his novels are extremely amusing. Among the most characteristic is *Redheap* (London, 1930; as *Every Mother's Son,* New York, 1930). At the other end of the scale, polished, witty, sophisticated, is *The Montforts* (London, 1928; as *The Madeline Heritage,* New York, 1928), by Martin Mills Boyd (b. 1893). Everything about this novel is easy, entertaining, and assured, and some of its satire is penetrating.

The short stories of today, in Australia as in other countries, are far less formal than those of the 'nineties, and deal with episodes that are felt to be attached to the larger life of their characters. The best of them are the work of the principal novelists, and in particular Katharine Prichard, Vance Palmer, and Frank Davison.

Most of the younger poets tend to radiate from certain centres: the *Bulletin; Meanjin Papers,* which, beginning as a tiny periodical of verse, has become one of Australia's two leading literary magazines; the Jindyworobak Club, preacher of a culture supposed to be derived in some half-mystical manner from the soil; *Southerly,* the organ of the Sydney branch of the English Association, which represents a more academic point of view than that of *Meanjin;* and *Angry Penguins,* which claims that it "fulfills the rôle in Australia of New Directions in America and of John Lehmann's New Writing in England." Whatever these writers lack, it is not assurance. Apart from the Jindyworobaks, there is no sign of a deliberate Australianism among the poets of today, but it would be difficult to imagine their work coming from any country except their own.

The leaders are two intellectuals, Robert David FitzGerald (b. 1902) and Kenneth Slessor (b. 1901). A thinker with a lyrical gift, FitzGerald has published two books, *To Meet the Sun* (Sydney, 1929) and *Moonlit Acre* (Melbourne, 1938). In the first, the lyrical predominates; in the second, the thoughts are riper and the lyrical element has diminished. FitzGerald is an adventurer of the spirit who has a strong sense of the marvellous and of mystery and a natural gift for imagery. He is unmistakably a modern, yet no individual modern poet seems to have influenced him. His work is distinguished by vigour and exuberance and by an essential simplicity, though he is not always easy reading. Slessor, on the contrary, is a sophisticated poet; his dry and cynical humour conveys a disillusion that seems in part assumed, and he has a sensitive ear for sound and rhythm. His verse has been collected in *One Hundred Poems; 1919–39* (Sydney, 1944).

Two of the most notable of the intellectual poets are James Philip McAuley (b. 1917), author of *Under Aldebaran* (1946), and Alec Derwent Hope (b. 1907), who has not yet published a book. McAuley's work is essentially modern and occasionally obscure, but it always has meaning, conciseness, and logical structure. Hope is an outspoken and pitiless social satirist, particularly of sex; he reminds one of an unillusioned but grimly humorous scientist recording the antics of men and women with arctic impartiality.

Melbourne Odes (Melbourne, 1934) is the work of a satirist of a very different kind, Frank Wilmot ("Furnley Maurice," 1881–1942), who obviously hates and is hurt by the evils he underlines. In most of his other verse, and particularly in *The Gully* (Melbourne, 1929), Wilmot is a nature poet, but indignation at social injustice informs all his work and he has written some powerful antiwar poems. The most notable of Australian war poets is, however, Leon

Gellert (b. 1892). His *Songs of a Campaign* (Sydney, 1917) move slowly and with dignity, and he has a remarkable faculty for the pictorial representation of moods. Another intellectual was John Alexander Ross McKellar (1904–1931), whose volume of *Collected Poems* (Sydney, 1946) is evidence of the loss Australian poetry has suffered by his early death. The Second World War has inspired a great deal of verse, but it awaits critical winnowing.

Of the lyrists, Tom Inglis Moore (b. 1901), who is linked with the intellectuals, is a worshipper of sensuous beauty, a lover who, in *Adagio in Blue* (Sydney, 1938), analyses his raptures. The verses of Kenneth Mackenzie, in *Moonlit Doorway* (Sydney, 1944), are sophisticated, sensuous, passionate, and flow more freely than Moore's. Another link with the intellectuals is Ronald McCuaig (b. 1906). In his *Vaudeville* (Sydney, 1938) he is an unrestrained sardonic realist of the tribe of Eliot, but in *The Wanton Goldfish* (Sydney, 1941) he is a simple and musical lyrist in the manner of the seventeenth century.

Australia has been late in developing essay, criticism, and drama. The only essays of the period that call for mention are contained in Wilmot's *Romance* (Melbourne, 1922). Their subjects are literary, for the most part, and they show imaginative insight and the gift of illuminating phrase. No critic of the calibre, durability, and energy of A. G. Stephens has appeared in recent years.

Plays for radio and stage are now appearing in numbers, and two playwrights are outstanding. Douglas Stewart, also a poet and critic, has published *Ned Kelly* (1943), a poetic drama of the life of the famous bushranger; and, in one volume, *The Golden Lover* and *Fire on the Snow* (Sydney, 1944). They are a poet's plays, and the first and second have had to be cut for production; the third is the best radio play that has yet come out of Australia. Sydney Tomholt (b. 1884) has the poet's imagination but not his method. The plays in his single volume, *Bleak Dawn* (Sydney, 1936), are short and concise, characterised by drabness, passion, or mysticism.

This rich and rapidly growing young literature, almost entirely the work of dwellers in cities, harks back constantly to the soil from which its individuality derives. In form, its principal characteristic is conciseness, with a tendency toward the episodic and the picaresque. It is marked, beneath whatever craft and sophistication, by an essential freshness, simplicity, and desire for action, and by a humour that is definitely ironic. Something of the uncertainty of the future, perhaps arising in part from its country's wide, incalculable rhythms of fertility and drought, may be felt in it also, but, along with this, a willingness to take a risk with things, and a determination to see them through.

〰〰〰〰〰〰〰〰〰〰〰〰〰〰〰〰〰〰〰〰〰〰〰〰

CHAPTER XXI

Art

BY BERNARD SMITH

FOR THE ART HISTORIAN the peculiar interest of the art of Australia is to be found in the adaptation and transformation of a European tradition in a new geographical and social context and its gradual acquirement of national characteristics. The art of no other country in history began from more humble or more unfavourable sources. Australian art history began when the eighteenth-century art of England was in its ascendant (1788), but by the time the colony had developed an independent economy capable of supporting artists, the general level of English taste had begun to decline to the extraordinary low level revealed by the Great Exhibition held in London in 1851.

The early colonial period of Australian art (1788–1809) covers the time from the beginning of the penal settlement until the arrival of Governor Lachlan Macquarie. During this period the small colony had to fight famine, disease, and loneliness. Artistic production was confined to topographical drawing and scientific recording.

The interest in biological science is plainly indicated by the great number of drawings of Australian plant and animal life made by governors, army officials, and convicts in the first years of settlement. The Linnaean Society of London was founded in the same year as the settlement. More than a thousand scientific drawings now extant were made in Australia before 1800. Created chiefly as important additions to scientific records, many reveal exceptionally high skill, discrimination, and taste. Drawing was an accomplishment of the eighteenth-century gentleman, and for the eighteenth-century sailor it was a necessity.

The linear precision and symmetry of the topographical style introduced into England by Canaletto was the first style on the continent. The convict John Eyre (arrived at Sydney 1804) and the army officer Major Taylor (arrived at Sydney 1817) produced capable work in the topographic manner. Most of the contemporary work was produced by amateur artists, either in pencil or water colours. Work was sold to itinerant sea-captains or collected by an officer to illustrate his diary or memoirs. In England there was a small but assured demand for mezzotints representing the fauna and flora of the new land.

The eighteenth-century tradition in Australia reached its fruition during the governorship of Colonel Lachlan Macquarie. Macquarie had many of the virtues and some of the faults of an enlightened despot of the eighteenth century. He widened and straightened many of Sydney's streets and planned the new towns of Windsor, Liverpool, and Bathurst. He developed for the first time a viceregal patronage of the arts, appointing Francis Howard Greenway (1777–1837) as government architect, making Michael Massey Robinson (1747–1826) Australia's first and only poet laureate, and helping such artists as the convict Joseph Lycett (arrived at Sydney 1810) and the freeman John William Lewin (1770–1819), who was appointed artist to the Macquarie Progress over the Blue Mountains in 1813.

In the Macquarie period (1810–1821) a small but distinct school of colonial portraiture came into being. Retired army officers, Sydney merchants, and some free settlers who were laying the foundations of large fortunes provided the first local market for art works. Richard Read (arrived at Sydney 1814) painted many portraits of colonial personages. Miniature painters were also active, one of the best known being Richard Read (the Younger) (arrived at Sydney 1819); but the introduction of the daguerrotype into Sydney in 1843 cut short the development of a school of miniature painters.

Characteristic of the period is the large number of commissions for drawings and water-colour paintings of country houses. The country-house landscape provided a bridge from the purely urban topographical drawing to the romantic landscapes of the latter part of the century. Joseph Lycett drew a series of these landscapes which were engraved and published in England.

The influence of the English romantic movement had been operating from the earliest days of Australian settlement. The first landscape in oils produced in the country, a painting of Sydney Cove in 1794 by the convict Thomas Watling, with a heavy foreground and dramatic emphasis, possesses affinities with the work of Richard Wilson. Romantic landscape became prominent in the 'thirties and 'forties, the years of the extension of Australia's pastoral economy. Conrad Martens (1801–1878), who settled in Sydney in 1835, was the most important of Australia's colonial artists. His best work has a delicate lyrical tenderness and a sensitive feeling for atmosphere and light, for he was an admirer of Turner. A capable draughtsman, Martens was always more at home with water colour than with oil. Indeed, the history of Australian painting until the middle of the nineteenth century is mainly the history of the colonial continuation of the English water-colour tradition. Frederick Garling (1806–1873) and Samuel Elyard (1817–1910) also produced many competent landscapes in the romantic manner, though their work tends to revert frequently to topographical tradition.

A number of artists, sustained by a small but intelligent circle of Englishmen, were working in Australia in the 'thirties and 'forties. It was in this period that the first art exhibitions and art societies were organised. The first exhibition of paintings in Australia was organised by John Skinner Prout (1806–1876) in Hobart in 1845. Two years later the Society for the Promotion of Fine Arts was established in Sydney.

The art of Australia from 1788 to 1851 is a colonial art of English origin, produced by English artists for Englishmen exiled in a harsh and uncongenial environment. It differed from English art only in its subject matter, and even that was seen in a European context. Martens placed English castles upon Australian hills. Colonial mansions with battlemented turrets rose amid Australian gums when the Gothic style was revived in the late 'thirties. William Charles Wentworth's mansion at Vaucluse is an instance of the impact of Gothicism upon colonial pseudoaristocratic taste. The gentility, finesse, and pretentiousness of an aristocratic culture grounded in a pastoral economy are to be observed in their infancy in this period of Australian art. While the tradition persisted well into the second half of the nineteenth century, the discovery of gold in 1851 changed the direction of Australian cultural development as surely as it changed the character of many of its institutions.

Between 1851 and 1861 all classes of people came to the country in search of quick and easy fortunes. The potential market for the artist was thereby increased enormously. The new populations of the diggings demanded illustrations and cartoons dealing with incidents in their own lives. In the 'fifties and 'sixties a number of illustrated periodicals came into existence. They were concerned with economic, social, political, moral, and religious questions of the day. Illustrations of contemporary Australian life and political cartooning were in great demand. This flowering of the graphic arts developed a mid-century realism (1851–1863) possessing national characteristics. The most important artist of the period was S. T. Gill (1818–1880). In the 'fifties lithography became popular as a method of reproduction, and by this means Gill's drawings circulated widely. He depicted all phases of life on the diggings, and the life of contemporary Melbourne and Sydney. A capable draughtsman, Gill expressed in his work the democratic activities of the day.

Although Charles Abrahams began working in the 'forties, the history of Australian sculpture actually begins with the arrival in Australia in the early 'fifties of Thomas Woolner (1825–1892), a Pre-Raphaelite; John Simpson Mackennal (1832–1901); and Charles Summers (1825–1878).

In 1863 the McCulloch Ministry of Victoria appointed a commission to investigate the promotion of the fine arts in Victoria. It was a time when both Victoria and New South Wales were assuming the dignity of national states. The sudden influx of wealth through the gold discoveries resulted in the rapid growth of the two largest centres of population, Melbourne and Sydney. In 1867 the Artisans' Schools of Design were established in Melbourne and the suburbs. These helped to train several of Australia's best-known artists, including Tom Roberts (1856–1931) and Frederick McCubbin (1855–1917). In the next decade many art and technical schools were founded in the provincial centres of Victoria. The National Gallery of Victoria was established in 1873, the oldest in any British Dominion. The Felton bequest, one of the most munificent endowments made to any art museum, provides this gallery with an annual income, enabling it to build up a representative collection of European art. The National Gallery of New South Wales was established in 1876; that of South Australia, in 1879.

These developments made it possible for the first time for students to receive a formal art training in their own country. Teachers from abroad became instructors in Australian art schools. Eugene von Guerard (1811–1901), George Frederick Folingsby (1830–1891), Lucien Henry (?–1896), and Louis Buvelot (1814–1888) are among those who brought the fruits of a Continental training to the new country. It is from this period that the exclusive predominance of the English tradition began to wane. Australian artists became aware of the importance of Paris, Rome, and Munich as art centres. In the 'seventies the sculptor Achille Simonetti (1840–?) and the painter Giulio Anivitti (1850–1881), both of Rome, were responsible, as teachers at the Academy of Art of New South Wales, for the introduction of the tastes and methods of the nineteenth-century European academies.

The years from 1863 to 1885 may be considered the academic period of Australian painting. A large number of sentimental genre paintings after the manner of the English painters Luke Fildes (1844–1927) and Frank Dicksee (1853–1928) were hung in the newly established galleries. And several local artists painted gallery pictures characterised mainly by their photographic naturalism, morbid sentimentality, and acreage. Fortunately there were not many of them.

The finest artist of the period was Louis Buvelot (1814–1888), a Swiss, whose work both in oils and water colours reveals sound craftsmanship and keen observation of the peculiarities of the local atmosphere and scene. It was Buvelot who attempted to translate for the first time the high-pitched hues of Australian landscape and the anatomy of the gum tree on canvas.

The increasing wealth and population, the formation of schools and galleries, and the growth of an intelligent audience possessing some claim to critical standards made possible, by the end of the 'eighties, the rise of a native school of Australian landscape painting. John Lhotsky, a visiting German scientist, had written in the English journal *Art Union* in 1839, "Australian sky and nature

awaits and merits real artists to portray it. There is a whole system of landscape painting of the most striking character yet available for human art." And as Lhotsky suggested, the growth of a
native tradition came in the solution of the landscape problem.
Tom Roberts, after his return to Australia in 1885 from studying
and painting abroad, and Girolamo Nerli (1863–1926) introduced
to Australia the direct methods of painting advocated by the
French impressionists. Roberts was mainly responsible for the inauguration of plein-air painting in Australia. He emphasised the
importance of seizing quickly and honestly the fleeting vision of
the moment. A group of young painters associated themselves with
Roberts, and so began the famous period of impressionist groups.

Painters' camps were established at Box Hill, Mentone, Heidel-
berg, and Charterisville, all near Melbourne. A new approach to
landscape based on impressionist techniques became the order of
the day. The first exhibition of impressionist painting held in
Australia was shown in Melbourne in 1889. It was roundly abused
by conservative newspaper critics. Among those who exhibited were
Tom Roberts, Arthur Streeton (1867–1943), Frederick McCubbin
(1855–1917), and Charles Conder (1868–1909), who later became
famous in Paris and London. The early work of Roberts and Streeton appeals most strongly today. These paintings reveal the tenta-
tive searchings for the solution of the landscape problem that had
baffled earlier artists: the rendering of an atmosphere drenched in
blinding sunlight, dust, heat-haze, and the delicate pastellate violet
and turquoise hues that characterise much of the Australian landscape.

The growth of a native school of landscape painting was closely
associated with the production of the first Australian genre paintings. Roberts, in his "Bailed Up," and "The Breakaway," McCubbin, in his "The Pioneers," and "Down on His Luck," sought to
bring the life of contemporary Australia within the vision of
their art, which may be seen as the continuation in a new idiom of
the mid-century genre lithography of S. T. Gill. It is in such work
that the egalitarian and democratic vein which has run consistently
throughout Australian cultural traditions may be traced most
clearly. In this respect Roberts and McCubbin expressed in their
painting much of that developing nationhood which is revealed

so clearly in the writings of Henry Lawson and Joseph Furphy ("Tom Collins").

Although the close examination of nature in the light of impressionism brought new energy to Australian painting, the romanticism of an older generation persisted among those who desired to retain a poetic and literary element in their work, who still read Ruskin and admired Turner and the delicacy of Corot. The neoromantics of the late nineteenth and early twentieth century followed many practices of the school of Roberts and Streeton, but, instead of accepting direct observation as the end of painting, used the techniques they had learned from the impressionists to elucidate and portray the subtler moods of Australian landscapes. They were the painters of the dawn and the afterglow, of the mists and the mystery of the Australian bush. John Ford Paterson (1851–1912) was a forerunner of this tendency; David Davies (1863–?) is a romantic in his best work; and a similar approach is to be found in many of the landscapes by Walter Withers (1854–1914). At the turn of the century the desire to reveal the soul of the Australian landscape led to an attempt among writers and some artists to create a local mythology. In his "Pan," Sydney Long (b. 1878) brings Greek mythology to Australian landscape. The Australian aborigine is seen as a delicate, faunlike creature, a view which owed far more to the *fin de siècle* aestheticism of England than to accurate observation or intensity of feeling.

An interest in eighteenth-century manners and customs, realised in a style of pseudorococo flamboyancy, is seen in the art of Norman Lindsay; in much of the work of the group of artists and writers who were influenced by his method and personality the tenuous linearity of *art nouveau* decoration appears. The most important artists of the tradition were Norman Lindsay (b. 1879) and Blamire Young (1862–1935) to whom may be added J. J. Hilder (1881–1916) in the realm of a pure aetherealised landscape in water colours.

In the same period an interest in etching developed. The purchase of Whistler etchings by the National Art Gallery (Melbourne) in 1892 attracted John Shirlow to the possibilities of the medium. Etchings had been produced earlier, but they were not widely accepted as a serious art form until the beginning of the twentieth century. Much of the acceptance by a local public was due to the work and influence of Sir Lionel Lindsay (b. 1874). H. van Raalte (1881–1929), Sydney Ure Smith (b. 1887), and John B. Godson (b. 1882) have worked with success as etchers.

Australian impressionism became the dominant tendency in Australian art. George Lambert (1873–1930) became one of the most accomplished painters of portraits in Australia. A skillful draughtsman and an able sculptor, Lambert's mature style resulted from the welding of the impressionist methods he learned as a student of Julian Ashton (1851–1942) and the severe academic training to which he subjected himself in Paris and London. Although not a modern painter, Lambert did much to encourage the younger Australian painters interested in the modern movement when he returned from abroad in 1921.

In Australia, as in so many other countries, the assimilation of impressionist techniques by the schools and the parallel development of photography led to an increasing emphasis on the study of tone. The cult of Velásquez and the popularity of the work of Sargent are a part of this development. In Australia the work of Hugh Ramsay (1877–1906), Bernard Hall (1859–1935), and both the painting and theories of Max Meldrum (b. 1875) show three distinct approaches to the impressionism of tonal values. A later generation of impressionists who derive far more directly from French impressionism includes Will Ashton (b. 1881) and Charles Bryant (1883–1937).

The influence of the modern movement in Australia may be traced from the year 1913, when Roland Wakelin (b. 1887), Grace Cossington Smith, and Roi de Mestre, art students in Sydney, became interested in the work of Paul Cézanne and other postimpressionist painters known to them, however, only in reproductions. A few years later George Bell (b. 1878) and several young painters in Melbourne, including Arnold Shore (b. 1897) and William Frater (b. 1890), began painting in a modern manner in Melbourne. Postimpressionist painting with its emphasis on design, colour, and the validity of distortion was bitterly resisted by conservative painters and critics, whose "emotional vested interests"—as Adrian Lawlor, the forthright and effective champion of the "moderns," termed it—were outraged by the new aesthetic. Modernism in painting was vociferously denounced by such well-known critics as J. S. MacDonald (b. 1878), Howard Ashton (b. 1877), and Sir Lionel Lindsay. The almost universal acceptance of the impressionist tradition in Australian landscape long after it had passed beyond its creative stage fettered the normal development of art in Australia for almost two decades.

Apart from those already mentioned, the influence of modern painting brought with it a greater interest in the formal qualities of pictorial composition. These are to be found in the work of many artists still among Australia's leading painters: N. Buzacott and Lina Bryans of Melbourne, John D. Moore (b. 1888) of Sydney, and Kenneth Macqueen (b. 1897) of Queensland.

Abstract and constructivist art had little influence in Australia until the 'thirties, when excellent work was achieved by Rah Fizelle, Frank Hinder (b. 1906), Grace Crowley, Eric Thake, and Eric Wilson (b. 1911). Surrealist painting has had few followers in Australia, James Gleeson (b. 1915), a young artist of unusual imaginative power, being the only artist to be influenced strongly by surrealist theories.

The return of William Dobell (b. 1899) from England in 1938 had a marked effect on the painting of the younger generation of Australian artists. An outstanding draughtsman and an able technician, Dobell possesses the sardonic humour and penetrating insight necessary to reveal the character of his sitters—his best works are portraits—and to perceive the artistic significance of the most commonplace situations and subjects. His "Irish Youth," "Mrs. South Kensington," and "Joshua Smith" show his range and ability as an artist. The award of the Archibald Prize of 1943 to Dobell for the Smith portrait resulted in the greatest controversy known to the history of art in Australia. The lawsuit which resulted from two rival competitors contesting the award, on the ground that Dobell's painting was not a portrait but a caricature, must stand beside the Whistler-Ruskin case for the degree of public interest aroused, its historical significance, and the aesthetic issues involved. The judgement was given in favour of the trustees of the National Art Gallery of New South Wales who made the award.

In the war years, cleavages within the ranks of the younger Australian painters affected by the modern movement became apparent. The concentration on formal design and the constructional elements of painting, which occupied the attention of artists in the 'thirties, was replaced during the war by greater preoccupation with subject matter. Partly owing to the impact of war and partly to a reaction from formalism evident for several years before the war, the tendency at present is manifesting itself in two opposing directions, a school of contemporary realism and a school of contemporary romanticism.

Russell Drysdale (b. 1912) has painted a new, if at times uncompromising, Australian landscape of droughts, soil erosion, destitution, and loneliness. A capable draughtsman and fine colourist, he is one of the most promising artists painting in Australia today. Noel Counihan (b. 1913) and Roy Dalgarno (b. 1911) have used a contemporary idiom to portray industrial life. Their work may be compared in some respects to that of the American artist William Gropper. The S.O.R.A. group of Sydney, which includes James Cant (b. 1911), Herbert McClintock (b. 1906), Roderick Shaw (b. 1915), and Hal Missingham (b. 1907), are seeking to bring art closer to Australian life. Apart from this group may be noted such artists as Jean Bellette (b. 1909), David Strachan (b. 1919), Francis Lymburner (b. 1916), Wolfgang Cardamatis (b. 1917), all of whom are essentially romantic in their artistic approach. Some of the most interesting landscapes in a romantic vein, strangely reminiscent of the Norwich school, are those of Lloyd Rees (b. 1895).

A somewhat similar cleavage between romanticism and realism exists in Melbourne. There is great integrity in the sombre political realism of Victor O'Connor (b. 1914) and V. Bergner (b. 1920). The work of Albert Tucker (b. 1914) and Arthur Boyd (b. 1920) comes closer to European expressionism than any other painting in Australia, and leans a little too heavily on literary symbolism for its effect. These Sydney and Melbourne groups form the *avant-garde* of contemporary painting in Australia. The postimpressionist painters of the Bell-Wakelin generation occupy a central position and have become widely accepted by the buying public.

The growth of an indigenous ballet in Australia in recent years has provided the opportunity for a group of competent and at times inspired ballet designers to develop a field of art previously unknown to the country. Loudon Sainthill (b. 1918), William Constable, Amie Kingston, and Elaine Haxton have produced excellent work in this field. The last artist has gained distinction also for her mural painting, a field that is still almost untouched in Australia.

Lack of commissions and a poor tradition have discouraged the production of good sculpture, but that of Raynor Hoff (1894–1937) is outstanding, particularly in architectural sculpture. The most important Australian sculptor working today is Lyndon Dadswell (b. 1905), who should be provided with the projects that his craft and intuitive powers deserve. Fine work has also been done by Daphne Mayo; and in small domestic sculpture the artistry of G. F. Lewers (b. 1905) is notable.

Public interest in the work of Australian artists is greater today than ever before. The nation has recently experienced the most serious threat to its existence. From that threat has grown an increasing respect for creative work on the part of many Australians. If Commonwealth, state, and municipal governmental authorities will recognise and foster this appreciation, Australian art should soon reach a new level of achievement, for even today there are many talented young artists producing first-class work, and some whose work would command respect in any international exhibition.

CHAPTER XXII

Journalism

BY CLIVE TURNBULL

AUSTRALIAN journalistic history divides itself into three periods: the early nineteenth century, when a subservient quasi-official press ministered to the needs and caprices of the dictatorship that controlled the penal settlements; the century from the 1820's to the 1920's, which saw the rise of the family-controlled newspaper through a series of struggles with officialdom to a position of political and financial power; and the last quarter of a century, which has seen (with two noteworthy exceptions) control pass into the hands of joint stock companies with an increasing tendency to amalgamation and popularisation. The development of journalism parallels the economic development of Australia itself. Today the financial power of the press is greater than ever, but its political power has waned. The didactic function, the *raison d'être* of many newspapers when the interests of an emergent commercial class ran contrary to those of colonial authority, takes a secondary place now that the position of this class has been consolidated. The newspaper industry offers commodities in return for immediate gains rather than policies designed to attain profitable ends; nor has this been found incompatible, in the best Australian journalism, with a sincerely held conception of public responsibility.

Australia's first newspaper, the Sydney *Gazette,* a weekly production of four foolscap pages, appeared on March 5, 1803. It was printed by George Howe (1769–1821), a convict and the second Australian printer, under the direction of Governor Philip Gidley King (1758–1808). The government controlled the *Gazette* and dictated its policy, but the financial responsibility fell upon Howe, who, while endeavouring to appeal to a public sufficiently wide to make the undertaking a commercial success, was nevertheless inhibited on every hand by the exacting requirements of official policy—requirements which were to make the *Gazette,* in the opinion of its critics, a repository of "fulsome flattery of Government officials and . . . inane twaddle on other matters." The *Gazette* was the principal representative of what has been termed the "convict press," the first of a group which included, in Tasmania, the Derwent *Star* (1810), the Van Diemen's Land *Gazette* (1814), and the Hobart *Town Gazette* (1816).

Such publications were by their very nature distasteful to the increasing proportion of free inhabitants in the penal colonies of New South Wales and Tasmania. To this class the government of the colonies by dictatorship of the governor and a military caste was odious. They sought citizen rights, and their desire to set up a normal abode of free Englishmen conflicted with the intent of the British authorities that the smooth functioning of the penal settlement should be paramount. When a free press did make its appearance it was subject to rigid censorship; the struggle of the early editors for liberty of the press is coterminous with the struggle of early politicians for democratic institutions.

Old and worn type, inferior paper of various sizes and colours, and defaulting subscribers, who were sometimes plaintively invited to make payment in wheat, added to the difficulties of the pioneer editors. Andrew Bent (1795–1850), the "Tasmanian Franklin," who had printed the Hobart *Town Gazette and Southern Reporter* from 1816, under government authority and with government resources, obtained his own type, and in 1824 changed the title of his paper to the *Gazette and Van Diemen's Land Advertiser,* venturing even upon some criticism of public affairs. The arrival of Colonel George Arthur (1784–1854) as Governor in 1824 put an end to the limited privileges which Bent had been allowed. Arthur, a martinet, prosecuted Bent for criminal libel arising from a letter he had published. The "poor printer" and "plain man," as he described himself, was fined the ruinous sum of £500 and sent to gaol while the government set up a new paper and appropriated the name of *Gazette* for it. Bent was refused a publisher's licence and relentlessly hounded by Arthur, who not only frustrated all his attempts at publication but again secured his imprisonment. "The unfortunate man lost altogether the savings of many years."

Bent was the first of many rebels against the colonial autocracy. Henry Melville, editor of the *Colonial Times,* was likewise persecuted. He lived to see the emancipation of the press but, like Bent, was ruined financially; he became "a dependent old man in London." The struggle continued on a larger stage. The antagonists now were Governor Sir Ralph Darling (1775–1858) of New South Wales and William Charles Wentworth (1793[?]–1872). Darling was a lawful tyrant of Arthur's school. Wentworth was the spokesman of the new Australianism. In London Wentworth had met Dr. Robert Wardell (1793–1834), the editor and proprietor of a London evening newspaper, the *Statesman,* and had induced him to accompany him to Sydney, bringing materials for a paper. This was the *Australian*—a significant title—launched on October 14, 1824.

Both the *Australian* and the *Monitor,* established in 1826 by Edward Smith Hall (1786–1860), vigorously attacked Darling. Darling, like Arthur, took every means in his power to curb this liberty. Under an Act of 1827 he instituted a series of actions for criminal libel against journalists who criticised his actions. As these were tried before a jury of military officers the Governor usually won. Hall spent three and a half years in gaol and is said to have appeared in the dock seven times for his criticisms of Darling. By the beginning of 1830 Darling was able to report to his superiors in London that "the radical press and its supporters" were "miserably reduced." While Hall was in gaol, four libel actions had been decided against him. Wentworth (a barrister), who had foreseen the effects of the Act and had parted with his interest in the *Australian,* was able to assist the victim of Darling's policy by his eloquence both within and without the court. In 1831 Darling was recalled, to the delight of the populace and especially of the *Australian* and the *Monitor.* Arthur was recalled in 1836 after a term of twelve years. Not for many years were the struggles of the colonists with the Colonial Office to end; but the struggles of the editors were virtually over. The battle for a free press had been won. There were to be no more Arthurs or Darlings to exercise the unique powers of the colonial adminstrators while those powers remained. In the rise of Australian democracy the powers themselves disappeared.

To regard the early colonial press as inevitably right, inevitably heroic, and inevitably democratic would, of course, be wholly wrong. Some of the fugitive papers of the time were scurrilous and vindictive. The governors were sometimes right by other people's lights as well as by their own. The newspapers were sometimes wrong. But time was on the side of the newspapers. The development of the penal colonies to self-governing lands of free men was inevitable. In that development such men as Bent, Melville, and Smith, who were prepared to suffer for their views, and Wentworth, as the spokesman of at least some of them, deserve all honour. Not one of these early periodicals—most of them weeklies or biweeklies—remains. The material reward of the founders was little or nothing at all. But they made articulate the new spirit of Australia, they pressed for, and brought about, reform—and they made possible the fortunes which were to be created from newspapers in the years to come.

The lifetime of only one newspaper still published overlaps this eventful period. In the last year of Darling's governorship three young men were preparing to publish a newspaper. They were Ward Stephens and Frederick Michael Stokes, clerks on the obsequious *Gazette,* and William McGarvie, a bookseller. On April 18, 1831, a few months before Darling's recall, they issued a four-page weekly, the Sydney *Herald* (to become in 1840 a daily and in 1842 the Sydney *Morning Herald* under which name it prospers to this day). The early *Heralds* belong to an interesting transitional stage. The paper was close enough to the crudities and cruelties of the first penal days to contain some matter which would now be considered in execrable taste. But it was no fire-eater like the *Monitor* and the *Australian*. It solemnly reproved the "reprehensible conduct" of some of the enemies of Darling. As early as 1842, its historian records, it was "Aunty" to the facetious, a foretaste of the title of "Granny" later bestowed in acknowledgement both of years and of sedateness. In 1841 its form was fixed. The paper was acquired by Charles Kemp and John Fairfax, to pass in 1853 completely into the hands of the Fairfax family, by whom it has been controlled ever since.

John Fairfax (1804–1877) stamped his character upon the *Herald*. A member of a Warwickshire family, trained as a journalist and printer, he became part proprietor of a paper at Leamington, England. An article protesting against an injustice by a local official resulted in a libel suit. Fairfax won the action but was ruined by the costs. Insolvent (he later paid all his creditors), he migrated to Australia, arriving in Sydney in 1838 with £5. Three years later, in partnership with Charles Kemp and with the help of friends, he was able to acquire the Sydney *Herald*. It was to be the first of the great family newspapers.

The new proprietorship of John Fairfax coincided with the beginning of a period of colonial consolidation. The colonists were taking on the appearance of free settlements. There was no longer the need or the desire for the violent feuds of the period which had ended with the departure of Darling and of Arthur. The colonial autocracy was reluctantly relaxing its hold. The ruling caste, military in tradition, Anglican in religion, and aristocratic in ambition, was being challenged by another, a middle class of rising merchants and landowners whom Fairfax, a nonconformist business man, was well fitted to represent. Cautious, responsible, devout, he embodied the most respectable traditions of his class and time. Under his management and that of his successors, the Sydney *Morning Herald* has pursued the noiseless tenour of its way, neither too far ahead of, nor too far behind, the fashion, a broadsheet whose sedateness is tempered by typographical improvements—an institution in Sydney, where it is viewed with a species of affection even by those who do not agree with its conservative political opinions.

Meanwhile, in the 'thirties and 'forties, there had grown up to the south of New South Wales the pastoral province of Port Phillip, later the colony, and now the state, of Victoria. Its chief town had produced a newspaper in 1838, the Melbourne *Advertiser,* issued by John Fawkner, an hotelkeeper, the first nine numbers in manuscript. The first of the papers still surviving, the Port Phillip *Herald,* was issued as a biweekly on January 3, 1840, by George Cavenagh, a former editor of the Sydney *Gazette*. Its descendant is the Melbourne evening *Herald* of today, but there has been no continuity of control.

June 2, 1846, saw the first issue of the second surviving Victorian journal, the *Argus,* established by William Kerr and bought in 1848 by Edward Wilson (1814–1878), a London clerk who had become a landholder in Port Phillip. Under the firm of Wilson and Mackinnon the *Argus* remained a family-controlled paper until 1936, when control passed into the hands of the Argus and Australasian, Ltd., a public company. The third surviving journal, the *Age,* was first issued on October 17, 1854, by two merchants, John and Henry Cooke. After various changes—one involving its being run for a short time as a printers' coöperative venture—it was acquired in 1856 for £2,000 by David and Ebenezer Syme, sons of a Scottish schoolteacher, reared in a household compounded equally of piety, a necessary frugality, stern discipline, and the Scottish love of learning. The first issue by the new management was made on June 12, 1856. The *Age* has remained ever since in the ownership of the Syme family.

It was the gold rush which provided the basis of the prosperity of the colony of Victoria and thus, in time, of the *Argus* and the *Age.* The circulation of the *Argus* was unprecedentedly large; it was said to approach that of the London *Times,* then a remarkable achievement. Its price, also, was low—threepence a copy compared with sixpence and even a shilling which had been charged in the early days of the Australian press. Its policies were those of the newcomers; Wilson wanted to "unlock the lands"—given over to vast pastoral holdings—for the settlement of the people; and he supported the gold-diggers in their agitation against obnoxious conditions on the gold fields, a support which led to the reviling of the *Argus* by its enemies when it subsequently condemned the unsuccessful revolt of Eureka. With the years Wilson acquired in equal proportions an increasing prosperity and an increasing conservatism. The *Argus* and the *Age* found themselves rivals not only in newspaper-selling but in politics. The *Argus* came to be regarded as the organ of "The Melbourne Club," otherwise of the large wool-growers and of the importers of Flinders Lane, the *Age* of the more radical elements in the community and of the slowly increasing group of Australian manufacturers seeking customs protection. David Syme (1827–1908) impressed himself upon the community as a political power, a dour Scotsman of high moral courage, whose chief claim to remembrance as a public figure is as "the father of protection." Syme, as it proved, was on the winning side politically. The *Argus* was forced to fight a series of rear-guard actions for low tariffs. Today protection is the settled policy of the country and as such is accepted; there is no free-trade newspaper.

With their increasing circulations and personal fortunes, the newspaper proprietors of Sydney and Melbourne strove with one another in the improvement of their services. Good objective reporting and editorial comment at what now seems inordinate length made up the bulk of their papers—papers in which the shipping advertisements on the front page were as much news to a community anxiously awaiting the arrival of friends and of mail from home as were the local events chronicled within. Editors were as enterprising as their modern equivalents. In the days before the electric telegraph the biweekly overland mail from Sydney to Melbourne reached a hamlet about twenty miles from Melbourne late in the evening, where ordinarily it remained overnight. This sufficed for the general public but not for the newspapers, whose waiting couriers gathered up their mailbags and rode hell for leather through the dark bush; if one were unhorsed by a tree branch on the way, so much the better for the others. In Sydney, representatives of the newspapers boarded English vessels as they entered or approached The Heads and commandeered all available English papers. When Sydney, Melbourne, and Adelaide were linked by telegraph, an elaborate method of news-getting was adopted by the Sydney *Morning Herald:* a representative of the paper boarded the incoming vessel at Albany in Western Australia, a couple of thousand miles away, and travelled in her to Adelaide, where he telegraphed to the Sydney office a summary of the news which he had prepared during his passage. This procedure was followed regularly until the completion of the submarine cable from England to Darwin in northern Australia and of the connecting overland telegraph from Darwin to Adelaide. When the first press cable message was received at Darwin, on July 1, 1872, the overland link, through the "dead heart" of Australia, was still incomplete and a horseman carried the message across a gap of about sixty miles. The Sydney *Morning Herald* received it the next day.

In earlier years the Australian papers had published pages of news extracted from English papers; and they themselves published long summaries for despatch to England. The dominance of European news in the early colonial press is frequently surprising to casual readers of old files who find Australian events, of which they would like to know more, subordinated to comparatively minor events in England. Cable messages were expensive, however, and an Australian-born generation lacked the keen personal interest of its fathers in occurrences in Great Britain. The English mail was no longer full of wonder and surprise for those who had already been apprised of events by cable, and the huge masses of reprint dwindled. But until comparatively recent years shipping advertisements still appeared on the front pages and, in a lingering colonialism, many papers continued to give cabled trivialities precedence over significant local news—a custom which has its legacy today in the publication in Australian papers of summaries of lucubrations in the American and English press on matters on which Australians are sometimes better informed themselves.

But if the editors of the now great dailies were no longer the fire-eaters and reformers of the young century, there were others who were. The *Bulletin,* a weekly founded in Sydney by Jules François [John Feltham] Archibald (1856–1919), a Victorian and no Frenchman in spite of his name, bore the motto "Australia for the Australians" and campaigned for "more humanity in the laws, more freedom in the Parliaments, more healthy independence in the Press." It expressed revolt against existing conditions in Sydney—cant, snobbery, and the legacies of the convict system. Strongly radical, zealous in the encouragement of Australian literature and the arts generally, the *Bulletin* gave expression to the new spirit of the common man in an Australia in which events were on the march—the birth of the Australian Labour Party as a political force, and of a passionate faith in the future of Australia as a nation. The *Bulletin* attained an Australia-wide reputation and its pink covers were familiar on the remotest frontier.

When Archibald retired, its critics said, the spirit went out of it. Under its altered motto, "Australia for the White Man," it appeals to a different public today. On March 7, 1945, the Minister for Information, Mr. Arthur Augustus Caldwell, a member of the Labour Party, said in the House of Representatives, "The *Bulletin* is undoubtedly the most anti-Australian of all newspapers published in Australia," a pronouncement which would have astounded the Labourites of the 'nineties.

No less influential in its fashion was the *Worker,* established by the labour unions of Queensland and issued in Brisbane in March, 1890, under the editorship of William Lane (1861–1917), the protagonist of the New Australia settlement in Paraguay and a burning idealist. The *Worker* had enormous effect on the politico-industrial situation of its day, particularly as it concerned workers in primary industry. A kindred paper was published in New South Wales, first as the *Hummer,* issued at Wagga, on October 18, 1891, and subsequently as the *Worker* (now the *Australian Worker),* transferred to Sydney. In 1898 the *Barrier Truth,* a Labour weekly, was established at Broken Hill, the New South Wales silver-lead centre; in 1908 it became, as the *Barrier Daily Truth,* the first Labour daily newspaper in Australia, and most of the time since then, the only one.

The first quarter of the twentieth century saw a quiet if steady development in the newspapers of the capitals. Sydney became the largest of the Australian cities, but the use of Melbourne as the federal capital from 1901 to the opening of the Parliament at Canberra in 1927, gave the Melbourne papers certain advantages and prestige. In the smaller capitals the newspapers followed the Sydney and Melbourne models—broadsheets, with advertisements on the front page and a main news page known as the "cable page." All maintained (and still maintain) large reporting staffs. Domestic news has never been syndicated to any great degree in Australia, though a beginning has lately been made with federal parliamentary news. Reporting staffs are consequently far larger than on corresponding English papers. Newspapers in different cities, however, do exchange news over leased wires. Since the opening of the submarine cable to Great Britain, British and foreign news has been distributed by various syndicates.

The period since the First World War has been one of great change. All the metropolitan dailies except one have replaced the advertisements of their front pages by news. Several have been converted from broadsheet to tabloid form. Even the most conservative have introduced comic strips. The long verbatim reports of proceedings have been so much curtailed that it has been complained that Parliament in some instances is inadequately reported. The models for change have been English rather than American. The

Max Dupain

WHEAT COUNTRY NEAR PARKES, N.S.W.

Australian National Publicity Association

LOADING SUGAR CANE, GORDONVALE, QUEENSLAND

Australian National Publicity Association

MUSTERING SHEEP FOR SHEARING, QUIRINDI, N.S.W.

Milton Kent

STEEL WORKS, NEWCASTLE, N.S.W.

prewar London *Daily Telegraph* and the London *Daily Express* have provided examples by which, it would seem, Australian newspapers have profited while retaining their own individuality.

Newspapers have been forced to adapt themselves to new conditions. A conspicuous example is the Sydney *Daily Telegraph,* which began life, under different ownership, as a broadsheet rival of the Sydney *Morning Herald* and is now the most ardent innovator in Australian newspaper practice; from the same office there issues the *Australian Women's Weekly,* a highly coloured pictorial weekly, the circulation of which (650,000 in 1945) has made Australian publishing history. Newspapers which failed to adapt themselves suffered drastic financial reorganisation, absorption by other papers, or extinction. The list of papers which have ceased publication for various reasons in comparatively recent years is extensive. It includes at least five papers financed by various sections of the Labour movement, political or trade union. With the single exception of the *Barrier Daily Truth,* no Labour daily has survived; lack of advertising from politically hostile sources and, in some instances, amateur management, have not been counterbalanced by circulation.

Much of the activity in Australian newspaper production since the end of the First World War may be ascribed to Sir Keith Arthur Murdoch, an Australian Scot. Appointed editor of the Melbourne *Herald* in 1920, he became chairman of the directors of the company by 1942. The rise of the *Herald* from a commonplace journal with a long history of financial vicissitude to the status of one of the great evening papers of the world may be ascribed mainly to Sir Keith Murdoch's flair for both journalism and business—a flair reflected in the success of the Melbourne *Sun News-Pictorial,* a pictorial tabloid which combines illustration with a news covering of unusual completeness for a journal of its kind; it has the largest circulation in Australia (325,565 in July, 1945). The rise of these papers, and of the Herald and Weekly Times, Ltd., which publishes them, is the major development of Australian journalism in the last quarter-century. The influence of the "Murdoch press," as it is known to its critics, extends over half of Australia. The Herald and Weekly Times, Ltd., is a large shareholder in Advertiser Newspapers, Ltd., of Adelaide, which publishes the *Advertiser,* though its interest is not sufficient for complete voting control. Advertiser

Newspapers, Ltd., is likewise a large shareholder without voting control in News, Ltd., which publishes the *News* of Adelaide and the *Barrier Miner* of Broken Hill; the Herald and Weekly Times, Ltd., has a very small direct shareholding in News, Ltd. The Herald and Weekly Times, Ltd., has also a very small interest in the preference capital of Queensland Newspapers, Ltd., publishers of the *Courier-Mail* of Brisbane. Sir Keith Murdoch has a large personal interest in Queensland Newspapers, Ltd.; he is a director in all these companies. No other combination approaches a chain in Australia, though the Norton interests of Sydney publish editions of the weekly, *Truth,* in Sydney, Melbourne, Brisbane, and Adelaide, and an evening paper, the *Daily Mirror,* in Sydney. The extra-journalistic ventures of newspapers include control, whole or partial, of various commercial broadcasting stations throughout the Commonwealth, and partnership in Australian Newsprint Mills (present capacity 26,000 long tons a year) of Tasmania, in which the Melbourne *Herald* is the largest shareholder.

Several important labour unions cover employees in the newspaper industry. The Australian Journalists Association was founded in 1911 to take advantage of the Commonwealth Conciliation and Arbitration Act; membership is obligatory by arrangement with the employers. The late Prime Minister John Curtin was a member. Toward the end of 1944 the Australian Journalists Association for the first time became involved, in Sydney, in a major industrial dispute when the Association directed its members not to produce copy for a composite newspaper issued by the proprietors after a printers' strike; the Association expressed no opinion on the merits of the original dispute. During the journalists' dispute, described by the proprietors as a strike and by the Association as a lockout, the Association and the Printing Industry Employees Union produced nine issues of a daily paper called the *News* which shared the honours of the streets of Sydney with the composite paper produced by the proprietors.

The Second World War brought severe cuts in newsprint, but circulation mounted. The leading newspapers found it desirable to send correspondents not only to the fighting fronts but to other world centres; they began to receive reports direct from the source instead of the observations of British and American correspondents filtered through London or New York. Contact with American troops on Australian soil led to wider interests, and features by American and English columnists began to appear regularly in Australian papers. An overseas weekly edition of the New York *Times* was published in Brisbane for American servicemen.

The increased circulation of the profit-making newspapers (with, as its complement, the failure of the Labour dailies) has not been accompanied by any increase in political influence; indeed, there has been, rather, a decrease from the days when such men as Syme were able to sway limited electorates. In spite of a predominantly non-Labour press a Labour Government was returned to power in 1943. The relations with members of this Government have not been wholly happy. In April, 1944, issues of certain newspapers in Sydney and Melbourne were seized by the Federal Government, which claimed breaches of the wartime censorship regulations. The newspapers concerned contended that a "security" censorship was being misused for political reasons, and they challenged the Government on this ground in the High Court. The dispute was settled by agreement, and a censorship code was drawn up, the first principle of which set forth that "Censorship shall be imposed exclusively for reasons of defence security." A further dispute between newspaper proprietors and the Government occurred in May, 1945, when the Postmaster General refused to grant the use of land lines for a news service with which the newspapers proposed to replace the Government news session previously broadcast by their associated radio stations.

In all but technique the comparison of Australian newspapers is with American rather than with English journals. Distances are too great for any one newspaper to exercise a nation-wide influence; circulation is confined to states and, in Queensland, mainly to the city of publication. Hostile critics are concerned rather with the extension of financial ramifications and the subservience of the commercial broadcasting system. The newspapers have recently shown themselves politically hostile to a majority of electors and hence to the government in power. It is perhaps reasonable to assume that a second period of conflict between the press and the executive, this time of the left instead of the right, resembling that in Britain, has begun.

CHAPTER XXIII

Religion

BY E. H. BURGMANN

RELIGION in Australia still reflects the sources in the British Isles from which it sprang. Anglicans are, for the most part, of English origin; Roman Catholics, of Irish; Presbyterians, of Scotch; Methodists, Baptists, Congregationalists, Salvation Army, and Friends (Quakers), of English and Welsh origin. The only denominations of numerical importance which have origins other than in the British Isles are the Lutherans, mainly from Germany; the Church of Christ and the Seventh-Day Adventists from the United States; and the Greek Orthodox from Greece, Russia, and the Middle East.

In a total population at the last census (1933) of 6,629,839, about 38 per cent were Anglican; 19 per cent, Roman Catholic; 11 per cent, Presbyterian; 10 per cent, Methodist. About 13 per cent did not state their religion. No other denomination reached 2 per cent of the population. It does not follow that these small denominations are unimportant. The Salvation Army, for instance, has made its presence felt by its social work, and the Congregationalists and the Society of Friends have had an appreciable influence; but the four major denominations naturally have dominated the religious scene in Australia.

Besides the denominations, there are various well-known associations like the Y.M.C.A., the Y.W.C.A., and the Australian Student Christian Movement (founded by Dr. J. R. Mott in 1896), which have a religious background and inspiration and carry on vigorous and important work. The A.S.C.M. is probably the most important Christian witness in the universities and holds an annual nation-wide conference of students which greatly strengthens interdenominational fellowship. It is affiliated with the World's Student Christian Federation and is thus an important link in the ecumenical movement. A similar zeal for fostering a Christian outlook in the universities is manifested by the graduate and undergraduate groups of the Roman Catholic Newman Society.

The major denominations have many fine churches, following almost entirely the architectural traditions of the British Isles. There are signs that a type of building more suited to the Australian climate and natural environment is in process of being evolved, but the older forms still prevail.

So far the Australian churches have shown little originality in thought or in forms of worship. They have felt bound to carry on the traditions they have inherited. Although the first two bishops and many of the early clergy of the Roman Catholic Church were English, that church and all others have leaned heavily on their places of origin for personnel and in many instances for financial support. This state of affairs is now coming to an end. Australian churches not only support themselves financially, but raise large funds for missionary work, especially in the Pacific. They also recruit and train their ministries locally. For this purpose large funds have been raised to provide training colleges. None of these has been established long enough for a tradition of real scholarship to emerge. Staffs have been overworked and libraries have been inadequate. The market for serious theological books is too small to make publication in Australia possible without loss.

Although churchmen of various denominations took a leading part in founding the several state universities, in none of them did theological studies find a place worthy of mention. This meant an absence of standards in, and a bias against the study of, religious thought. There is little doubt that this has impoverished Australian culture. Australia is a part of Western Christendom culturally. Cut the story of the church out of the history of European civilisation and what is left? Yet there is not a chair of divinity in any Australian university. There are signs, however, that more enlightened policies will prevail. A comparatively recent study of ecclesiastical subjects is now directed by a Board of Studies in the University of Sydney. Something has also been done in the universities of Melbourne and Queensland.

The sectarian warfare that raged in Great Britain had its counterpart in Australia, where the problem soon became the issue around which the major denominations fought for status and position within the state. The original attempt to follow prevailing English patterns at the beginning of the nineteenth century and thus to give the Church of England a privileged position with respect to education brought about a union of forces in which Scottish and Irish elements combined to pull down the privileged Anglicans from their seats. It was a contest worthy of the fighting qualities of the national elements engaged in it. The upshot was that the Anglicans were deposed from their place of privilege, which was certainly a good thing for them, but the price of the victory was the virtual secularisation of national education—a doubtful achievement.

It was natural, in an English convict colony ruled by naval and later by military officers, that English laws and customs should be taken for granted. The Church of England was established in England. The early rulers assumed that the same Church should be established in Australia. But conditions in Australia were vastly different from those in England.

In the first place, Australia contained a large number of Irishmen, many of them political prisoners, who had no love for English ways and little respect for the Church of their oppressors. These found an able leader in the Rev. John Joseph Therry (1790–1864), who arrived in Sydney as an official Roman Catholic chaplain in 1820. Father Therry well deserves the title of "Apostle of Roman Catholicism" in Australia. He was able and courageous and as irrepressible as any good Irishman. He fought against great odds with untiring devotion and won the respect of many outside his own flock. In his demand for the right to teach all Roman Catholic children and to have them excluded from contact with the Established Church he was inflexible. This was clearly a challenge to the right of the Church of England to control education in the colony. The Catholic Emancipation Bill (1829) had not yet been carried in England, and it took time for English-trained administrators to see the justice in the Roman Catholic plea.

Men like the Rev. Samuel Marsden (1764–1838), the "Apostle of New Zealand," and Archdeacon Thomas H. Scott (1773–1860) were convinced that the Established Church was a good thing in itself, and necessary in its English form for the organisation of the very untidy life of the young colony. In 1824 Scott, who had been in New South Wales in 1820 as Secretary to John Thomas Bigge, returned as Archdeacon with wide powers to organise the education of the colony under the aegis of the Church of England. He was promised much financial support through the short-lived Church and School Corporation. It looked as if the wealth of the colony would be poured into Anglican coffers and that administrative pressure was to be used to ground the youth of the colony in the tenets of the Church of England.

This fear brought the non-Episcopalians into alliance with the Roman Catholics, and the Presbyterians found a doughty champion in John Dunmore Lang (1799–1878). Lang arived in Sydney in 1823, and for more than fifty years was a highly significant person in the life of the colony. What Therry did for Roman Catholicism, Lang did for Presbyterianism. Lang had a better position than Therry from which to fight. He had behind him the prestige of the Established Church of Scotland and therefore a recognised status in public life. He was an able and stormy person who fought for the right with an enthusiasm that sometimes amounted to violence. Within his own denomination he caused much tension, even if he did make it count, and in public life he was a weighty influence on the side of an increasing liberalism.

Against the controversial skill of Dr. Lang and the tenacious resistance of Father Therry the attempt to maintain the Church of England in a privileged position had little chance. In England the Established Church was maintained, and a way was found to give full freedom to other denominations. But in Australia, where the balance of population was very different, such a compromise could not be reached. The rising tides of liberalism and secularism were also strongly with those who opposed any privileged denominationalism.

It was relatively easy to depose Anglicanism. It was not so easy to keep a satisfactory place for religion in education and in the national life. In 1836 all churches were given the right to found their own schools partly at public expense. This ended the tenuous reign of Anglicanism.

The nature of the controversy now began to change. Anglicans and Roman Catholics continued to fight for denominational schools. For the most part the non-Episcopal groups joined forces with the liberals and pleaded for national education under government control. Dr. Lang was a forceful exponent of this view. It is significant that in 1848, the year of the revolution in Europe, the first state schools were founded under a National Education Board. Subsidised denominational schools continued under a separate board.

But the tide was running strongly against the denominational schools. There was little or no provision for the training of teachers and there was much inefficiency. The defects in practice were regarded as evidence of wrongness in fundamental principle. The state schools were fortunate in discovering an able educational pioneer in William Wilkins (1826–1892), who wisely set about training teachers and improving their social and economic status. Under his guiding hand the state schools became far more efficient than the denominational schools. The latter had not evolved a satisfactory organisation and failed to move with the spirit of the times. Anglican and Roman Catholic bishops fought with conviction and delayed state action, but they did not succeed in beating the state schools on their own ground. The only argument that would have carried weight would have been greater efficiency in the church schools, and this was not forthcoming.

In 1866 Henry Parkes (1815–1896) put through Parliament his Public Schools Act, which abolished dual control and aimed at raising standards. A Council of Education was put in complete control of education in New South Wales. State schools became known as public schools. Certified denominational schools continued to receive state aid. Visiting clergymen were permitted to give special religious instruction in public schools for one hour a day. The liberal movement was not antireligious. It was trying, among other things, to solve the sectarian problem in education.

The 1880 Act, which still prevails, seems to have arisen from a fit of exasperation on the part of Parkes. The Roman Catholic Archbishop Vaughan (1834–1883) had made a violent attack on the public schools, and the Parkes' Act replied by withdrawing state aid from all denominational schools. The public accepted the Act, which represents the status attained eventually by the Australian states. Church schools remain, but they receive no financial aid from the state. The large denominations are represented by fine secondary schools, some of them the best in Australia. The Roman Catholics set to work to educate their children at their own expense. They have spent millions of pounds on this work, which constitutes one of the greatest achievements of any denomination in Australia. It is a chief source of strength to this Church. Anglicans and Presbyterians have also received magnificent bequests for educational work.

There is a general uneasiness about educational matters in Australia. It may well be a tribute to the work done in the past that it no longer satisfies the more alert and sensitive minds. The fear of rousing sectarian passions has kept politicians away from educational reform. But the end is not yet. The Church stands for an abiding element in human nature, and heaving the sectarian baby out with the bath water just because he is a noisy brat is no real solution.

The controversy over education was a chief factor in the alignment of the churches in their relations one with another. The Roman Catholics concentrated on the task of building up their schools and other institutions. It was a herculean undertaking and tended to turn them in on themselves and give them the appearance of being a race apart. Fears of popery also came in with the settlers from the Old World and died hard. But the Catholic Church had able leaders who pressed on with the work of organisation until the entire continent was divided in the traditional way into provinces and dioceses. It is the best-organised church in Australia and in bishops, priests, religious brothers, and nuns has by far the greatest number of official workers of any church in the land. It has a vigorous press, and is served by its own radio station. Roman Catholicism in Australia is a growing power.

The Presbyterians and Methodists are well organised and have maintained their position and influence in the national life. They are not now particularly identified with the radical movement in politics, and their onetime hostility to the episcopate is dying down. They are still definitely Protestant, but, as fear recedes, the cutting edge of their ancient sectarian sword is dulled. A crisis would sharpen it again, but security makes for peace.

The Anglicans have covered the continent with their parochial, diocesan, and provincial organisations. As with the other denominations, this has meant following the settler into the remotest parts of the country. The pioneer parson of every church is fit to stand beside the men who explored and opened up this rough land. As a matter of fact, the bush parson was often the only representative of culture and decency in exceedingly crude places. These men of God ministered to all sorts and conditions and kept the faith alive where men most needed it. In due time the ecclesiastical organisation took shape. The Anglican Church tried to keep dioceses and parishes on Old World models, even when a parish was half the size of England. The apostolic journeys of Bishop William Grant Broughton (1788–1853) tell vividly of the work entailed in planting an ancient church in a new land.

The Anglicans are probably the least-well organised of the major denominations. The tradition of Establishment left the impression that the Church was a wealthy institution and therefore was in no great need of support from its members. The Anglicans, therefore, have never been trained to support their church on the same scale as those who do not carry the incubus of the Establishment tradition. But much has been done, and the Anglican Church holds strongly to that middle position between Romanism and Protestantism which she feels it is her historic mission to maintain.

The Anglican is the most mixed in its members of all the churches. It holds within its fellowship persons of all shades of theological opinion, and manages to derive from the Book of Common Prayer a wide range of forms of worship. The Church is as full of contradictions as the English usually are. Somehow the strongly Catholic type and the violently Protestant type can live together in this ancient ecclesiastical household, and, what is still more strange in these days, every possible variety of political opinion can claim membership in this traditionally conservative institution. In Australia the Tory cannot depend on Anglican prayers for his political salvation. Some of the most radical political thinkers are to be found among the Anglican clergy.

In the fashioning of the political and social thought of the nation the churches have always played their part. Cardinal Moran (1830–1911) strongly sympathised with the rising Labour movement. He was also a stout advocate of federation. James S. T. Mc-Gowen (1855–1922), the first Labour Premier in New South Wales, was for more than thirty-two years a teacher and superintendent in an Anglican Sunday school. His rector, Archdeacon F. B. Boyce (1844–1931), took a leading part in forcing the attention of governments to such questions as old-age and invalid pensions, slum clearance, and liquor reform. The humanitarian legislation for which Australia has been noted in the past has had Christian inspiration as its principal sanction and support. This is true even if official church leaders often appeared lukewarm. The churches have maintained a steady and beneficial influence on the life of the nation and have been taken for granted as part of its heritage. There has been no other moral influence of equal importance.

But when all this is recognised it must be admitted that the influence of the churches has been weakened in the last half-century. In this respect Australia does not differ from the rest of Western Christendom. The rising tide of secularism has spread abroad the vague impression that somewhere in science there is an alternative to religion. The word "science" has attached to itself mythical associations and is used to settle all questions. The achievements of scientists are accepted as proof that science alone is a sufficient guide to life. The defenders of religion in the past were themselves confused and too often defended the wrong positions. When they were forced to retreat it was taken for granted that they had lost the whole contest, and their cause suffered accordingly. For a time traditional moral sanctions kept a sceptical society fairly steady, but eventually the attack was extended to the ethical field. Social cohesion began to dissolve, and there seemed to many to be no compelling reason why they should seek anything but their own interests. Gambling, which is essentially anarchic, greatly increased. So did age-old superstitions like astrology, and purveyors of lucky charms flourished on the folly of a witless crowd that waited hungrily on luck. Two world wars and a major depression within a generation have shaken confidence in the sufficiency of secular culture.

But it does not follow that people are returning or will return like lost sheep to the folds of the traditional churches. That will depend mainly on the churches themselves. At present most people are profoundly ignorant of the teachings of the churches. They have been out of touch for more than a generation. Their ideas—if they have any—are derived from vague memories of what interested the church folk of fifty years ago. Only the minority which has remained in the churches has any conception of the nature and meaning of the Christian faith. The rest are products of that new paganism which constitutes the greatest challenge to the church.

But even when the secular mind has feasted to the full on all that science can give, a hunger remains for something that will give life a more richly personal and a wider social significance. In Australia this void has been filled to some extent by the sentiment of "mateship." It grew in the bush and in lonely places, and for many it attained almost the quality of a religion. Its chief apostle was the short-story writer, Henry Lawson (1869–1922), who did more than any other writer to put the flavour of Australian democracy into the national life and literature. At its best, mateship could rise to something very fine and human, and it gave a tone to much in an Australian life that was singularly devoid of music. The sentiment also had practical results. That a man must stick to his "cobbers" was emphasised in early trade unionism and the beginnings of the Labour Party. It gave human warmth and something of the blood of life to these movements, but in the long run it was not able to sustain them in the rough places. The delinquent cobber, known as a "scab," found restoration to the brotherhood hard indeed, and the passions of party politics too often exposed the inadequacy of the gospel of mateship once mates got infected by the itch for power. The churches themselves felt, sometimes dimly, that these intense human emotions were related to the passions that had roots in religion. Many bush parsons were very good cobbers.

The fact that the Irish came to Australia with a grievance, with a background of Celtic tribalism, and with training in the art of rebellion made them fine material for a party which challenged the groups entrenched in economic privilege. The Irish provided much of the exuberant energy that found expression in the Labour movement. The leaders of the Labour Party were an Englishman (Holman, 1871–1934), a Welshman, (Hughes, 1864–), and a Scotsman (Fisher, 1862–1928), but the Party's most solid support came from the Irish Roman Catholics. This fact tended to make the other churches suspicious of the Labour movement. Economic considerations, however, prevailed, and the Party fought the battle of the underprivileged, irrespective of religious denomination. As the Irish have come to share in Australian prosperity, they have tended to become more sensitive to the rights of property.

As the Labour Party grows more and more socialistic in doctrine and aim, a tension arises in the minds of many Roman Catholics between their traditional politics and their traditional religion. Right-wing Labour will probably continue to appeal to them, while left-wing Labour will draw on the radicals of other denominations. The conflict over communism has great significance for religion in Australia because it forces a clear-cut division. The Roman Catholic Church is officially opposed to socialism and communism, and Communists are now the most vigorous element in left-wing Labour. Events are driving the Roman Catholics farther and farther to the right, and history may yet record that the strength of the Australian conservatives, now known as Liberals, will be found in the Roman Catholics of Irish origin.

An event even more strange historically will come to pass if Anglicans in large numbers support left-wing Labour. This is not so unlikely as it may appear. Many young Anglican priests are interested in socialism as an economy more expressive of Christian brotherhood than an economy that has been lavish in wars and depressions. The late Archbishop of Canterbury (William Temple, 1881–1944) was a powerful influence throughout the whole Anglican communion, and he described himself as an English socialist.

Several years ago the Roman Catholic Hierarchy in Australia presented to the Federal Government a statement on reconstruction called "Pattern for Peace." It is the most elaborate statement made by any church in response to an invitation from the Minister for Post-War Reconstruction to interested persons or bodies to contribute suggestions for shaping the postwar world. Its insistence on the "recognition of the dignity and personality of man" and of his right to freedom and justice would seem to imply that if a socialistic economy alone could carry out these principles the Hierarchy would encourage its realisation.

Australians in general are ready to listen to the churches as voices of the better conscience of the nation. They expect the churches to expose evils and injustices, and to give moral and spiritual direction. They realise that the churches must carry on their pastoral work, and would agree that the making of saints is their highest occupation. They expect them also to contribute to the enrichment of the national culture, and welcome the inspiration that can flow from church architecture, music, drama, and literature. But the average Australian feels that once a church becomes actively involved in party politics its morals quickly regress to the standards tolerated by the most secular-minded politicians. Even the suspicion of a religious organisation seeking political power stirs sectarian passions and bedevils political action. Australians look to churches to cleanse the currents of political life, and thus to be in politics but not of them. It will be impossible for churches to remain indifferent to political issues, but some will probably become more deeply involved than others. The future alone will work out the relation of socialism to the alignment of religious bodies.

There is little active hostility to religion in Australia. On the contrary, there is widespread respect, even where little understanding exists, and there is also the feeling that religion ought to be a very important influence and that it might actually become so at any time. The Australian has not made up his mind about religion, and has never felt himself seriously challenged by it. The continent is vast and it is easy to escape from the inherited traditions. There are wide seas between Australia and the lands where the ancestral religious traditions were fashioned.

The older traditions do not quite fit the new generations in a very different land. As Australians become Australian they sense a kind of foreignness in most of the influences that come from overseas, and religion is no exception. The "faith of our fathers" is no doubt a very good faith, but the time has come when the Australian is beginning to realise that he needs a version of the faith that he can feel to be his own. Australia is arriving at nationhood, and, however universal the Christian faith may be, it must take local colour in its expression and become native to every soil. The people in Australia who have remained most loyal to their traditional churches are in danger of getting outside the main currents of the rising tide of national life. These currents need the enrichment of a vigorous religion, but this must come from Christians who know not only their faith but also their native land.

CHAPTER XXIV

Education

BY K. S. CUNNINGHAM

EDUCATION is so much a part of the social fabric of a country that it cannot be understood without reference to the historical, geographical, economic, and political influences which have produced the total pattern of social life. So far as Australia is concerned, we must start with the fact that the culture is a transplanted and not an indigenous one—a position which it shares with the United States, Canada, South Africa, and New Zealand. Some day a master hand will trace and compare the development in these areas of transplanted European culture, giving particular attention to the influence of local conditions. In Australia the relevant local factors would include its geographical remoteness from similar cultures, the homogeneity of its settlers, the presence of a small and primitive native population unable to offer organised resistance to the occupation of its territories, the relatively unwatered nature of the mass of the continent, and perhaps above all the maintenance of close relations, subject only to evolutionary changes, with what Australians still call the Mother Country.

The only external influence of marked character, other than the British, has been the American. Indeed, Australia has drawn from either source with nearly equal readiness, much more readily than England and America have drawn from one another. There have been few important educational movements in the United States which have not had repercussions in Australia; and the Australian student of education is likely to know Dewey and Cubberley as well as he knows his Nunn and his Norwood.

In the last one hundred years the central feature of Australian education has been the emergence of free and compulsory education for all citizens. When the Australian colonies were settled, education was still regarded as a rightful privilege for those whose wealth or position placed them in the upper classes. Education was extended, in a limited or inferior form, to less-privileged members of society as a matter of religion and philanthropy. In the nineteenth century, however, the state realised with increasing clearness that the universal franchise would be either meaningless or dangerous unless universal literacy were achieved.

It was natural that the first attempts by the state to raise the level of education should have taken the form of grants to schools established and supervised by churches. Thus in Australia we find that the Church and Schools Corporation Act of 1826 granted £20,000 yearly to Anglican clergy for educational purposes. The settlement at Sydney then comprised about 50,000 people, of whom roughly half were free settlers and the other half convicts. Among other reasons, this first attempt met with much opposition because Australia did not adhere to the tradition of having an established church.

As in other English-speaking countries, however, later attempts to provide popular education through the endowment of church schools on a broader basis proved unsatisfactory. In Australia it was particularly so because denominations often set up rival schools even in areas where it was difficult to sustain one school of reasonable size. In more settled areas many children, in the absence of compulsory attendance, remained outside school altogether. A Select Committee appointed in 1844 by the New South Wales legislature found that under the denominational system half of the children between four and fourteen years were receiving no education.

The Committee advocated the adoption of the well-known Irish national system. Under this system public funds were made available to schools which were open to children of all denominations. Suitable extracts from the Scriptures were read, but no other form of religious instruction was given by the teachers. The clergy of various denominations visited the schools once a week to instruct their respective flocks. Education remained voluntary and small fees were charged. Not all the recommendations of the Select Committee were accepted, and the opposition of the churches necessitated a compromise. A National Education Board was set up in 1848, but the former Denominational Board was retained and grants to church schools were continued. Thus there were two boards, both supported from public funds. The compromise, with its resulting competition for pupils, proved unsatisfactory, and Henry Parkes (1815–1896), in a bill passed in 1866, succeeded in abolishing the dual system.

The new bill placed the control of education in New South Wales under a Council of Education of five members. The national schools were called "public" schools;[1] visiting clergy were given the right of entry for one hour a day; attendance was still voluntary. The New South Wales national system finally took shape in the Act of 1880, which abolished the Council of Education, set up a Department of Public Instruction under a Minister of the Crown, employed teachers as public servants, withdrew aid from all denominational schools, and made education compulsory from seven to fourteen years. Fees were still charged, but they were paid into revenue instead of being used to supplement teachers' salaries. In 1883 the first state secondary schools (high schools) were opened.

The problem of providing trained teachers was not an easy one. Until local systems of training were established under the state departments of education, several of the Australian colonies imported teachers from time to time from the British Isles. In New South Wales about thirty teachers were imported in the few years before 1860. Special mention must be made of the work of one of these teachers, William Wilkins, who arrived in 1851 and exercised a profound influence for thirty years thereafter. His training was obtained at Battersea College, England, under Dr. Kay (later Sir James Kay Shuttleworth) and Carlton Tufnell. Kay and Tufnell had studied at first hand the work of Pestalozzi, Froebel, and other reformers in Europe, and through Wilkins, who became Chief Inspector for New South Wales, the ideas and methods evolved at Battersea achieved more in the new colony than they did in England itself.

---

[1] At present New South Wales and one other state officially employ this term for schools supported and controlled by the state. Elsewhere in Australia the term is used, in the main, for church schools based on the model of the English "public" school. In this article they will be referred to hereafter as private schools.

We have traced the evolution of public education in New South Wales partly because it is typical and partly because its position as the senior colony tended to determine the course taken by the other settlements. Yet no colony (later state) has slavishly followed another. Victoria, after its separation from New South Wales in 1851, soon showed vigorous developments of its own. The Victorian Act of 1872 was the first educational legislation in the British Empire to make public education at once free, compulsory, and secular. Although the compulsory-attendance age was afterward lowered (it is still fourteen years in Victoria), this early Act required attendance from six to fifteen years.

The concept of an education equally available to all fell on fertile soil. The central core of the Australian nationalism which developed vigorously in the last fifty years of the century had two main roots. One was a determination to avoid class privilege, with the corollary that all men are entitled to a reasonable chance in life; the other was the growth of a generation which could appreciate Australia for its own sake without distortion by the nostalgia which prevented the early settlers from feeling truly at home. It is interesting to trace the educational ramifications of each of these lines of influence.

The general movement toward state socialism resulted, perhaps inevitably, in the evolution of highly organised state departments of education. The primary production on which Australia depended required extensive rather than intensive settlement. There was no tradition of local government. Australian democracy accepted the view that the best method of avoiding educational inequality of geographic and economic origin was for each state to provide from its revenue all costs of national education and to establish a system of inspection and supervision to ensure the efficient expenditure of the money. The states set up their own institutions for the training of teachers, controlled all school appointments and transfers, worked out schemes of promotion and inspection, and paid all salaries.

The development of national school systems under the auspices of the states and the removal of state aid to church schools by no means resulted in their demise. Indeed, these schools as a group have played, and continue to play, an important part in the educational life of the community, especially at the secondary level. There is a certain amount of state supervision, but it is little more than a safeguard against the establishment of schools by unqualified persons in unsuitable premises. Two states have a system under which all teachers must be registered, registration being based on completion of an acceptable course of training. In other areas, bursaries awarded by the state are tenable only at approved schools. In the main, provisions of this type have eliminated or prevented the establishment of undesirably weak schools, but have probably strengthened the remaining private schools without interfering essentially with their autonomy.

The independent church schools of Australia provide an obvious link with the British tradition—a link strengthened by the fact that up to recent years it was fairly common to import heads of schools from the British Isles.

The Australian scene reveals rather marked variations in the strength and status of the private school vis-à-vis the state secondary system. The accompanying table indicates this variation, as well

CHILDREN IN STATE SCHOOLS IN PROPORTION TO THOSE IN PRIVATE SCHOOLS

State	Age group 11–12 years		Age group 16–17 years	
	State	Private	State	Private
New South Wales............	395	100	188	100
Victoria.....................	324	100	56	100
Queensland..................	475	100	82	100
South Australia..............	627	100	123	100
Western Australia............	441	100	97	100
Tasmania....................	595	100	77	100
	Av. 405	...	Av. 104	100

as the general shift in proportion of pupils as between state and private schools with increased age of pupil. The shift is caused by two factors, the relative importance of which is unknown: (1) the transfer of pupils from state to private schools at twelve or thirteen years of age; (2) the fact that a majority of parents of higher income, who can more easily afford to meet the costs of continued education, send their children to private schools. An over-all factor is the variation in degrees of development in secondary-school facilities offered by the respective state authorities.

The table shows that for every child between eleven and twelve years of age attending private schools there are four times that number attending state schools. There are, however, about equal numbers of sixteen–seventeen-year-old pupils in the two types of school. Thus the proportion of children of the higher age group educated in private schools is about four times what it would be if there were no transfers and if both types of schools lost pupils at the same rate after the age for compulsory attendance is passed. The figures for private schools include attendance at Roman Catholic schools. This Church attempts to provide a complete system of schools at the primary level. If such pupils were omitted, the discrepancy shown in the table would be increased.

State variations are most marked in New South Wales and Victoria. In the former the state is educating almost twice as many sixteen–seventeen-year-olds as are the private schools. In Victoria at this age level the state is educating only slightly more than half the number of pupils attending private schools. Account may also be taken of the shift in proportion from the primary age group to the seconday group. This emphasises the relative "holding power" of the state secondary system in New South Wales, and tends to bracket Tasmania and Victoria as the two states in which private secondary schools are strongest.

The Roman Catholic Church has adopted the policy of providing, so far as possible, a complete system of its own schools running somewhat parallel to the state system. Altogether there are about 200,000 children attending such schools, or about 14 per cent of the total number of children in the same age groups, whereas some 19 per cent of the total population belongs to the Roman Catholic faith. The Church has consistently sought state aid for its schools on the ground that if it were not meeting the cost of teaching these children the state would have to pay the bill. There is unwillingness to agree that any form of religious instruction other than that given in their own schools can meet essential requirements. Each large centre has at least one Roman Catholic secondary school which in public thought, and for combined public-school sports, forms part of the private secondary system. It is reasonable to speak of three systems: a state system, a Roman Catholic system, and a third less coherent one comprising the remaining non-state schools.

Many people, including some associated with the private schools, are concerned about reproducing in Australia, in however modified a form, the dichotomy which is found in English education between schools for the classes and those for the masses. This questioning attitude is not necessarily incompatible with an appreciation of the accomplishments of private schools or, indeed, with a preference for what they embody, namely, a large measure of independence and explicit recognition of religion in the work of the school. In Australia the issue has not received anything like the public attention it has aroused in England. This may well be because of the greater accessibility of the private school in Australia. At the university the two streams reunite without observable discrimination. There are but slight evidences in Australia of the granting of vocational preferences by certain employers to those who have attended the "right" school.

It has been suggested that in the states where private schools are strong, a large proportion of the influential members of the community lack the direct interest in the national schools which they would have if their own children attended them, and that this makes it difficult to secure public pressure to raise the standards of state educational expenditure. The situation in Tasmania does not seem to confirm this view, but in that state it has been a Labour Government, with education as one of its main concerns, that has raised expenditure per head on state education over the last ten years from the lowest of all the states to the highest in the Commonwealth.

On the other hand, the independent schools have autonomy and are in a position of advantage if they wish to indulge in experimentation. However, they have, in the main, been educationally more conservative than schools under the state systems. The primary aim of instruction has frequently been that of securing a high percentage of passes at the state-wide examinations leading to university entrance. (A regrettable feature in most of the states is the publication in the daily press of the results of the annual examinations in such a way that the public can judge the relative success of each school in the competition.) In recent years there have been a few striking examples, and a greater number of more moderate ones, in which independent schools have used their freedom for showing educational leadership either through the school methods adopted, or through the public activities of their headmasters, or through both. Some private schools now offer far more than do the state schools in music, art, crafts, and nonexamination courses.

The Australian answer to the problem of the types of schools and courses which should be provided for children from about twelve years and older has been to provide separate institutions and to make at least the academic secondary school fairly selective in character. There are multilateral high schools in some of the country centres of Victoria. One institution offers practical and trade courses as well as foreign languages. But the private schools and the ordinary high schools are typically academic in character.

The states maintain a system of junior and senior technical schools and colleges. The senior technical colleges cover a wide range of courses which at their highest level run somewhat parallel to the courses in the faculties of engineering and chemistry at the universities. Some reciprocal arrangements exist, but there are problems to be solved in the demarcation of function between the two institutions.

Technical education made big strides during the war. Australia's munitions production was made possible through the use and expansion by the Commonwealth Government of existing institutions. All told, some 119,000 men received special training for work in munitions factories or for specialist branches of the armed forces. It is interesting to note that an aircraft industry was established by a country which, although it has made its own motor-car bodies, has so far imported all its automobile engines. The establishment of an optical-glass industry in the short space of two years was another striking development.

The table on the opposite page shows for the whole of Australia, and for all types of schools, the proportion of the respective age groups receiving full-time instruction. Australia has far to go before it attains anything approaching secondary education for all. The drop in the thirteen–fourteen-year group suggests that the exemptions from compulsory attendance which are granted in some states under special circumstances after the thirteenth birthday are more freely employed than would be expected. There is nothing very attractive about the last two years of schooling for those who intend to leave school as soon as possible. No recognised secondary course of schooling ends at fourteen. The whole content of education at this level seems to need drastic revision, especially in view of the intended raising of the leaving age. Australian wage laws, which require a basic wage to be paid by the age of twenty-one, tend to make employers anxious to maintain their full quota of junior workers and thus to encourage early recruitment of young people, pulling them from school.

In proportion to its population Australia has a bigger problem of educating children living in sparsely populated areas than has any other country in the world. At least two-thirds of its schools

PERCENTAGE OF RESPECTIVE AGE GROUPS ATTENDING SCHOOL

11–12 years	12–13 years	13–14 years	14–15 years	15–16 years	16–17 years
99.9	99.1	88.1	56.6	26.7	6.7

employ only one teacher, though they serve only 14 per cent of the total school population. There are schools in Queensland which cannot be reached by mail from the head office in Brisbane in less than a fortnight. Yet centralised control has made it possible to do a much better job of rural education than would otherwise have been possible. The six state authorities have been given the responsibility of building all schools and training and appointing all teachers. Particular attention is paid in teachers colleges to training in the best methods of running one-teacher schools. At times model schools are established in the city near the college so that students can observe and obtain practice in the simultaneous teaching of several classes, each containing five or six pupils.

This development of technique and the system of correspondence instruction for still more scattered pupils represent Australia's two main contributions to educational method. Starting about 1916, Victoria and New South Wales independently showed that, given literate parents who were prepared to coöperate, it was possible, by carefully prepared instruction and guidance, to teach children who had never seen a school or a teacher, and to maintain a rate of progress not far short of normal. Today about 20,000 children who would otherwise be without instruction are taught in this way throughout the Commonwealth. In each of the capital cities one can visit a school containing from forty to eighty teachers but no visible pupils. Through letters, exchange of photographs, and other ways the contacts between teacher and pupil are made as personal as possible. Indeed, the correspondence teacher knows more about her pupils as individuals than does the average city teacher who meets her class face to face five days a week. Many other countries, from Soviet Russia to Rhodesia, have studied and imitated the correspondence system.

In spite of its relatively good status, the one-teacher school is less favoured today than it was ten or fifteen years ago. It is realised that it cannot offer all the facilities of a modern education. There is consequently an increasing amount of consolidation in larger units. This will develop still more in future, though in many parts of the Commonwealth roads and distances will make consolidation virtually impossible.

The other point of criticism is that the rural school has not provided an education sufficiently adapted to the needs and interests of the country child. It may well be that the common programmes of study followed—though not rigidly prescribed in detail—in each state are not suitable for the city child, but they are certainly not drawn up with the specific and widely diversified needs and interests of the country areas in mind.

Both with respect to the consolidation movement and to changes in the curriculum, the most striking developments are those associated with "area" schools. There are some on the mainland, particularly in South Australia, but Tasmania has been the pioneer. The essential features of these schools are the provision of an area of from ten to fifty acres which is developed as a school estate; the removal and reërection of the closed one-teacher schools on the central site to provide extra buildings for crafts and activities; the spending by the pupils of about half of their time in such activities as building barns, laying concrete, growing crops and vegetables, keeping sheep, pigs, poultry, bees; the linking of most of the classroom work with work on the estate; and the provision (by Australian standards) of a good library. Each headmaster is free to develop special activities relevant to the life and interests of the district.

The first area school in Tasmania was opened in 1936. There are now fifteen. Their establishment has resulted in closing a number of one-teacher schools in the state. The usual opposition to the closing of small schools was encountered in the first year or two, but since then educational authorities in Tasmania have not been able to keep up with the requests from districts desirous of having area schools. A documentary film on these schools has been in great demand throughout the mainland states, and parents have formed associations to obtain similar schools for their children.

For many years in each state a body known as the Free Kindergarten Union has provided informal educational facilities for a number of children below school age. Funds are obtained from state grants and from money-raising projects. Such kindergartens have been located chiefly in industrial areas so that children of working mothers would not be neglected. The war greatly accentuated this phase of the problem and the Commonwealth Government took steps to provide facilities for children of women in war factories. No state yet provides for more than a fraction of the children between two and six years old.

There has been much opposition to the idea that young children should for any part of the twenty-four hours be removed from the influence of home and mother, but the view now seems to prevail that even on strictly educational grounds the nursery school is a good thing, even for—and sometimes especially for—children from privileged homes. The changed attitude has been brought about partly by the much higher standards of training for teachers of preschool children (elevating their work far beyond the baby-minding work of the old crèche), and particularly by the establishment by the Commonwealth Government in each capital city of a model centre known as a Lady Gowrie Pre-School Child Centre. The centres were set up just before the war and have done excellent work in demonstrating the educational possibilities, both for children and for their parents, of well-planned and well-conducted facilities.

At the other end of the ladder, Australia has a university in each capital city and university colleges at Canberra and at Armidale, New South Wales. The Canberra College is a locally controlled institution affiliated with Melbourne University. For a long time to come Canberra is unlikely to provide a full range of university courses, except, perhaps, in the liberal arts faculties. The Commonwealth Government has recently announced proposals for developing a postgraduate university at Canberra. It will presumably offer facilities in such fields as international affairs and public administration. Armidale College is an offshoot of Sydney University and students in arts courses can enroll for three years of work leading to a degree.

Each of the six universities functions under a state charter and receives a substantial part of its financial resources from an annual vote. This may fluctuate from year to year, but roughly a third of the income is derived from this source and the balance, in about equal amounts, from fees and endowments. The cost to a student in tuition fees for a full year's work is about £35. Western Australia, however, charges no fees. The question of fees apart, the Australian university resembles the American state university, although Australia has not followed American precedent in setting up as a separate institution a college which grants a first degree only. Another point of contrast is the provision in Australia for the completion of degree courses by students who are allowed to take more than one calendar year to complete a full year of academic work. Most of them hold jobs. Some are able to attend duplicate evening lectures. The student body may include a rather large proportion of part-time students. Admission to the universities is controlled by an examination conducted by the university itself for candidates in all parts of the state. The average quality of the Australian undergraduate is probably as good as it is in universities anywhere.

The universities are autonomous bodies under the control of a statutory council or senate. The nature of the representation varies from state to state, but typically includes representatives of the teaching staff, graduates (in some instances undergraduates also), the government, and important public bodies. Some concern has been felt over recent legislation in one state which altered the constitution of the controlling body and gave the government power to nominate a majority of members. There have been no instances in Australia of actual restraint of freedom of teaching at the universities, though there was a recent case in which the state legislature passed a motion of censure for views on religion expressed by a professor at a public meeting. The university authorities refused, however, to take any disciplinary action.

The universities have made an essential contribution to the intellectual, professional, and scientific development of Australian communities. Standards of admission and of attainment have been high and graduates who have gone abroad have usually achieved excellent records at overseas universities. In the main, Australia has followed the rather conservative traditions of British universities, with emphasis on established disciplines and studies. The link with British traditions is not surprising in view of the fact that most professional appointments in the past have gone to English scholars. As Australian scholarship has developed, a larger proportion—amounting in the last ten years to possibly 50 per cent—have gone to native-born Australians. In almost all instances the appointees have won their academic spurs in graduate study overseas.

It is generally conceded that the universities are not so well developed as they might be in social sciences. Among the universities there is one professorship each in anthropology, in public administration, in political science and philosophy, in political science and history, and in geography; three each in psychology and in education; and none in sociology. Economics and history are the only social studies for which full chairs are found at all universities. This relative weakness is unfortunate for a country which faces peculiar socioeconomic problems in rural settlement, regional development, transportation and communication, racial assimilation, and migration. In the last fifty years, hundreds if not thousands of capable young Australians have studied the language and culture of ancient Greece or Rome, but next to none have been trained to study and record the life of the Australian aboriginal whose ancient culture was passing away forever. Nothing could more dramatically illustrate the preoccupation with the past, the neglect of local material, and the lack of interest in sociological studies.

Australian universities seem to lack that close relationship with the communities they serve which is typical of most American universities. Yet they are not old enough to have the background of traditional culture which might be held to warrant a measure of detachment, not to say aloofness. A common criticism, but perhaps an overharsh one, is that the typical Australian student regards the university as a place where one obtains as quickly as possible the professional qualifications which enable him to earn a higher salary. Be that as it may, Australian universities do not enjoy the tremendous financial and moral support which most American universities receive from their communities, and particularly from their alumni. Australian facilities, equipment, and staffing permit of little in the way of extension services. This may well have something to do with the relative indifference of the community; but university leaders fear that any attempt at such expansion would interfere with the central functions of their institutions.

Of particular interest was the action of the Commonwealth Government in setting up a wartime Universities Commission, and the payment through it of substantial allowances to ensure the training of capable students in the "reserved" faculties of medicine, dentistry, engineering, physical science (including chemistry), agricultural science, and veterinary science. Full allowances amount to £104 a year and taper off until they disappear when parental income, after recognised deductions, amounts to £500. The activities of the Universities Commission are continuing in the postwar period. The hope has frequently been expressed that financial aid to students will be retained and extended to all faculties. A point of special interest is whether such assistance will be made available at a lower age level so that able students will be encouraged to continue their studies long enough to reach the stage for entrance to the university.

Many are hopeful that the experience and equipment of the educational services of the armed forces during the Second World War will be turned to account in developing postwar adult education. No one denies the need of such expansion and of a new outlook. The Workers Educational Associations (again a title and plan adopted from England), linked with extension departments of the universities, have done good work. But they have gone but a short distance and have not captured the public imagination.

There is now great interest in the community-centre idea, which seems to offer an opportunity not only of raising cultural standards but of elevating the status of local government. Many municipal authorities have drawn up plans or have taken the first steps toward the development of community-centre projects. So great is the interest that the eyes of the entire continent have concentrated on the small township of Nuriootpa in South Australia where community ownership and activity have developed in interesting fashion. The Commonwealth Government authorities have arranged for a report on adult education (as yet unpublished) and have established in the Department of Post-War Reconstruction a section to advise on the development of community centres.

Another step which could result in putting new life into education at all levels, especially adult education, is the recent establishment of a National Film Board with an income of £50,000 a year. The era of visual education has only begun, but Australia has scarcely kept up with developments. The new Board will act as a central agency for producing and collecting instructional and documentary films and distributing them to state educational centres and authorities.

The Royal Society provides an old standing link with English science—the Hobart branch being the first to be set up outside England itself. Its activities are confined principally to the publication of scientific papers.

The Australian Association for the Advancement of Science, again on the British pattern, before the war held biennial conferences in the chief centres in rotation. These have provided the main gatherings of workers in both the physical and the social sciences. An offshoot of the A.A.A.S.—being comprised of its Fellows—is the Australian National Research Council, which functions as a permanent body in the interest of science as a whole. It has administered grants from American foundations, especially in anthropology. It publishes every two months the *Australian Journal of Science*. Reorganisation of the A.N.R.C. is now being discussed with a view toward establishing strong committees or sections for physical, biological, and social sciences.

In 1938 the Australian Association of Scientific Workers was established. Membership is open to all workers in the field of science. Through conferences and in other ways it concerns itself with the place of science in community life and the status and remuneration of scientists.

The Council for Scientific and Industrial Research was established by the Commonwealth in its present form in 1926. It has conducted major research in physical and biological sciences, often in conjunction with the universities. Mention must also be made of the researches sponsored by the National Health and Medical Research Council, operating under the auspices of the Commonwealth Department of Health.

What may be an important development is the recent establishment of an Australia-wide Committee for Research in the Social Sciences. This Committee is representative of all the social disciplines. It functions under the auspices of the Australian National Research Council.

An Economics Society and an Association of Psychology and Philosophy have existed for a number of years; both publish journals. An Australian branch of the British Psychological Society was established in 1944.

There is no widely supported national educational association which unites the teaching profession as a whole. Each state has a well-organised union or federation of teachers employed by the state. There is also a loose association between these unions in the Australian Teachers Federation. So far as private schools are concerned, the only association overriding state boundaries is the Headmasters Conference. The New Education Fellowship, affiliated with the international organisation of that name with headquarters in London, has branches in each state which have recently linked themselves into an Australia-wide body. There have been several recent local conferences following a major one held in all states in 1937.

The Australian Council for Educational Research was established in 1930 as the result of an endowment from the Carnegie Corporation of New York. It has conducted various surveys, published about seventy reports, and acts as a recognised channel of information on educational developments between Australia and the outside world. It is also the major agency in Australia for the construction and distribution of mental and scholastic tests.

Australia is now struggling to stand on her own feet in cultural and scientific affairs. But so far as the content of education is concerned, careful revaluation is needed at all levels from primary school to university. The educational institutions have a triple obligation: (1) to transmit necessary elements of universal culture; (2) to incorporate, sustain, and develop the essential framework of British culture and British democratic evolution; (3) to cultivate an understanding of Australia and an emotional attachment to an acceptable Australian ideal. In the writer's opinion, there has not been a sufficiently bold recognition of the fact that, to be sound, education must have strong and deep local roots. A transplanted tree may give a quicker result, but it will remain sickly unless it adapts itself to local conditions and draws its nourishment therefrom.

The situation may change more quickly now that Australia has been forced by the startling events of the war to realise the sociological and geographical implications of wide separation from the parent culture. She will almost certainly rectify the failure to study the problems, the languages, and the customs of the races of the Pacific area. In the last twenty years there has been a great increase in serious studies of Australian historical, economic, and political development; of problems of migration, population, and land settlement; of cultural life; of the unique flora and fauna. Australia has become self-conscious, but the new knowledge has not yet been effective in vitalising the content of studies. Nothing less is needed than a team of competent workers constantly translating such material into a form which can be used by teachers and scholars. At the same time, nothing essential must be lost from the golden heritage of the past.

The second great problem is the administration and control of education. In the first twenty years of the twentieth century the state systems of education, under the influence of men like Frank Tate (1863–1939) and Peter Board (1858–1944), directors of education in Victoria and New South Wales, respectively, were in the formative period and made advances in many new directions. By comparison with national systems in other countries, they had much to contribute and little to be ashamed of. But the "best in the world" was a phrase which unfortunately gained currency.

Any such complacency is now rudely shattered. The need for educational development, if not for educational reform, is admitted on every hand. Australia's expenditure on education per head of population rose from £1.0s.11d. in 1901 to £1.17s.8d. in 1938. But this has not been nearly enough to enable Australia to keep pace with other countries. At present it is handicapped by many old buildings which should have been replaced twenty or thirty years ago. The ratio of teachers to pupils is such that classes of fifty and larger are not uncommon. The remuneration of teachers is poor compared with that of other professions. The standards of equipment and of facilities such as school libraries are much lower than is required for modern education. Even the universities are handicapped by shortages of personnel and inadequate equipment.

It is important to consider whether these features are due chiefly to lack of interest on the part of the public or whether they result from the structure of the educational system. They are highly centralised so far as each state is concerned. They differ from those of every other democratic country in the absence of effective local participation. There is no specific taxation for education. There is no particular political party which has identified itself with major advances in education. In theory the system of control by the government of the day should be responsive to public demand for improvement and for increased expenditure, but in practice it may be doubted whether the state governments have rightly interpreted the willingness of the community to pay for better educational facilities.

In recent years the situation has been affected by changing relations between the states and the Commonwealth, especially in respect to taxation. The Victorian Government, which has had for a number of years a standard of educational expenditure well below the Australian average, refuses to go "cap in hand" to the Commonwealth because it objects to what it regards as an infringement of its sovereign rights. The future of national education in Australia is obviously bound up with the decisions made on such questions. The recent establishment by the Commonwealth Government of an Office of Education has aroused great interest. One of its chief functions will be that of coördinating relationships between the Commonwealth and the states in educational affairs.

Another basic problem in Australia is the effect produced on the professional aspects of education by the closely knit system within each state—a system which makes all teachers public servants, which controls all developments from the capital city, and which places educational progress very much in the hands of the government of the day. Is it true, as stated by Leicester Webb in his *Control of Education in New Zealand* (New Zealand Council for Educational Research, 1937), that such a system tends to produce a situation which can be likened to "an army immobilised by its own defence works"? It seems certain that the promise of freshness and enterprise of the early years of the century has not been sustained.

It seems, too, that there has been an increased tendency to deal with professional problems at the political level. Even changes in school curricula and general organisation can be regarded as matters of policy not to be decided without Cabinet approval. The professional officers of the departments of public instruction, even if they feel that there are serious weaknesses, cannot easily give publicity to their opinions. They are often placed in a position of explicitly or implicitly defending the government. This is sometimes rendered easier by the fact that criticisms may be extreme or the critics uninformed. Again, the state educational services now tend to be closed systems with all appointments given to those who grew up in the service. In earlier days it was not uncommon to fill a higher post by making appointment from another state and occasionally even from another country.

Various suggestions have been made for the establishment of some policy-forming agency which would have greater permanency than a single government and greater freedom than a body of public servants. A board of enquiry into general educational problems, appointed by the South Australian Government, has recently recommended the establishment of an educational-policy board whose function it would be to draw up long-term plans and to advise the Minister for Education of the day.

It is obvious that Australia has educational problems broadly similar to those of other countries, but that these assume special aspects in the light of the historical, geographical, economic, and political background. The chief hope for the future lies in the general heart-searching which the war years brought, in the widespread dissatisfaction with things as they are, in a strengthening of the belief that no child should suffer through lack of educational opportunity, in the impulses toward a genuine national unity brought about by the imminent danger of invasion and the experiences of common service, in the demonstrations by service defence authorities of what can be done in education if resources are provided in proportion to the necessity and the demand, and, finally, the prospect of much greater contact with developments overseas. A serious test of Australian democracy is what it will accomplish in the field of education in the next twenty years

Part Six:

AUSTRALIA AND THE SOUTHWEST PACIFIC

CHAPTER XXV

Native Peoples

BY A. P. ELKIN

A USTRALIA'S RESPONSIBILITY for native peoples dates from the first British settlement at Port Jackson in 1788. At that time began the dispossession and depopulation of the aborigines—a process that still continues as settlement is pushed into the uttermost and least hospitable parts of the continent. An aboriginal population of about 350,000 in 1788 has dwindled to a little more than 50,000 full-bloods. There are also nearly 30,000 persons of mixed European and native descent.

Australia is not proud of this sad story; but where lies the guilt and what were the causes? The explanation is complex, for an intricate set of human relationships is involved, including government officials, missionaries, settlers (pastoralists, miners, pearlers, and others), and the aborigines.

Until full self-government was established in the Australian colonies, beginning with New South Wales and Victoria in the 1850's, the British Government, through the Colonial Office in England and the Governor or Lieutenant-Governor in the Australian colony, was responsible for the policy regarding the aborigines and the contact of the settlers with them. The policy was always benign and just, and at times contemplated civilising the natives as well as using them. When Arthur Phillip was appointed the first Governor of New South Wales he was instructed "to endeavour by every possible means to open an intercourse with the natives, and to conciliate their affections, enjoining all our subjects to live in amity and kindness with them." He was to punish British subjects who wantonly destroyed them or unnecessarily interfered with "the exercise of their several occupations." And, finally, he was to advise how intercourse with natives might be turned to the advantage of the colony. A later Governor of the same state, General Ralph Darling (1825–1831), was enjoined not only to see that the natives were "protected in the full enjoyment of their possessions, [and] preserved from violence and injustice," but also to take measures for "their conversion to the Christian faith and their advancement in civilisation."

The Home Office, located twelve thousand miles away, could not envisage the problem. The representatives of the British Government, willing as they were to carry out the official policy, were doomed to failure because of the self-contradictory nature of that policy. To protect nomadic, food-gathering tribes "in the full enjoyment of their possessions" was impossible, once they had been dispossessed of their land. The very act of dispossession involved serious, if not total, interference with their livelihood. Ignoring the rights of the natives as landholders, the government appropriated their land, which it regarded as Crown property. Nor was any land returned to them on new terms. White settlers took possession of all that was worth while in each district.

The aborigine quickly realised what had occurred. To hunt and gather native foods over his tribal country became trespass; to hunt the white invader's animals or gather some of his crops was stealing and, indeed, was regarded almost as the predatory raid of an enemy. The alternative was to become a landless employee, a type of life which had no meaning for the aborigine. His land had been more than a place of living and a source of food; it was the symbol of his spiritual life.

The aborigine might have fitted into the white man's scheme if he had been assured of an adequate food supply, if his totemic shrines had been respected, and if his ceremonial gatherings had still been possible. But once agriculture and the pastoral industry were established, the settlers needed all the available good land and water, irrespective of its sacred or sentimental associations; and they needed native labour for seasonal or emergency work, without regard to ceremonial occasions and duties. Thus the sequence of ritual observances, with the social and economic values which had given significance and emotional tone to native life, was replaced by dependence on the white "invader" and by subservience to his timetable. The impasse resulted in either clash or parasitism, in sudden or lingering death.

Governors and lieutenant-governors in their short and busy terms of office could not get to the roots of the problem—a problem which, as white settlement spread, was soon removed from other than transient observation on their part. The frontiers were advancing ever farther from the seats of administration. The settlers realised, as the home government failed to do, that they were occupying the country of unknown numbers of nomadic natives whom they did not understand, but whose labour they would like to use as cheaply as possible; that they were far from government protection in case of conflict, and, consequently, were out of reach of the administration of justice if they took the law into their own hands. Seldom did they have qualms about doing so, for the aborigine was uncivilised and had not developed the country. He should therefore either assist as labour, thus becoming more civilised, or should make way for the superior newcomer.

This attitude of superiority was frequently combined with fear, arising from lack of understanding of the natives and isolation on the frontier. It often led to an exhibition or use of force when there was no real danger. Thus originated the dogma that the natives "had to be taught a lesson" whenever events (e.g., cattle-spearing, or conflict over a white man's relations with a native woman) seemed to demand it. Such a "lesson" meant the death—usually by shooting— of half-a-dozen to a score or more of aborigines, both male and female. Each state, including the Northern Territory, has been the scene of "punitive expeditions," as they are sometimes called. The first occurred very early in the history of settlement, the latest in the 1930's.

In 1814 the Governor, after reviewing past occurrences, admonished settlers from "taking the Law into their own hands for the future, and to beware of wanton Acts of Oppression and Cruelty against the Natives."[1] In spite of this and similar pronouncements, however, the idea has prevailed in all the marginal regions that the settlers should deal with the natives in their own way, and that the local police, if any, should coöperate with them in making the natives afraid of, and subservient to, the white man.

---

[1] Sydney *Gazette,* June 18, 1814.

In this atmosphere of force and fear, clashes and killing were inevitable. There were no battles; the aborigines in their own feuds did not indulge in campaigns or seek many deaths. One usually sufficed. And unlike the Maoris of New Zealand they did not think of fighting for their country. To spear cattle or sheep for a feast or to take farm produce, and to kill the shepherd, boundary-rider, drover, or hut-keeper whom they thought to be an obstacle to this design; to kill the white man who had interfered with their women or failed to keep his word; and sometimes to cast their spears at their pursuers, or defend themselves when at bay—such motives led to the spearing or clubbing of individuals, not to attack in battle array.

Between 1842 and 1844, however, there seemed to be an uprising of aborigines from Port Phillip on the south to Wide Bay in south-eastern Queensland. Incidents occurred along the frontier of settlement with such frequency that observers thought they must be planned. Flocks were driven away, sheep speared, shepherds and hut-keepers wounded or killed (four in one district), and pioneers driven back to more closely settled areas. Various reasons were given for these "simultaneous uprisings," the only satisfactory one being that they expressed "the explosion of long-pent feelings of revenge and hatred toward the whites, resulting from a long course of violence and injustice on the part of the latter toward them."

A predisposing cause was the famous Myall Creek Massacre in New South Wales in 1839. Some stockmen and shepherds, enraged at the depredations of the natives among their flocks and herds, sallied out in force, killed a score or two of natives—men, women, and children—and burned the bodies. Acquitted once, the seven men were retried, found guilty, and executed. The sentence was widely disapproved. Similar accounts are available for other localities. In Victoria[2] from 1838 to 1841 forty-three aborigines were murdered in one district and nearly the whole of two tribes in another. In 1841–1842 eleven were killed in two districts and "many" in another.

The literature of the time (1850–1880) in Eastern Australia suggests that the extermination of the natives—as of other "pests"—

---

[2] R. J. Flanagan, *The Aborigines of Australia* (1888), pp. 130–137; reprinted from the Sydney *Empire,* 1853–1854.

would not have been regretted by many of the settlers, especially
after a sufficient number of labourers had been brought in from
Great Britain. Extermination was thought of as a positive process,
not as a negative dying out. The complete story has yet to be written, but the attitude is clear. It was well expressed by the Rev.
J. H. L. Zillman, who, while admitting that many natives had been
killed, maintained that the extermination of from fifty to a hundred natives for the murder of one white family was neither unde-
served or unnecessary.[3] It is doubtful whether the killing of natives
accounted directly for more than a small proportion of their decrease. But indirectly the loss of men from economic and ceremonial
activities, and of potential fathers and mothers, caused a severe
disturbance of tribal cohesion and continuity.

Other causes contributing to the decline in native population
were: the upsetting of dietary balance by interference with food-
gathering and hunting habits over tribal lands, and the substitution of flour, tea, and sugar, which had a bad effect on fertility and
on resistance to disease; the introduction of diseases against which
no immunity had been built up; and the loss of interest in life
which resulted from the breakdown of social and ceremonial organisations, for the aborigines can die by "faith."

Missions, too, unwittingly contributed to the decline by disturbing too suddenly some of the social and moral customs of the
aborigines, principally by undermining their fundamental beliefs
and sacred rites, especially among the youth, who thus ceased to
share a common spiritual experience with their elders. The natives
were unable to understand the Christian Gospel when it was not
related to their own way of life; consequently they were left without spiritual directive and sanction. This missionary approach,
however, has been abandoned for the most part, and missionaries
now receive training in anthropology and the problems of culture-
contact. But whatever be the criticism of their past methods, credit
must be given them for playing (often very courageously) the rôle
of protector and adviser to the natives in the clash of white and
black. Their very presence and attitude often acted as a check,
though they themselves were much criticised.

Apart from some overlapping, four phases stand out in the

[3] *Past and Present in Australian Life* (1889), p. 125.

history of contact in Australia. In the first phase, official policy was positive in aim, seeking to advance, civilise, and Christianise the natives, as well as to treat them with that justice which is the right of all British subjects. The settlers, dispossessing the natives of their land, took away the basis of aboriginal progress. But unaware of this, local officials and missionaries tried through schools, farms, exhortation, friendship, and employment to civilise them. Gradually, however, it was realised that the attempt was not successful. Moreover, the advancing and lengthening frontiers, following the increase of immigration from the 1820's, focussed official and public attention far more on the clash between settler and aboriginal than on the apparently hopeless task of civilising the natives. The transition period may be placed at about 1850–1855.

The second phase was one of pacification. Governments sought to prevent conflict in the marginal regions, mainly by convincing the aborigines, usually by force, that they must not interfere with white settlement. They were either to assist with their labour when this was wanted or to retire further inland. Otherwise there were clashes, punitive expeditions, trials by local or visiting magistrates, gaol, and depopulation. Official policy could do no more than declare that the natives be not harshly treated. That employers punished natives and that natives were "taught lessons" were well-known facts; but as governments did not have a policy or trained officers to deal with the sociological and economic situations of the frontier they were prepared to ignore these illegal occurrences unless there was a public outcry of political significance. During this phase the settler was allowed to be responsible for race-relations.

This gradually passed into a negative, protecting, and relieving phase. The new science of anthropology, from the 1870's on, was slowly recording evidence that the aborigines had a complex social organisation and ritual system and therefore were not so low as some had asserted. Public opinion was aroused from time to time by reports of atrocities in the marginal regions. And in closely settled regions there were remnants of full-blood groups and increasing numbers of mixed-bloods, living often as derelicts and wanderers on the outskirts of towns and settlements. To meet the situation aboriginal protection boards were set up in all states, by the end of the nineteenth century, to protect the natives against the grosser forms of abuse, and to supply rations, clothes, and medical treatment to those in need. In the first decade of the twentieth century a view which had been expressed occasionally in the preceding fifty years became established—that the aborigines were a dying race and that the best that could be done for them was to smooth their dying pillow.

The negative outlook of the third phase implied that the day of experiment on behalf of the aborigines had gone. Public opinion, however, perhaps through sympathy for the "dying," became more and more susceptible to reports of what occurred on the frontiers. Enquiries, commissions, and reports became frequent and interested bodies made repeated representations to governments. Moreover, after the establishment of a chair of anthropology at the University of Sydney in 1926 and the carrying out of a well-organised plan of research on aboriginal life and culture and contact problems, the scientific approach and the results of research became available to governments, humanitarian and missionary societies, and other interested bodies.

Again it was felt that something should and could be done for the natives. The renewed conviction found expression, in the 1930's, in the inauguration of a positive phase, the fourth. It was symbolised in three states and the Northern Territory by changing the title of the chief executive officer from chief protector to commissioner, director, or superintendent. The Protection Board in New South Wales became the Welfare Board. The objective, in all instances, is now positive in nature—the advance of the full-bloods to citizenship and the assimilation of mixed-bloods in the economic life of the community. The tendency of the latter is to remain predominantly endogamous in their several castes, but to play such increasing part in the life of the community as social prejudice permits.

With regard to the full-bloods, who in the Northern Territory performed valuable wartime service in reconnaissance and patrol units, assembly lines, and all sorts of semiskilled and labouring work, the army administration has shown that they can advance in a short time from bush life to well-ordered communal village life. Under instruction they adopted satisfactory methods of hygiene and sanitation, built well-made huts and beds, and took regular baths, physical exercises, and meals at tables with knives and forks. They worked well and were happy, for they had a well-balanced diet and medical attention, social life with their families and fellows in the villages, regular pay and controlled canteens, appreciation of their services, and open friendliness on the part of the Australian soldiers. Thus life was full, interesting, and worth while.

The test of statesmanship has now come: Will the Australian governments build on this experience, or will they let the natives drift back to life on the protected reserves or to an aimless existence around townships and stations?

There are at present six separate aboriginal policies and administrations—the five mainland states and the Northern Territory—with differences in immediate aims and in regulations, and with almost no sharing of experience. A unified national policy has been contemplated for more than twenty years. But a state government, with its large pastoral constituency, finds it almost impossible to change from a policy which makes natives cheap, though protected, labour, to one which rules that they are to be treated and paid as white labour and educated to play a full part in the country's economic life.

The Commonwealth Government, however, with most of its electorates in great urban centres and in rural regions where aboriginal labour does not present a problem, can take a broader view and a stronger stand. If progress is to be made, financial responsibility will have to be borne, at least in part, by the Commonwealth as a whole for the implementation of a positive policy in Western and South Australia, if not also in Queensland.

It therefore remains for the states, by referendum or by legislative action, to hand over to the Commonwealth their responsibility and powers regarding the aborigines or else, after conference with the Commonwealth, to agree by separate state acts to implement a common policy and to be subsidised for so doing.

Finally, it may be asked whether, apart from humanitarian reasons, the effort in behalf of the natives is worth while. The answer is Yes. The northern parts of Australia, west of the Great Dividing Range, and the central and arid regions would not have been developed to the present limited extent if aboriginal labour had not been available. And there is no reason to think that it will be developed further without the aborigines, unless Australia is prepared to import coloured labour, a very unlikely contingency. The aborigines make good stockmen, drovers, shearers, fencers, mechanics, windmill-attendants, motor-drivers, well-sinkers, boatmen, butchers, laundrymen, and general labourers. Given health, good diet, proper conditions for expectant and nursing mothers, community life, a sound policy of education, just treatment, and respect, they will prove to be Australia's greatest asset in the northern and central regions.

Australia first influenced the South Sea Islanders in the early 1840's, when an unrecorded number were brought to work on pastoral settlements in southern and southwestern New South Wales. The difference in climate and the loneliness made the experiment a failure. But in 1863 they were successfully employed in an agricultural venture near Brisbane. For the next forty years nearly 60,000 islanders were recruited for, and indentured to, Queensland employers. They came mainly from the New Hebrides and the Solomons, with a few, in the early 1880's, from New Guinea and the islands near by. By their labour the sugar industry was built up, though nearly half of them worked on cattle stations, on wharves, and in towns. They came under contracts, usually for three years.

Unfortunately, here as elsewhere, recruiting and indenturing of labourers from primitive communities involved many abuses, especially in the early years, and the death rate was high. But from 1868 the Queensland Government endeavoured to supervise the recruiting, and in 1875 a British High Commissioner for the Western Pacific was appointed with power to check abuses in the case of British subjects. After 1884 abuses both in recruiting and in the conditions of employment became rare.

In Queensland, however, opposition to the use of coloured labour developed among white workers and humanitarian groups, and became a political issue. Their opposition was strengthened by the growth of a "White Australia" sentiment which in Queensland prevented the indenturing of Indian labourers in 1882, when, after years of discussion, agreement had just been reached with the Indian Government. This meant the end of the indenturing of South Sea Island, or Kanaka, labour. Indeed, legislation to this effect was passed in 1890, but the system was revived under an old Act in 1892 for what Queenslanders regarded as cogent practical reasons.

Strong criticism came from the other Australian states; when the Commonwealth was formed in 1901, it took steps to ensure the cessation of recruitment of island labour by March, 1904, and the return to the islands by 1906 of all labourers, except a few hundred who were permitted to remain. To enable the sugar-growers to carry on with white labour the Commonwealth undertook to pay them a bounty. "By 1912 only four per cent of Queensland's sugar was grown by coloured labour." The next year the bounty was withdrawn.

There are three main racial groups among the natives of New Guinea. The pygmy or near-pygmy Negritos of the highlands are good gardeners, often practising irrigation and cultivation-drainage. They live in villages or in homestead fashion, and use the bow and arrow. The taller Papuans have characteristically long heads, sloping foreheads, long arched noses, and chocolate skin. They inhabit Papua west of Cape Possession and most of its inland region, and reach the coast at some points on the mandated side of New Guinea. They are found also in parts of New Britain. The rest of the inhabitants of both territories are the black to light coppercoloured Melanesians, who also occupy most of the rest of the arc of islands called Melanesia. They are mixed in some regions with the Papuans and in others with Polynesians. Melanesians all speak related languages of Indonesian stock, whereas the Papuan languages are complex and unrelated. Both Melanesians and Papuans live in villages and are gardeners and fisherfolk; the Melanesians are also a trading, seafaring people. The Papuans have only "oldman" rule; Melanesian leadership is usually based on wealth and prestige. Ceremonial and club life is important in all tribes.

Papua, which is the southeast "quarter" of the island of New Guinea, together with a few groups of islands (D'Entrecasteaux and Louisiade), was proclaimed a British Protectorate in 1884. In 1888 it was annexed as British New Guinea by Dr. (later Sir)

William MacGregor (1846–1919), who became its first administrator. The keynote of his policy was "to deal righteously and justly with the natives, to pacify the country, and develop it into a British colony." Queensland was responsible for the administration, but received financial assistance from New South Wales and Victoria. In 1902 general authority was transferred to the Commonwealth, and in 1905, by the Papua Act, British New Guinea became the Territory of Papua, as from September 1, 1906.

Before the annexation in 1888 there had been a few traders, miners, and missionaries in the Territory; up to the end of 1941 the white population, apart from a military establishment in 1940–1941, seldom numbered more than 1,200. The area under cultivation by whites averaged about 60,000 acres. Copra and rubber were the most important products. The natives number about 300,000, of whom never more than 12,000 were employed by Europeans at one time.

The administration policy laid down in Papua by Sir William MacGregor was developed by Sir Hubert Murray (1861–1940), Lieutenant-Governor from 1908 to 1940, who proceeded on the principle that the native's interest must be paramount and maintained that only if white settlers acted on this principle would their own interests in the long run be served. He "reigned" long enough to see his point of view accepted and vindicated. Because of the absence of native chiefs in almost the whole of Papua, Hubert Murray could not use the method of indirect rule. But by appointing a local man, the headman if suitable, as village constable and government representative, with a few limited powers, and later setting up a few village councils, he was working slowly for the day when the natives could be associated with the work of administration.

The characteristic of the Papuan administration was its personal emphasis. Governor Murray knew and influenced his staff, all the white residents, and seemingly most of the natives. His resident magistrates, assistant resident magistrates, and patrol officers knew and dealt personally with everyone in their own districts. Formality was dispensed with as much as possible, though familiarity was avoided. But a native labourer with a grievance against his employer would not hesitate to approach the magistrate and state his case. It was his right. Pidgin English was tabu, and the missions, which were responsible for all the education, were subsidised to teach English to a required standard.

The Mandated Territory of New Guinea includes the northeast "quarter" of the island of New Guinea, together with the Bismarck Archipelago and the northern Solomon Islands. In the 1870's German trading firms established themselves in the region; in 1884 it became a German Protectorate, and a colony in 1885. Plantation settlement then began, but there were only about 1,200 European residents, mainly German, and 1,400 Chinese in 1914, when the region was occupied by Australian troops. At the end of 1920 it was entrusted to Australia as a Class C mandate. By 1940 the white population had increased to 4,000 and the Chinese numbered 2,200. The area under cultivation, mainly for copra, had increased from 173,000 acres in 1920 to 273,000. The discovery and development of rich gold fields at Bulolo, Wau, and Edie Creek enabled much progress to be made, especially in native administration, as the royalty on gold provided a large source of revenue. The natives numbered about 700,000, of whom 40,000 were indentured to work mainly on plantations and in mines.

The Australian administration in the Mandated Territory followed on the lines of the German system, for the military officers, responsible for law and order from 1914 to 1920, were inexperienced in native affairs and adhered mainly to the system in operation. Some of the officers stayed on with the Mandate administration. It was not until the late 1920's that they were assisted and gradually succeeded by younger men with some specialist training in anthropology. Even so, the German attitude toward force as essential in "keeping natives in their place" was not entirely banished, and the use of pidgin English as the sole means of converse with them became a mark of their inferior caste or racial position. The personal approach of the Papuan system was not attempted and was suspect. The emphasis was rather on organisation.

The reason for the difference lay, no doubt, in the German and military history of the Territory, in its much greater area and population, in the necessity for presenting concise annual reports of methods and results to the League of Nations, and in the absence of a dominating personality at the head for a long period,

such as Sir Hubert Murray, who became sure enough of his policy
to trust its application and to inspire his whole team—officers, employers, and missionaries—with the same trust.

The administration was organised under a director of district
services, district officers, assistant district officers, and patrol officers, together with a village *luluai* (or head), usually nominated
by the natives, a *tultul* to assist and interpret for him, and a superficially trained native medical assistant for each village. District
chiefs were set up also, and several satisfactory experiments were
made with village councils.

The objective of both systems was the same. As Australia declared to the League of Nations a few years ago, the whole of the
legislation of the Territory of New Guinea had for its main object
the promotion of the welfare of the native population.

Neither Papua nor New Guinea have proved to be very attractive to white settlers. The tropical climate, the endemic diseases, the
uneven distribution of good soil, and the distance from the amenities of the great centres of population were the chief reasons. The
welfare of the natives, therefore, has not been jeopardised through
infiltration or invasion by great numbers of non-natives. Moreover, both administrations have taken care not to alienate for the
use of settlers any land that might conceivably be required by the
natives. For the general aim would be unattainable if a great proportion of them became landless and if village economy disinte-
grated through loss of productive land. As it happens, however,
only a third of the land set apart for lease by non-natives has been
used by them.

Another factor which has an important bearing both on white
settlement and on native welfare is the use of native labour. The
indenture system has prevailed for more than fifty years. The employer or his representative and the native employee sign a contract
before a government official, who must make certain that the native
understands the terms of the contract. This states the length of
service; the type, conditions, and place of work; and the rate of pay.

The native labour ordinances of both territories were very
thorough; on paper, at least, both parties knew where they stood
and that the government would see that justice was done. But, as
Sir Hubert Murray said long ago, the indenture system indicated

that settlers and natives did not trust one another; the criminal penalty—gaol for absenteeism—for a civil offense was an anomaly. The real trouble was the impossibility of policing the ordinances satisfactorily, especially with respect to the recruiting and the return of labourers to their own villages at the end of the term.

Much opposition to the indenture system developed in Australia in the 1930's and during the war. The long absences of a large proportion of labourers from their villages, frequently up to seven years in New Guinea, though seldom more than three years in Papua; the deleterious effects of absence on family and village life; the occasional over-recruiting of districts; the recurrent resort to force on plantations or to the courts to compel employees to work to the satisfaction of their employers, especially in the larger Mandated Territory in which many unsatisfactory indentured labourers were fresh recruits from villages, probably hundreds of miles away; and the realisation that basically the system was a means for providing controlled and comparatively cheap labour for white settlers in an uncomfortable climate—these were among the main arguments levelled against the system. In reply were the assurances, for the most part true, that Papuan planters were paternal-minded toward the natives, and the New Guinea employers' arguments that regular work was "good for the natives" and, with the prescribed diet, built up their health, and that the labour ordinances were admirable. But humanitarian, most missionary, anthropological, and Labour opinion was arrayed against the system.

The Papuan official policy had aimed consistently at replacing indenture by the free or "casual" labour system, and had done so by 1940 to the extent of one-third of the natives employed. As a result the Australian Government announced to the International Labour Organisation in 1944 that the indenture system would be abolished. When civil administration was restored in Papua–New Guinea in 1945, the system was drastically modified with a view to its abolition in about five years. Professional recruiters were disallowed and the term of contract was limited to one year. Thus the employer or one of his staff must come into personal contact with the natives he desires to employ, and, because of the one-year limit, he endeavours to obtain natives from as near as possible. His success depends on satisfactory personal relationships with the natives—the point on which the Papuan administration always laid stress. This policy, if adhered to, will pave the way to the complete abolition of the system.

Missions have functioned in these territories for seventy years. About one-third of the population is Christian and another third is under the influence of missions. Up to 1941 education was left almost wholly in their hands, and in this, as in evangelistic work, they relied primarily on native teachers and pastors. The standard varied, but the administrations did not suggest any alternative or supplementary agencies, no doubt because of cost. Collaboration between all missions and the government is necessary in order to formulate and implement an effective system of native education if the natives are to meet the increasing responsibilities of postwar policy.

The missions have played an important rôle, also, in civilising, and in maintaining law and order. Their staffs, knowing the native language of their districts, understood and influenced the natives to a degree unattainable by administrative officers on occasional brief visits. But in many instances the very nature of the missionaries' work, which involved close personal association with the natives, and their emphasis on the value of human personality, irrespective of skin colour, caused adverse criticism, especially from those who regarded natives simply as labour or as an inferior caste.

The staffs of most missions now receive anthropological and specialist training parallel to that provided for administrative officers, and so both should be able to coöperate more and more in the realisation of Australia's trust, which, in the words of the Anzac Pact, is "the welfare of the native peoples and their special economic and political development."

CHAPTER XXVI

Australia's Interest in the South Pacific Islands

BY GORDON GREENWOOD

THROUGHOUT the greater part of Australia's history, interest in foreign affairs has been no more than intermittent, mainly because attention was concentrated on internal development. But if geographical position was in part responsible for the tendency to ignore world politics, it also made unavoidable the early adoption of an attitude toward the islands of the Southwest Pacific. Yet even in an area so obviously vital to its interests, concern was occasional, in the sense that Australian public opinion was thoroughly aroused only when specific problems appeared likely to become a serious menace to local interests. The possibility of war, a threat to Australian security, the transportation of criminals to the French islands near by, any challenge to the right to maintain cherished immigration restrictions in Australian Pacific territories, and the presence of powerful neighbours in islands adjacent to its coasts—these were the issues which quickened public interest and about which Australian statesmen were most outspoken. But if such matters represented the high-water mark of Australia's concern it is well to emphasise that Australian interest in the Pacific—and especially in the control of the islands of the southwestern area—was far more constant than that displayed in any other aspect of external relations.

From the time of the first settlement the one inescapable fact was that the future of the colony was indissolubly linked with developments in the South Seas. Indeed, all early plans for the settlement of New South Wales included references to the use which

[374]

could be made of the islands of the Southwest Pacific. Both James
Mario Matra (?–1806) and Sir George Young (1732–1810), who
outlined some early projects for the settlement of the continent,
suggested that native families, and especially women, could be
secured from the islands, notably from New Caledonia, Tahiti,
and the Friendly Islands. Both emphasised, also, the advantages
which would accrue from the cultivation of the New Zealand flax
plant and from the use of New Zealand timber for ship-building.

The all-important motive in the foundation of New South
Wales was the necessity of discovering a solution of the penal
problem, yet once the decision to colonise had been made, other
inducements were speedily discerned. An opportunity was afforded
to establish a new commercial base in the South Seas; annexation
would forestall French designs in the area; and in time the new
settlement might, in the event of war with Holland or Spain, become valuable as a base from which to attack the Dutch islands or
Spanish America.

The instructions issued by the British Government to Captain
Arthur Phillip, the founding Governor, included references to the
policy that he should adopt toward the Southwest Pacific Islands.
Perhaps the most important point was the extent of his jurisdiction, which included "all the islands, adjacent in the Pacific Ocean,
within the latitude aforesaid of 10°37′ South and 43°39′ South."
Just what the British Government intended to convey by the use
of the term "adjacent" is not clear, but the early governors adopted
a broad interpretation, since occasional references are made to the
inclusion of Tahiti, New Zealand, the Fijis, and the Friendly
Islands as being "within the limits of this territory." Both Governor
Philip Gidley King (1758–1808) and Governor Lachlan Macquarie
(1761–1824) appointed a justice of the peace at Tahiti, and Macquarie made a similar appointment for the North Island of New
Zealand. It would seem that jurisdiction over the adjacent islands
did not entail an extension of sovereignty, but was rather "intended
to mark out a sphere in which the Governor might represent the
Crown."[1] It was a recognition by the British Government that there

---

[1] This is the view adopted, after detailed analysis of the evidence, by J. M.
Ward of the History Department, University of Sydney, in an unpublished
master's thesis, "Development of British Policy in the Islands of the Southern
Pacific to 1893."

might be circumstances in which the governors would have to exercise authority in the neighbouring islands in the interests of the new colony.

The British Government had no intention of permitting the development of trade by private merchants between New South Wales and the islands since this would have involved an infringement of the East India Company's monopoly rights to trade and navigation between the Cape of Good Hope and the Straits of Magellan. It was, in fact, specifically forbidden in the instructions issued to Phillip. This, however, did not imply that the colonial government was debarred from utilising the resources of neighbouring islands for the welfare of the colony, since the Governor was given permission to despatch vessels to the islands to augment his supplies and to recruit native women for the settlement. Nothing came of the latter suggestion, but the early governors did attempt, with some success, to supplement their food supplies from Norfolk and Lord Howe islands and from Tahiti.

Whatever the intentions of the British Government, the early history of New South Wales demonstrated that it was impossible to ignore the facts of geography. Though the colony was a British outpost, it was still a Pacific settlement. Almost at once the factors which have remained constant motivating forces in moulding an Australian outlook toward the Pacific began to operate; it is astonishing how early these basic motives appear. In spite of the discouragement of the home government, a trade connection was established between New South Wales and the islands. Sydney merchants like Simeon Lord (1771–1840) carried on a clandestine traffic in sandalwood obtained from the Fiji Islands and destined for the China market. But the major factor in making regular contact unavoidable was the establishment of the whale and seal fishery in which Sydney colonists competed with their British and American rivals. It was apparent that there was marked hostility to what was regarded as a United States invasion of a British preserve. Ample evidence exists in the colonial press to show that even in the early years of the nineteenth century the residents of New South Wales regarded the oceans surrounding Australia and the adjacent islands as a British area, and looked upon foreigners engaged in island trade and fishing as unwanted intruders.

This attitude was closely linked with questions of imperial rivalry and the security of the Australian settlements. The colonists wanted to see first Australia, then New Zealand, and finally the other islands of the Pacific placed under the British flag. They believed that only thus could the possibility of foreign empire in the South Seas be eliminated and Australia itself made secure. Suspicion of French intentions, however ill founded, was rampant just before and after 1800. Phillip was instructed to take possession of Norfolk Island to "prevent it being occupied by any other European power," and numerous settlements on the Australian coast were prompted by the same consideration.

The fear that Australian security would be threatened if the adjacent Pacific Islands passed under non-British control was strengthened during the Anglo-Spanish War of 1796 and the Anglo-American War of 1812. The activities of British whalers, carrying letters of marque and raiding Spanish commerce in the Pacific, made the Governor of New South Wales anxious about the possibility of reprisals against the settlement. The successful raids against British shipping in the Pacific carried out from a base in the Marquesas by Captain David Porter (1780–1843), who commanded the United States frigate "Essex," seemed to lend weight to the contention that the island groups would continue to represent a threat to Australia until they were annexed to the British Crown.

The belief that the future of the Australian settlements was intimately bound up with the control of the islands of the Pacific led early to the enunciation of the two-part view which has remained a feature of the Australian outlook: that no foreign power should be permitted to become entrenched near Australia, and that it was the destiny of Australia to control the outlying islands. A leading article in the Sydney *Gazette* in 1827 accused both France and the United States of endeavouring to extend their influence in the Pacific to the detriment of Great Britain. Such endeavours were condemned as destructive of Britain's influence among the islands in the vicinity of Australia and as an encroachment upon "the innumerable isles that bespeck that ocean of which Australia is destined to hold the imperial sway."

Foreign nations and the British Government doubtless found this attitude difficult to understand. Britain herself was reluctant

to add to her overseas possessions—though by 1840 she had agreed
to annex New Zealand—and her statesmen implied that it would
be more fitting if the Australian colonists were to concentrate on
the development of their enormous and largely unexploited continent rather than plague the home government with entreaties to
acquire new territory. But the Australian attitude derived principally from the belief that their chance of being free to develop the
continent without interference might well depend upon what happened elsewhere in the Pacific, and notably upon their success in
preventing other powerful nations from acquiring a foothold in
the islands.

Commercial and strategic interest in the islands was reinforced
before 1850 by considerations of a somewhat different kind. The
Pacific was, from the point of view of international regulation, a
no man's land, but it became increasingly clear that some method
would have to be devised whereby law and order might be enforced. The governors of New South Wales were almost immediately confronted with the problem of policing the Pacific, and
made repeated recommendations. In the face of British unwillingness to engage in large-scale annexation, the question was not solved
until the latter part of the nineteenth century. Australian interest
in the islands was accentuated by the British Act of 1817, which
declared that offences committed in the islands could be regarded
in the same category as offences committeed on the high seas; and
by the Acts of 1824 and 1829, under which the courts of New South
Wales and Van Diemen's Land were given authority to deal with
such offences.

Missionary activity also stimulated Australian interest. Samuel
Marsden (1764–1838) commenced his mission to New Zealand in
1814 and the British societies operating in the South Seas established links with New South Wales. Moreover, the missionary societies and their workers were opposed to the acquisition by foreign powers of the groups in which they operated, and when their
policy of establishing stable native kingdoms broke down they invariably favoured the establishment of a British or Australian administration.

Though an Australian attitude was formulated at an early date,
what counted most in the determination of policy was the inter-

pretation which the home government placed on British interests
in the Pacific. This remained true until the coming of self-government in 1855, was only slightly less true up to federation in 1901,
and even thereafter the disproportion in power between Australia
and Great Britain meant that until recent years Britain has been
dominant in moulding policy. Australians were not unwilling to
entrust the British Government with the handling of foreign policy
and defence, but whenever it was felt that Australian interests in
the Pacific were threatened, Australian politicians sought by protest or direct action to influence policy. At once it became obvious
that there were serious obstacles in the way of pressing the Australian standpoint with determination. The colonies were virtually
dependent on Britain for their defence; control of the foreign relations of the Empire was in the hands of the British Government,
which meant that issues in the Pacific would be viewed mainly in
the light of their effect on Britain's relations with other world
powers; and the Australian colonies, until federation, were dis-
united and therefore weak.

From about 1850 a changing Pacific and a changing Australia
brought a heightened interest in the islands and a stronger affirmation of an attitude previously existing but only occasionally expressed. Changes in the Pacific were brought about by the increasing concern betrayed by the major powers in the future of the
island groups and by the expanding activities of their respective
nationals.

Heightened interest was displayed in a variety of ways: in the
struggle to influence native rulers and establish a specially favoured position, as in Tahiti; in the rivalry for missionary spheres
between Protestant and Catholic organisations; in the competition for commercial supremacy, especially after Theodor Weber
inaugurated the trade drive which paved the way for the startling
successes of Godeffroy and Son and the "D.H. & P.G." (the Long-
handle firm); and, finally, in the clash of rival powers for island
empires in the Pacific. By the end of the nineteenth century, native
independence had vanished and all the important Pacific groups
had passed under European or American control.

Within Australia a more alert interest and a more outspoken
policy toward the neighbouring islands may be discerned. Self-

government gave the colonies a new status, and Australian politicians took advantage of their enlarged opportunities. Oceanic communications were of vital importance. Improvements in sea transport and the completion of the Panama railway in 1855 aroused the anxiety of Australian governments as they watched the struggle of the powers. Their anxiety was heightened by the fact that the Australian stake in the Pacific had increased immeasurably.

The same attitude also may be seen in relation to missionary activity. At first the Australian churches coöperated with their parent bodies in Great Britain in the task of evangelisation among the islands, but more and more they came to accept primary responsibility for work in the Pacific field. Thus in 1855, at the first Australasian Wesleyan Conference, control of the South Sea missions (Tonga and Fiji) was entrusted to the newly constituted church, and the Australasian Wesleyan Methodist Missionary Society came into being. In much the same way the Presbyterian Church acquired important mission interests in the New Hebrides. The Australian churches, through their missionary zeal, were not only establishing contacts of the utmost significance with many important groups, but were fostering in Australia an attitude favouring government annexation of groups in which their missionary societies were operating.

Commercial penetration of the islands by Australian traders and companies also proceeded rapidly after 1850, and, though the island trade formed only a small percentage of Australia's external trade, it was sufficiently significant to arouse governmental interest and support. The exhaustive report of the Interstate Commission in 1918 on British and Australian trade in the South Pacific, the object of which was to recommend methods of increasing Australian and British control of island traffic, in itself testified both to the strength of the commercial interests engaged in the trade and to the concern of the Commonwealth Government. No doubt governmental interest was engendered by the realisation that more than profits were at issue, since the activities of Australian firms maintained Australia's connection with the groups and enhanced its claim to consideration when political issues arose, as, for instance, in the New Hebrides.

Australian commercial ventures in the islands were far from negligible. Shipping services operating from Australian ports, especially Sydney, maintained regular connections between the conti-
nent and the more significant Pacific groups. Burns Philp and
Company, Ltd., the Australasian United Steam Navigation Company, Ltd., and the Union Steamship Company of New Zealand,
Ltd., provided services linking the mainland with the islands.
Numerous firms were engaged in island commerce (e.g., W. R.
Carpenter and Company, Ltd., carrying on a general island trade;
W. Gardiner and Company, Ltd., wholesale importers and manufacturers; Robert Reid and Company, Ltd., soft-goods merchants;
Nelson and Robertson, shipping agents and island merchants) or
owned plantations or other industrial enterprises. Burns Philp and
Company, founded in 1883, was the most important company engaged in the island trade and had branches at almost all the major
groups, including New Guinea, the New Hebrides, the Solomons,
Tonga, Samoa, and the Gilbert Islands. Mention should also be
made of the extensive plantations acquired in the Solomons in
1905 by Lever Brothers, and of the even more important sugar
plantations and mills in Fiji owned by the Colonial Sugar Refining
Company, Ltd., which before 1918 had invested about £3,000,000
in the cane-sugar industry in Fiji.

The Australian reaction to the changes occurring in the Pacific
was in keeping with the stage of development which the country
had reached, for it was marked at one and the same time by adoles-
cent irresponsibility and by the ardour and intrepidity of youthful
nationalism. Most Australians desired that Great Britain should
extend its imperial sway in the Pacific and, by a policy of annexation, exclude other European powers. No doubt the governments
of the Australian colonies would have been prepared in some instances to act on their own initiative rather than permit the annexation of adjacent groups by European powers, had it not been for
the realisation that such acquisitions must be sanctioned by the
British Government if they were to have any validity in the eyes
of other nations. Their policy therefore became one of attempting
to force Britain to act in the Pacific in accord with Australian senti-
ments. Continual pressure was brought to bear on reluctant British
governments.

Australians argued that colonial advice concerning the islands should be heeded, for Australia, through its trade and missionary contacts and its geographical location, was able to furnish accurate information about the practices and intentions of Britain's rivals. Few British ministers were willing to concede that this was true, but the German annexation in New Guinea in 1885 at least showed that the Australian warnings had more substance than the British Government had realised. There were repeated requests for action in particular groups and exasperated criticism whenever the British Government decided against acquiring further responsibility. Thus the Inter-Colonial Conference which met in Melbourne in 1870 passed a resolution, subsequently submitted to the British Government, favouring the establishment of a British Protectorate over Fiji. In 1885 Sir H. B. Loch (1827–1900), the Governor of Victoria, forwarded a suggestion, which he believed might appease an Australian opinion inflamed by the German annexation, that negotiations should be opened with the Netherlands Government with a view to acquiring their part of New Guinea.

Another and more extreme method of exerting pressure was direct action by colonial governments which hoped that Britain would sanction a *fait accompli*. A conspicuous example is the abortive annexation of New Guinea by the Queensland Government in 1883. Queensland had been exerting constant pressure on the British Government to annex New Guinea. When no satisfactory guaranty was forthcoming, Queensland decided to force the issue by taking possession in its own name. This determined bid to stampede the home government failed mainly because the Foreign Office assured Lord Derby that no foreign power had territorial designs in New Guinea. This assurance, unjustified by events, induced the British Government to disavow Queensland's action. About 1888 the Victorian Cabinet, alarmed by rumours of a projected French occupation, contemplated a similar plan for the annexation of the New Hebrides, but abandoned the project when it was convinced that the French did not intend to act.

Within Australia, governmental pressure on the British authorities was supported by the mobilisation of public opinion behind an active policy of intervention in the islands. This was principally the work of organised missionary and commercial bodies backed

by powerful newspapers. A notable instance is the contributions
to the Sydney *Morning Herald* between 1883 and 1907 of "Carpe
Diem," whose identity was later revealed as George Brown (1835–
1917), the celebrated Wesleyan missionary. A further step, designed
to ensure that the Australian colonies should speak with a single
voice and so force Great Britain to pay heed to Australian views,
was the holding of intercolonial conventions on matters connected
with the Pacific.

In spite of repeated demands for British action, the Australian
governments were curiously reluctant either to shoulder the responsibility or to bear the cost entailed by the policy which they advocated. When the annexation first of Fiji and then of New Guinea
was mooted, although the Australian interest was obviously more
vital than that of Great Britain, the colonies were unwilling to
defray a reasonable share of the cost and tended to argue that, since
these were matters of imperial concern, the responsibility obviously
lay with Britain. They were unable, moreover, to appreciate the
reasons for British reluctance to acquire additional territory. When
Alfred Deakin contended at the Colonial Conference of 1907 that
Britain had once held a vague suzerainty over most of the Pacific
but by subsequent actions had surrendered its rights, he was met by
the rejoinder, "When you convert indefinite interests into actual
interests you assume an amount of responsibility, and you become
liable to an amount of cost which does not apply to the indefinite
possession."[2]

Australians were gradually shedding their colonial outlook, for
with greater maturity came a willingness to accept both administrative and financial responsibility and share in the burden of
Australia's defence. Queensland, for example, after the annexation
of British New Guinea, participated in the work of administration
and, with New South Wales and Victoria, contributed to the cost.
With federation the Commonwealth assumed financial responsibility and, by the Papua Act of 1905, the colony of British New
Guinea was transformed into the Australian Territory of Papua.

With the outbreak of war in 1914, Australian fears in regard to
German possessions in the Pacific were, for the most part, proved
false. The Pacific outposts of the German Empire were weakly held

---

[2] *Proceedings,* Colonial Conference, 1907, p. 560, the Earl of Elgin speaking.

and Australian expeditionary forces easily occupied New Guinea and the neighbouring islands. The original intention was that the Australians should also take over the German islands north of the equator, but this was precluded by arrangements between the Japanese and British governments. Once the enemy strongholds had been eliminated, Australian attention was concentrated upon the peace settlement and the future disposition of the German islands.

The strength of the stand taken on this issue by the Australian Prime Minister, W. M. Hughes, backed on the whole by Australian public opinion, astonished Great Britain and the rest of the world. The main Australian aims were to ensure that enemy territory in the neighbourhood of Australia passed under Australian, or at least British, control; that no new "bad neighbours" obtained possessions which might threaten the continent; and that the nature of the control established over former enemy territory was satisfactory. The Australian Government would, no doubt, have liked to acquire German territory north of the equator, but, since there was little likelihood of support for such claims, its efforts were directed to securing as full control as possible over the areas to the south. Hughes himself favoured outright annexation and fought the suggestions for international control, fearing that it might not effectively guarantee Australian security and might have the further disadvantage of permitting large-scale Asiatic immigration to areas near Australia's coast. The adoption of the principle of a Class C mandate, which would enable Australia to apply its immigration laws to the Mandated Territory of New Guinea, did much to reconcile Australian opinion to the mandate system. Australia, though not successful in all her aims, did achieve her basic objectives at the Peace Conference; she acquired German New Guinea under mandate and, with Britain and New Zealand, control of Nauru. She had thus undertaken new responsibilities in the Pacific and achieved an enhanced international status.

Between the First World War and the Second, Australia showed rather less concern than formerly about the islands of the Pacific until new fears were aroused by Japan's imperialistic designs. The Commonwealth administered the Pacific territories under her control with reasonable success; she remained dissatisfied with the Anglo-French condominium in the New Hebrides, where Australian missionary interests pressed for its replacement by British or Australian jurisdiction; she welcomed, for the first time in her history, possession by a non-British power of a chain of island bases in the Pacific in the belief that United States power would act as an effective counter to Japanese pretensions; but she was alarmed by Japanese activities in their mandated islands and by Japanese plans for a southward drive. Japanese aggression in the Pacific found Australia, along with other nations, ill prepared, but the Japanese threat to Australia was defeated by the aid extended by the United States and by determined defence of the New Guinea bastion.

What lessons did Australia learn from the extremity of her danger in 1942, and what attitude has her government subsequently taken toward the Pacific? Light can best be thrown on these questions by a consideration of the Anzac Pact concluded between Australia and New Zealand in 1944. The clauses dealing with security and defence show that Australian attention is still concentrated on the islands fringing her coast, but, whereas until the Second World War the emphasis was upon the Southwest Pacific, there is today a realisation that the islands farther north are equally vital to Australia's security. Australia and New Zealand have therefore asserted their right to assume primary responsibility for the defence of "the arc of islands north and northeast of Australia to western Samoa and the Cook Islands." Concern was also felt lest changes should be brought about in the Pacific without full representation at the highest level by both countries. Australia has repeatedly declared that her contribution to the war in the Pacific entitles her to the fullest say on "the interim administration and ultimate disposal of enemy territories."

Nor is the Australian Government willing to concede that the establishment of Allied war bases in the Pacific itself bestows a right to claim sovereignty in the islands concerned. Indeed, Dr. H. V. Evatt, Minister for External Affairs, has asserted his belief that French, Dutch, and Portuguese sovereignty should be restored over prewar territories—an attitude which, in view of past Australian policies, can only mean that the Australian Government no longer believes that the possession of territory close to its shores by these powers constitutes a threat to security.

Three other points bearing on island administration should be noted: the insistence that every government has the right to control immigration in all territories within its jurisdiction, the emphasis on trusteeship in the government of native peoples, and the insistence on establishing regional machinery for the South Pacific.[3]

What emerges most clearly from the Anzac Pact and other recent official pronouncements upon the Pacific is the determination of Australia to accept a leading rôle in the Southwest Pacific. The long-held belief that this was an area not only vital to Australia's security but one in which she was destined to play a determining part has been reaffirmed in even stronger language. Australia's material interests in the islands reinforce that determination, but there is also the belief that the Commonwealth can make a valuable contribution through enlightened administration, missionary enterprise, and cultural stimulation. Australians believe that their vital interests in the area are greater than those of Great Britain and that, along with New Zealand, Australia should become the legatee of British influence in the Pacific.

From the time of the early settlements the basic interests of Australia in the islands have altered little, but a changing world will force Australia to reorient her policy in many directions. If the conquest of distance indicates that the islands have acquired new importance as links in the world's air routes, from the point of view of defence that same conquest, as seen in the rocket and the atomic bomb, implies that the old concepts of strategy based on the theory of the island fringe are outdated.

The egotistical nationalism which marked Australia's earlier outlook will need to be replaced in a Pacific in which regional and international agreements will have high priority if there is to be an orderly future. Australia, if she can shed her parochialism, can contribute much to the life of the Pacific by making trusteeship a reality, by exerting her influence against a too-ruthless exploitation of the islands, and by exemplifying that small nations as well as large may, through the ideas which they disseminate, add to the advancement and well-being of the peoples of the Pacific Islands.

---

[3] An agreement for the establishment of a South Pacific Commission was signed at Canberra on February 6, 1947, by Australia, New Zealand, the United Kingdom, France, the Netherlands, and the United States.

Part Seven:

THE SECOND WORLD WAR
AND AFTER

CHAPTER XXVII

Australia in the Second World War

BY GAVIN LONG

WHEN GREAT BRITAIN declared war on Germany on September 3, 1939, Australia followed her example within a few hours. In the Federal Parliament which met three days later, no voice was raised against the Government's decision. "We are together in this struggle," said Prime Minister Robert Gordon Menzies (b. 1894), "and we are confident that our unity and determination, being based upon justice, are bound to succeed." John Curtin (1885–1945), the leader of the Labour Party in the House and official Leader of the Opposition, described the outbreak of war as "a most dreadful calamity," but said that his party would support "measures having for their object the welfare and safety of the Australian people and the British Commonwealth of Nations." Indeed, though legally Australia had the right to choose whether she would go to war, all but a fraction of the Australian people felt that morally there was no choice and that, in 1939 as in 1914, Australia must stand beside the parent nation. An overwhelming majority of Australians were convinced that the cause was just and that it was Australia's business to help protect the weaker countries of Europe and perhaps of the whole world against Nazi tyranny.

Although Australia had steadily increased her expenditure on defence in the six years before September, 1939, the forces with which she entered the war were still small and gravely short of equipment. The army comprised 80,000 militiamen organised into five under-manned divisions of infantry and two of cavalry, with a cadre of only 2,800 professional soldiers. The navy included six cruisers and was manned by 4,600 officers and ratings. The standing air force had a strength of 3,100 officers and men and was equipped with obsolescent machines. It did not possess within itself the resources needed even to train the vastly larger air force which Australia was soon to offer to the British Commonwealth as a whole.

A beginning had been made with the manufacture of munitions; in 1939 some 3,000 workers were employed in government-owned armament factories and some private corporations were making war equipment, but it was not until March, 1939, that the first modern military aircraft to be built in Australia had been flown and the making of other types was only beginning to be organised. Shortage of equipment was to be a constant anxiety from 1939 to 1942.

Moreover, in all their plans the Australian leaders had to consider a factor which had been absent in 1914. Then Japan had been allied to Great Britain, but in 1939 Japan was an ally of Germany, and, though she was for the moment an inactive partner, Australia could not disregard the possibility that Japan would strike when she saw a favourable opportunity.

Some Labour members of Parliament had made it clear from the first days of the war that they would oppose any plan to send an Australian expeditionary force to Europe, arguing that to do so would lead eventually to attempts to introduce conscription for oversea service, to which Labour was traditionally opposed, and that, in any event, Australia's first duty was to defend her own shores at home. Several of the Labour leaders in Parliament, including Mr. Curtin himself, had been ardent opponents of conscription in the First World War, and the bitter controversies of 1916 and 1917 were echoed in Parliament and press as soon as it was suggested that Australian forces be sent overseas.

However, before the war was a fortnight old, Mr. Menzies announced that a volunteer force of 20,000 men, including one complete infantry division, would be raised for service at home or abroad. In the next few weeks it was decided also to reintroduce compulsory military training for home defence so as to maintain within Australia a militia of 75,000 men. Moreover, Australia soon agreed, as her share in a vast Empire air training scheme, to train 57,000 men, including 30,000 pilots, air gunners, and navigators, and soon ships of the Royal Australian Navy were operating under the command of the British Admiralty and far from Australian waters.

Before the end of the breathing space which came between the outbreak of war and the German offensive in western Europe the Sixth Australian Division (the first five divisions were militia formations) was in Palestine preparing for service in France, and another division was being formed, the two, with corps troops equal in strength to another division, comprising a corps commanded by Lieutenant-General Sir Thomas Albert Blamey (b. 1884), an experienced soldier who had been Chief of Staff of the Australian Corps in France in 1918.

The fall of France and the intervention of Italy changed the whole complexion of the Australian war effort. Great Britain was in danger of invasion and had no surviving allies except the remote British Dominions. The Middle East, the halfway house between the Orient and Britain, was threatened by Italian power. The French forces in Africa and Syria now being neutral, Italy possessed naval, land, and air strength which on paper was superior to the slender forces which Britain was maintaining in and around the western Mediterranean. The threat to Britain herself was so dangerous that she could spare few reinforcements to oversea theatres, and the defence of the Middle East became, for the time being, a responsibility chiefly of forces from south and east of Suez—India, Australia, South Africa, and New Zealand.

Broadcasting on May 14 Mr. Menzies said, "Australia can make a splendid and perhaps a decisive contribution to victory. The time presses. Let no man delay." He expressed the mood of the Australian people. The ranks of new army formations filled quickly, and an Eighth Division was raised. Volunteers for service as air crew enlisted so rapidly that the schools could not cope with them, and often they had to wait a year or more before being summoned to begin training. A convoy of Australian troops on its way to Egypt was diverted to England, where it arrived early in June. It was organised into a force somewhat less than a division in strength and served there during the critical period of 1940.

At the same time, munition production in Australia was accelerated. Great quantities of war matériel had been lost in the retreat from France and Belgium and it was apparent that in future Australia would have to rely chiefly on her own factories to equip her forces. The government decided to build at Sydney, the main naval base, a dry dock which could accommodate the largest ships afloat and thus would enable the battleships of a British or Allied power to be repaired in the South Pacific in the event of a war with Japan.

On May 22, 1940, Essington Lewis (b. 1881), the general manager of the Broken Hill Proprietary Company, the largest heavy-industry firm in Australia and the chief producer of steel, was appointed with almost dictatorial powers to organise Australian industry for the maximum production of munitions. Much had already been achieved in making weapons and other equipment for the growing army, but the defeat in Europe was recognised as demanding an all-out effort. Mr. Lewis set out to multiply by five within a year the number of workers engaged in making munitions and to produce within Australia most of the requirements of modern war.

By calling on men aged up to twenty-four the militia was maintained at a strength of 250,000. During 1941 these troops spent ninety days in and then ninety days out of camp, the object being to ensure that a force of 125,000 was always available to meet sudden attack by Japan, yet without robbing industry of more men than it could afford to lose.

In the tense months which followed the overrunning of Europe, Mr. Menzies, a confident and eloquent leader, attempted without success to form an all-party Government. The Labour Party had held from the beginning that the Opposition should be "watchdogs over the public interest." Mr. Menzies eventually announced that a general election would be held in September. The election gave the parties supporting him a bare majority in both the Senate and the House of Representatives, depending on the support of two independents.

In 1940 ships of the Australian navy had been in action in the Mediterranean, notably on July 19, when the cruiser "Sydney" and four destroyers fought two Italian cruisers and sank one of them, the "Bartolomeo Colleoni." The initial test of the Second A.I.F. (Australian Imperial Force) did not come, however, until January 3, 1941, in the first British drive into Italian Cyrenaica, when the

Sixth Australian Division, under Major-General Sir Iven Giffard Mackay (b. 1882), who had been an outstanding young battalion commander in the First World War, assaulted and, after two days of hard fighting, captured the Italian fortress of Bardia. The Australians, supported by British tanks and other British troops, took 45,000 prisoners. On January 21 the division broke through the defences of the similar fortress of Tobruk and took 26,000 prisoners. By March 6 it had fought its way through Derna and on to Benghazi, south of which, at Beda Fomm, the British Seventh Armoured Division, which had been operating on the desert flank throughout the campaign, destroyed the retreating remnants of the Italian army.

The Sixth Division, now an expert and confident fighting force, was replaced in western Cyrenaica by the partly equipped, partly trained, and incomplete Ninth Australian Division. As soon as it returned from the desert the Sixth Division, with the Second New Zealand Division and a British armoured brigade, was sent to Greece to help defend its northern frontier against an imminent German attack. Militarily, this expedition offered little hope of success, but honour and national prestige demanded that the British Commonwealth should give what help it could to its only surviving ally. When Germany attacked Greece in overwhelming strength, General Blamey's Anzac Corps, as he named it, was able to fight only a series of rear-guard actions from a line near the Yugoslav frontier to the Gulf of Corinth. Finally, in a coolly organised withdrawal, 44,000 of a total British and Dominion force of 55,000 were brought out in naval ships and transports, often under heavy air attack; in the succeeding months many hundreds of those who then remained in Greece escaped to Palestine.

Part of the force from Greece was landed on Crete and was retained there to supplement the garrison. In the first large airborne invasion in history, the Germans struck at Crete with paratroops, air transports loaded with soldiers, and a small armada of sea-borne troops, and used hundreds of bombing and strafing aircraft to pin down the defenders. The sea-borne force was destroyed by the navy and large numbers of the paratroops were killed by the defenders, but enough remained to hold a vital aerodrome and make possible the landing of transport aircraft loaded with troops.

After days of bloody and often confused fighting, a withdrawal was ordered and the navy managed to remove most of the defending troops to Egypt.

Meanwhile, a German-Italian force had counterattacked in North Africa, and the Ninth Australian Division with some British armoured troops had been driven east. A stand was made within the old Italian perimeter defences at Tobruk, where, surrounded on the landward side by Field-Marshal Erwin Rommel's powerful German-Italian forces, but supplied by small craft which braved the much-bombed route to Alexandria, a composite force, commanded until October, 1941, by Major-General Leslie John Morshead (b. 1889; a forceful young leader of Australian infantry in the First World War), held the fort for eight months and was finally relieved by a new British counteroffensive from Egypt. At Tobruk, for the first time in the war, an advancing German army, strong in armour and possessing almost unchallenged command of the air, was halted and its repeated attacks were defeated.

While part of his army was locked up in Tobruk and part of it was holding precariously east of the Egyptian frontier, General Sir Archibald Wavell, the British commander at Cairo, decided that to secure his right flank he must occupy Syria, whence had come evidence of German penetration. At dawn on June 8 he attacked with such forces as he could command—the raw Seventh Australian Division and some British, Indian, and Free French brigades. General Dentz's Vichy French troops, mainly Foreign Legionnaires and African regulars, fought skillfully and well, and it was not until July 11 that he admitted defeat. The Australians, including some who in the previous six months had fought in Libya, Greece, and Crete, lost 411 men in six weeks of bitter fighting against a former ally.

After the relief of Tobruk all the Australian divisions in the Middle East were out of the line, either retraining and refitting in Palestine or standing along a defensive line in northern Syria. They had played a major and sometimes a decisive part in the defence of the Middle East during an anxious year. This force of volunteers, eager to equal the performances of their fathers in 1914–1918, had been forged into a skilled and confident force— certainly, in the summer of 1941, the most widely experienced force of such size on the Allied side. In that year it had fought against three enemies—Italians, Germans, and French—in three continents, in desert and mountain, in snow and in parching heat.

The fighting in 1941 represented a double gain to Australia. Not only had she played a large part in holding this vital area but in doing so had built an army which, though small, was of superb quality. On the debit side were the casualties that had been suffered, including 2,200 killed or missing and 6,000 prisoners of war.

In 1941 long casualty lists, shortages and restrictions, and increasingly frequent warnings that Japan might strike brought the war close to the life of the citizens at home. A strict control of man power and manufacturing was introduced, transport was curtailed, and house-building virtually ceased. The petrol ration imposed in 1940 was further reduced. Newsprint was rationed at little more than half the prewar level.

After another unsuccessful attempt to form a national Government, Mr. Menzies, who was having increasing difficulties with his own supporters, resigned. In August, 1941, his Government was replaced by one led by the genial Arthur William Fadden (b. 1895), leader of the Country Party. This endured, however, only until October 7, when, after defeat on the budget, it was replaced by a Labour administration with Mr. Curtin as Prime Minister. Close on the heels of a revised budget the new Cabinet was faced with the crisis produced on December 7, 1941, by the long-feared Japanese attack on British, American, and Dutch possessions.

The Japanese, with a powerful and well-trained army, a large fleet well supplied from bases near at hand, and an air force of almost first-class size and quality, advanced rapidly in the Philippines, Malaya, and the Indies. Great Britain, under attack at home and still uncertain whether she could hold on in the Middle East, could not spare adequate forces for the war against Japan. India had a large population and growing industrial resources, but years would be needed to organise these for war on a large scale. At home Australia had one armoured division with very little armour and seven semiequipped and semitrained militia divisions. She had a numerically large air force, but it was chiefly a training organisation, and most of its few operational squadrons were still equipped with obsolescent aircraft.

Australia's contribution to the land defence of Malaya and the Indies was two brigades in Malaya, a few battalions in Java, and small garrisons in the Dutch island bases of Amboina and Timor. A small Australian air force fought in Malaya (it was aircraft of this force which first saw and attacked the Japanese invading convoy). Australian naval units, which formed a substantial part of the inadequate British-American-Dutch naval force fighting in East Indian waters, lost heavily there.

The Australian brigades in Malaya came into the battle late, since their original rôle was to prevent a possible landing on the southeast of the peninsula. However, southward from Gemas, 150 miles north of Singapore, the Australians for a while bore the brunt of the attack. Japanese encirclement tactics, supported by a monopoly of the air, forced the defenders back to Singapore Island where, after bitter and bloody fighting, the commander of the British forces capitulated. Of the Australians, about 22,000 were taken prisoner, either here or in the Indies, and the Eighth Division ceased to exist.

After discussions with the British Government it was decided that two of the three Australian divisions in the Middle East should be transferred to stiffen the defence against the Japanese advance. They were hurriedly embarked with the intention of landing them in Burma or Java, but the Japanese moved too fast. Eventually two of the six brigades that had been recalled from the Middle East remained in Ceylon, which appeared to be one of Japan's next objectives, and the remainder were disembarked in Australia. Meanwhile the Japanese advance moved on virtually unchecked until Java, Timor, and Rabaul had fallen. By the end of February no substantial military force stood between the edge of the Japanese southward advance and Australia except a semitrained garrison of little more than a brigade at Port Moresby in Papua and some tiny detachments in the island chain to the east of the Coral Sea. Nor, at this stage, had Japanese sea and air power been seriously challenged.

It was apparent that Australia, with such aid as New Zealand could give, would not be able to defend the Southwest Pacific alone or even to hold Australia if it was attacked. On December 28 Mr. Curtin, who had shown himself a prudent and devoted leader, issued a New Year's message in which he appealed to the United States for help:

Without any inhibitions of any kind, I make it quite clear that Australia looks to America, free of any pangs as to our traditional links or kinship with the United Kingdom. . . . We know that Australia can go and Britain can still hold on. . . . The Australian Government's policy has been grounded on two facts. One is that the war with Japan is not a phase of the struggle with the Axis Powers, but is a new war. The second is that Australia must go on to a war footing.

In the following months the Government adopted drastic measures to prepare the nation for a war which might have to be fought on Australian territory and with limited help from overseas. By the end of the year it was estimated that two-thirds of the males between eighteen and forty had been called up for military service. A part-time Volunteer Defence Corps, armed at the outset with single-shot rifles and other antiquated weapons, some of them home-made, reached a strength of 98,000, and 300,000 men and women were organised for air-raid precautions and other forms of civil defence. Large numbers of men from forty to sixty, many of them sedentary workers, were recruited into a Civil Constructional Corps to build camps, roads, aerodromes. Tens of thousands of women were enlisted in the fighting services, and the supply of workers for essential industries was increased by directing women from domestic service to the factories. The sight of troops digging and wiring defences on the outskirts of the cities and towns of the east coast, and the news that (on February 19, 1942) Darwin, the capital of the Northern Territory, had been heavily bombed by Japanese aircraft, aroused excitement and renewed determination.

In February and early March the Japanese continued to advance from island to island in the Dutch East Indies and New Guinea. On March 17 General Douglas MacArthur (b. 1880) arrived in Melbourne, having been ordered by President Roosevelt to transfer his headquarters from the Philippines to Australia. At the invitation of President Roosevelt, Mr. Curtin nominated General MacArthur as commander of all Allied forces in the Southwest Pacific. General Blamey became commander of the Allied Land Forces and the American Major-General George H. Brett (b. 1886) of the Allied Air Forces.

By this time the forces in Australia had increased substantially. American troops, eventually to total two infantry divisions, with many air-force and ancillary units, had been arriving since February, and veteran units of the A.I.F. returned to Australia in March. In the three months that had passed since Japan entered the war the training and equipment of the Australian militia had improved rapidly. At the same time, after the conquest of the Indies and Rabaul and the occupation of the northern Solomons, the Japanese southward advance lost its impetus. For the next three months the Allied strength in Australia was slowly built up almost without interference.

The lull ended with two naval-air battles—the Battle of the Coral Sea early in May, and of Midway a month later—in which the Japanese navy suffered defeats so severe that thereafter American command of the sea was secure. In July, however, in spite of these setbacks, the Japanese began to thrust forward again in New Guinea.

A Japanese force landed at Gona on the northern coast and soon afterward came into contact with a small force of Australian and Papuan infantry which had marched over the Owen Stanley Range from Port Moresby. The little Australian force withdrew and the Japanese force continued to climb the mountain track toward Port Moresby, reaching Kokoda, the principal village and plantation area on the northern slopes of the range, on August 10. Experienced infantry of the A.I.F., hurriedly sent to Port Moresby, met the Japanese in the ranges south of Kokoda on August 26 and, later reinforced by additional A.I.F. and militia battalions, fought a bitterly contested withdrawal to Eoribaiwa Ridge, thirty-five air miles from Port Moresby, and there the Japanese advance was halted.

Meanwhile, on August 25 the second prong of the Japanese advance had struck at Milne Bay, a plantation settlement at the eastern tip of the island. In the previous few weeks a militia brigade and a brigade of the A.I.F., with fighter squadrons of the R.A.A.F., had been sent to Milne Bay. The Japanese landed troops and tanks, but, after ten days of hard fighting in the course of which the Japanese, supported by frequent naval bombardments, had the main air strip under small-arms fire, the attack was defeated.

These successes, which were accompanied by American landings in the Solomons, were soon followed by an offensive against the Japanese force at Eoribaiwa. More reinforcements had been sent to Port Moresby, until, by the end of August, all the Seventh Division, a brigade of the Sixth, and several militia brigades were in New Guinea. At the same time regiments of the two American divisions in Australia—the Thirty-second and Forty-first—were on the move. The battlefield had been chosen, the legend of the Japanese soldier's invincible skill as a jungle fighter had been dispelled, and the long campaign begun which was to result in the reconquest of New Guinea and the disastrous defeat of Japan's southern armies. In six weeks of merciless fighting along a track which climbs precipitous forest-clad mountains, the Australian force drove the Japanese back to their base in the Buna-Gona area on the northern coast. Here the Japanese clung to their deeply dug positions for two months against a series of costly attacks by Australians and American troops, together approximating three divisions, until the entire Japanese force was exterminated. The Allied Air Force, now rapidly gaining strength and skill, had been able to prevent the reinforcement or withdrawal of the Japanese troops.

The pattern of the coming war in the Southwest Pacific could now be discerned. Increasing air and sea power could isolate the enemy's strongholds, and the troops which had already bettered the Japanese in jungle fighting could destroy them. When cornered, however, the Japanese fought with the utmost doggedness, counting it an honour to die in the forlornest of forlorn hopes and reckoning it a deep disgrace to be taken prisoner.

Before General MacArthur's forces had recuperated sufficiently to continue the offensive, the Japanese made one last throw. In January and February they advanced swiftly from Salamaua against Wau, in the rich gold-field area on the tablelands of southeastern New Guinea. By this time General MacArthur's reservoir of experienced troops was almost empty. To meet the new threat, battalions of one of the two remaining A.I.F. brigades were flown north. The reinforcements arrived just in time, for Japanese bullets were reaching the aerodrome as some of the transport aircraft arrived. The Australian veterans swiftly drove the Japanese out of the area. Then began one of the most exacting campaigns the

Australians fought in New Guinea, as a force of A.I.F. and militia, supported in the later stages by an American combat group landed at Nassau Bay, slowly thrust the Japanese back through the rugged, forest-clad ridges between Wau and Salamaua.

Anomalies had been created by the existence in the same theatre of two Australian armies, one a volunteer force ready to fight anywhere in the world, and the other consisting partly of conscripts who could legally be employed only in Australia and its New Guinea territories. It was a problem of exceptional difficulty for a Labour Government among whose supporters were many who were firmly opposed to conscription for oversea service. After consulting his party and persuading it of the necessity of his intended move, Mr. Curtin, in February, obtained from Parliament an amendment of the Defence Act authorising the employment of conscripted militiamen not anywhere in the world but anywhere in General MacArthur's Southwest Pacific zone.

By the end of February, 1943, the tide had turned in the Pacific as definitely as in Europe and Africa. The Japanese had at last abandoned Guadalcanal after a long series of counterattacks which had cost them dearly. They were on the defensive and it was apparent that they no longer possessed enough sea and air power to maintain their scattered island strongholds. On January 24 General MacArthur had publicly stated that the most striking lesson of the campaign was "the continued and calculated application of air power, employed in the most intimate tactical and logistical union with ground troops." A new form of campaign had been tested, he added, and it pointed the way to the eventual defeat of the enemy in the Pacific.

Proof of the pudding was provided in the virtual destruction by American and Australian aircraft of a Japanese sea convoy believed to be transporting 15,000 troops across the Bismarck Sea to Lae in New Guinea, and by the opening, on September 4, of a large offensive against Japanese bases in that territory.

In February the Ninth Australian Division had returned to Australia from Egypt, where, from July to November, it played an important part in stopping Rommel's advance on Alexandria and in the victory of El Alamein. This division, rapidly retrained for tropical warfare, and the Seventh were chosen as spearheads of the new offensive, which was on a scale hitherto unprecedented in the war against Japan, and was aimed, in a first phase, at the recovery of Lae, the Huon Peninsula, and the Markham Valley. Success in this undertaking would rob the Japanese of most of their main bases in eastern New Guinea and would provide the Allied force with aerodromes from which to protect a landing on New Britain.

The Ninth Division was landed on the shores of Huon Gulf north of Lae; on the following day the Nadzab aerodrome in the Markham Valley west of Lae was seized by American paratroops and Australian paratroop artillery, and by Australian pioneers and engineers who had marched overland to the same objective. Two days later the Seventh Division began to land at Nadzab by air. Salamaua was captured on September 11 and Lae five days later. Promptly a brigade of the Ninth Division was taken along the coast to Scarlet Beach, north of Finschhafen, the next Japanese base, and landed there from American assault craft. Troops of the Seventh Division began moving toward the elevated Ramu Valley which led northward to Japanese bases west of Finschhafen.

In a boldly conducted campaign fought against a stubborn foe in precipitous mountains densely covered with rain-forest, this force, which gradually increased in strength until it included several strong American and militia formations, fought its way for seven hard months to the Japanese bases of Madang and Alexishafen. Heavy tanks were employed in the operations, and artillery was used on a scale previously unattained in New Guinea. The advance both along the coast and through the Ramu Valley, where the Seventh Division was entirely maintained by air, was made possible by the increase in American air strength, which by this time (with the help of the smaller Australian air force) had subdued the Japanese air power and made the seas around New Guinea and the Solomons perilous for Japanese shipping.

The effort required for this campaign left the greater part of the Australian army in need of a long rest and reinforcements. By September, 1944, it had suffered 70,000 battle casualties; the air force had lost 12,000 men and the navy 2,500. The Australians who were or had been in uniform totalled 975,000. In spite of the threat to the homeland, Australia had continued to send her promised contributions of trained air crew to the R.A.F. until, in August,

1944, there were 21,000 men of the Australian air force serving outside the Pacific Theatre and mostly in Europe, the Middle East, and Burma. More than 52,000 women were in the services.

All this represented an excessive drain on the man power of a nation of 7,300,000 people, which was called on to provide increasing quantities of food, munitions, and clothing for the American army and the armies in India and Burma, and was striving to remedy its shortage of shipping and aircraft by building its own. The Curtin Government (which was returned with a large majority at a general election in August, 1943) decided that the nation's civilian workers would have to be reinforced at the expense of the fighting services, and that in 1944–1945 there would be a net transfer to civil life of about 57,000 men.

To maintain the effort throughout 1943 and to continue it for the following years cost civilians, particularly the young mothers, much weariness and discomfort. Always there is an element in a community which dodges restrictions imposed for the general good. In Australia, however, the great mass of the people went short of many things from 1942 onward. While meat, butter, sugar, tea, clothing, and petrol were rationed, shortages of other goods such as eggs, bacon, rice, beer, canned foods, tobacco, electrical gear, and a wide variety of other manufactured articles were even more keenly felt. Travel was restricted under a system of priorities. Life was made drabber by restrictions aimed at simplifying and standardising clothing and manufactures. To save labour and fuel the delivery of household supplies, except bread and milk, was forbidden, and the young housewife, already unable to obtain help to care for the children or do the washing, had to carry her stores home, perhaps to a house into which several families were crowded because, as a result of the restriction of building, Australia was gravely short of homes.

Evidence of a greater assertiveness in international affairs—a condition to be expected after the anxieties of the past few years—was given when an agreement was signed between Australia and New Zealand in which they pictured, within a general scheme of world security, a regional zone of defence based on Australia and New Zealand, and declared that the use in wartime by any power of the territory of another did not provide a basis for subsequent territorial claims. At the same time, evidence of a growing return of interest in internal affairs was provided when the Government sought the approval of the people for amendments of the constitution to empower the Commonwealth to carry out its plan of post-war reconstruction. However, at a referendum held in August the electors voted against it, though by a relatively small majority.

In the summer of 1943–1944 the American army took over the main burden of the land fighting in the Southwest Pacific hitherto borne chiefly by Australian troops. Supported by overwhelming naval and air forces, American divisions captured bases in New Britain and the Admiralty Islands, and at Hollandia, Biak, and elsewhere in Dutch New Guinea.

Late in 1944 Australian forces, now rested and reinforced, took over the operations against the three Japanese strongholds by-passed in General MacArthur's rapid advance toward Manila, namely, Bougainville Island, New Britain, and Wewak. With the change came a new policy. Where hitherto the rôle of the American garrisons had been to hold wide defensive perimeters around their bases in these areas, four Australian divisions now began operations aimed at annihilating the isolated Japanese forces, estimated to total 90,000 men.

In April, May, and June, 1945, while these three campaigns were still in progress, the Seventh and Ninth Australian divisions made a series of landings in Borneo on the western flank of the American advance, which by that time had swept through the Philippines and secured a chain of island bases between those islands and Japan. In the Philippines operations the Australian navy and the Australian First Tactical Air Force and other units had taken part. Indeed, in the first three and a half years of the war against Japan, Australian ships and aircraft had taken part in most of the major actions in the Southwest Pacific and the Indies.

By the end of the German war, Australia had lost in action three of the six cruisers which she possessed in 1939 and seventeen smaller ships. Throughout the war it was the rôle of the Australian navy and air force to serve as parts of larger Allied forces. It is impossible in this brief narrative to give more than a general picture of their services. To the end of May, 1945, the small but efficient navy lost 1,964 killed or missing; the air force suffered 14,394 casualties, including 10,032 dead or missing, and the army's losses were 75,018, including 15,938 dead or missing. The figures do not include the heavy losses caused by death from disease.

In the first five years of the war the national debt rose from £1,295,000,000 to £2,427,000,000. The material cost of the war was heavy. Shortages developed, notably of houses, which may take years to replenish. Farms, roads, and buildings were neglected. A vast quantity of the equipment of the nation, which normally would have been scrapped, demanded replacement. Education and health suffered as a result of overwork and strain at home as well as among the fighting men—a condition indicated by an increasing tendency to industrial unrest in the later years of the war.

The nation was given telling proof of the strain the war had placed on its leaders when, on July 5, 1945, Mr. Curtin died, after having been too ill to work for some months. With singular wisdom and prudence, he had steered Australia through perhaps the most critical years of its history. The extent to which he had won the confidence of the people was believed to have been demonstrated by the results of the general election of 1943, which many considered to have been a personal victory. Mr. Curtin was succeeded by John Benedict Chifley (b. 1885), a former railway worker, who had been regarded as the sagest of Curtin's lieutenants.

The end of the fighting in Europe offered Australians the prospect of only a limited relief from the wartime anxieties and discomforts. It brought the rescue of the prisoners who were in German hands, but a far larger number were still prisoners of the Japanese. All but a small proportion of Australians in the navy, the army, and the air force were serving in the Pacific Theatre when Germany surrendered, and relatively large Australian forces were committed to important rôles in the war against Japan. Australia could hope only for a limited release of men and materials for peaceful reconstruction until Japan had been overcome. Only when Japan capitulated in August, 1945, was it possible for Australia to begin to think of relaxing her war effort.

In its effects on the Australian people at home the Second World War was in sharp contrast to the First. In 1914–1918 Australia developed her manufacturing power a little, and was useful as a remote and untroubled supplier of raw materials. Since 1939, however, Australian life and industry have been radically changed. By the regimentation of her people and the conversion of industry she achieved a war effort comparable (in proportion to the size of her population) with that of Great Britain. It is safe to assert that the Second World War has affected the international relations and internal economy of the Commonwealth far more deeply than did the relatively remote struggle of a generation ago.

〰〰〰〰〰〰〰〰〰〰〰〰〰〰〰〰〰〰〰〰〰〰〰〰〰

CHAPTER XXVIII

The Pattern of Reconstruction

BY H. C. COOMBS*

THE WORD "reconstruction" may mean either "building again" or "building afresh." In Australia, the approach to the task of postwar reconstruction represents a synthesis between the two definitions. It is, on the one hand, a matter of adapting the economy so as to catch up as quickly as possible on wartime arrears of production and maintenance; and, on the other, an attempt to lay sound foundations for a more satisfactory environment than existed before the war.

Although the need for a smooth and rapid adjustment to the conditions of peace was by no means overlooked, the principal emphasis in Commonwealth planning was deliberately placed on the need to maintain (in Lord Beveridge's phrase) "full employment in a free society." It is believed that, under full employment, problems which otherwise would threaten the very structure of society may prove comparatively easy to solve within the framework of existing institutions. Full employment, however, will not be attained by schemes designed to make work for work's sake; the aim will be to make efficient use of Australia's relatively limited man power in ways which will contribute most to the raising of living standards and the development of national resources.

Two kinds of factors set limits to what Australia can expect to achieve by a full employment policy. The hard facts of comparative geography make it clear that not even the fullest development of resources can gain for Australia the standard of living which

* Mr. Coombs wishes to acknowledge the assistance of G. G. Firth, Senior Research Officer, Ministry of Post-War Reconstruction, in preparing this paper. Mr. Firth is B.Sc. (Econ.) of the University of London and was Ritchie Research Fellow at the University of Melbourne from 1938 to 1940.

now seems within the reach of the favoured populations of more generously endowed countries. Australian soils, climate, and mineral resources offer a prospect of worth-while return on developmental expenditure; but, in the main, progress must depend on the more intensive use of resources already partly exploited. The "open spaces" are a myth indeed.

How much can be done within the limits set by nature, however, will depend on the degree of success in overcoming the second type of limiting factor—the sheer inertia of a human society. The political institutions of Australia, a federation of six sovereign states, are by no means ideal for carrying out a balanced programme of development; already attempts to modify the Constitution so as to facilitate such a programme have failed with the referenda of 1944 and 1946. It remains to be seen how much can be done through agreement between the governments of the Commonwealth and the states. But neither Commonwealth nor state governments have yet evolved the machinery needed to work out and to coördinate the policy essential to a full-employment economy.

The problems which faced Australia on the cessation of hostilities were, in the main, the same as those faced by the other United Nations which took an active part in the war. Apart from Australian territories outside the mainland, only at Darwin in the Northern Territory was there any extensive war damage to be made good; but the demobilisation and reëstablishment in civilian life of more than half-a-million members of the armed forces was in itself a considerable task. Because Australia was committed to the maintenance of a full war effort after the defeat of Germany, and because the defeat of Japan was unexpectedly early, much of the conversion and detailed planning had to be done in a hurry to make possible the speedy reëmployment of those released from the services and from war industries. Japan's early surrender, however, merely changed the scale and urgency of the immediate task: it did not alter the need to ensure that the task was properly related to the long-term objectives of national policy.

Some danger existed that the social and political urgency of reëmployment would lead to action which might stereotype a pattern of expenditure and employment inconsistent with the pattern which, on a longer view, is necessary to ensure a satisfactory standard of living and a steady rate of development. Australia might have been tempted to use too high a proportion of its available resources in building factories and cinemas, and too low a proportion in remedying the appalling shortage of dwellings which existed even before the war and which was greatly worsened by the almost complete cessation of civilian building activity since 1941. The building industry, in any event, needs to be expanded until it employs about 50 per cent more labour than in 1939, if progress is to be made in overcoming the housing shortage. A greater expansion than this, however, might well necessitate a sharp contraction in the not distant future; so it may be desirable for the community to wait for building and construction of lesser urgency. Even the 50 per cent expansion, moreover, will take time to accomplish in view of the difficulty of increasing the supply of key materials (especially timber).

During the war certain secondary industries—particularly the metal trades—were expanded beyond peacetime capacity. Some contraction was recognised as inevitable and, indeed, gave rise to a significant part of the reëmployment problem. Apart from these instances, however, there remain a number of industries which were either expanded or newly established in Australia during the war, or which could use some of the plant and equipment that had been installed for war purposes. It was necessary to decide which of the possible new industries could be permanently maintained; the decision depended partly on costs of production as compared with similar industries in other countries, and partly on Australia's obligations to other countries under relevant international agreements. Secondary industry offers the best prospect of employment for whatever increased population Australia may be able to attract through immigration on a substantial scale; but, if that population is to enjoy a satisfactory standard of living, the new industries must be operated at the lowest possible cost.

During the war all rural industries were seriously embarrassed by the acute shortage of man power, and there are large arrears of maintenance to be made good. But this is a purely temporary problem. Much more serious is the risk that a period of comparatively high prices in oversea markets in the immediate postwar period will encourage expansion in primary production and a structure of rural capital values and debts which, in the long run, may prove to be unjustified. Although the Commonwealth is responsible for oversea marketing and has set up a Bureau of Agricultural Economics, effective control of primary production rests mainly with the states, the governments of which in the past have tended to take an optimistic view of long-term market prospects. A possible source of overexpansion, however, was recognised in the Commonwealth-state agreements concerning the land settlement of former service personnel, which are based on the principle that settlement should be undertaken only when economic prospects are reasonably sound. By the Wool Use Promotion Act of 1945 the Commonwealth Government increased the levy on Australia's staple export to finance research on the production and manufacture of wool, in order to meet the increasing competition from synthetic fibres with new blends and improved quality of materials based on the natural product.

In view of the comparatively wide scope of public enterprise in Australia, new public works and deferred maintenance will play a substantial part in solving the immediate problem of reëmployment. The National Works Council, consisting of the state premiers meeting under the chairmanship of the Prime Minister for the Commonwealth, was set up in 1943 to plan works projects for the postwar period. In spite of difficulties in obtaining experts for this planning, much of the programme of "urgent and important" works was ready by the time of the Japanese surrender. The experience gained in its preparation will, of course, be of the utmost value to the long-term policy of full employment. The National Works Council will probably become a permanent part of the machinery for collaboration between Commonwealth and state governments, serving to ensure that a "shelf" of works projects for wide distribution throughout Australia is kept in readiness against the threat of depression.

On May 30, 1945, the Minister for Post-War Reconstruction (the Hon. John J. Dedman, M.P.) introduced in the House of Representatives a Parliamentary Paper entitled "Full Employment in Australia" (No. 11, Group H; printed and published by the Commonwealth Government Printer, Canberra, A.C.T.). This document states unequivocally that "full employment is the fundamental aim of the Commonwealth Government," and that "in peacetime the responsibility of Commonwealth and State Governments is to provide the general framework of a full employment economy, within which the operations of individuals and businesses can be carried on." The case for this policy rests on the judgement that "to prevent the waste of resources which results from unemployment is the first and greatest step to higher living standards"; and that therefore the governments of the Commonwealth and the states "should accept the responsibility for stimulating spending on goods and services to the extent necessary to sustain full employment."

The significance of this statement of policy can be fully appreciated only in relation to the policy which was pursued in the Great Depression of the 1930's. After the catastrophic fall in export receipts which took place from 1928 to 1930, the Commonwealth Bank refused to finance government deficits on the scale necessary to avert a high percentage of unemployment; so, in spite of a 25 per cent depreciation in the external value of the Australian pound and appreciable but inadequate deficits in the majority of state budgets, Australia experienced the full rigours which world depression can bring to a country dependent mainly on export markets for primary products. Wage cuts further reduced incomes and added to unemployment, which at its worst affected almost a third of the working population and left social and political scars which even yet have not completely healed. It is against this background that the full-employment policy of Australia must be evaluated.

The view is now becoming generally accepted that no country can afford a banking system which is not subject to public control in the interests of employment policy. By Acts Nos. 13 and 14 of 1945, the Commonwealth Treasurer is given, respectively, wide powers of control through the Commonwealth Bank over the private banking system and the power eventually to determine the monetary policy of the Commonwealth Bank. Responsibility for this crucial element of economic policy is thus squarely placed where, in a democracy, it properly belongs—with the government of the day. By the same legislation the Commonwealth Bank is given full power to discharge effectively the functions of a modern central bank.

Needs unsatisfied and savings accumulated during the war will probably ensure that the over-all demand for labour is maintained for some time during the transition, at least so long as a ready market can be found for Australia's staple exports. Indeed, the immediate problem is rather to prevent the excess of effective demand over available supplies from bringing about inflationary increases in the prices of many goods and services. In view of the transfers of labour which are required to reëstablish production on a peacetime basis, however, the potential threat of inflation is, under the circumstances, quite compatible with rather large unemployment. Yet the full-employment policy will be held to apply as much to the transition as to the normal conditions which still lie in the future.

It was to meet this situation that Parliament enacted in June, 1945, the Reëstablishment and Employment Act, which among other things provides for training, reinstatement, and preference to former members of the services. Besides this legislation, demobilisation plans provided for early release of key men required to prepare for the speedy reëmployment of those who will need to find new jobs. Although most man-power controls were quickly removed, a limited supervision of engagements and dismissals was designed to encourage the movement of labour from war industries to peacetime employment. Particularly important was the Commonwealth Employment Service which was set up under the Reëstablishment Act to assist servicemen and women to find suitable employment and to carry out functions which in the United Kingdom are performed by the employment exchanges of the Ministry of Labour.

No one can tell how long postwar prosperity will last under the stimulus of deferred demand, but past experience would lead one to expect the initial threat to full employment in Australia to originate in depression overseas, and to show itself first in falling markets for Australian exports. It is partly for this reason—for net export receipts still average about 15 per cent of the national income— that Australian representatives in recent international discussions have emphasised the need for the more advanced nations to collaborate in maintaining high and stable levels of employment within their economic systems. It was, in fact, mainly owing to the efforts of the Australian delegation to the United Nations Conference at San Francisco in 1945 that an employment policy is prominent among the declared objectives of the Economic and Social Council of the United Nations.

However, international efforts to maintain employment at a satisfactory level throughout the world may not at first succeed. If Australia experiences a sharp decline in export receipts, owing to a temporary slump in employment and expenditure overseas, it will be necessary to prevent the decline from reducing employment in Australia. This will be done by maintaining the incomes of primary producers so far as may be practicable, by stimulating private investment expenditure, and by taking the opportunity to employ idle resources in accelerating and expanding public programmes for national development, housing, improvement of capital equipment, and providing facilities for social and cultural activities. Australia is fortunate in having a wide range of developments requiring public expenditure on capital equipment and development, and in which public activity is generally accepted as desirable. The recent establishment of an Industrial Development Department of the Commonwealth Bank to provide capital for small and growing enterprises widens the scope of investment in which direct public action can be taken. A policy of this kind will be less difficult to carry out than might be true in countries where public enterprise is more narrowly restricted.

Nonetheless, the difficulties likely to beset Australia in effecting full employment can be predicted. The purely institutional problems of a federal constitution have already been noted. To some degree the difficulties of the constitutional position are mitigated by the existence of some machinery for, and an established practice of, collaboration. The legally established Loan Council is perhaps the most important instrument of collaboration. It consists of Commonwealth and state treasurers, and has constitutional authority to decide how much Australian governments shall borrow and how loans shall be allocated. In practice, moreover, contacts between the seven governments are far more effective than might be supposed. The Loan Council has been supplemented by the National Works Council, which may continue to plan public investment and development policy.

Much more threatening to the success of a full-employment policy are the twin problems of wages and industrial relations. For complete success the policy should maintain such a pressure of demand on resources that for the economy as a whole there will be a tendency toward a shortage of men instead of a shortage of jobs. The implications of the situation for wage policy and industrial relations need to be studied carefully. It may well be that the problems cannot be fully resolved without a fundamental change in the traditional attitudes of both employers and employees, but it is too early to predict how the change could be brought about. In the meantime the existing evidence suggests that in this respect the course of full employment is unlikely to run entirely smooth.

In the later 'thirties, after the Australian economy had emerged painfully from the depression, constant difficulty was experienced in preserving equilibrium in the balance of payments. The difficulty may have arisen from special factors, but it will certainly reappear should the need arise to maintain full employment in Australia when employment in important oversea countries is declining. Under these circumstances Australia's demand for imports would be kept up at a time when export receipts were falling off; once exchange reserves have been exhausted, restriction of spending on imports will be the only policy consistent with the maintenance of full employment. Unless the reasons for it are understood, the policy is likely to be popular neither at home nor overseas; but of course it will not be necessary so long as a high level of employment is maintained by the major industrial countries of the world.

AUSTRALIA

By Mrs. C. J. Carleton

There is a land where summer skies
Are gleaming with a thousand dyes . . .
Blending in witching harmonies . . .
In harmonies:
And grassy knoll and forest height
Are flushing in the rosy light
And all above is azure bright,
Australia, Australia, Australia.

There is a land where honey flows,
Where laughing corn luxuriant grows:
Land of the myrtle and the rose . . .
Land of the rose;
On hill and plain the clust'ring vine
Is gushing out with purple wine,
And cups are quaffed to thee and thine!
Australia, Australia, Australia.

There is a land where floating free,
From mountain-top to girdling sea,
A proud flag waves exultingly . . .
Exultingly;
And freedom's sons the banner bear,
No shackled slave can breathe the air,
Fairest of Britain's daughters fair!
Australia, Australia, Australia.

MY COUNTRY

By Dorothea Mackellar

The love of field and coppice,
Of green and shaded lanes,
Of ordered woods and gardens
Is running in your veins.
Strong love of grey-blue distance,
Brown streams and soft, dim skies—
I know, but cannot share it,
My love is otherwise.

I love a sunburnt country,
A land of sweeping plains,
Of rugged mountain ranges,
Of drought and flooding rains.
I love her far horizons,
I love her jewel-sea,
Her beauty and her terror—
The wide brown land for me!

* * * * *

An opal-hearted country,
A wilful, lavish land—
All you who have not loved her,
You will not understand—
Though Earth hold many splendours,
Wherever I may die,
I know to what brown country
My homing thought will fly.

A SELECTED BIBLIOGRAPHY

Series V. Exploration papers. None issued.
Series VI. Scientific papers. None issued.
Series VII. Ecclesiastical, naval, and military papers. None issued.

7. A. W. José, H. J. Carter, and T. G. Tucker (eds.), *The Australian Encyclopaedia* (Sydney, 1927), in 2 vols.

This work, of which a revised and enlarged edition is promised, contains a mass of data on a wide variety of topics, but it is nevertheless not so comprehensive as an encyclopaedia should be.

8. *The Cambridge History of the British Empire,* Vol. VII, Part I: *Australia.* (Ernest Scott, Advisor for Australia; New York and Cambridge, Eng., 1933).

Professor Crawford and Mr. James, in a joint evaluation, state that the text of this volume "reflects fairly the state of Australian historical research when it was published." It may be added that, even so, it is more notable for factual richness than for interpretative suggestiveness. It contains a rather full bibliography. Part I (Manuscript Sources and Official Papers and Publications: A, Great Britain; B, Australia; C, France) is still a valuable guide; but Part II (Other Works) was always a very uneven performance, lacking in critical discrimination, and is now badly out of date.

9. Brian Fitzpatrick, *British Imperialism and Australia: An Economic History, 1783–1833* (London, 1939), and *The British Empire in Australia, 1834–1939* (Melbourne, 1941).

These two volumes taken together constitute a detailed socioeconomic history of Australia, with much attention to the international context of developments. Professor Crawford and Mr. James remark that it is "the most considerable individual contribution since the appearance of *The Cambridge History of the British Empire* [see No. 8] to our knowledge of Australian history."

10. Edward Shann, *An Economic History of Australia* (Cambridge, Eng., 1930). Most useful if read in conjunction with No. 9, above.

11. Gordon L. Wood (ed.), *Australia: Its Resources and Development* (New York, 1947).

12. C. E. W. Bean (ed.), *The Official History of Australia in the War of 1914–1918* (Sydney, 1921–1942), in 12 vols. See, alternatively, C. E. W. Bean, *Anzac to Amiens: A Shorter History of the Australian Fighting Services in the First World War* (Canberra, 1946).

13. H. L. Harris, *Australia's National Interests and National Policy* (Melbourne and London, 1938).

14. W. K. Hancock, *Australia* (London, 1930, 1945).

15. C. Hartley Grattan, *Introducing Australia* (New York, 1942; rev. ed., 1947).

16. Alexander Brady, *Democracy in the Dominions: A Comparative Study in Institutions* (Toronto, 1947).

A brilliant study in comparative institutional democracy. Part Two deals with Australia. The other Dominions discussed are Canada, New Zealand, and South Africa.

17. *Economic Record.* Journal of the Economic Society of Australia and New Zealand.

No. 1 appeared in November, 1925. It contains many articles on public economic affairs which are extremely useful to the nonspecialist.

18. *Australian Geographer.* Journal, Geographical Society of New South Wales.

No. 1 appeared in August, 1928.

19. *Australian Quarterly.* Published by the Australian Institute of Political Science.

No. 1 appeared in March, 1929. The best general periodical issued in Australia.

20. *Australian Outlook.* The quarterly Journal of the Australian Institute of International Affairs.

No. 1 appeared in March, 1947. Successor to *Austral-Asiatic Bulletin,* published 1937–1946, though only occasionally during the war.

21. *Public Administration.* The Journal of the Australian Regional Groups of the Institute of Public Administration.

No. 1 appeared in December, 1937.

22. *Historical Studies, Australia and New Zealand.*

No. 1 appeared in April, 1940.

23. *Australian Public Affairs Information Service.* A Subject Index to Current Literature. Published by the Commonwealth National Library.

No. 1 appeared in July, 1945.

24. *Australian Social Science Abstracts.* Published by the Committee on Research in the Social Sciences of the Australian National Research Council.

No. 1 appeared in March, 1946.

CHAPTER I

LAND AND PEOPLE

Sir T. W. Edgeworth David, *Explanatory Notes to Accompany a New Geological Map of the Commonwealth of Australia* . . . (Sydney, 1932); Griffith Taylor, *Australia: A Study of Warm Environments and Their Effect on British Settlement* (London, 1940), and *Australian Meteorology* (Oxford, 1920); H. A. Hunt, Griffith Taylor, and E. T. Quayle, *The Climate and Weather of Australia* (Melbourne, 1913); J. Bartholomew and K. R. Cramp, *The Australasian School Atlas*; Geoffrey C. Ingleton, *Charting a Continent* (chiefly a history of hydrographical surveying), (Sydney, 1944); Gordon L. Wood, *The Tasmanian Environment* (Melbourne, 1929); Charles Fenner, *South Australia: A Geographical Study* (Melbourne, 1931); J. Macdonald Holmes, *The Geographical Basis of Government* (especially applied to New South Wales), (Sydney, 1944), and *Soil Erosion in Australia and New Zealand* (Sydney, 1946); H. H. Dare, *Water Conservation in Australia* (Sydney, 1939).

A "Bibliography of Australian Geographical Literature from 1926" appears in successive numbers of No. 17, above, beginning with Vol. III, No. 3. See also Nos. 7, 8, 11, 13, 14, 15, above.

CHAPTER II

The Coming of the British to Australia, 1770–1821

G. Arnold Wood, *The Discovery of Australia* (London, 1922); Eris O'Brien, *The Foundation of Australia (1786–1800)*, (London, 1937); George Mackaness, *Admiral Arthur Phillip, Founder of New South Wales* (Sydney, 1937), and *The Life of Vice-Admiral William Bligh* (Sydney, 1931); H. V. Evatt, *Rum Rebellion: A Study of the Overthrow of Governor Bligh* (Sydney, 1938); Sibella Macarthur Onslow (ed.), *Some Early Records of the Macarthurs of Camden* (Sydney, 1914); Ernest Scott, *The Life of Captain Matthew Flinders* (Sydney, 1914).

See also Nos. 1, 2, 3, 5, 6, 7, 8, 9, 10, 21, above.

CHAPTER III

The Triumph of the Pastoral Economy, 1821–1851

Stephen H. Roberts, *The Squatting Age in Australia, 1835–1847* (Melbourne, London, and New York, 1935), and *History of Australian Land Settlement* (Melbourne, 1924); R. C. Mills, *The Colonization of Australia (1829–42)*, (London, 1915); A. Grenfell Price, *The Foundation and Settlement of South Australia, 1829–1845* (Adelaide, 1924); R. B. Madgwick, *Immigration into Eastern Australia, 1788–1851* (London, 1937); Marion Phillips, *A Colonial Autocracy: New South Wales under Governor Macquarie, 1810–1821* (London, 1909); M. H. Ellis, *Lachlan Macquarie: Some Aspects of His Life* (Brisbane, 1942); Marjorie Barnard, *Macquarie's World* (ltd. ed., Sydney, 1941; pop. ed., Melbourne, 1946).

See also Nos. 1, 3, 4, 5, 6, 7, 8, 9, 10, 21, above.

CHAPTER IV

The Gold Rushes and the Aftermath, 1851–1901

For this period secondary works are extremely scarce. The main printed records are the Parliamentary Debates and Parliamentary Papers of the several colonies, the British Parliamentary Papers, and the files of colonial newspapers. Reminiscences of the gold-rush days are very numerous, and a critical survey of them would be useful. See Myra Willard, *History of the White Australia Policy* (Melbourne, 1923).

See also Nos. 3, 4, 7, 8, 9, 10, 21, above.

CHAPTER V

The Commonwealth, 1901–1939

The principal sources for this period are the *Official Year Book of the Commonwealth,* the Commonwealth Parliamentary Debates and the Commonwealth Parliamentary Papers. A useful running commentary is provided by the quarterly articles in the *Round Table* (London, since 1910). There are three good general surveys of Australia at different points in the period, by a Frenchman, an Australian, and an American: Albert Métin, *Le Socialisme sans doctrines: la question agraire et la question ouvrière en Australie et Nouvelle-Zélande* (Paris, 1901; 2d, rev., ed., 1910); and Nos. 14 and 15, above. The following are the most important special studies: E. H. Sugden and F. W. Eggleston, *George Swinburne: A Biography* (Sydney, 1931), useful for Victorian politics from 1900 to 1913 and also for the Inter-State Commission; H. V. Evatt, *Australian Labour Leader: The Story of W. A. Holman* . . . (Sydney, 1940), a detailed account of the rise of the Labour Party and of New South Wales politics; L. F. Fitzhardinge *et al.*, *Nation Building in Australia: The Life and Work of Sir Littleton Groom* (Sydney, 1941), the fullest study of federal politics from 1901 to 1930; Walter Murdoch, *Alfred Deakin: A Sketch* (London, 1923); Nettie Palmer, *Henry Bournes Higgins: A Memoir* (London, 1931); A. Grenfell Price, *Australia Comes of Age* (Melbourne, 1945); Arthur Norman Smith, *Thirty Years: The Commonwealth of Australia, 1901–1931* (Melbourne, 1933).

See also Nos. 3, 4, 7, 8, 9, 10, 11, 12, 14, 15, 16, 18, 19, 21, above.

CHAPTER VI

The Constitution and Its Problems

John Quick and Robert Randolph Garran, *The Annotated Constitution of the Australian Commonwealth* (Sydney, 1901); W. Harrison Moore, *The Constitution of the Commonwealth of Australia* (2d ed., Melbourne and London, 1910); *The Commonwealth of Australia Constitution Act (As Altered to 1 July 1936)*, (Canberra, 1936); F. L. W. Wood, *The Constitutional Development of Australia* (London, 1933); *Report* of the Royal Commission on the Constitution (Canberra, 1929); W. A. Holman, *The Australian Constitution* (Sydney, 1928); G. V. Portus (ed.), *Studies in the Australian Constitution* (Sydney, 1933); D. A. S. Campbell (ed.), *Constitutional Revision in Australia* (Sydney, 1944); R. R. Garran, "The Development of the Australian Constitution," in *Law Quarterly Review*, Vol. XL (April, 1924); Herbert Vere Evatt, "Constitutional Interpretation in Australia," in *University of Toronto Law Journal*, Vol. III, No. 1 (1939); Gordon Greenwood, *The Future of Australian Federalism* (Melbourne, 1946).

See also *Record of Proceedings* of a Convention of Representatives of the Commonwealth and State Parliaments on Proposed Alteration of the Commonwealth Constitution, held at Canberra, November 24–December 2, 1942 (Canberra, 1942); and Nos. 3, 7, 8, 14, 15, 16, 18, 20, above.

CHAPTER VII

Australian Party Politics

Most Australian political history to date has been written from one or the other partizan side and few standard biographies of political figures exist. See bibliographies of historical chapters. *The Australian Encyclopaedia* covers in separate articles many phases of Australian politics before the First World War. There is one fine, full-scale political biography, *Australian Labour Leader,* by Dr. H. V. Evatt (Sydney, 1940). It deals with a New South Wales Labour Premier, W. A. Holman, who was a great figure in his own day, and gives as background most of the early political history of the Labour movement. Walter Murdoch's *Alfred Deakin* (London, 1923) is subtitled *A Sketch,* and does not attempt a critical review of its subject's career. Arthur Norman Smith's *Thirty Years: The Commonwealth of Australia, 1901–1931* (Melbourne, 1933) is a political history, close to the events it recounts, written by a journalist. Warren Denning's *Caucus Crisis: The Rise and Fall of the Scullin Government* (Parramatta, 1937) is a journalist's account of why Labour failed in the interwar period. Denning's *Inside Parliament* (Sydney, 1946) is an attempt to tell the average citizen how Parliament actually works. But a full-dress political history, written as a non-partizan investigation of the subject, does not exist.

See also Nos. 3, 7, 8, 13, 14, 15, 16, 18, 19, 20, 22, 23, above.

CHAPTER VIII
Public Administration and Its Problems

There is no systematic study of the history and development of public administration in Australia. The early history of Australian government is effectively treated by Edward Jenks in *The Government of Victoria (Australia),* (London and New York, 1891). Small monographs on the history of local government include A. W. Greig, *Notes on the History of Local Government in Victoria* (Melbourne, 1925); C. H. Bertie, *The Early History of the Sydney Municipal Council* (Sydney, 1911); F. A. Bland, *City Government by Commission, The Story of Sydney's First Commission Government, 1853–1857;* T. Wornsop, *A History of the City of Adelaide* (Adelaide, 1878). E. H. Sugden and F. W. Eggleston, *George Swinburne: A Biography* (Sydney, 1931), throw light upon the administrative problems of government from the angle of a Minister of State in Victoria from 1886 to 1928. F. W. Eggleston, *State Socialism in Victoria* (London, 1932), gives the experience of a Minister of State in administering government statutory corporations, as well as the story of the growth of such corporations in Australia. D. A. S. Campbell (ed.), *Constitutional Revision in Australia* (Sydney, 1944), deals with the administrative problems of Australian federalism.

See also the files of No. 20, above.

CHAPTER IX
Foreign Policy

Discussion of foreign policy in Australia is usually conducted in the newspaper press, in periodicals and pamphlets, or over the radio, and much of this material soon becomes rather difficult of access. Books which illustrate the state of opinion at the time they were issued include W. G. K. Duncan (ed.), *Australia's Foreign Policy* (Sydney, 1938); I. Clunies Ross (ed.), *Australia and the Far East* (Sydney, 1936). There is no comprehensive study of the genesis and evolution of Australian ideas on foreign policy since colonial times. Jack Shepherd, *Australia's Interests and Policies in the Far East* (New York, 1939), is an important introduction to that phase of the matter. See also H. V. Evatt, *Foreign Policy of Australia: Speeches* (Sydney, 1945), and *Australia in World Affairs* (Sydney, 1946);

United Nations Conference on International Organization: Report by the Australian Delegates (Canberra, 1945); Werner Levi, *American-Australian Relations* (Minneapolis, 1947).

See also Nos. 7, 8, 12, 13, 14, 15, 18, 19, 22, 23, above.

CHAPTER X

The Growth of the Australian Economy

A. G. L. Shaw, *The Economic Development of Australia* (London and New York, 1944); D. B. Copland, *Australia in the World Crisis, 1929–1933* (Cambridge, 1934); P. D. Phillips and Gordon L. Wood (eds.), *The Peopling of Australia* (Melbourne, 1928); F. W. Eggleston *et al.* (eds.), *The Peopling of Australia* (further studies), (Melbourne, 1933); W. G. K. Duncan and C. V. Janes (eds.), *The Future of Immigration into Australia and New Zealand* (Sydney, 1937); W. D. Forsyth, *The Myth of Open Spaces: Australian, British and World Trends of Population and Migration* (Melbourne, 1942); J. B. Brigden *et al.*, *The Australian Tariff: An Economic Inquiry* (Melbourne, 1929); Gordon [L.] Wood, *Borrowing and Business in Australia* (London, 1930); E. Ronald Walker, *The Australian Economy in War and Reconstruction* (London, 1947).

For basic statistical information see the *Bulletins* on Production, Demography, Finance, Transport, and Communications, and the *Labour Reports,* published by the Commonwealth Bureau of Census and Statistics, Canberra.

See also Nos. 7, 8, 9, 10, 11, 13, 14, 15, 16, 18, 22, 23, above.

CHAPTER XI

Australia and the World Economy

The most useful material in the field of this essay is to be found in general economic histories of Australia mentioned elsewhere in these bibliographies, in studies of particular aspects of the matter like Gordon [L.] Wood, *Borrowing and Business in Australia* (London, 1930); Roland Wilson, *Capital Imports and the Terms of Trade* . . . (Melbourne, 1931); in the books of documents assembled to illustrate the conflict of opinion during the Great Depression, notably D. B. Copland and C. V. Janes (eds.), *Australian Trade Policy: A Book of Documents, 1932–1937* (Sydney, 1937); and through the references cited in such books.

See also Nos. 7, 8, 9, 10, 11, 13, 14, 15, 16, 18, 19, 22, 23, above.

CHAPTER XII

Primary Industries in the Economy

W. G. K. Duncan (ed.), *Marketing Australia's Primary Products* (Sydney, 1937); D. B. Copland and C. V. Janes (eds.), *Australian Marketing Problems: A Book of Documents, 1932–1937* (Sydney, 1938), and *Australian Trade Policy: A Book of Documents, 1932–1937* (Sydney, 1937); W. D. Forsyth, *The Myth of Open Spaces: Australian, British and World Trends of Population and Migration*

(Melbourne, 1942); *Reports* of the Rural Reconstruction Commission, as follows: First, A General Rural Survey; Second, Settlement and Employment of Returned Men; Third, Land Utilisation and Farm Settlement; Fourth, Financial and Economic Reconstruction of Farms; Fifth, Rural Credit; Sixth, Farming Efficiency; Seventh, Rural Amenities; Eighth, Irrigation, Water Supplies and Land Drainage. See also S. M. Wadham, *Necessary Principles for Satisfactory Agricultural Development in Australia* (Joseph Fisher Lecture in Commerce, University of Adelaide), (Adelaide, 1946).

See Commonwealth *Production Bulletin* passim, and Nos. 7, 8, 9, 10, 11, 13, 14, 15, 16, 18, 22, 23, above.

CHAPTER XIII

SECONDARY INDUSTRIES IN THE ECONOMY

See the *Production Bulletin* and the *Labour Report,* issued annually by the Commonwealth Bureau of Census and Statistics, Canberra. The literature in this field is remarkably scanty, the author of the chapter stating, "There is no literature of Australian manufacturing." His reference is to critical historical studies.

See also Nos. 7, 8, 9, 10, 11, 13, 14, 15, 16, 18, 22, 23, above.

CHAPTER XIV

TERTIARY INDUSTRIES IN THE ECONOMY

This essay represents an original investigation of the field. There is no book devoted to the subject. The general concept of primary, secondary, and tertiary industries, reflected in this essay and the two immediately preceding, will be familiar to students of economic literature.

See also Nos. 16, 22, 23, above.

CHAPTER XV

BANKING, FINANCE, FISCAL POLICY

The most recent general survey of Australian banking is the *Report* of the Royal Commission appointed to inquire into the monetary and banking systems at present operating in Australia (Canberra, 1937). A briefer account is to be found in R. C. Mills and E. Ronald Walker, *Money* (7th ed., Sydney, 1941). Leslie C. Jauncey, *Australia's Government Bank* (London, 1933), is a readable but not entirely satisfactory account up to that time. On the period of the Great Depression see the books by D. B. Copland and E. Ronald Walker cited in the bibliographies of other chapters. There is no history of Australian banking. For current statistics see the *Finance Bulletin,* published by the Commonwealth Bureau of Census and Statistics, Canberra. Beginning in 1945, the Commonwealth Government has issued annually a paper entitled *National Income Estimates,* carrying the figures back to 1938–1939.

See also Nos. 7, 8, 9, 10, 11, 13, 14, 15, 16, 18, 20, 21, 22, 23, above.

CHAPTER XVI
THE RÔLE OF LABOUR

There is no complete history of Australian trade unionism or of labour in politics, nor any collection of labour documents. The following books may profitably be consulted: J. T. Sutcliffe, *A History of Trade Unionism in Australia* (Melbourne and London, 1921); Brian Fitzpatrick, *A Short History of the Australian Labor Movement* (Melbourne, 1940; new enl. ed., 1944); E. W. Campbell, *History of the Australian Labour Movement: A Marxist Interpretation* (Sydney, 1945), a Communist Party document; H. V. Evatt, *Australian Labour Leader: The Story of W. A. Holman* (Sydney, 1940); Lloyd Ross, *William Lane and the Australian Labour Movement* (Sydney, 1938); Clive Turnbull, *Bluestone: The Story of James Stephens, Leader of the Early Eight Hours Movement* (Melbourne, 1945).

See also Nos. 7, 8, 9, 10, 11, 13, 14, 15, 16, 18, 22, 23, above.

CHAPTER XVII
THE DEVELOPMENT OF THE SOCIAL SERVICES

"There is a paucity of literature on the Australian social services," states the author of the chapter. The only general work on the subject is W. G. K. Duncan (ed.), *Social Services in Australia* (Sydney, 1939). See also E. Ronald Walker, *Unemployment Policy* (Sydney, 1936); Annual *Report* of the Commonwealth Director-General of Social Services, 1942–; and Nos. 7, 8, 9, 11, 14, 15, 16, 20, 22, 23, above.

"There is a wealth of literature on the subject of wage fixation in Australia." Consult the following: George Anderson, *Fixation of Wages in Australia* (Melbourne, 1929); F. W. Eggleston *et al.*, *Australian Standards of Living* (Melbourne, 1939); Orwell de R. Foenander, *Towards Industrial Peace in Australia* (Melbourne and London, 1937), *Solving Labour Problems in Australia* (Melbourne and London, 1941), *Wartime Labour Developments in Australia* (Melbourne and London, 1943); and *Industrial Regulation in Australia* (Melbourne, 1947); H. B. Higgins, *A New Province for Law and Order* (London, 1922), an extremely useful background book.

See also Nos. 7, 8, 9, 11, 14, 15, 16, 18, 20, 22, 23, above.

CHAPTER XVIII
THE SOCIAL STRUCTURE OF AUSTRALIA

This essay is based on wide general reading rather than on consultation of specialised books of an historical character, for none has been written, so far as the writer knows, with this kind of analysis in mind. From an earlier period there is F. R. E. Mauldon, *A Study in Social Economics: The Hunter River Valley, New South Wales* (Melbourne, 1927). Only in recent years have sociological studies been made, and as yet but a handful have found publication: A. J. and J. J. McIntyre, *Country Towns of Victoria* (Melbourne, 1944); Alan

Walker, *Coaltown: A Social Survey of Cessnock,* [New South Wales] (Melbourne and London, 1945); Charles A. Price, *German Settlers in South Australia* (Melbourne, 1945); Alan J. Holt, *Wheat Farms of Victoria* (Melbourne, 1946); Brian Fitzpatrick, *The Australian People, 1788–1945* (London, 1947). These books give a conception of the tone and texture of Australian life. Also in recent years much information of value has been collected for other purposes, as in housing surveys, and since there is a distinct increase in interest in the sociological approach, many useful publications are fairly certain to appear in the immediate future.

See also the relevant sections of books in the general list.

CHAPTER XIX
ON AUSTRALIAN CULTURE

There is no book that traverses the ground covered in this essay. The items cited in the bibliographies for chapters on cultural affairs open up the field incidentally and should be consulted. See also Nos. 4, 7, 8, 14, 15, 18, above.

Concerning the ballet, see the sumptuous illustrated volume, *Borovansky Ballet in Australia and New Zealand* (Melbourne and London, 1946), by Norman Macgeorge.

CHAPTER XX
LITERATURE

The only textbook on the subject, H. M. Green, *An Outline of Australian Literature* (Sydney and Melbourne, 1930), is out of print. Mr. Green hopes to have ready soon a critical history of Australian literature. E. Morris Miller's No. 4, above, is a useful reference book. M. Barnard Eldershaw, *Essays in Australian Fiction* (Melbourne and London, 1938), deals with H. H. Richardson, Katherine Prichard, Christina Stead, Eleanor Dark, Leonard Mann, Vance Palmer, F. D. Davison, and the Montforts. T. Inglis Moore, *Six Australian Poets* (Melbourne, 1942), deals with Christopher Brennan, Bernard O'Dowd, J. S. Neilson, Hugh McCrae, William Baylebridge, and R. D. Fitzgerald. H. M. Green, *Fourteen Minutes: Short Sketches of Australian Poets and Their Work* (Sydney, 1944), which is based on radio talks, deals with these and a number of other poets. Mr. Green asked that it be stated that "C. Hartley Grattan is the only non-Australian, so far as the writer is aware, who has studied Australian literature, and he knows more about it than all but a few Australian critics." See, for example, the essay on Australian literature in the *Encyclopedia of Literature* (New York, 1946).

The best anthologies are, for short stories, A. G. Stephens (ed.), *The Bulletin Story Book* (Sydney, 1901); Nettie Palmer (ed.), *An Australian Story Book* (Sydney, 1938); George Mackaness (ed.), *Australian Short Stories* (London, 1928, 1932); for verse, Percival Serle, Frank Wilmot, and Robert H. Croll (comps.), *An Australasian Anthology* (London, 1927; Sydney and Auckland, 1946); George Mackaness (comp.), *Poets of Australia* (Sydney, 1946). Since 1941 there has appeared an annual anthology of short stories, *Coast to Coast* (Sydney), and one of verse, entitled *Australian Poetry* (Sydney).

Recent editions of the work of writers mentioned in the essay are as follows: *Selected Poems of Charles Harpur* (ed. by Kenneth H. Gifford and Donald F. Hall; Melbourne, 1944); Henry Kingsley, *The Recollections of Geoffry Hamlyn* (1886; Everyman's Library, London and New York, 1924); *The Poems of Adam Lindsay Gordon* (London, 1912); *Poems of Henry Clarence Kendall* (Melbourne, 1890; Sydney, 1924); Marcus Clarke, *For the Term of His Natural Life* (London, 1886), has been reprinted frequently; Rolf Boldrewood, *Robbery under Arms: A Story of Life and Adventure in the Bush and in the Goldfields of Australia* (London, 1897); *A. G. Stephens: His Life and Work* (ed. by Vance Palmer; Melbourne, 1941), consists chiefly of selections from Stephens' essays; Henry Lawson, both prose and verse available in many editions; Tom Collins, *Such Is Life* (1903; 2d ed., Melbourne, 1917; reprinted, Sydney, 1944), is to appear in an American edition (Chicago, 1947); *The Collected Verse of A. B. Paterson* (Sydney, 1927; Sydney and London, 1946) and other popular editions of selected verse are commonly available; H. H. Richardson, *The Fortunes of Richard Mahony*, is still in print; Christopher Brennan, a collected edition of verse and prose will appear in 1947; *The Poems of Bernard O'Dowd* (collected ed., Melbourne and Sydney, 1944); William Baylebridge, available only in privately printed, limited editions; Mary Gilmore, available only in original editions; Hugh McCrae, *Poems* (Sydney, 1939); *Collected Poems of John Shaw Neilson* (ed. by R. H. Croll; Melbourne and Sydney, 1934).

The work of living writers is usually available only in the original editions, though occasionally in popular reprints. The Australian Pocket Library, a paper-covered series published during the Second World War to meet popular demand, includes books by M. Barnard Eldershaw, F. D. Davison, Miles Franklin, Mrs. Aeneas Gunn, Leonard Mann, Vance Palmer, Katherine Prichard, Kylie Tennant, and others. There is an acute need for a standard reprint series with biographical and critical prefaces.

CHAPTER XXI
Art

William Moore, *The Story of Australian Art* (Sydney, 1934), in 2 vols. Vol. II contains a "Dictionary of Australian Artists"; Bernard Smith, *Place, Taste and Tradition: A Study of Australian Art since 1788* (Sydney, 1945); Sydney Ure Smith (ed.), *Art in Australia* (New York, 1941), contains illustrations and a useful bibliography. There are many monographs on individual artists.

CHAPTER XXII
Journalism

"There is no general work on journalism in Australia," states the author of the chapter. Individual newspapers are dealt with as follows: for the Sydney *Gazette*, see J. A. Ferguson, Mrs. A. G. Foster, and H. M. Green, *The Howes and Their Press* (Sydney, 1936); for the *Age* of Melbourne, see Ambrose Pratt, *David Syme, the Father of Protection in Australia* (London, 1908); for the Sydney *Morn-*

ing Herald, see J. F. Fairfax, *A Century of Journalism: The Sydney Morning Herald and Its Record of Australian Life* (Sydney, 1931), and *The Story of John Fairfax* (Sydney, 1941), which, taken together, constitute the fullest record of any Australian newspaper. Special numbers containing historical matter were issued by the *Bulletin* on January 29, 1930, and by the Melbourne *Herald* on January 3, 1940. On the labour press see: W. G. Spence, *Australia's Awakening: Thirty Years in the Life of an Australian Agitator* (Sydney and Melbourne, 1909); George Dale, *The Industrial History of Broken Hill* (Melbourne, 1908); Lloyd Ross, *William Lane and the Australian Labour Movement* (Sydney, 1938); G. H. Pitt, *The Press in South Australia, 1836–1850* (Adelaide, 1946).

CHAPTER XXIII

RELIGION

R. A. Giles, *The Constitutional History of the Australian Church* (London, 1929); Eric Ramsden, *Marsden and the Missions* (Sydney, 1936); F. T. Whitington, *William Grant Broughton, Bishop of Australia* (Sydney, 1936); Eris O'Brien, *The Foundation of Catholicism in Australia* (Sydney, 1922), in 2 vols., and *The Dawn of Catholicism in Australia* (Sydney, 1928), in 2 vols.

See also Nos. 4, 7, 8, 14, 18, 23, above.

CHAPTER XXIV

EDUCATION

G. S. Browne (ed.), *Education in Australia* (London, 1927); K. S. Cunningham, G. A. McIntyre, and W. C. Radford, *Review of Education in Australia, 1938* (Melbourne, 1939), contains a full "Bibliography of Australian Educational Reports and Studies"; Percival R. Cole (ed.), *The Primary School Curriculum in Australia* (Melbourne, 1932), and *The Rural School in Australia* (Melbourne, 1937); C. C. Linz, *The Establishment of a National System of Education in New South Wales* (Melbourne, 1938); I. S. Turner, *The Training of Teachers in Australia* (Melbourne and London, 1943).

See also Nos. 7, 8, 14, 15, 18, 22, 23, above.

CHAPTER XXV

NATIVE PEOPLES

On the background of aboriginal policy within the Commonwealth see Paul Hasluck, *Black Australians: A Survey of Native Policy in Western Australia, 1829–1897* (Melbourne and London, 1942); Edmund J. B. Foxcroft, *Australian Native Policy* (Melbourne and London, 1941). With regard to the latter Professor Elkin states: "Chapters iv–vii only; the sections dealing with states other than Victoria are based on insufficient data and are unreliable." The aborigines' departments in the states and the Northern Territory issue annual reports. There is a voluminous anthropological literature on the aborigines, but perhaps the most useful general volume is A. P. Elkin, *The Australian Aborigines: How to Understand Them* (Sydney and London, 1938).

Essential texts on the situation in New Guinea: see the annual *Report* on British New Guinea rendered to the Queensland Government from 1886 to 1906; and the annual *Report* on the same area as the Territory of Papua to the Commonwealth Government from 1906 to 1941. On the mandated portion of New Guinea see the *Reports* to the Council of the League of Nations on "Administration of the Territory of New Guinea" from 1921 to 1940. See also J. H. P. Murray, *Papua, or British New Guinea* (London, 1912), and *Papua of To-Day* (London, 1925); F. W. Eggleston (ed.), *The Australian Mandate for New Guinea* (Melbourne, 1928); S. W. Reed, *The Making of Modern New Guinea* (Philadelphia, 1943).

There is no comprehensive critical study of policy with regard to the Pacific Islanders in Queensland, but see relevant passages in Myra Willard, *History of the White Australia Policy* (Melbourne, 1923).

See also Nos. 7, 8, 9, 10, 13, 14, 15, 18, 19, 22, 23, above.

CHAPTER XXVI
AUSTRALIA'S INTEREST IN THE SOUTH PACIFIC ISLANDS

J. W. Burton, *Brown and White in the South Pacific* (Sydney, 1944); R. M. Crawford (ed.), *Ourselves and the Pacific* (Melbourne, 1941); T. Dunbabin, *Slavers of the South Seas* (Sydney, 1935); C. Brunsdon Fletcher, *The Black Knight of the Pacific* [George Brown], (Sydney, 1944); Gordon Greenwood, *Early American-Australian Relations* ... (Melbourne, 1944); Jean I. Brookes, *International Rivalry in the Pacific Islands, 1800–1875* (Berkeley and Los Angeles, 1941); Guy H. Scholefield, *The Pacific: Its Past and Future, and the Policy of the Great Powers from the Eighteenth Century* (London, 1919); J. M. Ward, "Development of British Policy in the Islands of the Southern Pacific to 1893" (unpublished thesis, University of Sydney, 1945).

See also Nos. 6, 7, 8, 13, 14, 15, 18, 19, 22, 23, above.

CHAPTER XXVII
AUSTRALIA IN THE SECOND WORLD WAR

There is an increasing literature of the war, but the following items appear to be the most interesting of those available at the moment of writing: H. Gordon Bennett, *Why Singapore Fell* (Sydney and London, 1944); D. B. Copland, *Towards Total War* (Sydney, 1942); H. V. Evatt, *Foreign Policy of Australia: Speeches* (Sydney, 1945); John Hetherington, *Airborne Invasion: The Story of the Battle of Crete* (Sydney and London, 1944); Paul and Frances McGuire, *The Price of Admiralty* (Melbourne and London, 1944); Ian Morrison, *Malayan Postscript* (London, 1942; Sydney, 1943); John F. Moyes, *Scrap-Iron Flotilla* (Sydney, 1944); A. F. Parry, *H.M.A.S. Yarra* (Sydney, 1944); Chester Wilmot, *Tobruk 1941:Capture—Siege—Relief* (Sydney and London, 1944); Rohan D. Rivett, *Behind Bamboo: An Inside Story of the Japanese Prison Camps* (Sydney and London, 1946); E. Ronald Walker, *The Australian Economy in War and Reconstruction* (London, 1947).

See also Nos. 14, 16, 18, 19, 20, 22, 23, above.

CHAPTER XXVIII

THE PATTERN OF RECONSTRUCTION

The basic document for the chapter is *Full Employment in Australia* (Canberra, 1945), a Commonwealth Government publication. There is voluminous periodical literature on full employment and other phases of reconstruction, as well as pamphlet literature. See also H. C. Coombs, *Problems of a High Employment Economy* (Joseph Fisher Lecture in Commerce, University of Adelaide), (Adelaide, 1944); D. A. S. Campbell (ed. and co-author), *Post-War Reconstruction in Australia* (Sydney, 1944); L. G. Melville *et al., Australia's Post-War Economy* (Sydney, 1945); Cyril Smith *et al., Repatriation and Rehabilitation* (Sydney, 1946); E. Ronald Walker, *The Australian Economy in War and Reconstruction* (London, 1947). For the last see especially Part Three, "Toward Reconstruction."

See also Nos. 15, 16, 18, 19, 20, 22, 23, above.

INDEX

Index

ACKNOWLEDGEMENT

The General Editor desires to record here his sincere appreciation of the splendid coöperation he has received from the staff of the University of California Press in the editing of the manuscript and the making of this book. In particular he is indebted to Mr. Harold A. Small, the Editor of the Press; to Mr. Amadeo R. Tommasini, Designer and Production Manager; to Miss Genevieve Rogers for editorial assistance in every part of the volume; and to Mrs. Chester J. Wolf for accurate and painstaking typing and secretarial work.

THE GILLICK PRESS • BERKELEY • CALIFORNIA